The First of the Modern Ottomans

The eighteenth century brought a period of tumultuous change to the Ottoman Empire. While the Empire sought modernization through military and administrative reform, it also lost much of its influence on the European stage through war and revolt. In this book, Ethan L. Menchinger sheds light on intellectual life, politics, and reform in the Empire through the study of one of its leading intellectuals and statesmen, Ahmed Vâsıf.

Vâsıf's life reveals new aspects of Ottoman letters – heated debates over moral renewal, war and peace, justice, and free will – but it also forces the reappraisal of Ottoman political reform, showing a vital response that was deeply enmeshed in Islamic philosophy, ethics, and statecraft. Tracing Vâsıf's role through the turn of the nineteenth century, this book opens the debate on modernity and intellectualism for those students and researchers studying the Ottoman Empire, intellectual history, the Enlightenment, and Napoleonic Europe.

Ethan L. Menchinger is currently a lecturer at the University of Michigan. He was previously a postdoctoral fellow at the Forum Transregionale Studien and Freie Universität, Berlin, and a visiting scholar at the University of Toronto.

"Situating the historian Vâsıf within the revolving core of Ottoman modernity, Ethan L. Menchinger gives us a thoroughly researched and often entertaining book that uncovers the links between the Ottoman worldview, literary culture, and international power politics. This is an engagingly written, sympathetic portrait of a man at once immensely gifted and deeply flawed – an impressive work of new scholarship."

Douglas A. Howard, Professor of History, Calvin College

"Although there are a few good biographies of well-known Ottoman bureaucrats and intellectuals, intimate accounts of Ottoman individuals have not proliferated in modern scholarship. Ethan L. Menchinger's *The First of the Modern Ottoman* is therefore a very welcome and well-executed contribution to this genre. The book is an eloquently written reconstruction of the life of a relatively obscure bureaucrat, diplomat, and court historian whose life spanned one of the most eventful and transformative periods for Ottoman society: the end of the eighteenth and early years of the nineteenth centuries. It is the story of an ambitious but unconnected youth from Baghdad who developed himself into a member of the elite class of bureaucrats invested in resuscitating a failing empire.

Menchinger bases his study on thousands of pages of personal writings by the historian – both published works and manuscripts from the Ottoman archives – and makes effective use of sources in a number of languages. He thus admirably manages the difficult task of recreating the details of Vâsıf's professional career: the offices he held, his duties, his diplomatic missions, even his day-to-day activities at various periods. However, the study is more than just a personal professional history of this bureaucrat; it successfully weaves the progress of his career into an account of a speedily changing political climate, a modernizing empire, and a rapidly transforming zeitgeist. The work also evokes the human side of Vâsıf: his rather selfish, uncollegial character; his easy alienation of his peers; the philosophical questions in his mind; his outlook on life; and how he coped with the onset of modern times.

The study as such is required reading for all who want to understand the intellectual history of the period. Through depicting the inner workings of Ottoman bureaucracy in times of war and peace, as well as the intellectual preoccupations of its bureaucrats, Menchinger provides a good glimpse of a reforming empire through the lens of one of its functionaries, as steps toward an Ottoman modernity were being taken."

Hakan Karateke, Professor of Ottoman Turkish Culture, Language and Literature, University of Chicago

"This is the return of narrative history and the genre of biography with a vengeance, but a sweet vengeance at that. Based on painstaking research in scores of manuscripts and archival documents, it tells the story of the prolific and rather odious Ottoman chancery officer and court historian, Ahmed Vâsıf (d. 1806). We follow Vâsıf and watch him cook up justifications for Ottoman compromises and territorial losses and provide validations for reform initiatives from the assemblies of Baghdad, to the chancery offices of Kars and Van, to the royal court at Istanbul, to the army camps of Shamen, to the negotiation tables in Bucharest, to the opera houses of St. Petersburg, to the parks of Madrid, to exile in Lesbos, and to the residential neighborhood of Çamlica. In the process, Vâsıf arrives at a historiographical and philosophical outlook that reconstitutes the Ottoman polity from a divinely ordained exceptional and unilateral order to a reciprocal and necessarily bilateral state based on human will. In short, this is a coming of *modern* age story, which is a must read for Ottomanists and comparativists alike."

Dana Sajdi, Associate Professor of History, Boston College

Cambridge Studies in Islamic Civilization

The First of the Modern Ottomans

The Intellectual History of Ahmed Vasıf

ETHAN L. MENCHINGER

University of Michigan

CAMBRIDGE
UNIVERSITY PRESS

CAMBRIDGE
UNIVERSITY PRESS

University Printing House, Cambridge CB2 8BS, United Kingdom

One Liberty Plaza, 20th Floor, New York, NY 10006, USA

477 Williamstown Road, Port Melbourne, VIC 3207, Australia

314-321, 3rd Floor, Plot 3, Splendor Forum, Jasola District Centre, New Delhi - 110025, India

79 Anson Road, #06-04/06, Singapore 079906

Cambridge University Press is part of the University of Cambridge.

It furthers the University's mission by disseminating knowledge in the pursuit of education, learning and research at the highest international levels of excellence.

www.cambridge.org
Information on this title: www.cambridge.org/9781316647943
DOI: 10.1017/9781108181990

First published 2017
First paperback edition 2020

A catalogue record for this publication is available from the British Library

ISBN 978-1-107-19797-8 Hardback
ISBN 978-1-316-64794-3 Paperback

For Natalia

Contents

Illustrations

Maps

Acknowledgments

I first "met" Ahmed Vâsıf in the fall of 2006 while writing an undergraduate thesis at the University of Toronto. That I am now his biographer many years later is due to the timely aid and generosity of more people and institutions than I can fairly thank. I wish to own my debt first to Gottfried Hagen and Virginia Aksan, who read the full study both in its first guise as a doctoral dissertation at the University of Michigan and later as a book manuscript. Their help and sensible criticism have been invaluable. Michael Bonner and Rudi Lindner, too, helped to shape this book with their feedback. The Department of Near Eastern Studies and Rackham School of Graduate Studies, University of Michigan, funded the first stages of my research in Turkey. The program "Europe in the Middle East – the Middle East in Europe" at the Forum Transregionale Studien in Berlin gave me time and support as a 2014/15 fellow to rethink, rewrite, and visit libraries across continental Europe. Much of the revision itself took place at the Graduate School for Muslim Cultures and Societies, Freie Universität, to whose staff and students I owe special thanks. Finally, a 2015 Summer Fellowship from the American Research Institute in Turkey let me finish the research where it began, Istanbul, while a 2015/16 visiting affiliation in the Department of Near and Middle Eastern Civilizations, University of Toronto, brought it full circle.

This book would have been impossible but for the help of many good librarians and archivists. The Hatcher Graduate Library in Ann Arbor; the Staatsbibliothek zu Berlin; the Newberry Library in Chicago; the Başbakanlık Osmanlı Arşivi, Beyazıt Devlet Kütüphanesi, İstanbul Üniversitesi Nadir Eserler Kütüphanesi, Millet Kütüphanesi, and Süleymaniye Kütüphanesi in Istanbul; the British Library in London; the

xiii

John Rylands Library in Manchester; the Bibliothèque nationale de France in Paris; the Robarts and Thomas Fisher Rare Book Libraries in Toronto; the Österreichische Nationalbibliothek in Vienna – I wish to thank their respective staffs for cheerfully (and accurately) filling my requests. The Biblioteca Nacional de España, Thomas Fisher Library, and National Portrait Gallery, London, also kindly gave me permission to reproduce images in their collections.

No lesser thanks must go to colleagues and friends who aided this project along its way. Virginia Aksan lent me key microfilms from her personal library. Kemal Beydilli, Mustafa Bilge, and Seyfi Kenan at the İslâm Araştırmaları Merkezi (İSAM) in Istanbul shared their hospitality, advice, and deep knowledge of Vâsıf and eighteenth-century sources; Kemal Bey, too, provided files that made this book possible. Noah Gardiner secured a rare manuscript for me in Cairo, Günhan Börekçi, Kahraman Şakul, Will Smiley, and Aysel Yıldız sent other documents, and Victor Ostapchuk lent the guidance of a true *hoca*. Maria Marsh and her team at Cambridge University Press also worked on my behalf with efficiency and enthusiasm, while two anonymous readers helped to improve the final product markedly. I would most of all like to thank my family, however – Dad, Mom, Stefan, Olivia, my extended family, and my in-laws Мама, Батько, і Ляриса – who have always supported me. Lastly, to my wife Natalia go the greatest thanks for her years of love and encouragement. It is to her that I dedicate this book.

Note on the Text

TRANSLITERATION AND SPECIAL TERMS

This study uses a modified Modern Turkish script to render Ottoman Turkish names, titles, terms, and constructs. In general, I adhere to the original orthography and indicate long vowels with a circumflex (Â, â, Î, î, Û, û); I omit the glottal consonants ʿayn (ʿ) and *hamza* (ʾ), which are unvoiced in Turkish, except where absolutely necessary, as in the transliteration of key technical terms. For non-specialists, the following letters may be unfamiliar:

C, c   pronounced "j" as in "jam."
Ç, ç   pronounced "ch" as in "cheese."
Ğ, ğ   this "soft g" is mostly unvoiced and lengthens the preceding vowel.
I, ı   pronounced like the first syllable in "early."
Ö, ö   pronounced as in the German "schön" or the French "seul."
Ş, ş   pronounced "sh" as in "shoe."
Ü, ü   pronounced as in German or the French "tu."

For Arabic and Persian names and terms, I have followed the transliteration system employed by the *International Journal of Middle East Studies* (*IJMES*), which uses diacritics to more accurately reflect the script. In all cases I have preferred, where they exist, Anglicized versions of place names and titles like "sultan," "Sufi," and "ulema." To make the text more accessible to non-specialists, I have also tried to translate terms and quotations into idiomatic English. While this may arguably reduce scholarly "accuracy," interested readers are free to consult original texts in my 2014 doctoral dissertation. All other special terms are listed in the glossary. Unless otherwise noted, source translations are my own.

NAMES AND DATES

A study like this one as a rule contains many personal and place names. To reduce confusion, I have added a Dramatis Personae to the front matter with information on major figures in Ahmed Vâsıf's life and career and arranged it alphabetically. The reader will find place names on the maps.

For ease of access, I have favored Anno Domini (AD) dating in the text proper according to the Gregorian calendar. The notes list dates in both AD and in the Muslim lunar hijri or Anno Hegirae (AH) system. I use the following abbreviations for hijri months:

M	Muharrem/Muḥarram
S	Safer/Ṣafar
Ra	Rebiülevvel/Rabî' al-awwal
R	Rebiülâhir/Rabî' al-âkhir
Ca	Cemâziyelevvel/Jumâdâ al-awwal
C	Cemâziyelâhir/Jumâdâ al-âkhir
B	Receb/Rajab
Ş	Şaban/Sha'bân
N	Ramazan/Ramaḍân
L	Şevvâl/Shawwâl
Za	Zilkade/Dhû al-qa'da
Z	Zilhicce/Dhû al-ḥijja

CURRENCY

It is hard to accurately convey value in a pre-modern society. The Ottoman Empire was agrarian, without a full cash economy, and did not have a unified system of currency in the eighteenth century. Local and foreign coinages circulated freely, while the century saw runaway inflation in the wake of the Ottoman-Russian wars. That said, some words on Ottoman coins and their equivalencies will give the reader a basic sense of value.

The smallest unit of Ottoman coin was the silver asper or *akçe*. However, the *akçe* had become so devalued by the late seventeenth century that it gave way in daily exchange to the more valuable *para* and to the silver piaster or *kuruş*. The exchange rate for these denominations was set at one *kuruş* = 40 *para* = 120 *akçe*. The relative value of Ottoman to European currency is more complex. In 1768, for example, a Venetian ducat was worth about four *kuruş* and a British pound sterling eight *kuruş*. By Ahmed Vâsıf's death in 1806, the *kuruş* had slipped to about eight to the ducat and fifteen to the pound sterling. Vâsıf at the height of his career probably earned no more than 15,000 *kuruş* a year, or some 1,000 pounds. To put this into perspective, recall that Jane Austen's eligible bachelors Mr. Bingley and Mr. Darcy had yearly incomes of 5,000 and 10,000 pounds each and that they lived in a far wealthier country. Due to lower prices, Vâsıf's buying power with 15,000 *kuruş* was likely higher than a British contemporary with 1,000 pounds. See Şevket Pamuk, *A Monetary History of the Ottoman Empire* (Cambridge, 1999), pp. 163, 168.

FINAL NOTE

In the last stages of this study, I acquired a new dissertation on Vâsıf submitted at Istanbul University, a critical edition of part of his chronicle: Hüseyin Sarıkaya, ed., "Ahmed Vâsıf Efendi ve *Mehâsinü'l-Âsâr ve Hakâîkü'l-Ahbâr'ı,* 1209–1219/1794–1805" (Istanbul University, 2013). Since Sarıkaya's archival work on Vâsıf largely reproduces my own, I cite him only where we disagree or where he has uncovered documents that eluded me.

Dramatis Personae

Abaza Paşa, Mehmed (??-1771/72): Soldier and vizier. Fought in the 1768–1774 war at Bender, Falça, and Kartal. Mutinied in Crimea, fled to Anatolia, and was executed. Vâsıf's patron.

Abdülhamid I (1725–1789): Son of Ahmed III and twenty-seventh sultan of the Ottoman line. Reigned from 1774 to 1789.

Argyropoulos, Yakovaki (1774–1850): Phanariot. Translator and interpreter born in Istanbul. Worked for years at the Sublime Porte.

Ârif Efendi, Dürrîzâde Mehmed (1740–1800): Jurist and judge from an eminent ulema family. Served as *şeyhülislâm* twice, in 1785/86 and from 1792 to 1798.

Âsım Efendi, Ahmed (1755–1819): Poet, littérateur, and historian. Famed as the Turkish translator of two lexicons, one from Arabic, one from Persian. Served as court historian from 1808 to 1819. Vâsıf's jealous rival.

Âşir Efendi, Mustafa (1729–1804): Judge, jurist, and scholar. Served as *şeyhülislâm* from 1798 to 1800. The brother Ahmed Azmî Efendi and Abdürrezzâk Bâhir Efendi and Vâsıf's friend.

Âtıf Efendi, Ahmed (??-1806): Scribe and high-ranking bureaucrat. Chief scribe in 1798.

Ayşe (??-??): One of Vâsıf's younger daughters. Married either Seyyidâ Efendi or Sâlih Efendi.

Azmî Efendi, Ahmed (??-1821): Scribe and ambassador. Followed Ahmed Resmî Efendi to Berlin in 1763/64 and was ambassador to Morocco (1787) and Prussia (1791/92). Abdürrezzâk Bâhir Efendi's brother.

Bâhir Efendi, Abdürrezzâk (1730–1780): Scribe, bureaucrat, man of letters. Held high office and served as chief scribe from 1772 to 1774 and from 1779 to 1780. Vâsıf's friend and patron.

de Bassecourt, Francisco González, conde del Asalto (1726–1793): Spanish nobleman. Capitan general of Barcelona and Cataluña during Vâsıf's embassy.

Bouligny y Paret, Juan (1726–1798): Spanish statesman and diplomat. Served as envoy and ambassador in Istanbul from 1779 to 1793.

Callimaki, Scarlat (1773–1821): Phanariot noble. Grand dragoman of the Porte from 1801 to 1806. Was prince of Moldavia three times (1806, 1807–1810, 1812–1819) and prince of Wallachia in 1821.

Canikli Paşa, Ali (1720/21–1785): Soldier and Trabzon notable. Held military commands in the 1768–1774 war and led failed expeditions to Crimea in 1778/79. Wrote the *Rare New Stratagem*.

Charles III of Spain (1716–1788): Duke of Parma and Piacenza, King of Naples and Sicily, King of Spain. Enlightened despot who ruled Spain from 1759 to 1788, enacting reform.

Dürrî Efendi, Mehmed (??-1795): Chancery scribe and reformer. Negotiated the Treaty of Sistova and served as chief scribe in 1794/ 95. Author of the *Choice Desire to Correct Disorder*.

Dürrîzâde Efendi, Ataullah (1729–1785): Judge and jurist. Named *şeyhülislâm* in 1783. Implicated with Grand Vizier Halil Hamid Paşa in a plot to dethrone Abdülhamid I, deposed, and exiled. Perhaps poisoned.

Edîb Efendi, Mehmed (??-1801): Scribe, poet, and historian. Served as court historian from 1787 to 1790 and again from 1791 to 1793. Vâsıf's rival.

Enverî Efendi, Sadullah (1736?–1794): Scribe and court historian. Held office in the Ottoman bureaucracy. Vâsıf's chief rival as court historian, which post he held five times (1769–1774, 1776–1783, 1787–1791, 1791–1793, and 1794).

Esma Sultan (1726–1788): Daughter of Ahmed III, sister of Abdülhamid I, and wife of Muhsinzâde Mehmed Paşa. Tightfisted. Took Vâsıf's landed income in 1774.

Fâiz Efendi, Ahmed (??-1807): Reformer and scribe. Selim III's longtime privy secretary and Vâsıf's patron. Murdered in the 1807 rebellion.

Feyzî Efendi, Süleyman (??-1793/94): Chancery scribe and vizier. Chief scribe twice from 1779 to 1781 and 1787 to 1788. Later "turned paşa" and was a provincial governor. Vâsıf's friend.

Gazi Paşa, Hasan (Cezayirli) (??-1790): Influential Grand Admiral and vizier. Won fame during the 1768–1774 war as a naval hero and served as Grand Admiral from 1770 to 1790. Grand Vizier in 1790.

Gravina y Nápoli, Don Federico (1756–1806): Spanish seaman. Captain of the *Santa Rosa*, which returned Vâsıf to Istanbul in 1788. Later an admiral. Died from wounds at Trafalgar.

Gül Ahmedpaşazâde Paşa, Ali (1706/7–1769): Vizier and soldier. Rose through the palace to become Grand Admiral. Later exiled and a provincial governor. Vâsıf's first patron.

Hâfız Paşa, İsmail (1757/58–1807): Vizier. Served a term as Grand Vizier in 1806.

Hakkı Bey, Mehmed (1747–1811): Vizier and governor. Suppressed rebels in Rumelia in late 1790s. Target of Vâsıf's resentment.

Hamid Paşa, Halil (1736–1785): Scribe, reformer, and vizier. Chancery product who served as chief scribe in 1780. Later was Grand Vizier from 1782 to 1785 and set out to reform the military. Dismissed, expropriated, and killed in 1785 for an alleged plot.

Hanîfe (??-mid-nineteenth century): One of Vâsıf's younger daughters. Married Ahmed Feyâzî Efendi.

al-Harbûtî, Ebülbekâ Hasan (??-??): Baghdadi teacher and scholar. Vâsıf's father.

Hayrî Efendi, Mehmed (1734?-1789): Scribe and poet. Held high office in the chancery and served as chief scribe three times (1781, 1785/86, 1788/89). Drowned in the Boze river. Author of poetry edited by Vâsıf.

Italinskii, Andrei Yakovlevich (1743–1827): Russian diplomat. Served for many years as ambassador in Istanbul. Negotiated with Vâsıf in 1805/6.

İvazpaşazâde Paşa, Halil (1724?–1777): Grand Vizier during the 1768–1774 war. Blamed for the rout at Kartal and dismissed in 1770.

İzzet Paşa, Mehmed (1723–1784): Courtier and vizier. Rose to become Grand Vizier in 1774/75. Not to be confused with Safranbolulu İzzet Mehmed Paşa, Grand Vizier from 1794 to 1798.

Koca Yusuf Paşa (??-1800): Georgian by birth. Soldier and vizier. Protégé of Gazi Hasan Paşa who was Grand Vizier from 1786 to 1789 and 1791 to 1792. Led the army during the Maçin defeat and boycott.

Küçük Hüseyin Paşa (1758/59–1803): Georgian or Circassian by birth. Became Selim III's court chamberlain and later Grand Admiral. Led the naval expedition against the French in Egypt. Vâsıf's patron.

Mabeynci Ahmed Efendi (??-1807): Court chamberlain and confidant to Selim III. Vâsıf's patron and one-time neighbor. Murdered in the 1807 rebellion.

Mekkî Efendi, Mehmed (1714–1797): Judge, jurist, and scholar. Was *şeyhülislâm* in 1787/88 and 1791/92. Wrote works of exegesis, law, theology, and poetry. Vâsıf's friend.

Moñino y Redondo, José, conde de Floridablanca (1728–1808): Spanish noble, statesman, and reformer. First minister under Charles III and leader of an Enlightened reform program.

Mourouzi, Demetrius (Beyzâde) (1768–1812): Phanariot noble. Son of Constantine Mourouzi, Grand Dragoman and prince of Moldavia. Brother of Alexander Mourouzi, Grand Dragoman and prince of Moldavia and Wallachia. Colluded with Italinskii.

Müftîzâde Efendi, Ahmed (??-1791): Jurist and judge. Influential religious figure during the 1780s. Served as *şeyhülislâm* in 1786/87.

Muhsinzâde Paşa, Mehmed (1704–1774): Soldier, vizier, and governor. One of few capable viziers during the 1768–1774 war. Served twice as Grand Vizier (1765–1768, 1772–1774) and pushed for a negotiated peace.

Münib Efendi, İbrahim (??-1786): Chancery scribe. Served as chief scribe in 1774 after Abdürrezzâk Bâhir Efendi's dismissal. Signed the Treaty of Küçük Kaynarca with Ahmed Resmî Efendi.

Mustafa III (1717–1774): Son of Ahmed III and the twenty-sixth sultan of the Ottoman line. Reigned from 1757 to 1774. Older brother of Abdülhamid I and father of Selim III.

Nesîm Efendi, İbrahim (??-1807): Courtier and statesman. Influential confidant of Selim III who served as corresponding secretary and the Grand Vizier's steward. Murdered in the 1807 rebellion.

Nûrî Bey, Halil (??-1799): Scribe and historian. Replaced Vâsıf as court historian in 1794, serving till his death.

Obreskov, Aleksei Mikhailovich (1718–1787): Russian diplomat. Resident envoy at Istanbul from 1751 to 1768. Negotiated with Abdürrezzâk Bâhir Efendi and Vâsıf on two occasions.

Râgıb Paşa, Mehmed (Koca) (1698/99–1763): Scribe, poet, vizier. Important eighteenth-century man of letters and administrator. Chief scribe from 1741 to 1744. Served as Grand Vizier from 1757 to 1763. Famed as a stylist, letter-writer, and poet.

Râif Efendi, İsmail (??-1784/85): Scribe. Served twice as proxy chief scribe (1768/69–1772/73, 1774) and once in full (1774–1776). Briefly taken with Vâsıf.

Râif Efendi, Mahmud (??-1807): Scribe and reformer. Traveled to London between 1793 and 1797 and served as chief scribe from 1800 to 1805. Wrote *Tableau des nouveaux règlemens de l'empire*

Ottoman and the *Handbook of Geography*. Murdered in the 1807 rebellion.

Râşid Efendi, Mehmed (1753/54–1798): Scribe, poet, and printer. Held high chancery office and was chief scribe three times (1787–1791, 1792–1794, 1797–1798). Reestablished and operated the imperial press. Vâsıf's erstwhile ally and enemy.

Râtib Efendi, Ebubekir (1750–1799): Scribe, courtier, and influential reformer under Selim III. Traveled to Vienna as ambassador between 1791 and 1792.

Repnin, Nikolai Vasilevich (1734–1801): Russian statesman and soldier. Successful general in the 1768–1774 and 1787–1792 wars. Ambassador to Istanbul in 1775/76.

Reşîd Efendi, Mustafa (??-1819): Scribe, courtier, and adviser to Selim III. Held many high offices, including steward to the Grand Vizier, head of the New Revenue treasury, and proxy chief scribe.

Resmî Efendi, Ahmed (1700–1783): Scribe and reformer. Elder statesman during the 1768–1774 war who signed the Treaty of Kaynarca. Wrote *A Summary of Admonitions*.

Ruffin, Pierre-Jean-Marie (1742–1824): French orientalist and diplomat. Envoy in Istanbul while Vâsıf was chief scribe. Collector of manuscripts and professor of Turkish and Persian.

Rumiantsev, Petr Aleksandrovich (1725–1796): Russian field marshal. One of the best generals of the eighteenth century. Led the Russian army in the 1768–1774 war and met with Vâsıf several times.

Selim III (1761–1808): Son of Mustafa III and twenty-eighth sultan of the Ottoman line. Reform-minded and author of the "New Order" reforms. Deposed in 1807 and murdered in 1808.

Silâhdar Mehmed Paşa (1735/36–1781). Courtier and vizier. A palace confidant of Abdülhamid I who was Grand Vizier from 1779 to 1781. Vâsıf's patron.

Tatarcık Efendi, Abdullah (1730/31–1797): Scholar, judge, and reformer. Influential voice under Selim III and rival of Mehmed Râşid Efendi. Friend to Vâsıf, with whom he was exiled in 1794/95.

Ümmü Gülsûm Hanım (??-??): Vâsıf's wife and the mother of his children. Perhaps related to Abdürrezzâk Bâhir Efendi's family.

Yenişehirli Osman Efendi (??-1784): Chancery scribe. Served as chief scribe in 1768/69. Led failed peace talks during the 1768–1774 war and obstructed Vâsıf.

Yusuf Ağa, Mühürdâr (??-1807): Cretan by birth. Influential courtier and steward to Selim III's mother Mihrişah Sultan. Leader of a faction opposed to Vâsıf and his patrons.

Ziyâ Paşa, Yusuf (??-1819): Georgian by birth. Grand Vizier from 1798 to 1805 and again in 1809. Led the military expedition against the French in Egypt and Syria.

Züleyhâ (??-mid-nineteenth century): Vâsıf's eldest daughter. Married either Seyyidâ Efendi or Sâlih Efendi and was later part of a scandal with the daughter of Mehmed Mekkî Efendi.

Chronology

Ca. AH 1147 = 1735	Ahmed Vâsıf is born in Baghdad.
Ca. AH 1175 = 1761/62	Vâsıf pursues his studies in Aleppo.
AH 1180 = 1766/67	Vâsıf travels to Anatolia and studies in Van and Kars; he meets Gül Ahmedpaşazâde Ali Paşa and accompanies him to Sivas as a treasury scribe.
AH 1183 = 1769	Gül Ahmedpaşazâde Ali Paşa joins the imperial army on the Danube. Vâsıf follows in train to Bender, where in October, his master puts down a mutiny and dies.
AH 1184 = 1770/71	Vâsıf becomes Abaza Mehmed Paşa's private secretary. He witnesses major Ottoman defeats at Falça, Kartal, and İsmail and is captured by the Russians.
AH 1184/85 = 1770/71	Vâsıf is a prisoner-of-war in St. Petersburg. In the fall of 1771, Catherine II frees and sends him back to the Ottoman camp with peace proposals. Vâsıf then visits Istanbul and seeks patronage, attaching himself to Abdürrezzâk Bâhir Efendi.
AH 1185/86 = 1771/72	Grand Vizier Muhsinzâde Mehmed Paşa makes Vâsıf a clerk in the correspondence office at the rank of bureau chief. Peace talks at Foksani collapse. Vâsıf travels to the Russian camp to renew a truce with Field Marshal Rumiantsev and is rewarded.

AH 1186/87 = 1772/73	Vâsıf joins Abdürrezzâk Efendi at the second round of peace talks in Bucharest during the winter of 1772/73, serving as secretary to negotiations. His position as secretary to the left-wing cavalry is reconfirmed, while talks fail in the spring.
AH 1188 = 1774	Mustafa III dies. Vâsıf joins the final campaign of the war and is at the battle of Kozluca in June. He is trapped at Şumnu with the remnants of the army when peace is declared, and he negotiates with Rumiantsev at Jassy that fall.
AH 1188–93 = 1774–79	A factional realignment takes place at court, leaving Vâsıf out of favor and without post or income.
AH 1193 = 1779	Abdürrezzâk Efendi becomes chief scribe a second time and Vâsıf writes a gloss on al-Zamakhsharî's *Exceptional Aphorisms*. In October, he gains a post as first fortifications officer.
AH 1194 = 1780	Abdürrezzâk Efendi, Vâsıf's patron, falls out with the Grand Vizier and dies.
AH 1195 = 1781	Vâsıf is passed over for office in the yearly round of appointments.
AH 1196 = 1782	The chancery product Halil Hamid Paşa becomes Grand Vizier. In September, he makes Vâsıf the director of the outer documentation office.
AH 1197 = 1783	The Crimean Crisis erupts. Vâsıf is named court historian for the first time and begins to compile a chronicle.
AH 1198 = 1784	Vâsıf works as galley scribe in Galata. He and Râşid Mehmed Efendi buy İbrahim Müteferrika's old printing press and refurbish it, publishing an edition of the chronicle of Sâmî, Şâkir, and Subhî in the autumn.
AH 1199 = 1785	Halil Hamid Paşa is dismissed, exiled, and killed. Vâsıf adds to his chronicle while repudiating the late Grand Vizier and cultivating

	Gazi Hasan Paşa. Vâsıf and Râşid publish an edition of the chronicle of İzzî.
AH 1200 = 1786	Vâsıf is made temporary head of the suspended payments office. He fights with Râşid over the operation of the press and is ousted. In December, Râşid has him sent away from Istanbul as ambassador to Spain.
AH 1201 = 1787	Vâsıf leaves for Spain after long preparations. He tours Barcelona, Valencia, and La Granja, where in September, he is received by Floridablanca and Charles III.
AH 1202 = 1788	Vâsıf winters in Madrid, makes social rounds, and meets the Englishman William Beckford. He continues to observe the Spanish kingdom. He returns home in April and writes an embassy report, but finds himself removed from office.
AH 1203 = 1788/89	The empire is at war with Austria and Russia. Abdülhamid I dies and is replaced by his nephew, Selim III. Vâsıf serves in the treasury in Istanbul, where he is promoted to the head of the Anatolian accounts office.
AH 1204 = 1790	Selim makes Vâsıf his proxy court historian and asks him to record the events of the royal accession.
AH 1205 = 1791	Vâsıf is called to the war front in March. He serves Koca Yusuf Paşa as a courier and head of the general accounts office. He also writes a speech for the Grand Vizier and negotiates a truce with Nikolai Repnin, returning to take part in the Maçin boycott. In September, Vâsıf is sent away to Belgrade.
AH 1206 = 1792	In April, Selim recalls Vâsıf to Istanbul but, still angry, leaves him without a post. Vâsıf devotes himself to study and claims to be impoverished.
AH 1207 = 1793	Vâsıf most likely writes the *Perplexities in Vaṣṣâf's Vocabulary* and edits Mehmed Hayrî's poetry. He gains a name for himself as a poet, as well. In May, Vâsıf returns to the

	Anatolian accounts office and becomes court historian for a third time. He submits the first installment of *Charms and Truths*.
AH 1208/9 = 1794	Râşid Efendi feuds with Tatarcık Abdullah Efendi and targets his erstwhile partner Vâsıf, whom he accuses of sedition. The historian is dismissed from office and exiled to Lesbos.
AH 1209/10 = 1795	After a few months in exile, Vâsıf returns to Istanbul and resumes his work in the treasury as director of the Anatolian accounts office. His son Lebîb marries.
AH 1210/11 = 1796	Vâsıf fails to receive an appointment.
AH 1211/12 = 1797	In the spring, Vâsıf is made head of the general accounts office.
AH 1212/13 = 1798	Vâsıf again fails to receive an appointment. The French invade Egypt in July, on which occasion he writes the *Letter of Consolation* for the sultan.
AH 1213/14 = 1799	Returning to the Anatolian accounts office, Vâsıf gets a snap appointment and promotion to chief of the daily ledger. Halil Nûrî Bey dies in May. Vâsıf replaces him as court historian for a fourth and final term. He begins the second installment of *Charms and Truths* and edits Ebubekir Sâmî Paşa's poetry.
AH 1215 = 1800	Vâsıf submits the second volume of *Charms and Truths* and is made chancellor. He moves on to the third installment and probably writes the *Book of the Monk*.
AH 1215/16 = 1801	In February, Vâsıf is discharged as chancellor. His house burns down the next month and he moves to Çamlıca, while Selim commissions him to rewrite the works of Hâkim and Çeşmizâde. Küçük Hüseyin Paşa returns from Egypt that December in triumph.
AH 1216 = 1802	Selim approves Vâsıf's revisions and has him edit the work of Enverî. The historian also writes the *Gestes of Hüseyin Paşa* and is renamed chancellor.

AH 1217 = 1803	In September, the historian replaces Mustafa Râsih Efendi as chancellor.
AH 1218 = 1803/4	Selim commissions the *Final Word to Refute the Rabble* in defense of his reforms. Vâsıf also works with Mahmud Râif Efendi on the *New Atlas Translation*.
AH 1219 = 1804/5	Vâsıf prints his revisions of earlier chronicles as the fourth volume of *Charms and Truths*. Selim orders him to compile a fifth.
AH 1220 = 1805	Selim fulfills Vâsıf's lifelong dream by naming him chief scribe. The historian represents a "French faction" at court, but negotiates a treaty renewal with the Russian ambassador Italinskii, which is ratified in December.
AH 1221 = 1806	Early in the year, Vâsıf is forced to step down as court historian. His health failing, he moves the empire away from its alignment with Russia and sparks crises during the summer with threats to close the Bosphorus to shipping and the removal of the Phanariot princes. He dies in October, just before war is declared.

Abbreviations

A.DVNS.NMH	Nâme-i Hümâyûn Defterleri, BOA
AE.Abd	Ali Emiri, Abdülhamid I collection, BOA
AE.Slm	Ali Emiri, Selim III collection, BOA
A.RSK.d	Bâb-ı Asâfî, Rüûs Kalemi Defterleri, BOA
ATLAS	Mahmud Râif, *Cedîd Atlas Tercümesi*
AÜDTCF	Ankara Üniversitesi Dil ve Tarih-Coğrafya Fakültesi
BnF	Bibliothèque nationale de France, Paris
BOA	Başbakanlık Osmanlı Arşivi, Istanbul
C.ADL	Cevdet Adliye collection, BOA
C.DH	Cevdet Dahiliye collection, BOA
C.HR	Cevdet Hariciye collection, BOA
C.MF	Cevdet Maarif collection, BOA
C.ML	Cevdet Maliye collection, BOA
C.TZ	Cevdet Timar collection, BOA
D.BŞM.d	Bâb-ı Defterî, Başmuhâsebe Kalemi Defterleri, BOA
DİA	*Türkiye Diyanet Vakfı İslâm Ansiklopedisi*
EI²	*Encyclopaedia of Islam*, 2nd edition
GAZAVÂT	Vâsıf, *Gazavât-ı Hüseyin Paşa*. ÖN Cod. H.O. nr. 205
GOW	Franz Babinger, *Die Geschichtsschreiber der Osmanen und ihre Werke*
HADÎKAT	Osmanzâde Tâib, *Hadîkatü'l-Vüzerâ*
HAT	Hatt-ı Hümâyûn collection, BOA
HULÂSAT	Abdullah Uçman, ed., *Sekbanbaşı Risalesi, Hulâsat el-Kelâm fi Red el-Avam*
İA	*İslâm Ansiklopedisi*

İ.DH	İrade-i Dahiliye collection, BOA
IJMES	*International Journal of Middle East Studies*
İLGÜREL	Vâsıf, *Mehâsinü'l-Âsâr ve Hakâîkü'l-Ahbâr.* ed. Mücteba İlgürel
İÜ	İstanbul Üniversitesi Kütüphanesi, Istanbul
İÜEF	İstanbul Üniversitesi Edebiyat Fakültesi
KINÂLIZÂDE	Kınâlızâde Ali Çelebi, *Ahlâk-ı Alâ'î*
KK.d	Kâmil Kepeci Defterleri, BOA
MEHÂSİN 1	Vâsıf, *Mehâsinü'l-Âsâr ve Hakâîkü'l-Ahbâr.* İstanbul Arkeoloji Müzesi Kütüphanesi, nr. 355
MEHÂSİN 2	Vâsıf, *Mehâsinü'l-Âsâr ve Hakâîkü'l-Ahbâr.* İÜ TY nr. 5978
MEHÂSİN 3	Vâsıf, *Mehâsinü'l-Âsâr ve Hakâîkü'l-Ahbâr.* İÜ TY nr. 5979
MEHÂSİN 4	Vâsıf, *Mehâsinü'l-Âsâr ve Hakâîkü'l-Ahbâr.* İÜ TY nr. 6013
MEHÂSİN 5	Vâsıf, *Mehâsinü'l-Âsâr ve Hakâîkü'l-Ahbâr.* Istanbul, 1804. 2 vols.
MEHÂSİN 6	Vâsıf, *Mehâsinü'l-Âsâr ve Hakâîkü'l-Ahbâr.* TSMK Hazine nr. 1406
MERSH	*The Modern Encyclopedia of Russian and Soviet History*
MHM.d	Mühimme Defterleri, BOA
NEVÂBİG	Vâsıf, *Tercüme-i Şerh-i Nevâbigü'l-Kelim.* Süleymaniye Kütüphanesi, Pertev nr. 387
RÂHİBNÂME	Vâsıf, *Râhibnâme.* TSMK Hazine nr. 386
RESMÎ	Ahmed Resmî, *Hulâsatü'l-İtibâr*, trans. Ethan L. Menchinger
SEFÂRETNÂME	Vâsıf, *Sefâretnâme-i Vâsıf.* TSMK Hazine nr. 1438, fols. 327b-354b
SO	Mehmed Sürreya, *Sicill-i Osmânî*
SSA	İstanbul Müftülüğü Şer'iyye Sicilleri Arşivi, Istanbul
TESLIYETNÂME	Vâsıf, *Tesliyetnâme.* TSMK Hazine nr. 1625
TOEM	*Târih-i Osmanî Encümeni Mecmuası*
TSMA	Topkapı Sarayı Müzesi Arşivi, Istanbul
TSMK	Topkapı Sarayı Müzesi Kütüphanesi, Istanbul
ÖN	Österreichische Nationalbibliothek, Vienna
OTAM	*Ankara Üniversitesi Osmanlı Tarihi Araştırma ve Uygulama Merkezi Dergisi*
Y.EE	Yıldız Esas Evrakı collection, BOA

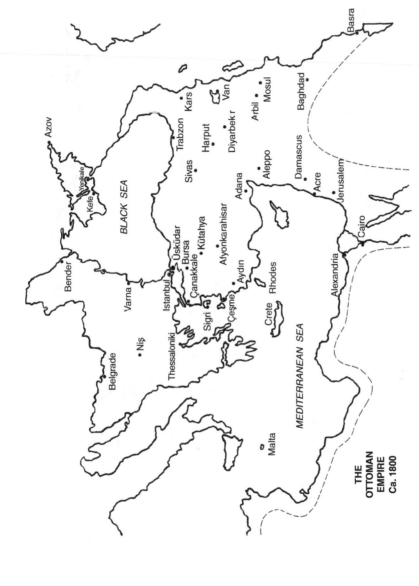

1. The Ottoman Empire, ca. 1800

THE OTTOMAN EMPIRE Ca. 1800

BLACK SEA

MEDITERRANEAN SEA

Azov
Basra
Kars
Van
Mosul
Baghdad
Arbil
Trabzon
Harput
Diyarbekr
Sivas
Aleppo
Damascus
Adana
Acre
Jerusalem
Bender
Yenikale
Kefe
Üsküdar
Bursa
Kütahya
Istanbul
Çanakkale
Afyonkarahisar
Aydın
Varna
Cairo
Rhodes
Sigri
Çeşme
Alexandria
Thessaloniki
Crete
Niş
Belgrade
Malta

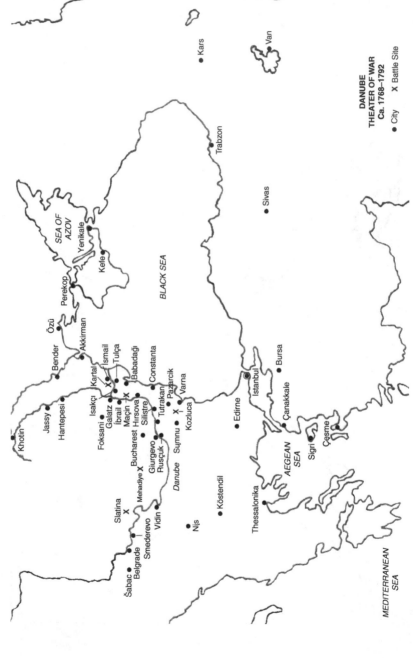

2. The Danube Theater of War, ca. 1768–1792

DANUBE
THEATER OF WAR
Ca. 1768–1792
● City   X Battle Site

SEA OF
AZOV

BLACK SEA

AEGEAN
SEA

MEDITERRANEAN
SEA

Kars
● Van
● Trabzon
● Sivas
Yenikale
Kefe ●
Perekop ●
Özü ●
Bender ●
Akkirman ●
Jassy ●
Hantepesi ●
Khotin ●
Foksani ●
Isakçı
Galatz
İbrail
Maçin
Hirsova
Silistre
Bucharest
Giurgevo
Ruşçuk
Mehadiye
Slatina
Smederevo
Vidin
Šabac
Belgrade
Niş ●
Köstendil ●
Thessalonika ●
Sigri
Çeşme
İstanbul
Edirne ●
Çanakkale ●
Bursa ●
Kartal
İsmail
Tulça
Babadaği
Constanța
Pazarcik
Varna
Tutrakan
Kozluca
Şumnu
Danube

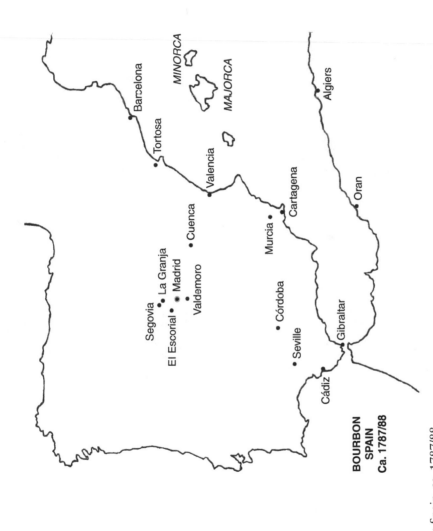

Barcelona
Tortosa
MINORCA
MAJORCA
Valencia
Cartagena
Algiers
Oran
Segovia
La Granja
Cuenca
El Escorial • Madrid
Valdemoro
Murcia
Córdoba
Gibraltar
Seville
Cádiz

**BOURBON
SPAIN
Ca. 1787/88**

3. Bourbon Spain, ca. 1787/88

Introduction

In a famous work called the *Sublime Ethics*, or *Ahlâk-ı Alâî*, the Ottoman moralist Kınâlızâde Ali Çelebi (d. 1571) counted two different kinds of ignorance: simple and compound. While the first type means simply not to know something, which itself is not overly blameworthy, the second is more pernicious. Compound ignorance is twofold in that a person does not know a thing, but wrongly thinks that he does; it is a vice because he is ignorant of his own ignorance.[1]

There is something about biography that lends itself to ignorance. A biographer on one hand has the impossible task of evoking a past life, in many cases one far from his own in time, gender, mentality, and culture, and lived in a complex web of social relations. There can be no total biography, just as there can be no total history. It goes without saying that major and minor gaps will remain no matter how carefully one reconstructs a subject's upbringing, career, opinions, and wider socio-cultural context. Sources, subjective experience, and the distance of time pose barriers that no one can fully overcome. At the same time, biographers run the risk of feeling too close to subjects as they dispel their initial ignorance – they risk trading simple for compound vices and trusting too much in the limited scope of their knowledge. We of course have no idea how Kınâlızâde might have solved the problem of biography. Very probably, however, he would have first advised us to know what we know, know what we do not know, and admit to our simple ignorance. It is only by grappling with these limits that a biographer can avoid more

---

[1] KINÂLIZÂDE, 170–174. See also Gottfried Hagen, "The Order of Knowledge, the Knowledge of Order: Intellectual Life," in *The Cambridge History of Turkey* (Cambridge, 2013), 2: 407.

serious pitfalls and begin to write an honest, if incomplete and imperfect, account of his subject.

In this study – a biography of the eighteenth-century Ottoman historian, courtier, and intellectual Ahmed Vâsıf Efendi (ca. 1735–1806) – I have taken Kınâlızâde's wisdom as a guide and solace. Indeed, his words hold doubly true for Middle Eastern lives. Whether from a cultural reticence, a "principled forgetfulness," or a different valuation of the life lived, Middle Eastern societies before the nineteenth century left much less in the way of biographical material than did their European counterparts. This is not to say that we lack sources, even first-person narrative. Literate early modern Ottomans wrote travel accounts as well as diaries and anthologies on poets, scribes, and scholars; some wrote embassy reports and poetry; and still others left autobiographical fragments, curricula vitae of a sort to describe an intellectual career. Rich as these sources are, though, they do not offer the level or type of detail to which European historians are used. Ottomans had no tradition of memoir or confessional autobiography, for example. While private letters survive, these, like their poetry and biographical writing, tend to eschew subjectivity for the language of moral trope and metaphor. The sources set parameters, then: by and large, we know Ottomans as public and professional figures, with little inkling of family, friendships, or personality, and still less of inner life. The would-be Ottoman biographer must thus make creative use of sources, follow archival trails, mine contemporary European accounts, and read his subject's own writings with care, patience, and a readiness to either admit defeat or speculate.[2]

It is perhaps little wonder that Ottoman historians rarely produce biography, so great is the bother and so meager are the rewards. Even so, it is a loss to the field. Biography gives our knowledge a human cast, or what Cornell Fleischer once likened to putting flesh on a skeleton: "not only bones, but organs, veins, emotions, rhythms."[3] While Fleischer took the sixteenth century as his period rather than the eighteenth, as told through the life of Mustafa Âli of Gallipoli, the reader will see that

---

[2] The problem of biography in Middle East and Ottoman history is by no means new. See Virginia Aksan, "The Question of Writing Premodern Biographies of the Middle East," in *Auto/Biography and the Construction of Identity and Community in the Middle East*, ed. Mary Ann Fay (New York, 2001), 191–200; Martin Kramer, ed., *Middle Eastern Lives: The Practice of Biography and Self-Narrative* (Syracuse, 1991); and İlber Ortaylı, "Türk Tarihçiliğinde Biyografi İnşası ve Biyografik Malzeme Sorunsalı," in *Osmanlı'dan Cumhuriyet'e Problemler, Araştırmalar, Tartışmalar* (Istanbul, 1998), 56–63.

[3] Cornell H. Fleischer, *Bureaucrat and Intellectual in the Ottoman Empire: The Historian Mustafa Âli, 1541–1600* (Princeton, 1986), 4.

I agree with his sentiment. How is it that thirty years later, we still know so little about the Ottomans? Why is Ottoman cultural and mental life still such a mystery to us? Our subject Ahmed Vâsıf served for nearly forty years in the imperial chancery and as court historian (*vekâyi'nüvis*), fought in two wars, went to Russia and Spain, wrote on poetry, ethics, politics, and printing, and left a vast history. Perhaps the greatest mind of his era, he lived at the same time as giants of the European Enlightenment like Immanuel Kant (1724–1804) and Joseph Haydn (1732–1809). How is it that we know so much less about his world, its rhythms, and its intellectual pulses? This book aims to evoke the human side of Vâsıf's world, an empire on the cusp of modernity, and to explore the life of an Ottoman thinker while dispelling our ignorance of a key juncture in that empire's history. Vâsıf is in this way both a subject and vessel for wider study. Through his life and writings, we can enter the cultural and intellectual ferment of his day, grasp his experiences, and see his world as a Muslim gentleman saw it; we can trace the career of an individual while sketching a panorama of élite Ottoman society at a time of great upheaval – the eighteenth century.

While we need not pause long, it may be useful first to say a few words about the Ottoman world in Vâsıf's lifetime. By the early 1700s, the empire was already ancient. Its rule in Anatolia, the Balkans, and the Arab lands of Egypt, Syria, and North Africa went back some four hundred years and, to members of the ruling Muslim élite, rested on the virtues of a dynasty that God had blessed over all others. The Ottoman Empire arose in the wake of the Mongol invasions. Led by semi-nomadic Oğuz Turks, and a line descended from a figure named Osman, the Ottomans began as plunderers, freebooters, and self-styled warriors for the faith or *ghâzi*s on the Byzantine frontier in northwest Anatolia. The enterprise took on a more organized aspect in the fourteenth and fifteenth centuries as the band, buoyed by success, gained followers and pushed into Thrace and the Balkans and seized neighboring Christian lands for Islam. By the sixteenth century, the Ottomans ruled a full-fledged empire – crowned by Mehmed II's 1453 capture of Constantinople (present-day Istanbul), as well as by his grandson Selim I's conquest of the Levant, Egypt, and the Holy Cities of Mecca and Medina. The Ottomans were a feared power. To the English historian Richard Knolles in 1603, they were the "terror of the world." Yet the conquest empire soon passed. Its vast reaches needed consolidation and, from the reign of Süleyman I (1520–1566), it turned its energies inward and slowly, if painfully, joined the ranks of early modern states. The realm changed so fundamentally during the seventeenth century that one scholar has called it a "second empire."[4] Sultans reigned but no longer ruled, trading military leadership for the role of figurehead and leaving power in the hands of great households and a developed scribal bureaucracy. Ottoman expansion ground to a halt with the 1683 siege of Vienna and a final closure of the frontier in the ensuing Treaty of Karlowitz (1699). The empire's power structure was also greatly altered. Where the conquest empire had been centralized in Istanbul, the bureaucratic empire of the seventeenth and eighteenth centuries more closely resembled a loosely spun web. Élites grew in number and spread deeper into the provinces, helped in part by the rise of tax-farming and the 1695 grant of lifetime freehold (*malikâne*), but the fabric wore thin overall. The empire in 1700 was more interconnected, but more decentralized, stronger in spots but weaker as a whole than its earlier incarnation.

To discern this polity's human side requires a closer look at those with a stake in government. Who made decisions? Who ruled the empire? Traditionally, Ottoman society was split into two groups: Muslim and non-Muslim taxpaying subjects (called the "flock" or *re'âyâ*) and a ruling élite (*'askerî*) who, in theory, protected the "flock," paid no taxes, and served one of three distinct but not exclusive career paths. Religious scholars (*'ilmiyye*), or "Men of Learning," were the bookmen who staffed the empire's courts and schools, its judges, jurists, teachers, and upholders of law. Soldiers (*seyfiyye*), or "Men of the Sword," held military rank. These were commanders, governors, viziers, and members of the realm's once crack infantry corps, the Janissaries, who by now had taken up trade, but still enjoyed nominal military status. Scribes (*kalemiyye*), or "Men of the Pen," meanwhile, the last career line to form, managed the empire's day-to-day affairs, kept bureaucratic records, and held chancery and treasury posts in the capital or provinces. Taken together, Ottoman political thinkers held that these groups formed a fixed "world order," a timeless, divinely-ordained hierarchy, the divisions of which each group had to respect for society to function and in which the élite acted as a linchpin. They were the "glue" that held the régime together.

It was to this latter group of élites that Vâsıf and his peers belonged. Soldier, scholar, or scribe, they were educated in the Islamic classics, shared a system of loyalties and beliefs, and knew up to three languages, Arabic, Persian, and Turkish, in addition to local dialects. The Ottoman

---

[4] Baki Tezcan, *The Second Ottoman Empire: Political and Social Transformation in the Early Modern World* (Cambridge, 2010).

élite ruled by consensus, not only representing the royal household and administration, but also other interest groups aligned with Istanbul. Outwardly, we know much about these men. We can often discover their names, trace their careers from office to office in archives or chronicles, and sometimes make out personal networks, factions, and enmities. We also know that the eighteenth-century élite was larger and more diffuse than before and extended far into the hinterlands. In Vâsıf's day, Ottoman powerbrokers included dynasts, scribes, tax-farmers, merchants, Janissaries, and local magnates. Yet realities were far from the ideal. Ottomans kept up the fiction of a military empire – indeed, the whole government joined the army on campaign – but in the eighteenth century, scribes held a decisive balance of power. In the 1700s, the bureaucracy grew larger and more powerful, especially the chancery and its head, the chief scribe, or *reisülküttâb*, who oversaw the realm's increasingly vital foreign affairs. So too did it yield a number of Grand Viziers, like Halil Hamid Paşa (d. 1785), who jumped career lines in striking though not always smooth transitions to "Men of the Sword." By contrast, scholars and military men faced increasing alienation and made it hard to sustain a governing consensus. The eighteenth century is thus in many ways this story: "a hundred-year struggle of the Ottoman dynasty and its affiliated households to preserve the old order."[5]

Educated Ottomans also felt a deep sense of historical and political mission. For them, the empire was nothing less than a worldly expression of God's will and favor for the Ottoman dynasty, a "manifest destiny" or exceptionalism for which they found proof in past events. The realm's rapid growth from a medieval frontier polity, its expansion into Europe and the Islamic heartlands, its capture of Istanbul – these feats proved that God had not only sent the dynasty to renew and spread the faith, but fated its success. The Ottomans had their origins in warfare. If expansion had mostly ceased by the eighteenth century, élites still paid lip service to an archaic warrior ethos and celebrated the realm's past and future conquests in poetry and prose, in panegyric and historiography. They seem to have believed their own press. The realm could not be beaten, they claimed; come what may, it would triumph and last until the end of time.

The eighteenth century did not unfold as these men hoped and envisioned, however. Not all was well. In fact, the Ottoman world would face an unprecedented crisis in several long-term trends: military defeat,

---

[5] Virginia Aksan, "War and Peace," in *The Cambridge History of Turkey* (Cambridge, 2006), 3: 113–114.

a breakdown in élite consensus, and the glaring failure of exceptionalism as an ideology. The 1700s began with promise. Despite the terms of Karlowitz, by which they ceded large territories for the first time, Ottoman rulers had enough success to feel a false sense of strength and security. Abroad, they balanced losses at Passarowitz (1718) with the capture of Azov (1711) and the Morea, regained in 1715 from Venice, while the 1739 Treaty of Belgrade rewarded a three-year struggle against Russia and Austria with Belgrade, parts of Wallachia, and thirty years of peace. At home, meanwhile, Ottoman fiscal policy triumphed. Alongside a general economic boom, tax-farm yields grew tenfold between 1703 and 1768 and made up some fifty percent of the empire's revenues, prosperity that was reflected in Istanbul as élites built waterfront pleasure domes and followed the royal household up and down the Bosphorus on seasonal villegiatura. This was the world in which Vâsıf and his peers grew to adulthood. They would look back on the time as an Edwardian summer of feasts, garden parties, and entertainments.[6]

The 1768–1774 Ottoman-Russian war put an abrupt end to this golden vision. It is fair to say that many Ottomans were overconfident and shocked by the war's outcome; it is also accurate to date to 1774 a cascading series of crises in the empire, both political and ideological. The Ottoman military had not kept pace with European tactics and weapons, nor did the empire's weak central authority work well under the strain of war in raising men, revenue, and supplies. Bankrupt and feeble, the realm needed some measure of reform to preserve the old order. The problem was that reform in the army or bureaucracy threatened vested interests and shifted power away from some élites – Janissary, grandee, tax-farmer – toward others, stirring up bitter resentment. As calls for reform grew louder in the century's final decades, then, the Ottoman élite bickered. The violent political life of the period points to a breakdown in consensus as well as a deep moral and intellectual crisis that not even the empire's putative savior could resolve. While Sultan Selim III (1789–1807) ended the vacillation of his predecessors Mustafa III (1757–1774) and Abdülhamid I (1774–1789), overseeing bold changes, his deposition and murder and the purging of his allies set Ottoman reform back by decades. By 1808, the régime was beset by paralysis and failing legitimacy, the old order unable to support itself.

[6] Shirine Hamadeh evokes this zeitgeist well in *The City's Pleasures: Istanbul in the Eighteenth Century* (Seattle, 2007). See also Ariel Salzmann, "An Ancien Régime Revisited: 'Privatization' and Political Economy in the Eighteenth-Century Ottoman Empire," *Politics and Society* 21 (1993): 393–423.

Historians know these details well, if they may quibble with my rather grim reading of the century as a whole. What we do not know is how Ottomans reacted. That these reverses challenged the empire's ruling ideology must only have made them harder for élites to rationalize and digest. Ottoman political beliefs brooked no middle ground. If God truly blessed the dynasty and realm, if He gave them special favor, how and why did they now fare so poorly? In fact, this question was not new. Ottoman thinkers since the late sixteenth century had worried about the empire's "decline" and how best to restore its former glory, devoting a genre of political advice literature to the issue with models by men like Mustafa Âli (d. 1600), Kâtib Çelebi (d. 1657), and Mustafa Naîmâ (d. 1716). Ottoman decline literature voiced a sense of loss at an imagined "golden age" when truth, order, and justice had prevailed. As often happens in changing societies, its authors sensed that their ideals and concept of the world no longer matched reality. They thus looked to the past, usually the reign of Süleyman I, and called for reform to rebuild the distinctions of class and estate that they believed once guaranteed the empire's order. It is not always helpful for us, with the benefit of hindsight, to dismiss these ideas or to point out that early modern Ottomans simply mistook historical change for symptoms of imperial "decline." The psychological effect was real. In the eighteenth century, too, Ottomans saw "disorder" and "decline" as the source of the empire's problems and tried vainly to hold on to their sense of mission. It was only as defeat built on defeat that the effort failed. In fact, for Vâsıf and his peers, the world did not just appear to be changing. It seemed to be sliding inexorably into chaos.[7]

It is probably true to say that the failure of Ottoman exceptionalism worsened the century's political turbulence. An eighteenth-century Ottoman had few options when faced with his worldview's bankruptcy. One was to ignore it; another, less forgiving, was to look for answers and assign blame. What had happened and why? The vitriol and recrimination in our sources seem to fit the pattern of a blame game, one that singled out different groups in the élite for moral or political failings and escalated as the century wore on. We would be wrong to focus only on the destructive,

---

[7] There is a large literature on Ottoman "declinism." See Douglas Howard, "Ottoman Historiography and the Literature of 'Decline' of the Sixteenth and Seventeenth Centuries," *Journal of Asian History* 22 (1988): 52–77; Cemal Kafadar, "The Myth of the Golden Age: Ottoman Historical Consciousness in the Post-Süleymânic Era," in *Süleyman the Second and His Time*, eds. Halil İnalcık and Cemal Kafadar (Istanbul, 1993), 37–48; and idem, "The Question of Ottoman Decline," *Harvard Middle Eastern and Islamic Review* 4 (1998): 30–75.

however. A third option remained: to seek out new and creative solutions. Collective anxiety drove much intellectual debate in the late 1700s as Ottomans of all stripes – military men, statesmen, shills, earnest objectors, and cynical opportunists – moved to save the old order. We see it at work in issues ranging from the legal and moral merits of peacemaking to the limits of human reason and political reform. We even find it in debate over historical causation and in theological disputes over free will and theodicy. Ottoman anxiety was highly productive.[8] Vâsıf and his peers met the period's challenges largely on the strength of their own resources by adapting, reinterpreting, and reshaping the capital of some thousand years of Islamic culture. While they did not intend to remake their society, preferring to see the empire's plight in familiar frameworks, their activity forces us to ask how the eighteenth century shaped Ottoman minds, how it eroded key legal, ethical, and philosophical concepts, and how it contributed to a looming Ottoman modernity. So formed, this question hangs over the following pages. We must look to this eighteenth-century *fin de siècle* if we choose to define "modern" not only by technological progress, but in terms of episteme and worldview, for it was then that Ottoman élites forged new ways of seeing themselves and the wider world.

While nearly inescapable to us today, modernity remains a loaded term in Islamic and historical scholarship. "Modern" means many things to a great many people. It can signify a discourse, a culture, a lifestyle, a mindset, or a historical period. It may be a parochial European phenomenon or bleed into all manner of local "modernities" and conflate with related but distinct issues like westernization, enlightenment, and secularism. Modernity as such tends to lose meaning as an analytical category.[9] I do not wish to get bogged down in the well-trod debates over Islamic and Ottoman modernity. However, the reader deserves to know upfront how I treat the concept. Historians have often linked the onset of modernity in the Ottoman Empire to the adoption of European arms, tactics, institutions, and mores starting in the late eighteenth and early nineteenth centuries, as a result of Western encroachment. The idea that modernity came via technological or institutional import is not entirely wrong, but it masks other useful perspectives and ignores the role of domestic actors. The very act of borrowing required deliberation on the part of statesmen and thinkers. It forced them to grapple with new and at times profoundly

---

[8] I treat the link between "decline," anxiety, and intellectual debate in "Free Will, Predestination, and the Fate of the Ottoman Empire," *Journal of the History of Ideas* 77 (2016): 445–466.

[9] Alev Çınar, *Modernity, Islam, and Secularism in Turkey* (Minneapolis, 2005), 1–9.

unsettling ideas. Modernity as an emerging intellectual mindset or attitude, then, or as episteme or worldview, must form part of our narrative. Focusing on intellectual development restores a good deal of agency to the Ottomans. It also highlights changes that occurred wholly or mostly through internal dynamics. The past three decades have seen heated discussion in the field about "Islamic Enlightenment" – whether the eighteenth century saw a native growth in scholastic rationalism, a valorization of philosophy, and a shift away from a theocentric to an anthropocentric worldview in the empire. While I hesitate to use the term "Enlightenment" – usually reserved for the intellectual-philosophical movement of eighteenth-century Europe – this complex of ideas offers intriguing parallels and seems to indicate a break with the past. My own study explores some of the contemporary trends in more detail, in contests over the limits of human reason and action and in showing a clear disjuncture with older conceptual frameworks.[10]

How does Ahmed Vâsıf illuminate these issues, then? What makes him a good subject and how does his life help us to grasp the intellectual history of the eighteenth-century Ottoman Empire? This is a fair question. For one thing, Vâsıf is uniquely fitted for biographical study. Born in Baghdad around 1735, he had a long career in government service and left a richly detailed paper trail: ten major and minor works totaling some 2,500 manuscript folia in poetry, ethics, geography, lexicography, politics, and history, as well as drafts, personal papers, and scores of archival documents. We know more about Vâsıf than perhaps any other pre-modern Ottoman statesman. We can trace his career almost continuously from his entry into state service in 1768 to his 1806 death, follow his formation and growth, and catch snatches of family and personal relations. There is also inner life. Vâsıf had a strong if complex personality, what some today might call an "over-developed ego." He wrote prolifically and enjoyed writing about himself and adding personal commentary, allowing us to judge his views on Ottoman state and society and a host of pressing issues. Vâsıf the intellectual emerges most clearly in the court chronicle that he began in the 1780s and continued, off and on, until

---

[10] On Islamic Enlightenment, see the provocative work of Reinhard Schulze: "Das islamische achtzehnte Jahrhundert: Versuch einer historiographischen Kritik," *Die Welt des Islams* 30 (1990): 140–159; and idem, "Was ist die islamische Aufklärung?" *Die Welt des Islams* 36 (1996): 276–325. B. Harun Küçük argues the Ottoman case in "Early Enlightenment in Istanbul" (Ph.D. diss., University of California, San Diego, 2012). See too Fatih Yeşil's study – also a good intellectual biography – *Aydınlanma Çağında bir Osmanlı Kâtibi: Ebubekir Râtib Efendi (1750–1799)* (Istanbul, 2010).

the year before his death. Called the *Charms and Truths of Relics and Annals*, or *Mehâsinü'l-Âsâr ve Hakâîkü'l-Ahbâr*, the work is a sprawling account of the latter half of the eighteenth century, a sort of tapestry in which he interwove his views with those of his patrons, the sultans, and his own courtly faction. *Charms and Truths* is as notable for its historical contents as for its interpretation. Vâsıf showed his benefactors in a fawning light, it is true, but he also took pains to support their policies with the intellectual means at hand. He mined the Ottoman canon for compelling arguments, created a coherent philosophical framework, and quite literally rewrote the dynastic history by reworking and annexing earlier accounts to his narrative. His is an intellectually forceful and partisan work – it is a historical monument to Ottoman reformism.

For Vâsıf wrote from a definite point of view. Indeed, he is well-suited to study insofar as he belonged to and spoke for an identifiable group of like-minded élites. Mostly scribes, these men had survived the Russian-Ottoman wars, tasted defeat firsthand, and believed in the need for centralizing and royal reform. They first held power as a loose coalition in the 1770s and 1780s, for a time under Grand Vizier Halil Hamid Paşa. However, it was only under Selim III that they came into their own and began to push for deeper change. With the sultan's help, they issued the "New Order," or *nizâm-ı cedîd*, a bold and wide-ranging reform program in the empire's military, administrative, fiscal, and social spheres. For the first time, the empire opened embassies in European capitals. For the first time, it joined the concert of non-Muslim foreign powers. Selim III and his courtiers even upstaged the Janissary corps by founding a new style army drilled in European arms and tactics, loyal to the sultan, and funded by its own treasury. Vâsıf spent his adult life with these men. His ideas formed and evolved as they worked, talked, plotted, squabbled, and (very often) died together. While a leading thinker, then, Vâsıf was fairly typical of the group and more successful as a systematizer of their ideas than as an innovator. His story is not uncommon. If we can say that he was an outsized personality, his ideas were less exceptional than representative of Ottoman reformist currents at large.

The fact that Vâsıf is so richly documented does not make the task of biography easy, nonetheless. His writing poses distinct obstacles. It is well to remember that Vâsıf lived in a patrimonial society, supported by sultans and Grand Viziers, and as such was limited in what he could or could not say. Court could be a dangerous place. A scribe or historian might offer criticism, but not usually of living, powerful figures, lest he lose his position or life, and he could not diverge too far from a patron's

FIG. 0.1: Ahmed Vâsıf Efendi (d. 1806) as Spanish ambassador.
Reproduced by kind permission of the Biblioteca Nacional de España.

directives. It is at times hard to discern where Vâsıf stood on particular issues or whether, in some cases, he withheld his views out of fear. I have hence tried to be mindful of these concerns and read between lines, noting when his position jars with those he held elsewhere. Nor did Vâsıf always tell the truth. Brilliant but conceited, he was not known for honesty and is sometimes belied by outside sources, Ottoman and European, usually in casting himself in a more favorable light. These issues do not render Vâsıf a wholly unreliable narrator, however, and the reader will note that I try to explore rather than condemn his deceits and to give him credit without overlooking his faults. Biography is in some ways equal parts art and scholarship. However careful I have been in research and documentation – and I have been meticulous – my portrait of Vâsıf will inevitably be an idiosyncratic and partial account of his person and society, and this, I feel, is no reason for discomfort. Vâsıf has always seemed to recede in the same measure that I move forward. The more I have learned about him and his world, the more I have come to accept how little I know and will ever know about them. It does no good to pretend otherwise – we should not fear a little healthy ignorance.

The Ottoman Empire at Vâsıf's death in 1806 looked largely as it had seventy years earlier in his youth. The loss of some lands aside, the realm remained intact and the line of Ottoman sultans still ruled, if precariously, from Istanbul. Dress, manners, customs, morés – the historian as a young man would have recognized all the outward trappings of early nineteenth-century Ottoman society as his own. Yet there were dramatic changes afoot. Vâsıf and his colleagues had lived through unprecedented trials, crises that eroded their very worldview, and they altered the empire's intellectual landscape for good in the search for a remedy. There was no going back. But it would not be wholly correct to date the "modern" empire from this period, at least as no self-respecting intellectual would have accepted such an idea. Vâsıf and his peers remained loyal Ottomans to the end, still committed to the traditions and ideals of the dynasty, its laws, institutions, social order, and unique mission in history. In this way, we can perhaps say that they were neither here nor there, unwittingly on the brink of a seismic shift, but not over it, the last of the ancients and first of the moderns.

I

Out of the East: Early Life (ca. 1735–1768)

The world was old when Ahmed b. Hasan was born in Baghdad in the early decades of the eighteenth century. God, it was said, had created the earth and Adam ages ago *ex nihilo* and revealed His final messenger Muhammad a thousand years past and more. For four hundred years, the dynasty of Ottoman sultans had reigned over a far-flung empire with Istanbul at its heart; just as the Prophet was the seal of prophets, so too would they, the seal of dynasties, rule till the end of time. Ahmed b. Hasan's birthplace on the margins of this empire was not terribly auspicious. Once the glittering center of a civilization and an empire in its own right, the Abbasid caliphate, Baghdad by the year of his birth ca. 1735[1] had dwindled to a provincial outpost along the Persian border, an area that after the collapse of Safavid power in the 1730s and 1740s suffered from instability and military incursions, most lately in the

---

[1] Vâsıf's birthdate has been a point of some error and conjecture, as it is nowhere specified. Ottoman biographies claim that he exceeded seventy years of age at his death in 1221/ 1806: Ahmed Cevdet, *Târih-i Cevdet* (Istanbul, 1891/92) 8: 77; Süleyman Fâik, *Sefînetü'r-Rüesâ* (Istanbul, 1853), 149; Davud Fâtin, *Tezkere-i Hâtimetü'l-Eş'âr* (Istanbul, 1854), 432; and Mehmed Cemaleddin Karslızâde, *Osmanlı Tarih ve Müverrihleri: Âyine-i Zurefâ* (Istanbul, 2003), 65. European sources are slightly more helpful. The *Diario de Madrid* reported on September 12, 1787, that he looked no more than forty-five years of age, while an official letter (August 15, 1787) from authorities in Barcelona to the central Spanish government stated that he was fifty-four years old. If we presume that the latter number is the more accurate information and work backwards, it yields a birthdate of AD 1733 or alternately AH 1147 (AD 1734/35). For these citations, see Antonio Jurado Aceituno, "18. Yüzyılda Bir Osmanlı Elçisinin İspanya'yı Ziyareti," *Tarih ve Toplum* 36 (2001): 34; and Mehmet Necati Kutlu, "İspanyol Belgelerine Göre İspanya Nezdinde Görevlendirilen (Eyüp'te Medfun) İlk Osmanlı Elçisi Ahmet Vâsıf Efendi," in *Tarihi, Kültürü ve Sanatıyla IV. Eyüpsultan Sempozyumu Tebliğler, 5–7 Mayıs 2000* (Istanbul, 2000), 109.

campaigns of the warlord Nadir Shah. A perception of history and faded glory surely touched the young man. If not consciously, he must have noticed on some level the gulf that divided past and present in his hometown, where relics of greatness stood amid stagnation, and from which a world empire had long since passed to others.[2]

What little we know about Ahmed's family comes through his father, a local religious scholar (*'âlim*) named Ebülbekâ Hasan al-Harbûtî. Although sources say nothing about his mother or possible siblings – either their names or personal details – this scant information does shed some dim light onto his life. Ahmed's full name was Ahmed b. Ebülbekâ Hasan al-Harbûtî.[3] The *nisba* adjective "al-Harbûtî" or "the one from Harbût" indicates that the family originally hailed from the city of Harput in eastern Anatolia, some 500 miles northwest of Baghdad near present-day Elâzığ. As Harput's population was historically mixed, one cannot extrapolate an ethnicity for them, Kurd, Turk, Arab, or Armenian. Ahmed's family must have been of modest means. That his father earned a living by teaching and does not feature in contemporary biographical dictionaries means that he probably did not hold any major posts in the city's ulema hierarchy and was not well-known.[4] However, by merit of his vocation, Ebülbekâ Hasan was certainly literate and a member, albeit a minor one, of the empire's learned religious institution (*'ilmiyye*). This social position afforded his son distinct educational and professional opportunities.

---

[2] On Baghdad and Iraq in the eighteenth century, see Tom Nieuwenhuis, *Politics and Society in Early Modern Iraq* (The Hague, 1981); and Robert Olson, *The Siege of Mosul and Ottoman-Persian Relations, 1718–1743: A Study of Rebellion in the Capital and War in the Provinces of the Ottoman Empire* (Bloomington, IN, 1975). A near-contemporary account is given by J.-B. Louis Jacques Rousseau in *Description du pachalik de Baghdad, suivie d'une Notice historique sur les Wahabis, et de quelques autres pieces relatives à l'Histoire et à la Littérature de l'Orient* (Paris, 1809), 1–122.

[3] Ismâ'îl Bâshâ al-Baghdâdî, *Hadiyyat al-'ârifîn: asmâ al-mu'allifîn wa âthâr al-muṣannifîn min kashf al-ẓunûn* (Beirut, 2008), 1: 166; M. Nuri Çınarcı, ed., "Şeyhülislâm Ârif Hikmet Bey'in Tezkiretü'ş-Şu'ârâsı ve Transkripsiyonlu Metni," (master's thesis, Gaziantep University, 2007), 108; and Mehmed Nâil Tuman, *Tuhfe-i Nâilî: Divân Şâirlerinin Muhtasar Biyografileri* (Istanbul, 2001), 2: 1139. Vâsıf is also called "Ahmed Vâsıf b. Hasan" in court records (*siciller*) after his death: e.g. SSA, Kısmet-i Askeriyye nr. 827, pp. 4b, 21a. My thanks to Aysel Yıldız for these documents.

[4] Çınarcı, "Tezkiretü'ş-Şu'ârâ," 108. I have consulted standard works as well as those specifically on Iraqi scholars: Muḥammad b. Muṣṭafa al-Ghulâmî, *Shimâmat al-'anbar wa'l-zahr al-mu'anbar* (Baghdad, 1977); Muḥammad Amîn b. Faḍl Allah al-Muḥibbî, *Khulâṣat al-athâr fî 'ayân al-qarn al-ḥâdî 'ashar* (Cairo, 1868) 4 vols.; Muḥammad Khalîl b. 'Alî al-Murâdî, *Silk al-durar fî 'ayân al-qarn al-thânî 'ashar* (Beirut, 1997), 2 vols.; 'Uthmân b. 'Alî al-'Umarî, *al-Rawḍ al-naḍir fî tarjamat udabâ al-'aṣr* (Baghdad, 1974–75), 3 vols.; Muḥammad Amîn b. Khayr Allah al-'Umarî, *Manhal al-awliyyâ wa mashrab al-aṣfiyyâ min sâdât al-Mawsil al-ḥadbâ* (Mosul, 1967), 2 vols.

Ahmed's education would have started early in life. Because Ebülbekâ Hasan was a scholar, it is safe to assume that the boy's earliest lessons took place at his father's side. In addition to his first language, spoken at home, probably the local dialect of Arabic,[5] he would have been introduced as a young child to the Quran and its language of classical Arabic and sent to a *mekteb*, or Quran school, where students read and recited scripture and learned basic religious precepts as well as the rudiments of Arabic grammar. The next step in a typical education, at least for those aspiring to the religious hierarchy, was to enroll in a college or *medrese*. Whether Ahmed took this step is not clear. We know that he studied with Baghdadi scholars, perhaps as an informal auditor, and recalled in later life observing local ulema refute the new Wahhabi creed.[6] It is likewise clear that he had a solid grasp of rhetoric (*belâgat*), dialectic and logic (*mantık*), scriptural exegesis (*tefsîr*) and traditions (*hadîs*), and speculative theology (*kelâm*), advanced subjects normally taught in the *medrese*.[7] Rather uncharacteristically, Ahmed wrote virtually nothing as an adult about his studies. "I spent the prime of my life learning the noble and technical sciences and perfecting my education," he said in one passage from the 1770s, "giving my nights to study and foregoing sleep."[8] Only once did he record a teacher's name: Mehmed Mekkî Efendi, a judge, two-time *şeyhülislâm*, and author of a popular commentary on the celebrated Arabic poem the *Ode of the Mantle* (*Kasîde-i Bürde*) whom he met much later in Istanbul. "Early in his career he was on familiar terms

---

[5] A Spanish source cited in Aceituno, 35, says that among other languages, Vâsıf knew Syriac. While this is plausible given his family's origins, Vâsıf would also have learned colloquial Arabic.

[6] Ahmed Âsım, *Târih-i Âsım* (Istanbul, 1870), 1: 255. Vâsıf probably saw this disputation (MEHÂSİN 4, fol. 152b) during his adolescence or early adulthood. Founded by Sheikh Muḥammad ibn 'Abd al-Wahhâb (d. 1792), this controversial creed focused on the divine unity and was rejected by members of all four Sunni legal schools. Written refutations began to appear as early as 1744–1745. Hamadi Redissi, "The Refutation of Wahhabism in Arabic Sources, 1745–1932," in *Kingdom Without Borders: Saudi Political, Religious, and Media Frontiers* (New York, 2008), esp. 165–167.

[7] On typical tuition in early modern Ottoman schools, see Madeline Zilfi, *The Politics of Piety: the Ottoman Ulema in the Postclassical Age (1600–1800)* (Minneapolis, 1988), esp. 43–80; Richard Chambers, "The Education of a Nineteenth-Century Ottoman Âlim: Ahmed Cevdet Paşa," *IJMES* 4 (1973): 440–464; and Shahab Ahmed and Nenad Filipovic, "The Sultan's Syllabus: A Curriculum for the Imperial Ottoman *Medreses*," *Studia Islamica* 98/99 (2004): 183–218. Vâsıf discusses analogical propositions in MEHÂSİN 2, fol. 13a. In MEHÂSİN 4, fols. 47b–48b, he recounts an exegetical debate over Quran verse 2:133, which he translated from Arabic into Ottoman Turkish.

[8] NEVÂBİG, fols. 1b–2a. The "technical sciences" like grammar and syntax were tools to acquire "noble sciences," such as traditions and exegesis.

with me," Ahmed recalled, marking Mekkî Efendi's 1797 death. "I always profited from his wisdom and solved difficulties in exegesis and other fields by referring them to him."[9] However, Ahmed later in life also voiced a palpable disdain for the ulema, calling them corrupt, unqualified, illiterate sponges.[10]

Why did Ahmed not follow his father's career path? Why, indeed, did he become openly contemptuous of it? Like many of his generation, it may well be that he was stymied in pursuing a religious career. The eighteenth-century *'ilmiyye* did not welcome sons of provincial scholars, however talented. Unique among Islamic states, the empire had co-opted the religious hierarchy and brought training and posting under its control in Istanbul; youths who wanted a formal teaching or judicial career had to go to the capital as a rule to access its system of schools and pious foundations. Starved of resources at home, these provincials often could not meet the standards for employment and found the going hard even when they did. It was typical for candidates to wait years to take the qualifying exam (*rüûs*) for a teaching post, for example, and while an entry-level grade conferred status, a stipend, and security, further advancement relied less on skill or seniority than on well-heeled patrons. Qualified candidates flooded the system. Nepotism also limited the higher ranks to a closed set of Istanbul families, whose sons could bypass the exams entirely and take over their fathers' posts by hereditary succession.[11] Ahmed's complaints about the profession were precisely these – it was corrupt and dominated by the ill-educated and undeserving – and his contempt may have masked some amount of lingering envy or resentment. The religious hierarchy in any case did not offer a promising career.

Other paths to advancement nevertheless remained open for Ahmed b. Hasan and, whether by choice or necessity, he turned increasingly to the literary and scribal arts. Scribal service (*kalemiyye*) in the Ottoman government remained an attractive career path in the mid-eighteenth century, and rather more open than the religious hierarchy. A prospective scribe usually entered a household or chancery department at a young age, where he was trained as an apprentice and learned the basics of calligraphy,

---

[9] MEHÂSİN 3, fol. 169a. Mekkî Efendi, Vâsıf's elder by thirty years, was born in Mecca in AH 1116 (1704/5). While it is perhaps possible that they met earlier, his career did not obviously overlap with Vâsıf's and they most likely knew one another in Istanbul. See SO, 4: 1080; and DİA, s.v. "Mekkî Mehmed Efendi."

[10] For example, MEHÂSİN 4, fols. 42a-42b.

[11] See Madeline Zilfi, "Elite Circulation in the Ottoman Empire: Great Mollas of the Eighteenth Century," *Journal of the Economic and Social History of the Orient* 26 (1983): 318–364.

composition (*inşa*), accounting, and other pertinent skills. In addition to a normal religious education, he was also expected to master a corpus of literature known as *adab*, an encyclopedic array of urbane, humane subjects encompassing everything from history and diplomatics to poetry, proverbs, and bons mots. With this education in hand, and with proper patronage and luck, he could hope in time for a regular position as a full scribe (*kâtib*).[12] Ahmed's journey was not usual in this sense. According to the historian Ahmed Âsım (d. 1819), the young scholar was naturally attracted to literature and applied himself to epistolography and the Arabic linguistic sciences (*'ulûm-ı 'arabiyye*), elements of belles-lettres that, along with other chancery skills, were equally useful to a budding littérateur as to a scribe. His studies were interrupted, however. For reasons unknown, perhaps his father's death, Ahmed soon found himself in need of money and put his pen to use for local élites as a copyist and scribe, for which he earned a reputation as a talented stylist.[13] It is at this time that Ahmed probably won a particularly meaningful honor – a pen name or *mahlas*. When an Ottoman scribe attained sufficient skill, he was normally given a new name reflecting his passage from novice to master and alluding to an outstanding personal quality.[14] Ahmed's new name – Vâsıf, meaning "one who describes or praises" or more colloquially a "wordsmith" – reflected success in his new career path as much as it did his eloquence with words. This was the name that he bore when he emerged into the full light of sources and that he carried until the end of his life: Ahmed Vâsıf Efendi.

We can gain a better idea of early modern scribal training from a miscellany, or *mecmû'a*, that belonged to another Vâsıf Efendi. Ottoman scribes learned through imitation and by studying the models of recognized calligraphers, poets, and stylists. The chancery language was not easy. Whether in Arabic or Turkish, scribes wrote in ornate rhymed prose that was dense with allusion, verse, figure, and metaphor. Prose blended with

---

[12] Scribal education has been treated extensively elsewhere. Examples include Virginia H. Aksan, *An Ottoman Statesman in War and Peace: Ahmed Resmi Efendi, 1700–1783* (Leiden, 1995), 1–12; Carter V. Findley, *Bureaucratic Reform in the Ottoman Empire: The Sublime Porte, 1789–1922* (Princeton, 1980), 93–100; Christine Woodhead, "From Scribe to Littérateur: The Career of a Sixteenth-Century Ottoman Kâtib," *Bulletin of the British Society for Middle East Studies* 9 (1982): 55–74; and Yeşil, *Ebubekir Râtib*, 21–26.

[13] Âsım, 1: 255; and Otocar von Schlechta-Wssehrd, "Die osmanischen Geschichtsschreiber der neueren Zeit," *Denkschriften der phil. hist. Klasse der Kaiserl. Ak. der Wissenschaften* 8 (1856): 5.

[14] Findley, *Reform*, 97.

poetry, indistinguishably at times, and required an ear for prosody and a grasp of the correct form for every occasion – how to write a daily report but also how to phrase petitions and letters of congratulations, consolation, thanks, and others. The miscellany in question was likely a private notebook. The owner, one Vâsıf, took down verse by famed poets like Seyyid Mehmed Sabrî (d. 1645), Mustafa Nâilî (d. 1666), and Ahmed Neşâtî (d. 1674). He included a specimen of calligraphy and letters by some of the top Ottoman stylists of the day, like the chronicler Tâlikîzâde (d. 1606), Veysî (d. 1628), the chief scribe Râmî Mehmed Efendi (d. 1708), and Yusuf Nâbî (d. 1712). He even appended one or two samples of his own work. Although he was an earlier Vâsıf, his notes offer an intimate look at the rote learning and wide-ranging knowhow involved in scribal education. Our Vâsıf, too, would have cultivated these skills.[15]

At some point as a young man, Ahmed Vâsıf left his natal city of Baghdad. He himself gives no indication why this was and it may be that the city had little left to offer him. Eighteenth-century Baghdad presented an ambitious but unconnected youth with limited prospects. Entrenched families controlled its highest religious posts and, though a regional center of learning, it could not compete with the empire's larger cities for scholars and students. Baghdad was also ruled by autonomous governors and their extended slave (*mamlûk*) households, who virtually monopolized military and civil positions in the province and whose independence made transferring to the scribal bureaucracy in another province or Istanbul a remote possibility. The same was true up and down the empire's eastern marches. While sovereigns of what is now Iraq and eastern Anatolia, the Ottomans most often ruled these areas through local tribes and urban notables and had never fully integrated them into the empire's regular provincial structure. Whatever control Istanbul held over cities like Baghdad, Basra, and Mosul had waned by the early eighteenth century, as the state came to rely on powerful clans and families to collect taxes and, in times of war, to recruit, mobilize, and supply armed forces. To be sure, these locals were part of the imperial fabric; they had good reason to be loyal and reaped political and financial rewards in return for

---

[15] Vâsıf, *Mecmû'a*, İÜ TY nr. 1555. Internal evidence suggests that this work cannot belong to Ahmed Vâsıf and instead dates from the late seventeenth or early eighteenth century. For example, one letter (fol. 72b) addressed to the chief scribe Bekir Efendi from a former chief scribe and "now lord of Rethymno" Mehmed Bey must be dated to ca. AH 1104 = 1692/93. Cf. Fâik, 45. Another (fols. 73b-74a) by Nâbî congratulates Râmî Efendi on one of his two appointments as chief scribe, either on 28 Ra AH 1106 = November 16, 1694 or 1 R AH 1109 = October 17, 1697.

their cooperation. Yet they made the decisions on the ground, not scribes in Istanbul. Outside of Baghdad, for example, the Jalîlî family effectively ruled at Mosul from 1726 onward. The situation was more complex in Kurdistan, where the Ottomans had long tried to co-opt tribes to consolidate power. In many inaccessible areas – as with the Bâbân clan near Shahrizôr and the Soran near Arbîl – the tribal emirs nevertheless acted with impunity and ruled what were more or less personal fiefdoms, cooperating with Ottoman authorities only when it suited them. It would have been obvious to Vâsıf that a religious or scribal career held little future for him here, along the frontier.[16]

In any event, biographical sources agree that the young Vâsıf traveled west and north to Aleppo, Kars, and Van to continue his education. His movements in these cities are obscure, nor do we know for sure in what order he resided in them. It seems most likely that he first followed the annual desert caravans west from Baghdad to Aleppo, called "the White," an ancient city dominated by its huge medieval citadel.[17] In moving to Aleppo, Vâsıf traded the moribund Baghdad for the empire's third city, a bustling hub of some 100,000 inhabitants which, though smaller than in centuries past, remained a significant commercial entrepôt and intellectual center. He was there by 1761/62 at the latest.[18] He then traveled northeast into the highlands of Anatolia. In April of 1767, for example, while studying near Kars and Van, he witnessed riots in Kars which led to the murder of the local warden, Gürcü Mehmed Paşa.[19]

---

[16] See Dina Rizk Khoury, *State and Provincial Society in the Ottoman Empire: Mosul, 1540–1834* (Cambridge, 1997); and Hakan Özoğlu, *Kurdish Notables and the Ottoman State: Evolving Identities, Competing Loyalties, and Shifting Boundaries* (Albany, NY, 2004).

[17] Joseph von Hammer-Purgstall, *Geschichte der osmanischen Dichtkunst* (Pest, 1837), 3: 552; Fâik, 146; Fâtin, 431; Karslızâde, 64; and Schlechta-Wssehrd, 5. These caravans made the journey once or twice per year. There were two routes: one through northern Mesopotamia and a shorter but more arduous path that forded the Euphrates at the city of Hit and traversed the desert. J.-B. Louis Jacques Rousseau made the latter journey in 1808 and took some two months in transit: *Voyage de Baghdad à Alep (1808), publié d'après le manuscrit inédit de l'auteur* (Paris, 1899). See also idem, *Pachalik de Baghdad*, 54, 77–78.

[18] In a chronicle entry for the year AH 1200 (MEHÂSİN 1, fol. 268a), Vâsıf notes that he was in Aleppo "twenty-five years previously," or in AH 1175 = AD 1761/62. Alexander Russell's estimate of mid-eighteenth-century Aleppo's population at 235,000 is probably much too high: *The Natural History of Aleppo*, rev. ed. (London, 1797), 1: 98. Cf. Maurits H. van den Boogert, *Aleppo Observed: Ottoman Syria through the Eyes of Two Scottish Doctors, Alexander and Patrick Russell* (Oxford, 2010), 185, 188. Rousseau's numbers for the smaller Baghdad (95,000 to 100,000 in *Pachalik de Baghdad*, 8) must also be inflated.

[19] This occurred in Za AH 1180: MEHÂSİN 5, 1: 289–290. Cf. Çeşmîzâde Mustafa, *Çeşmîzâde Tarihi*, ed. Bekir Kütükoğlu (Istanbul, 1993), 25–26.

To his Grace the Duke of S. Argyll. This Print of the City and Castle of ALEPPO is Inscribed by his most Obedient and devoted humble Servant. A.Drummond.

FIG. 1.1: City view of Aleppo in the mid-eighteenth century.
Reproduced courtesy of the Thomas Fisher Rare Book Library, University of Toronto.

These perambulations can best be interpreted within the Islamic tradition of "travel in search of knowledge (*riḥla fī ṭalab al-'ilm*)," whereby men augmented their education by traveling, sometimes very far afield, to seek out respected teachers. Although sources do not specify what or with whom Vâsıf studied, it is quite possible to speculate given the region's intellectual life and his subsequent interests. Theology thrived in eighteenth-century Syria and Anatolia in networks of pietistic Nakşbendî Sufi scholars like Davud-ı Karsî (d. 1755/56), Saçaklızâde Mehmed Maraşî (d. 1732/33), and Ebusaid Mehmed Hâdîmî (d. 1762), all of whom wrote extensively on willpower and human agency, subjects crucial to Vâsıf's mature thought.[20] Aleppo itself supported theology, but also the study of jurisprudence, exegesis, prophetic traditions, and philology; Anatolia, meanwhile, was known for the high level of its logic, philosophy, semantics, and other rational sciences (*'ulûm-ı 'akliyye*), particularly among Kurdish teachers, and attracted students from Baghdad, Aleppo, and elsewhere abroad.[21] Vâsıf certainly continued to study exegesis and theology in his mature years. So too was he well-read in philosophy, ethics, astronomy, and the natural sciences, all subjects taught outside of the *medrese* and for which he presumably found private tutors. Indeed, this is one obstacle in sketching his formation as a thinker. It is hard to associate him with any one "type" of intellectual figure. He was not a religious scholar like his father, though he was deeply familiar with the religious or "transmitted" sciences (*'ulûm-ı nakliyye*). He was not a philosopher, despite the space he devoted to philosophical concepts in his work. Neither did he have formal training as a scribe, at least not as a typical novice, even though this became his eventual profession. Vâsıf's education was certainly wide-ranging and profound, but does not seem to have been directed to any of these specific ends. If anything, he might best be

---

[20] Philipp Bruckmayr, "The Particular Will (*al-irâdat al-juz'iyya*): Excavations Regarding a Latecomer in Kalâm Terminology on Human Agency and its Position in Naqshbandi Discourse," *European Journal of Turkish Studies* 13 (2011), 2–20. Hilmi Kemal Altun has cataloged a large number of such scholars and their works in "Osmanlı Müelliflerince Yazılan Kazâ ve Kader Risâleleri ve Taşköprüzâde'nin *Risâle Fi'l-Kazâ ve'l-Kader* Adlı Eseri" (master's thesis, Marmara University, 2010).

[21] Russell is dismissive of contemporary learning in Aleppo, but his description suggests a lively intellectual scene. He also mentions (88 ff.) interest – though he insists that it was sterile – in geography, poetry, and the natural sciences. On Anatolian scholarly networks, see Khaled El-Rouayheb, *Islamic Intellectual History in the Seventeenth Century: Scholarly Currents in the Ottoman Empire and Maghreb* (Cambridge, 2015), 13 ff.; and idem, "The Myth of 'the Triumph of Fanaticism' in the Seventeenth-Century Ottoman Empire," *Die Welt des Islams* 48 (2008): 210–216.

considered a littérateur (edîb); at least, his interests in history, poetry, and ethics place him securely in this ambit.[22]

It is also fair to ask whether Vâsıf developed any interest in Sufism or a more formal affiliation to a dervish order, or tarîkat. This we really do not know. Mystical study was popular in all parts of the empire and offered a more esoteric experience of faith than the scriptural teachings of the college. Sufi orders followed distinct paths – mixtures of ecstatic, contemplative, or ascetic practice – toward a mystic union with God. The novice would seek out a spiritual master or sheikh, a mentor who would guide him in the order's rituals and mysteries and lead him ultimately to full initiation. Several major pathways flourished in the eighteenth century. Halvetî Sufis inclined to asceticism, including retreat, fasting, vigils, meditation, and the repetition (zikr) of devotional litanies, and had been closely linked to the dynasty in earlier days. The Bektaşîs, a heterodox order affiliated with the Janissary corps, venerated the Prophet's son-in-law 'Alî and practiced the sharing of bread and confession of sins to the sheikh, rituals possibly absorbed from Christianity. Mevlevîs, meanwhile, were famed for their music and whirling dances. Yet the foremost mystical order in Vâsıf's lifetime was the Nakşbendiyye. Nakşbendî Sufis took a "sober" tack in their devotions, which centered on silent litany and a rigid adherence to holy law and could, in an Ottoman context, draw on the monist doctrines of the philosopher Muḥyî al-Dîn ibn al-'Arabî (d. 1240). They also took an increasingly active role in public life. Nakşbendîs, particularly the Müceddidî sub-order, called for the moral reform of the Muslim community, insisted on the empire's defense against its enemies, and counted many a scribe and courtier in their influential ranks.

Vâsıf may well have flirted with some kind of mystical study, and more especially with the Nakşbendî order. Nakşbendî Sufis were "spectacularly" successful in Kurdistan, where they became local leaders and held political and intellectual sway from the seventeenth century onward. We know that Vâsıf's family came from this area and that he studied there as a young man. He was well read in Ibn al-'Arabî, whom he called the "greatest master (Şeyh-i Ekber)."[23] There is also a treatise compiled by

---

[22] The author of a rare work from the 1780s said that Vâsıf came "from out of the East," studied with many men of Aleppo, and honed his skill in Arabic, Turkish, and Persian poetry and prose. He hence focused on the literary aspects of Vâsıf's education: Mehmed Emîn, Dercü'l-Vekâyi', Dâr al-kutub, 152 M. Tarîkh Turkî, fol. 87a. My thanks to Noah Gardiner for securing this manuscript.

[23] SEFÂRETNÂME, fol. 348a. Vâsıf cited Ibn al-'Arabî elsewhere, e.g. MEHÂSİN 5, 1: 8. See also Dina Le Gall, A Culture of Sufism: Naqshbandis in the Ottoman World, 1450–1700 (Albany, 2005); and El-Rouayheb, Intellectual History, 257–261.

one "Vâsıf" on the teachings of Muḥammad Murâd al-Bukhârî (d. 1729), the sheikh who first spread the Nakşbendî-Müceddidî order into Ottoman lands, though the contents suggest that it was written before his time by someone of the same name. More concretely, the historian in later life spoke favorably of mystics and had close links to disciples of the popular Nakşbendî sheikh Bursalı Mehmed Emîn Efendi, like the courtiers İbrahim Nesîm, Ahmed Fâiz, and Mabeynci Ahmed Efendi. Linking him to the Nakşbendîyye makes some sense. However, while Vâsıf must have been familiar to some degree with the order and its ideas, any affinity on his part, if it existed, was probably casual.[24]

In the late 1760s, Vâsıf entered the service of a provincial governor, a connection that began his career. This man was Gül Ahmedpaşazâde Ali Paşa.[25] Whether in the bureaucracy or the service of a major household, advancement in the eighteenth-century Ottoman Empire depended in large degree on the strength of one's kinship or other personal relations usually subsumed under the term *intisâb* – "patronage" or "connections." In the realm's patrimonial society, these were more akin to a familial than a strictly professional bond. In exchange for position and influence, clients

---

[24] This treatise is found in Süleymaniye Kütüphanesi, Esad Efendi nr. 1419, fols. 29b-44b, and bears the title "The lectures of his grace Sheikh Muḥammad Murâd, which the late Vâsıf recorded as best he could so that his words might be properly understood and passed down." It seems to date from the late seventeenth or early eighteenth century and may, perhaps, be the work of the Vâsıf mentioned above. Âsım notes (2: 83) these three men, all Ahmed Vâsıf's later patrons, as followers of Mehmed Emîn. See also Vâsıf on the Nakşbendî sheikh Muradzâde Mehmed Efendi (MEHÂSİN 5, 1: 14–15, 51) and his praise of mystical ascetics (MEHÂSİN 6, fol. 63a).

[25] Modern reference works almost completely neglect Ali Paşa. Ottoman sources for his life include MEHÂSİN 5, 1: 55, 96–98, 181, 290, 294 and 2: 53–55; SO, 1: 17–18, 6: 1737, 1775; Çeşmîzâde, 19, 27, 37; Mehmed Hafîd, *Sefînetü'l-vüzerâ*, ed. İsmet Parmaksızoğlu (Istanbul, 1952), 51 f.; Şemdânîzâde Süleyman, *Mür'i't-Tevârih*, ed. Münir Aktepe (Istanbul, 1976–81), 2-a: 3, 10, 38, 58; 2-b: 8, 18; and Mehmed Hâkim, *Tarih-i Hâkim*, TSMK Bağdat nr. 231, fols. 212b, 215a, 216a, 255b-256a. Ali Paşa was born about 1706/7 (AH 1118), the son of Gül Ahmed Paşa and the grandson of Grand Vizier Çorlulu Ali Paşa. He married Hibetullah Hanım Sultan in the fall of 1740 (Ş AH 1153) and served early in his career as *mirahor-ı sâni*, *kapıcılar kethüdâsı*, and *mirahor-ı evvel*. Osman III appointed him governor of Rumelia on 5 M AH 1170 (September 30, 1756), with the rank of vizier, and shortly thereafter he became *kapudan-ı deryâ*. He was dismissed and exiled to Kos on 24 Ş AH 1171 (November 7, 1757). After thirty months, in March of 1760, he was restored to the rank of vizier to İçel. Ali then held posts at Jidda, Adana, Aydın, and Diyarbekir before being transferred to Aleppo on 5 L AH 1180 (March 6, 1767), to Kars on 28 Za AH 1180 (April 27, 1767), again, upon his own request, to İçel in late Z AH 1180 (late May), and few months after to Sivas. Ali served during the 1768–1774 war as commander (*serasker*) of İlsavet and Bender. He died at Bender in mid-C AH 1183 (October 1769). There has been some question over his correct name – Kel or Gül. It is correctly voweled in Hâkim (fol. 256a) and Çeşmîzâde (19, n. 3).

bolstered their patron by supporting his household and political interests, which were often indistinguishable, and frequently became confidants, favorites, or sons-in-law (damad). Vâsıf as an outsider needed such connections badly. Merit could bring preferment, but more often family ties, wealth, or the influence of powerful patrons eased the passage through the ranks, especially in the bureaucracy, where a well-connected candidate could hope for rapid promotion and even the chance to circumvent normal seniority for more prestigious appointments; an unsuccessful candidate, by contrast, could easily spend a lifetime toiling in the bureaucracy's lower strata.[26]

Ali Paşa offered this protection. Having begun his career in the palace service, Ali had survived the precipitous rises and falls common to a vizierial career, but persevered, married into the imperial family, and built up his household. Elevated by Osman III to vizier in 1756 and shortly after to Grand Admiral (kapudan-ı deryâ), his promising career was derailed a year later when the Chief Black Eunuch (kızlar ağası) Ebukûf Ahmed Ağa implicated him in a plot to oust the new Grand Vizier, Koca Râgıb Paşa. It seems that when Osman fell deathly ill in the autumn of 1757, the chief eunuch, one of the most powerful men in the empire, tried to consolidate his position in the coming reign by supplanting Râgıb Paşa with a more malleable creature, Ali Paşa, whose consent he secured. Râgıb Paşa, unaware, was then summoned to the palace where he was to be stripped of office. But the plot fell apart. A colleague warned the vizier and he went into hiding until the storm had passed, emerging unscathed when word of the sultan's death was announced to become the most powerful Grand Vizier of the century. For his part in the intrigue, Ali Paşa was dismissed, expropriated, and sent into exile on the island of Kos, where he languished for two and a half years until being pardoned in 1760. Thereafter, he moved between various provincial governorships. It was in one of these postings that he met Ahmed Vâsıf.[27]

[26] On patronage, see Aksan, Ottoman Statesman, 23–33; Findley, Reform, 30 ff.; Fleischer, Bureaucrat, 19–20; Bernard Lalor, "Promotion Patterns of Ottoman Bureaucratic Statesmen from the Lâle Devri until the Tanzimat," Güney-Doğu Avrupa Araştırmalar Dergisi 1 (1972): 78–80; and Joel Shinder, "Career Line Formation in the Ottoman Bureaucracy, 1648–1750: A New Perspective," Journal of the Economic and Social History of the Orient 16 (1973): 228.

[27] MEHÂSİN 5, 1: 96–98, 181. See also Henning Sievert, Zwischen arabischer Provinz und Hoher Pforte: Beziehungen, Bildung und Politik des osmanischen Bürokraten Râgıb Mehmed Paşa (st. 1763) (Ergon Verlag, 2008), 313–321; and Norman Itzkowitz, "Mehmed Raghib Pasha: The Making of an Ottoman Grand Vezir," (Ph.D. diss., Princeton University, 1959), 145–157. Other sources fail to mention this event. Hâkim

With what little we know about his travels, it is all but impossible to pinpoint where, when, and how Vâsıf encountered Ali Paşa and secured his patronage. In 1767, Ali held brief terms of office in Aleppo, Kars, İçel, and Sivas, all of which might have overlapped with the young scholar's itinerary. Most likely they met at Kars, where Vâsıf passed part of the year studying, or shortly thereafter in Sivas some 400 miles to the west. Once formed, however, their bond was strong. Now Ali's protégé, Vâsıf spent nearly two years at Sivas as his treasury scribe (hazîne kitâbeti), a position related to the management of the governor's household and its expenses for which he had previous experience at Baghdad.[28] As was often the case in Ottoman patronage, the link also proved less that of an employee than of a companion and perhaps son. Vâsıf admired the older Ali. "He was handsome," he remembered, "of average height, refined and dignified, a wise and unrivaled vizier ... He showed me respect and generosity beyond my expectations." He even tutored Ali in literary pursuits, leading him through the odes of the popular Persian poet 'Urfî and, in Arabic, al-Harîrî's Assemblies or Maqâmât, a tour de force of rhymed prose and verse, rhetoric, and sparkling wit. Ali in turn supported Vâsıf, monetarily and otherwise.[29]

It should be clear by now that Vâsıf's trajectory was not entirely usual for someone of his social background. His upward mobility in fact finds an instructive parallel in the career of an earlier historian, Mustafa Naîmâ, who also hailed from the realm's Arab lands. Naîmâ was born around 1655 in Aleppo. Like Vâsıf, he was a provincial who in time made his way to Istanbul, found employment as a chancery scribe, and served as the empire's court historian or vekâyi'nüvis. Yet Naîmâ gained entry into circles of power much more easily than Vâsıf. The son and grandson of Janissary officers, he took advantage of his family's local prestige and links to the capital and, while perhaps still a teenager, secured an apprenticeship in the palace service in Istanbul. Naîmâ's placement – in the halberdiers corps at

records Ebukûf's and Ali's dismissals, but claims (fols. 255a-256b) that they were based on malfeasance – lax oversight for the former, oppression for the latter. Ahmed Câvid is simply silent on the matter: HADÎKAT, suppl. 3: 6–7.

[28] This is corroborated by Âsım's use (1: 255) of financial metaphor. See also Fâik, 146; Hammer-Purgstall, 3: 552; and Schlechta-Wssehrd, 5. Vâsıf was not his librarian, as other sources indicate.

[29] MEHÂSİN 5, 2: 55. On 'Urfî Shîrâzî (d. 1590/91) see E.G. Browne, A Literary History of Persia (London, 1924), 4: 241–249. On Muḥammad al-Qâsim b. 'Alî b. Muḥammad b. 'Uthmân al-Harîrî (d. 1122) see Carl Brockelmann, Geschichte der arabischen Literatur (Weimar, 1898), 1: 276–277. An "assembly" was an elaborate work of prose telling a dramatic anecdote. Al-Harîrî's, the classic of the genre, included wordplay, enigmas, obscure expressions, and colloquialisms, and required textual commentaries.

the old palace – was desirable and helped him to forge links in the wider bureaucracy, in which he moved and worked for the rest of his life. Naîmâ never climbed as high as Vâsıf in the scribal service. However, his life illustrates the benefits that came with birth and family. Vâsıf's lack of this sort of social capital makes his entry into and success in the imperial system all the more striking; it may also help to explain his later support of systemic reform.[30]

In 1767, Ahmed Vâsıf was approximately thirty-two years old and about to embark on a career in state service. Tall, dark, and strapping, he was already highly learned.[31] He had traveled the Levant and eastern reaches of the empire, searching out scholars and knowledge, and by this point had become a practiced scribe and mastered the languages of culture and administration – Ottoman Turkish, Persian, and classical Arabic – in addition to his native dialect.[32] Even at this early age, Vâsıf took an incipient interest in surrounding events. When he recorded the history of these years as a much older man, three decades later, he drew heavily on Ali Paşa's memories and alluded to a practice of saving documents, either in the original or by copying them down in a daybook.[33] The historian within him was already forming. Vâsıf was furthermore well-positioned in a major statesman's entourage. Although Ali Paşa's career had stagnated in the eastern provinces, far from Istanbul, the empire's center of power, he was a first and crucial patronage link. He treated Vâsıf well, provided him a post, security, and a father-figure, and held out the promise of future advancement. Little did the young man know that this future would take him still further afield – out of the east, to the Danube, Russia, and the Gate of Felicity itself.

---

[30] Lewis V. Thomas' excellent *A Study of Naima* (New York, 1972) is the standard work on this figure. See further Bekir Kütükoğlu, "Vekayi'nüvis," in *Vekayi'nüvis Makaleler* (Istanbul, 1994), 111–112; and DİA, s.v. "Naîmâ."

[31] According to descriptions, Vâsıf was tall, burly, olive-skinned, well-comported, and had a full black beard and fastidious mode of dress. See Aceituno, 34; and Kutlu, 109.

[32] Persian was not taught in a typical *medrese* education. Vâsıf would have learned it through a dervish lodge, a private tutor, or daily exposure somewhere. Of these three languages, it was certainly his weakest. See also Chambers, 454–455.

[33] MEHÂSİN 5, 1: 314 and esp. 2: 232, where Vâsıf notes that he kept a verbatim copy of the minutes of certain peace negotiations, but lost it in a fire. At least while court historian, Vâsıf kept daybooks. These came into the possession of Ahmed Cevdet Paşa after his death, bear notations from Cevdet's son, and are now dispersed in various locations: BOA.Y.EE 90; Beyazıt Devlet Kütüphanesi, Nadir Eserler Bölümü nr. V3497–200; and Millet Kütüphanesi, Ali Emiri layihalar nr. 74.

2

At War (1768–1774)

2.1 THE DANUBIAN FRONT, 1768–1771

In June of 1769, Ahmed Vâsıf arrived in Gül Ahmedpaşazâde Ali Paşa's train at Hantepesi on the Pruth River in Moldavia. The imperial army was mustering. As the Sivas governor paraded into the city in full review, his men and retinue (*kapu halkı*) saw encamped the vast and disorderly host that the Grand Vizier, Mehmed Emin Paşa, would lead in that year's campaign season against their northern enemy Russia.[1] The long peace on the empire's European frontier was at an end. Russia's invasion of Poland in 1763 and its interference in Polish affairs had inflamed tensions between the two empires and renewed their mutual fear and distrust, latent since the 1739 Treaty of Belgrade. The Russians had also furnished a pretext when, the previous summer, their forces chased rebel Poles into Ottoman territory and sacked the border town of Balta. Buoyed by popular sentiment, the war's supporters predicted that Russia would wilt under the threat of force and that the empire might even regain territory in Poland. They expected a short and glorious affair. With former Grand Vizier Muhsinzâde Mehmed Paşa dismissed for his opposition, on October 4, 1768, Sultan Mustafa III declared war. It was to be, in fact, one of the most costly errors of the eighteenth century.[2]

---

[1] MEHÂSİN 5, 2: 12; Muharrem Saffet Çalışkan, ed., "(Vekâyi'nüvis) Enverî Sadullah Efendi ve Tarihinin I. Cildi'nin Metin ve Tahlili (1182–1188 / 1768–1774)" (Ph.D. diss., Marmara University, 2000), 30.

[2] Ottoman accounts of the war were generally written with hindsight by its opponents, especially chancery scribes like Vâsıf. As such, they can be quite critical. On the war's causes, see MEHÂSİN 5, 1: 314–315 and 2: 4–6; "Vekâyi'nüvis Enverî," 16–17; and RESMÎ, 34–37 (trans.), 92–95 (text). In the secondary literature, see Aksan, *Ottoman*

The 1768–1774 war proved to be a great shock to Vâsıf and his peers, for they shared an implicit faith in the empire. A certain militancy and sense of exceptionalism had long been central to the self-perception of the empire's élites, along with the belief that history had culminated in the Ottoman dynasty. Ottomans like Vâsıf felt that their rulers were blessed: that God had sent them to renew the faith and that the dynasty itself was just, divinely favored, and would endure, victorious, until the end of time. The fall of Constantinople and their far-flung conquests were proof of this. Ottoman exceptionalism was also enmeshed in the realm's frontier origins. It seemed to both grow out of and explain the early empire's ghazi traditions and dizzying expansion. Because of their devotion to jihad, as warriors for the faith, the Ottomans saw themselves as superior to Europeans and even to other Islamic dynasties. The "zeal of Islam" and duty of jihad supposedly made their soldiers more innately brave than non-Muslims and hence, all other things being equal, they could and would always prevail.[3]

Ottoman imperial ideology placed great weight on military success and on the pursuit of religiously sanctioned war, or *ghazâ*, merging the formulation of jihad in Islamic jurisprudence with Turco-Mongol notions of world domination and a belief in the empire's exceptionalism. The classical, juristic view of jihad is well-known. Islam as a universalizing legal tradition divides the world into two basic spheres, a "realm of war (*dâr al-ḥarb*)" and a "realm of Islam (*dâr al-Islâm*)" that exist in a state of continuous open or latent war. This division, which is "morally necessary, legally and religiously obligatory," will continue until the former is absorbed by the latter. While pauses in hostility can occur and are at times the rule, these are temporary and legal only when in the community's best interest. A permanent peace is theoretically impossible.[4] Ottomans additionally inherited a stock of prophecies and legends, some Islamic, some Central Asian, auguring a destiny of world conquest.

Statesman, 100–123; and Osman Köse, *1774 Küçük Kaynarca Andlaşması* (Ankara, 2006), 5–12.

[3] Gottfried Hagen and Ethan L. Menchinger, "Ottoman Historical Thought," in *A Companion to Global Historical Thought* (London, 2014), 100–101; and Hagen, "Afterword" in *An Ottoman Mentality: The World of Evliya Çelebi* (Leiden, 2004), 233–241. See further Colin Imber, "The Ottoman Dynastic Myth," *Revue d'etudes turques* 19 (1987): 7–27. Textual expressions of this belief appear frequently below.

[4] This quotation is from Bernard Lewis, *The Political Language of Islam* (Chicago, 1988), 73. The available literature on jihad is extensive. See Michael Bonner, *Jihad in Islamic History: Doctrines and Practices* (Princeton, 2006); Majid Khadduri, *War and Peace in the Law of Islam* (Baltimore, 1955); and relevant articles in EI². Articles in DİA often dispute this view in apologetic terms and argue that jihad was a response to Christian aggression.

These were epitomized by the myth of the "Golden" or "Red Apple (*kızıl elma*)." Originally an apocalyptic tale about the fall of Constantinople, the "red apple" took its name from an orb held by an equestrian statue of the emperor Justinian and became a byword for world domination and continual expansion. While they avoided defining its location, Ottomans from the sixteenth century on used this term in several distinct senses: for any distant goal of conquest, for the mythical place where their conquests would end, and for ensuing world domination.[5] Such, then, were the views of educated society. Myth and law – the predominant Hanafi school – stressed the world's division into *dâr al-ḥarb* and *dâr al-Islâm*, as well as a doctrine of *force majeure* in which peace could occur in but two situations, truce or submission to rule. The result was an imperial mythos in which war was perpetual, peace the exception, and the Ottomans "always justified – and always at war."[6] Yet while many scholars focus on the martial overtones of Ottoman exceptionalism, it must be said that this ethos was a more complex, pervasive worldview – one that avowed complete faith in the empire's superiority and its ability though God's aid to overcome all challenges, domestic or foreign. The troubles of the eighteenth century were not simply a blow to Ottoman military pride. They also opened a wide rupture between ideology and reality and between self-perception, aspiration, and the empire's real frailty. If military success vindicated Ottoman beliefs about history and their role within it, defeat bred dissonance, to accept which required a shattering alteration in the way élites saw themselves, the dynasty, and the surrounding world.[7] One of the greatest challenges for Vâsıf's generation was hence, somehow, to reconcile the empire's fortunes with what

---

[5] On legal notions of war and peace in the Ottoman Empire, see Colin Imber, *Ebu's-su'ud: The Islamic Legal Tradition* (Edinburgh, 1997), 67–70; Viorel Panaite, *The Ottoman Law of War and Peace: The Ottoman Empire and Tribute Payers* (Boulder, 2000), 80, 128–132; and Mouradgea D'Ohsson, *Tableau général de l'empire othoman* (Paris, 1788–1824), 1: 35–41. Osman Turan has written extensively on Ottoman concepts of world domination in "The Ideal of World Domination Among the Medieval Turks," *Studia Islamica* 4 (1955): 77–90; and idem, *Türk Cihân Hâkimiyet Mefkûresi Tarihi* (Istanbul, 1969), 2 vols. On the legend of *kızıl elma*, see Pál Fodor, "The View of the Turk in Hungary: The Apocalyptic Tradition and the Legend of the Golden Apple in Ottoman-Hungarian Context," in *Les traditions apocalyptiques au tourant de la chute de Constantinople*, eds. Lellouch and Yerasimos (Paris, 1999), 99–131; and Stéphane Yerasimos, "De l'arbre à la pomme: la généalogie d'un thème apocalyptique," in ibid, 153–192.

[6] John F. Guilmartin, "Ideology and Conflict: The Wars of the Ottoman Empire, 1453–1606," *Journal of Interdisciplinary History* 18 (1988): 726.

[7] Rifaat Ali Abou-El-Haj, "Ottoman Attitudes Toward Peacemaking: The Karlowitz Case," *Der Islam* 51 (1974): 134–136.

they knew and believed of its exceptionalism. War, peace, and peace-making were for them not academic, but issues of the highest psychological order.[8]

The war effort was already behind schedule when Vâsıf and Ali Paşa reached Hantepesi. The sultan's declaration had come so late in the season that it was impossible to mount a proper campaign, and Ali waited until the springtime to respond to his mobilization orders. As the government traditionally followed the Ottoman army on campaign, when he set out from Sivas to join the imperial army at Hantepesi, the major supply depot, he took his scribes and household along with his military levies. Vâsıf was of course included.[9] Grand Vizier Mehmed Emin Paşa welcomed the governor warmly upon his arrival, though he was late, happy to find someone at camp of a like refinement. "Having now met, it is a pity that I have not had your conversation. I thought it had gone extinct among the viziers!" he said. Mehmed Emin was in need of more than polite company, however. A product of the chancery with, by his own admission, no military experience, he was now expected to command the empire's lumbering war machine and lead it east to the fortress of Bender, on the lower reaches of the Dniester river, where the Ottoman command hoped to encounter the Russians.[10]

Vâsıf and his patron were soon alarmed by what they saw. Conditions on the front were poor and the road to Bender arduous. The commissary officers had failed to gather enough provisions for the march, which took three or four days through arid terrain, and the soldiers assumed that Bender would be better supplied, this being one reason why the Grand Vizier had chosen the route. They were wrong. When the army reached

[8] Some scholars question how committed Ottomans were to this ideology in war and diplomacy. While it would be foolish to ignore their flexibility, extensive relations with Europe, and increasing reliance on diplomacy in the seventeenth and eighteenth centuries, textual evidence signals that many did in fact espouse traditionally "Islamic" views of war and peace until quite late, perhaps the end of the eighteenth century. Readers interested in this historiographical debate may refer to my dissertation, "An Ottoman Historian in an Age of Reform: Ahmed Vâsıf Efendi (ca. 1730–1806)" (Ph.D. diss., University of Michigan, 2014), 114–117.

[9] It was common practice to appoint two redundant chanceries: "full" office holders who accompanied the army, and their proxies who stayed in Istanbul. See Aksan, *Ottoman Statesman*, 130–131. Vâsıf records these appointments in MEHÂSİN 5, 1: 322–323.

[10] Ali Paşa informed Vâsıf (MEHÂSİN 5, 2: 12) of this exchange orally. Yağlıkcızâde or Hindî Mehmed Emin (b. 1723/24) spent his youth in India with his merchant father. He joined the chancery and rose to *reisülküttâb* (22 S AH 1178 = July 21, 1764) before becoming a vizier. He was appointed Grand Vizier on October 20, 1768, but was dismissed ten months later and executed shortly thereafter. See "Vekâyi'nüvis Enverî," 25–26; Fâik, 105–106; HADÎKAT, supp. 3: 18–19; and RESMÎ, 44–45 (trans.), 100–101 (text).

Yassıtepe outside of Bender on June 30, they discovered that the provisions had been ineptly or corruptly organized and that there were not even ovens for baking the army's bread. Prices rose sharply and the army, gouged by local speculators, became mutinous. Within two days, a dismayed Vâsıf watched as five to six thousand men deserted southward toward the Danube.[11] What was worse, Mehmed Emin Paşa insisted in spite of these problems on offensive action. In early July, he held council in his pavilion and proposed that a force be sent to invest the fortresses of İlsavet, Orhankrad, and Mirhorad, which the Russians had recently built along the Bug River. The council nominated Gül Ahmedpaşazâde Ali as its commander (serasker). Ali Paşa openly objected. The soldiers' mettle could not be trusted in battle, he held, and he suspected that the lack of provisions would cause the force to disintegrate. Given the cost of food and fodder, he demanded five hundred purses of akçe to pay for supplies. Members of the council – notably the Grand Vizier's chief steward (sadaret kethüdâsı) Evliya Ahmed Ağa and the treasurer (defterdâr) – assured Ali at length that they would assist his operations and left him no choice. He crossed the Dniester a few days later with his entourage and several battalions of Janissaries. They were to have support from the Tatar Khan and a large contingent of Tatar horse.[12]

Vâsıf had agreed with his patron's concerns and now saw them realized. Ali did not receive the promised supplies, nor could he in any case remain in the field, for word came that the Russians were assaulting the northern fortress of Khotin, site of an Ottoman victory earlier that year. He returned to Bender perforce. On arrival, Vâsıf sensed that the city was in a state of near-panic. The air was rife with mutiny and rumor: the army continued to hemorrhage troops, scarcity made the soldiers demoralized and ungovernable, and the Grand Vizier was ill, some said mad. A false report that the enemy had cut off the city's roads caused frenzy; the situation was dire. In light of these difficulties, the ministers recommended

[11] Vâsıf wrote (MEHÂSİN 5, 2: 16–17) that the army reached Yassıtepe on 24 S AH 1183 = June 29 and estimated the number of deserters at "five to ten thousand." Enverî specifies (38–40) that the army actually arrived the next day, 25 Safer, and puts the numbers at five to six thousand infantry and cavalry. For additional detail, see RESMÎ, 39–40, 48 (trans.), 96–97, 103 (text); Aksan, Ottoman Statesman, 141–143; and Necîb Âsım, "Pîr Mehmed Efendi Muhtırası," TOEM 13 (1921–1923): 134–135.

[12] MEHÂSİN 5, 2: 18–19, 23; and RESMÎ, 49 (trans.), 104 (text). Enverî (41–42, 49) does not mention Ali Paşa's reservations and says that the council took place on 4 Ra, or July 8, with Ali leaving Bender several days later. According to a document issued to the Tatar Khan Devlet Giray, Ali left Bender on 5 Ra, or July 9: Uğur Ünal, ed., Kırım Hanlarına Nâme-i Hümâyûn (Istanbul, 2013), doc. 76.

that the army garrison Bender and return to Hantepesi, where they could gather supplies and try to relieve Khotin, and they invited Gül Ahmedpaşazâde Ali to accept command in Bender. This was too much for him. Ali made for Evliya Ahmed Ağa's pavilion and blankly refused, protesting the poor state of his troops and supplies. They argued for two hours before they were joined by the army judge advocate (*ordu kâdısı*) Abdullah Efendi and the chief usher (*kapu kethüdâsı*) Bayburdî Mustafa Ağa, who quieted the governor with promises of aid and 100,000 *kuruş* in funds from the central treasury and personal loans. Ali at last relented and went to the Grand Vizier, who invested him in office, and at the end of July 1769, the imperial army decamped for Hantepesi.[13]

The next few months passed uneasily for Vâsıf in this ill-provisioned, insecure outpost on the empire's frontier. His first taste of war had been disastrous. He blamed the army's failures not on his commanders, but on the soldiers who had undermined them through ignorance, greed, and a lack of discipline and devotion. To him, there could be no question otherwise.[14] Still, at this point, he had yet to witness a real engagement. That was to change. As the summer waned and the imperial army moved into winter quarters, Ali Paşa pillaged Polish towns across the Dniester that had collaborated with the Russians, who in turn, being informed by locals that Bender could be stormed, approached the fortress with some 15,000 men and made several assaults. Each time, Ali Paşa and the Tatar Khan drove them away. But the governor's good fortune did not last. The garrison's auxiliaries (*yamak*) remained restive and in late October, demanded an ad hoc council to air their grievances. Ali tried to defuse the situation, asking them to send one or two representatives, but the auxiliaries rebuffed him and moved in armed mutiny on his lodgings, where his retinue, in a display of strength, forced them to beat a hasty retreat. Several days later, the governor fell ill with dropsy and died; he was buried in the citadel. Vâsıf was sure that the mutiny had broken his health and killed him.[15]

---

[13] MEHÂSİN 5, 2: 23–26; "Vekâyi'nüvis Enverî," 49–53; RESMÎ, 49 (trans.), 104 (text); and Şemdânîzâde, 2b: 8. News of the Russian attack on Khotin evidently arrived the day after Ali Paşa left for İlsavet, on 6 Ra, or July 10: Ünal, doc. 76. The sources disagree on the date of the army's departure for Hantepesi, with Vâsıf saying 22 Ra AH 1183 (July 26, 1769), Resmî 27 Ra (July 31), and Enverî 25 Ra (July 29). Resmî and Câvid (HADÎKAT, supp. 3: 19) allege that by this time, Mehmed Emin Paşa had lost his mind, the former remarking that he had to be "forcibly borne away" from Bender.

[14] MEHÂSİN 5, 2: 32, 42.

[15] MEHÂSİN 5, 2: 50–51, 53–54. Vâsıf must have witnessed this mutiny firsthand, as it is not mentioned in other sources. Cf. "Vekâyi'nüvis Enverî," 83–84, 88–89. Şemdânîzâde claims (2b: 18), probably incorrectly, that Ali died in the month of Receb/November.

We do not know what steps the young scribe took in the months following Ali Paşa's death. Vâsıf was understandably devastated and succumbed to depression, having lost an employer, patron, companion, and mentor. "I did not leave his side for three years," he mourned. "After his death I was torn from him like a soul bereft of body and for some time wandered the wilderness, lost in my agony."[16] But he did not stay idle. Vâsıf's career and future depended on securing a new connection and in the winter of 1770, he attached himself to the service of another commander, one Abaza Mehmed Paşa. Like so many things, how Vâsıf made this connection is unclear. Abaza Paşa had served with distinction at Khotin the previous year but also, to his discredit, abandoned the fortress before the Grand Vizier ordered a general evacuation. He then spent the winter in Moldavia under the *serasker* Abdi Paşa and in late April or early May, transferred to İsmail, a fortress on the Danube. Vâsıf may have returned at this time to the imperial army, which was wintering in the town of Babadağı, or encountered him elsewhere. What is certain is that he became Abaza's private secretary (*mektûbcı*), handling his incoming and outgoing correspondence, a post that required frequent communication between the two. We likewise know that he avoided mentioning his time with the vizier and that the topic appears to have been a point of some pain or embarrassment. For this there was good reason, as Abaza Paşa's career and life would shortly end in disgrace.[17]

In the spring of 1770, the imperial army was preparing a major push northward. After moving out of winter quarters, the new Grand Vizier İvazpaşazâde Halil Paşa established his base of operations on the south shore of the Danube at Isakçı, directly across from a town called Kartal. The Ottomans sent a force of about 30,000 men north up the Pruth River under Abaza Mehmed Paşa and Dağıstanî Ali Paşa to reinforce the Tatar Khan and to move against the Russians in Moldavia. When they joined the army of Abdi Paşa, Vâsıf, in Abaza's entourage, had never seen such a concentration of men. To him, the plain seemed like a roiling sea.[18]

---

[16] MEHÂSİN 5, 2: 55.

[17] Sources confirm that Vâsıf was indeed in Abaza Mehmed's retinue between 1770 and 1771. See "Vekâyi'nüvis Enverî," 266; Fâik, 146; Karslızâde, 64; Schlechta-Wssehrd, 5–6; and Hammer-Purgstall, 3: 552. According to one account (SO, 4: 1039), Abaza served in Bender in August of 1769. This is incorrect and Vâsıf himself clarifies (MEHASIN 5, 2: 60) that the individual was a different Abaza Mehmed. See furthermore Aksan, *Ottoman Statesman*, 144–147; "Vekâyi'nüvis Enverî," 73, 83; Şemdânîzâde, 2b: 5–6, 16–17, 23, 27; and Mustafa Kesbî, *İbretnümâ-yı Devlet*, ed. Ahmet Öğreten (Ankara, 2002), 117.

[18] MEHÂSİN 5, 2: 85.

By July 18, after some initial skirmishing, he and Abaza Paşa were encamped near the ford of Falça along with the Tatar Khan and Abdi Paşa, awaiting the arrival of a third force from the imperial army with which they could attack the Russians. That evening, they posted sentries. However, in the early morning, the calm was shattered by gunfire and chaos. As Vâsıf oriented himself, he saw the soldiers in panic, abandoning their munitions and ordnance, and while some rallied to Abdi Paşa and for a time seemed to have the upper hand, they too turned tail. It later became obvious to Vâsıf what had happened: the Russians had learned of the army's plans, surprised the sentries, who had fallen asleep, and over-whelmed the stockades in two parties. The unexpected attack had sent the whole army into flight, including the Khan and Abaza Paşa. Indeed, some even hinted that the latter deliberately deserted the battle out of malice for Abdi Paşa. Vâsıf refused to fault his commanders in this way. The blame for the débâcle, he insisted, rested squarely on the soldiers' cowardice, sin, and failure in the duty of jihad, for which defeat was a divine punishment.[19]

The fugitive Ottomans eventually regrouped at the Janissary Ağa Kapıkıran Mehmed Paşa's camp a few hours away near Kartal and sent word to the Grand Vizier, who could see their forces from the southern shore. Concerned for the army's order and morale, İvazpaşazâde Halil Paşa decided to reinforce them in person. The second stage of the battle was about to begin. The bulk of the Ottoman army was now, on the last day of July, situated at a place called Gölbaşı, between two lakes and connected to the Kartal plain and Danube by a narrow tongue of land. The Grand Vizier had assigned Abdi Paşa, Abaza Mehmed Paşa, and Karslızâde Hasan Paşa to the skirmishers and right and left flanks, respectively. That night, Abaza Mehmed had sentry duty. Vâsıf may have had a premonition: their position was exposed and its defenses unfinished as evening wore on. In the small hours, the Russian general Petr Rumiantsev tested the Ottoman defenses, just as at Falça, but he retreated and attacked again at dawn as the two forces came to grips in a mortal struggle. As Vâsıf saw things, the Ottoman line initially held as the center and left checked the advance. But the Russians then trained their cannon on the cavalry in

---

[19] MEHÂSİN 5, 2: 84–89. Vâsıf's account responds directly to Enverî (133–135), who alleges that Abdi Paşa discovered that the Khan and Abaza Paşa were conspiring against him out of jealousy and so held his forces back until he could tell what was truly happening. He blames the latter for the outcome of the battle. Repeated in substance in Şemdânîzâde, 2b: 39–40, 42. See also Aksan, *Ottoman Statesman*, 148–151; RESMÎ, 52–54 (trans.), 106–108 (text); and "Pîr Mehmed Efendi Muhtırası," 137.

Abaza Mehmed's right flank. The horsemen scattered, and the commander could not hold his formation and withdrew. Thus began the rout.
The others fell back with Abaza – the infantry to Kartal, where they
waited in terror that the Russians would drive them into the Danube.
Some tried to swim to offshore ships, only to swamp them and drown, and
only slowly were the rest evacuated. Another group of about 30,000
cavalry, including Abdi Paşa, Abaza Mehmed Paşa, and Vâsıf, rode east
across country to the town of İsmail.[20]

The cavalry at İsmail expected to be transported across the Danube.
But as there were too few boats, the Grand Vizier decided in council
on August 5 that it would be better to use the force there and to send the
Tatar Khan from Isakçı with reinforcements and supplies. The Khan
arrived to find a sullen camp desperate to escape. They ignored his orders
and instead sent Abdi Paşa to intercede with the Grand Vizier, whose
response reiterated his earlier command and put Abaza Mehmed Paşa in
charge. It did no good. Before the reply could even arrive, a group of
soldiers tried to commandeer the supply ships. Most drowned; some
managed to cross the river to the fortress of Tulça. The next day, meanwhile, a few thousand Russians under the general Nikolai Repnin
appeared and put the cavalry and infantry to flight. Vâsıf recalled that in
retreat, the horse was pressed between a lake on their right and the
Russians on their left, "passing through hell and high water" and severe
trials. The Russians took many captive. Abaza Paşa then boarded a barge
with a handful of men and returned to the imperial army with news of
what had happened. The disaster of Kartal was finally over.[21]

The aftermath of the first two campaign seasons was a rude awakening
to members of the Ottoman hierarchy. Be what may, the war would be
neither glorious nor short. Its supporters had been overconfident.
The problem that they now faced was what to do and how to apportion

---

[20] MEHÂSİN 5, 2: 88, 90–97; "Vekâyi'nüvis Enverî," 137–142; RESMÎ, 54–55 (trans.),
108–110 (text); Şemdânîzâde, 2b: 43–45; and Aksan, *Ottoman Statesman*, 151–153. See
also MERSH, s.v. "Rumiantsev, Petr Aleksandrovich." Ottoman commentators feared
that the battle would be another St. Gotthard, where in 1664, the Ottoman army was
pinned against the Raab River, their bridge collapsed in a panicked retreat, and scores
drowned.

[21] MEHÂSİN 5, 2: 97–99. The force reached İsmail on 11 R AH 1184 (August 4, 1770) and
deserted the town on 14/15 R AH 1184 (August 7–8, 1770). The unique detail in Vâsıf's
account of the garrison, the Russian attack, and the cavalry flight suggests that he was an
eyewitness. Our other main sources, Enverî and Resmî, were with the imperial army in
Isakçı. Cf. "Vekâyi'nüvis Enverî," 143–150; RESMÎ, 55–56 (trans.), 110 (text); and
Şemdânîzâde, 2b: 46. See Köse, 30–35, for a summary of this campaign.

blame. What should be done? Who was responsible? More ominously, why, if the empire was divinely supported, had they been so entirely outmatched? These were questions without clear answers, questions that would reverberate until well after the war had ended. At this point, many Ottomans began to consider the option of a negotiated peace. The law, as Vâsıf knew, allowed the empire to make peace in a losing war to secure its territory and subjects' life and property. Rumiantsev raised this prospect shortly after Kartal, but the Grand Vizier deferred to Istanbul, and Vâsıf was bitterly disappointed when the sultan and his circle opted to fight rather than accept the overtures, ascribing them to weakness. Blame was another matter. A ready scapegoat for Kartal was İvazpaşazâde Halil Paşa, who lasted only a few months in office before his dismissal in December of that year. Although Vâsıf did not pity the Grand Vizier, he recognized that the source of defeat went beyond any one man. Years later, he wrote that the planning of Kartal had been sound – provisions, munitions, soldiers, and ready cash, all meticulously organized – but that the rout had reflected the army's moral failings as a whole. Again and again, the soldiers fixed on selfish gain and failed to fulfill their duty as Muslims. These were not the same troops who had won the empire great victories centuries ago.[22] Another victim of Kartal was Vâsıf's patron. By the early fall, Abaza Mehmed Paşa had earned a dubious fame. Whatever his merits, he had been involved in a string of collapses at Khotin, Falça, Kartal, and most lately İsmail, even admitting his failure in Vâsıf's hearing. He had also amassed large debts for his retinue, irregular soldiers that he thought were loyal but whom Vâsıf deemed little better than scum. Word came toward the end of November: the sultan was demoting him from the rank of vizier and exiling him to Köstendil, a city several hundred miles to the west of the front. Abaza Paşa was embittered. He had served for three years at great sacrifice for a reward of ignominy and exile. However, on the road to Köstendil, he and his retinue met the new Tatar Khan, Selim Giray, who was making his way to the imperial army's winter camp at Babadağı. Abaza Paşa lamented his fate to the Khan, who felt sorry for him, brought him along, and pleaded with the new Grand Vizier Silâhdar Mehmed Paşa to restore his rank. In January 1771, he did just that – a second and final chance. Abaza Paşa was soon appointed to the fortress of Yenikale and

[22] MEHÂSİN 5, 2: 95–96, 97–99, 113–115. Rumiantsev's proposal for negotiations reached the Ottoman army around 25 Ca AH 1184 (September 16, 1770). See also Aksan, Ottoman Statesman, 153–155; HADÎKAT, supp. 3: 20–22; and RESMÎ, 56–57 (trans.), 111–112 (text).

took his retinue to the Black Sea port of Constanta, boarded ship, and set sail for the Crimea.[23]

Whether Vâsıf followed Abaza Paşa to the Crimea is an unsolved and perhaps unsolvable problem, for at some point in 1770 or 1771, he fell into Russian hands. The usual narrative is as follows.[24] In the spring of 1771, Abaza Paşa anchored at Kefe on the peninsula's east coast to garrison Yenikale, a fortress guarding the Sea of Azov. On arrival, he asked his superior, the *serasker* İbrahim Paşa, whether he should go to Yenikale or if he was free to remain in Kefe or join the *serasker*'s army at Perekop, then called Orkapısı, the "key" to the peninsula. İbrahim Paşa replied that his orders were to defend the fortress, but Abaza Paşa did not go. He refused. The Ottoman army in the Crimea was ill-provisioned, the supply fleet three months late, and Abaza protested his lack of men, money, and supplies by insubordinately staying at Kefe. When a Russian army under Vasili Dolgurukii stormed Orkapısı in the early summer and overran the peninsula, Abaza Paşa decided to flee rather than fight and took ship to Sinope in Anatolia, where he was eventually apprehended and executed. İbrahim Paşa then staged a brave but doomed defense of the peninsula. By early July 1771, Kefe, Yenikale, and other fortresses had fallen and the *serasker* and a troop of 280 Ottomans were captured, of which the Russians sent a group of fifty-one to St. Petersburg as prisoners of war. Biographical sources generally include Vâsıf in this number. On closer inspection, however, the chronology is impossible.[25]

---

[23] Abaza Paşa's dismissal occurred on 8 Ş AH 1184 (November 27, 1770) and his reappointment on 10 L AH 1184 (January 27, 1771). Vâsıf closely follows (MEHÂSİN 5, 2: 110, 129, 141–142) Enverî in these events, but alters specific details like the number and state of Abaza's retainers. Cf. "Vekâyi'nüvis Enverî," 160–161, 165, 188, 211–212. See also Şemdânîzâde, 2b: 57.

[24] The primary source for these events is Necâtî Efendi, who served in the retinue of İbrahim Paşa and went with him to St. Petersburg: Erhan Afyoncu, ed., "Târih-i Kırım (Rusya Sefaretnâmesi)" (Master's thesis, Marmara University, 1990), 13–26; Faik Unat, "Kırımın Osmanlı idaresinden çıktığı günlere ait bir vesika: Necati Efendi Sefaretnâme veya Sergüzeştnâmesi," *Türk Tarih Kurumu Kongresi* 3 (1943): 370–374; and idem, *Osmanlı Sefirleri ve Sefaretnameleri* (Ankara, 1992), 116–128. Vâsıf (MEHÂSİN 5, 2: 166–169), Şemdânîzâde (2b: 71–73), and the Tatar historian Halim Giray Sultan (*Gülbün-i Hânân* [Istanbul, 1909], 183–186) also provide descriptions. See further Alan Fisher, *The Russian Annexation of the Crimea, 1772–1783* (Cambridge, 1970), 29–44; and Köse, 63–70.

[25] It seems that no one has ever bothered to check the internal chronology of Vâsıf's account (MEHÂSİN 5, 2: 176–177) with that given by Necâtî (26, 30). İbrahim Paşa's group left the Crimea on 15 Ca AH 1185 (August 26, 1771) and arrived in St. Petersburg on 6 L AH 1185 (January 12, 1772). Vâsıf's captivity by contrast ended in C AH 1185 = mid-September 1771. He could not in that interval have traveled to St. Petersburg and back.

While there is no reason to doubt that Vâsıf was sent to St. Petersburg
as a captive (a fact which evidence confirms), he was clearly not among
İbrahim Paşa's group that arrived in the city on January 12, 1772. Vâsıf
had by that time already returned to the Ottoman army. He must therefore have been captured earlier. Other Ottoman prisoners were in the
Russian capital, like Abdülcelilzâde Mehmed Emin Paşa, who surrendered the city of Bender in 1770 after a harrowing siege, and it is possible
that Vâsıf was taken the same year at Kartal.[26] Whatever the case, in
St. Petersburg, Vâsıf had his first real contact with the non-Ottoman
world. He had surely seen and interacted with Europeans before.
Baghdad and Aleppo, for example, each had foreign merchant enclaves.
But St. Petersburg was a different case, the capital of the empire's arch-
enemy and a city of alien religion, customs, language, architecture, and
morés. To grasp the magnitude of his experience, one must recall that
eighteenth-century Ottomans divided the world into starkly opposed
halves: their own civilization and a "realm of war" that was hostile,
godless, and patently inferior. We know that Vâsıf considered his captivity
a trial and harbored a lifelong dislike of Russians. We also know that,
apart from the physical rigors of captivity, he felt a deep psychological
displacement and found the northern climate harsh and desolate, his
captors coarse, boorish, and brutal. No less disturbing for him was the
paradox that these people were on the verge of an unprecedented victory
over his empire. How was it possible? Yet there is reason to think that
a prolonged stay, and his probably lasted months, would have upset any
simple notions he had about the infidel world. Indeed, Vâsıf remained
engaged and even curious in his surroundings. The prisoners in
St. Petersburg were treated honorably and Vâsıf may have joined them
in attending balls, the theater, and the opera, for which he later showed
a taste. He seems to have learned a limited amount of Russian, at least
enough to ask questions and make himself understood. Lastly, but tellingly, Vâsıf at this time began to take notice of the Russians themselves –
of their economy, their military discipline, and their skill in arms and
technology – if not from any sympathetic or human sentiment, then
simply because these qualities could, potentially, answer his paradox.[27]

---

[26] Necâtî, 31–33; and "Pîr Mehmed Efendi Muhtırası," 150. Vâsıf's presence in
St. Petersburg is attested by himself (MEHÂSİN 5, 2: 289) and by at least one contemporary source (Enverî, 265).

[27] Vâsıf hinted (MEHÂSİN 5, 2: 188) at the trauma of his captivity by referring to himself as
"disaster-stricken." During this period, he extracted what information he could from his
minders on the sources of their military success, anecdotes of which he recorded in a later

Графъ Петръ Александровичъ   Le Comte Pierre Alexandrowitch
Румянцевъ-Задунайскій,   Roumiantzeff-Zadounaïsky,
1725 — 1796   1725 — 1796

FIG. 2.1: Petr Rumiantsev (d. 1796), Russian field marshal and victor of Kartal.

Vâsıf's captivity ended in the summer of 1771. The war by then had taken a toll on both sides and Catherine II hoped to secure an advantageous peace, giving her commander-in-chief Rumiantsev instructions to negotiate with the Grand Vizier and returning Vâsıf to the Ottoman army with informal peace proposals. From St. Petersburg, the young scribe

work, HULÂSAT, 54–55, 79–80. One passage of his chronicle (MEHÂSİN 5, 2: 261) also displays a knowledge of Russian by translating and transliterating the term for a type of field gun, what he calls a "concealed cannon" or пушка скрытая (پشکی سکلیتی). See Necâtî, 30–51, on the conditions and activities of the Ottoman prisoners in St. Petersburg.

likely traveled overland through Poland to reach the Russian army on the Danube in early autumn. Here, for the first time, Vâsıf encountered the forty-six-year-old Rumiantsev, now a Field Marshal after his victories at Falça and Kartal, with whom he would develop a rapport and come to respect as a negotiator and statesman. During Vâsıf's stay, Rumiantsev gave him a personal letter for the Grand Vizier, as well as a satchel of missives from İbrahim Paşa's men in the Crimea to their families. He then crossed into Ottoman territory. Vâsıf must have felt untold relief at entering the imperial camp at Babadağı, his long trial over. He could not rest, though, and upon arrival, he was questioned by Silâhdar Mehmed Paşa and explained as best he could what he had seen and heard in Russia. Sensing the gravity of the situation, Mehmed Paşa decided to speed him to the sultan with his corresponding secretary (*mektûbî*), Abdürrezzâk Bâhir Efendi, who was on his way to Istanbul. The two therefore set out together for the capital on September 19, 1771.[28]

Vâsıf's captivity might be considered a fortunate stroke in that he came to Istanbul with a certain cachet, a certain celebrity that boded well for his career and future advancement. Istanbul was the empire's center of power and the site of the central administration. Not only was Vâsıf undoubtedly exhilarated by this visit to the city, his first, but he knew that if he acted wisely, he could gain access to career-altering influence. So far, his positions had been in the retinues of provincial grandees. A placement in the imperial chancery offered more lucrative opportunities, but also the prospect, given skill and luck, of one day rising to a position of power in his own right. The three months he spent in the capital were thus heavy with expectation. Vâsıf's first task was to report to the sultan, Mustafa III, who questioned him several times, took his report in writing, and awarded him cash emoluments to ease his hardship.[29] He also took pains to cultivate new patrons, especially in the major chancery offices. Power and influence in the late eighteenth-century Ottoman chancery resided in departments most closely connected to the person of the chief scribe, or *reisülküttâb*, the head of the chancery who was increasingly concerned with the empire's foreign affairs. The most prestigious

---

[28] MEHÂSİN 5, 2: 176–177; "Vekâyi'nüvis Enverî," 265; and Şemdânîzâde, 2b: 76. See further Aksan, *Ottoman Statesman*, 155–156; Fâik, 146; Schlechta-Wssehrd, 6; and Hammer-Purgstall, 3: 552. A route through Poland would conform to the return itinerary in Necâtî (52–56) and explain Vâsıf's claim (MEHÂSİN 4, fol. 10b) to have visited Poland, where he observed a pipe organ. This also appears to have been when he was in Babadağı, which he described (MEHÂSİN 5, 2: 77–78) in detail and said that he saw in person.

[29] MEHÂSİN 5, 2: 177, 279; and Âsım, 1: 255–256.

offices at this time were the correspondence office, or *mektûbî odası*, which assisted the chief scribe in foreign relations and handled the Grand Vizier's correspondence, and the office of the receiver, or *amedî odası*, which drafted reports issued by the chief scribe as well as ministerial correspondence with the sultan. Both offices dealt with the highest affairs of state; both were frequent stepping-stones to top office.[30] Vâsıf badly needed a patron and, with customary careerism, he aimed high. He started frequenting the proxy chief scribe Râif İsmail Efendi, who showed him favor, perhaps taken by his eloquence and close knowledge of the Russians. Râif quickly cooled to him, however.[31] The reasons for this are not known, but may follow a discernible pattern in Vâsıf's later behavior: the selfish and uncollegial alienation of his peers. The *mektûbî* Abdürrezzâk Efendi proved a more successful, ultimately more stable connection. Small of stature, but spirited and able, Abdürrezzâk had overcome doubts about his ability to forge a distinguished career. Koca Râgıb Paşa once pronounced him too short to employ: "He shall make the imperial council a laughingstock," he had said. Nevertheless, by 1771, Abdürrezzâk Efendi had served as corresponding secretary for a total of seven years and was Mustafa III's trusted advisor, acting as his courier between the capital and battlefront. This combination made him a key figure. He not only had the sultan's ear, but was poised for rapid advancement, likely to the head of the chancery, and represented a felicitous connection for the young scribe.[32] Thankfully for Vâsıf, Abdürrezzâk recognized his talent and the two shared a close working relationship in addition to common literary and professional ambitions. Upon leaving the capital, they appeared to have reached an understanding. Judging from later events, it was one based on shared interest and loyalty.

Events that autumn eventually forced Abdürrezzâk Efendi and Vâsıf back to the front. The *mektûbî* had made this latest trip to report on the restive army and to implore the sultan to act on the Grand Vizier's petition to winter in Edirne or Istanbul, meeting with him several times. The army in Babadağı was badly exposed; Abdürrezzâk urged the sultan to move its

---

[30] Findley, *Reform*, 70 ff.; Lalor, 78–88; and Norman Itzkowitz, "Eighteenth Century Ottoman Realities," *Studia Islamica* 16 (1962): 87–89. See also Recep Ahıshalı, *Osmanlı Devlet Teşkilatında Reisülküttâblık (XVIII. Yüzyıl)* (Istanbul, 2001), 136 ff.

[31] Fâik, 114–116, 146–147; and Karslızâde, 64.

[32] On Abdürrezzâk Bâhir Efendi see MEHÂSİN 5, 2: 194–195; Fâik, 108–112; and Şemdânîzâde, 2b: 53–54, 56, 60, 63, 76. Abdürrezzâk's shortness sometimes caused mirth, as when he invested the still smaller Ebubekir Râtib Efendi as *amedî* in 1779. "Praise God!" he said. "There is someone even shorter than me!" MEHÂSİN 6, fol. 100b. Yeşil repeats this story in *Ebubekir Râtib*, 36.

quarters south to shield it from attack. Mustafa III, however, wanted to keep the army along the Danube, lest the inhabitants of that region begin to flee their homes. In one meeting, Abdürrezzâk shocked the audience by questioning the sultan's judgment and warning him bluntly of the army's danger. He regretted his words as soon as the meeting ended and commiserated later that day with Vâsıf, who worried he would be exiled. The sultan then called. He had been right: reports had it that the army had been routed and was streaming southward from Babadağı. Abdürrezzâk set out at once to avert a disaster and reached Pazarcık, where the remains of the army were camped, with orders to remove Silâhdar Mehmed Paşa. In late November, he took the seal of office and sent it to Muhsinzâde Mehmed Paşa, now reinstated as Grand Vizier, in Rusçuk.[33]

Vâsıf himself tarried a while longer in Istanbul. In December, he took leave and made his way, letters of introduction in hand, to rejoin the army at the town of Şumnu, where Muhsinzâde Paşa planned to overwinter. Vâsıf found his chance when the vizier came from Rusçuk. Probably at Abdürrezzâk Efendi's instance, Muhsinzâde reviewed samples of his writing and gave him an appointment in the chancery, his first. Vâsıf later wrote that his style so pleased the Grand Vizier on the occasion that, without further suasion, he promoted him to the rank of bureau chief or *hacegân*.[34] The scribe's new position was as one of a score of clerks (*halîfe*) in Abdürrezzâk's correspondence office, a small but select bureau and a proving ground for talent, and he was now entitled to a base salary as well as other prerogatives like rations. The correspondence office served as the chief scribe's secretariat and Vâsıf's duties involved him in confidential correspondence as well as in the Grand Vizier's communications with other bureaus and the provinces, in drafting documents, preparing abstracts, and executing fair copies, often personally.[35] Vâsıf was now in a privileged position. The rank of bureau chief qualified him for future

---

[33] MEHÂSİN 5, 2: 175–177, 179–180, 187–188; "Vekâyi'nüvis Enverî," 259–265, 278–286; and Şemdânîzâde, 2b: 77, 81. See also HADÎKAT, supp. 3: 14, 22–25; RESMÎ, 61 (trans.), 115–116 (text); and Aksan, *Ottoman Statesman*, 156. Abdürrezzâk took Silâhdar Mehmed's seal of office on 20 Ş AH 1185 = November 28, 1771.

[34] MEHÂSİN 5, 2: 188, 279; and Âsım, 1: 256. Muhsinzâde Paşa arrived in Şumnu in mid-N AH 1185 = mid-December 1771.

[35] While there is no surviving archival evidence for the appointment, Vâsıf specified in his chronicle (MEHÂSİN 2, fol. 4a; MEHÂSİN 5, 2: 3) that he first served in this chancery office. See also Âsım, 1: 256; Fâik, 147; Fâtin, 432; Karslızâde, 64; Schlechta-Wssehrd, 6; and Hammer-Purgstall, 3: 552. On the upper scribal bureaucracy and the duties of the correspondence office, see Findley, *Reform*, 78–79, 83–84, 100 ff.; and Lalor, 79–83.

openings in the chancery's top stratum, in which he could expect increased compensation and status. He likewise remained Abdürrezzâk Efendi's protégé and was thus part of a circle that included the Grand Vizier and experienced ministers like Ahmed Resmî Efendi, Muhsinzâde's steward and Abdürrezzâk Efendi's brother-in-law. There was every reason to assume that he would rise alongside his patron, who on January 21, 1772, became chief scribe.[36]

2.2 FAILED PEACE EFFORTS, 1772–1773

The lines of communication between the Ottoman and Russian armies remained open during the winter of 1772. Muhsinzâde Paşa made no secret of his opposition to the war and his reappointment as Grand Vizier signaled the empire's readiness to negotiate. Peace seemed ever more likely. In late May, the two sides announced a three-month armistice to hold a summer peace conference in Moldavia, at Foksani, and in July, the Ottoman representatives arrived from Istanbul: the first delegate and former chief scribe Yenişehirli Osman Efendi and the second delegate Yâsinîzâde Efendi, a member of the ulema. Osman Efendi and Yâsinîzâde then crossed the Danube to meet their Russian counterparts, Catherine's favorite Grigorii Orlov and the longtime chargé d'affaires Aleksei Obreskov, and began talks in high summer. What made Foksani memorable was not its result, however. It failed to produce one. Osman Efendi refused the Russians' main demand of Crimean independence and bellowed wildly in negotiations, haranguing the Russian delegates who thought him unstable and his behavior incomprehensible. In fact, Osman was in fear of his life. The sultan and ulema had already rejected this stipulation as illegal according to holy law, which in most cases forbade the surrender of Muslim territory, and he dared not disobey. When neither side gave ground, the conference collapsed and the representatives prepared to return home.[37]

Foksani instead exposed major disagreement in the empire's hierarchy. War and peace formed divisive problems in the eighteenth-century

---

[36] MEHÂSİN 5, 2: 194; Fâik, 109; and Aksan, *Ottoman Statesman*, 27.

[37] According to Enverî (349–354) the proceedings at Foksani began on 7 Ca AH 1186 = August 6, 1772, and broke off on 27 Ca = August 26. See also Aksan, *Ottoman Statesman*, 156–158; RESMÎ, 62–63 (trans.), 116–118 (text); and Köse, 70–78. Fâik, 106–108, relates Osman Efendi's life and career. On Orlov and Obreskov, the latter of whom served as Russian legate in Istanbul from 1751 to 1768, see MERSH, s.v. "Orlov, Grigorii Grigor'evich" and "Obreskov, Aleksei Mikhailovich."

Ottoman Empire, as they were closely entwined with the dynasty's mystique and with an ideology that could not easily face defeat or a dictated settlement. Many were simply unable to reconcile the contradictions they saw in the conflict – between the empire's supposed martial exceptionalism and what had unfolded in the field – and they refused to admit defeat out of hand. This was one obstacle. Another was that in Ottoman notions of peacemaking, based on *force majeure*, the dignity of the empire required tangible concessions or a peace befitting its "abiding honor." Such a concern was not new, having arisen earlier in the century at Karlowitz (1699) and Passarowitz (1718). Of course, what an honorable peace meant in practice was contentious. If some felt it necessary to make concessions to salvage the empire's honor, they faced opponents who saw the negotiations as dictated and in violation of the law. To these, the only option was to fight for better terms and to hope to win a major battle and, thus, a "victorious peace."[38] Still others like Osman Efendi watched how the winds blew. Theirs was the narrow path of self-interest.

Vâsıf's involvement in negotiations that autumn in many ways marked a logical extension of his duties and the first real test of his career. At Şumnu, he had continued his work in the chancery. He soon transferred to the office of the receiver, a still smaller bureau which handled incoming and outgoing correspondence, the chief scribe's and the chief steward's reports, and the Grand Vizier's communications with the sultan. Like his first post, this clerkship made him privy to sensitive information and required close contact with Abdürrezzâk Efendi, Ahmed Resmî Efendi, and the Grand Vizier, among others. His inclusion in confidential matters, particularly foreign affairs, is also evident from the fact that he began to courier documents and even questioned Muhsinzâde about his misgivings over the war and the reasons for his prior dismissal.[39] Vâsıf felt certain that peace was in the empire's interest. When alarm rippled

---

[38] Such concerns at Karlowitz emerge visibly in the chronicle of Mustafa Naîmâ, *Târih-i Na'îmâ*, 1: 45–46. See also Abou-El-Haj, "Ottoman Diplomacy at Karlowitz," *Journal of the American Oriental Society* 87 (1967): 511; and idem, "Ottoman Attitudes," 134–135. For similar concerns in the Treaty of Passarowitz, see Rhoads Murphey's "Twists and Turns in the Diplomatic Dialogue: The Politics of Peacemaking in the Early Eighteenth Century," in *The Peace of Passarowitz, 1718* (West Lafayette, IN, 2011), 80–81, 90 n. 11.

[39] MEHÂSİN 2, fol. 4a; and MEHÂSİN 5, 1: 314–315, 2: 3. According to archival documents (BOA.A.RSK.d 1593, p. 60 and 1623, p. 37), Vâsıf also rose to the rank of the Avlonya tax collectorship on 13 Ra AH 1186 = June 14, 1772. See also Ahıshalı, 142 n. 198; and Erhan Afyoncu, "Osmanlı Müverrihlerine Dair Tevcihat Kayıtları I," *Belgeler* 20 (1999): 124. See Lalor on the office of the receiver, 83–88.

through the army in September that Osman Efendi and Orlov were abandoning talks, and that Osman Efendi had refused to extend the truce, set to expire on September 21, he duly hastened to the council called by the Grand Vizier and listened. Muhsinzâde Paşa had received a personal appeal from Rumiantsev proposing, in effect, to bypass official lines to extend the truce and begin a second round of negotiation. What should they do? The council urged action. A return to war was in no wise favorable for the state, they said, and they advised the Grand Vizier to draft a reply and renegotiate the truce before Osman Efendi could return to the army, sending a well-informed envoy that supported the decision. If nothing else, the empire would at least gain breathing room. The Grand Vizier agreed and had the letter prepared. He then chose an envoy. As Vâsıf recorded it decades later, likely with a deal of vain embellishment, Muhsinzâde singled out and addressed him: "Let me see what you are made of, young man," he said. "A truce is now a great service and blessing for the realm. But what will you say when you arrive? How will you carry out this task?" Vâsıf answered: "I have no idea what the enemy will say, but God willing I shall do everything in my power that is needed." Muhsinzâde gave him the letter, instructions to treat with the Field Marshal in Jassy, and a generous travel allowance. On the way, he was also to convey documents to Osman Efendi. Any lingering doubts that Vâsıf might have had on his departure were dispelled by Ahmed Resmî, an elder statesman and former ambassador, who waylaid him outside of the Grand Vizier's tent and forcefully repeated the value of a truce. Soldiers would surely desert once they learned of Osman Efendi's return, he pointed out; even a delay of ten days would be useful. With that advice, Vâsıf said a prayer and took to his coach. The truce was set to lapse in days.[40]

From Şumnu, Vâsıf raced toward the Danube and Rusçuk, where he had sent riders ahead to prepare boats for his crossing. On arrival, he found these ready and met the town's warden, Dağıstânî Ali Paşa, to explain the council's decision and that the warden was not to engage in hostilities till his return. Ali Paşa's reaction unsettled him. "Why should anyone want a truce?" he asked, derisively. "I have endless men and they are not only able to make sorties. Only let the Grand Vizier allow it and

[40] MEHÂSİN 5, 2: 225–226; "Vekâyi'nüvis Enverî," 355, 356–359; and RESMÎ, 63–64 (trans.), 118 (text). Vâsıf and Resmî claim that Osman Efendi was acting without proper authorization in breaking off negotiations and returning to the army. A document (BOA. C.HR 7849) dated 19 C AH 1186 = September 17, 1772, records that Vâsıf was given 250 kuruş as a travel allowance.

I shall cross and subdue the country all the way to Kiev!" Vâsıf answered impassively that the council had made its decision, but he hoped, if a truce could not be secured, that Ali would keep his vow. He then crossed to Giurgevo, where he boarded a calash and found Osman Efendi three hours ahead returning from Foksani. Vâsıf approached the carriage. He presented the Grand Vizier's letter and briefly described his mission, but Osman, too, was unhelpful: "Marshal Rumiantsev cannot grant a ten day truce," he said. "Not only have they troubled you to no end, but seeking this ludicrous truce will disgrace the empire and waste time." Vâsıf was aware of Osman's reputation – an influential courtier, he was said to hold grudges – and so he measured his words carefully. "I will follow your lead," he told him. "I will go if you say to go; if you say to stay, I will stay." While this undisguised flattery calmed Osman, Vâsıf listened to the minister bitterly criticize his colleague Yâsinîzâde Efendi as they returned together to Giurgevo. He anxiously reflected as they stopped at the camp outside of town. This was not a man to cross, he knew.

Osman Efendi called Vâsıf to his tent an hour later. Present were two envoys from Prussia and Austria who had followed him to Foksani, unsuccessfully, to mediate a settlement. "Was it not foolish to send this bureau chief they call Vâsıf Efendi from the army for a truce?" he asked the Austrian. "Can Rumiantsev even call a truce?" When the envoy refused to commit, noting that Rumiantsev was an agent of the Russian state, the Prussian spoke up and questioned Osman's motives. Why was he obstructing his own state's appointee? Truce or no, would the man not at least be useful for gathering intelligence? Vâsıf sensed that this rebuke struck home, as Osman blanched and turned to him, saying, "You must now be on your way." To sharpen the embarrassment, Vâsıf rather spitefully reminded Osman that he had returned on his orders: "God willing there is good in this. Pay no mind to these envoys' sophistries and silence them," he said. "You would have me in trouble, sir," Osman replied. "At all events, after what these envoys have said you must go." Vâsıf was not on his way without a final word from Osman Efendi, however. In case the mission failed, as Osman expected it would, he gave Vâsıf as a last resource several talismans sent by Mustafa III, a devotee of the occult, to bury in the ground so that Rumiantsev would walk over them and fall under their influence. He would thankfully not need them.[41]

---

[41] MEHÂSİN 5, 2: 226–227. Tahsin Öz describes these talismans and their instructions (TSMA.E 3809), found inside of a red satin pouch in the imperial palace archives. The charms consisted of white beeswax and were sewn inside thick white cloth and wrapped in paper, bearing seals and the names of the intended targets. According to the

Rumiantsev greeted Vâsıf's arrival in Jassy with guarded relief. Once he had read the Grand Vizier's letter and confessed that Osman Efendi and Orlov had foolishly forced the empires to the brink of war, damage he and Muhsinzâde could hopefully repair, he let the scribe rest for a few hours before recalling him to discuss the truce with Obreskov. The Field Marshal spoke first to warn against any double-dealing. The Ottomans must be sincere in their desire for peace, he said, and must not try to mislead him. Vâsıf insisted that the empire's aim was "a peace befitting its honor and welfare" and that he had no ulterior motives, but Rumiantsev suspected his visit might be a ploy to gain time. Having seen the dismal reality of Ottoman camp, Vâsıf was aware that such a suspicion was not unfounded. Bluffing, he therefore claimed the imperial army had 80,000 soldiers at its disposal as well as forty to fifty thousand in both Silistre and Rusçuk waiting for the word to attack. They had no need of manpower. He likewise related how he had been hard-pressed to restrain Dağıstânî Ali Paşa and that the Silistre warden had similar orders. "We would not make these proposals if we did not want peace," he concluded. Obreskov at that moment interposed. A seasoned diplomat whom Vâsıf respected, and who saw through his bravado, he advised that the situation was clear enough and that they must stop bandying about words and attend to the truce. They then asked Vâsıf how long the proposed agreement should last. Vâsıf requested a period of some months, as certain terms would need time for approval. Rumiantsev replied that he did not have the power to extend the truce, but that he could write to the empress. Since his request would take about forty days, he could give the Ottomans this time and add several more months later with her authorization. Vâsıf balked. The empire would accept nothing less than a seven-month truce, he said, and besides, they had no assurance that the empress would consent. That Rumiantsev had foreseen this objection was plain from the compromise he now offered: he would provide the Ottomans with a sealed guarantee, his word of honor, so long as they did the same. While Vâsıf had no such authority, he knew that the mission's success depended on his agreement and he accepted, promising a similar guarantee within ten days of his return. The truce was in hand. After taking Rumiantsev's voucher, Vâsıf raised one final matter. He reminded the Field Marshal that he had

---

annotated instructions, Osman Efendi was unable to use them and gave the remainder to Vâsıf. Osman also explains how the Foksani negotiations broke down and hints that he would have prevented Vâsıf's mission if he could have. See "Yerköy Mükâlemelerinde Murahhaslar için Gönderilen Büyüler," *Tarih Vesikaları* 2 (1942): 101–103.

instructed his own commanders to avoid hostilities unless under direct attack. "I think that it would be proper if you also sent these instructions to your men," he said. In truth, on the way to Jassy, Vâsıf had seen Russian troops moving toward the Danube and nearly lost his composure, knowing the parlous state of the frontiers and fearing a catastrophe. Much to his relief, Rumiantsev sent word to halt their advance, and he took to the road.

Even with the Field Marshal's guarantee, there remained a real danger that the truce would be upset before Vâsıf contacted the Grand Vizier in Şumnu. Making all speed, he reached Giurgevo two days out of Jassy and crossed to Rusçuk, where Dağıstânî Ali Paşa met him and demanded to know the outcome of the mission. Vâsıf noted a change in the garrison's morale. Callously, he toyed with Ali – "We are at war," he said – and urged him to carry out his earlier plan of attack. The warden went pale. He had merely put on a brave face in their last meeting for encouragement, he admitted. His men had either fled or died of disease and he had neither money nor provisions; he had no means to fight, much less take the offensive, and he begged that the Grand Vizier be informed of the situation. In view of his disclosure, Vâsıf told Ali of the guarantee and enjoined him to secrecy until the truce was formally announced. He also learned that Osman Efendi was undermining him. In Hezargrad, he encountered one Bekir Bey, who reported that Osman was spreading rumors that the truce was doomed – that Rumiantsev would not agree – and agitating for war with the claim that the Russians were reduced by illness. The other ministers complied, afraid he would influence the sultan against them, and they sent Bekir Bey with orders to reinforce Ali Paşa or, if possible, to cross the Danube. Vâsıf was surely disturbed by this news, but did not satisfy Bekir's queries. He merely directed him to proceed to Rusçuk slowly, lest his orders be changed from the rear. Vâsıf entered the imperial camp around dawn on September 24, 1772, and, after performing his morning prayers, went directly to Muhsinzâde Paşa's pavilion with Abdürrezzâk Efendi and Resmî Efendi. There, he explained the situation in detail. The scribe had every reason to hope for a kind reception and reward. According to his account, Muhsinzâde was so pleased by his conduct that he offered to promote him then and there to the head of the receiver's office or *amedî*. However, Vâsıf declined this opportunity with perhaps overweening modesty, with the excuse that he did not wish to slight his superior, the current receiver. Muhsinzâde nonetheless promised to repay him and later that day sent word that he had granted him a prebend (*zeamet*) in Anatolia valued annually at no less than 20,000 *akçe*, a tidy sum.[42] Vâsıf was well pleased with himself. The landed income was an immense boon, especially on campaign, and his service would allow negotiations to resume. His first diplomatic task had succeeded; he had earned his peers' admiration and, more importantly, justified the Grand Vizier's trust.

In the following weeks, the two empires acted on the truce's extension by organizing a new conference for the fall in the Moldavian city of Bucharest. For all his involvement in earlier negotiations, Vâsıf could reasonably expect to partake in this effort for the reason that his patron, Abdürrezzâk Efendi, was selected to negotiate on the empire's behalf, and he was accordingly in the chief scribe's retinue as secretary to negotiations (mukâleme kâtibi) when it left the imperial army in late October, crossing the Danube after a stay in Rusçuk to gather supplies.[43] At Bucharest, the Ottomans and Russians began intensive negotiations. Opening the conference on November 9, Abdürrezzâk and the Russian delegate Obreskov sat in a score of sessions through the winter and tried to broker compromises on the war's pressing issues. Vâsıf and a colleague, Hayrî Efendi, recorded these proceedings. However, as the two delegates painstakingly built up the framework for an agreement, it became clear that the terms would not be palatable. Obreskov and his government demanded, among other things, Crimean independence and the possession of key fortresses on the peninsula, points that required the sultan's approval. Muhsinzâde and his ministers endorsed these, but only against stout opposition in Istanbul. In his role as secretary to negotiations, moreover, Vâsıf was fully aware of the danger that he and others faced in drafting an unpopular treaty. This danger was not abstract. Abdürrezzâk Efendi's brother, a judge

[42] MEHÂSİN 5, 2: 228–232; "Vekâyi'nüvis Enverî," 358–360; and Schlechta-Wssehrd, 6. Ahmed Câvid preserves Vâsıf's detailed official report of this journey, the original of which he lost in a fire some years later. In this account, Muhsinzâde's offer of promotion is much vaguer. Vâsıf also tells Osman Efendi on his return that the truce had been foreordained: "I can still hardly believe it," Osman replies, "but God grant that it ends well." Osmanlı-Rus İlişkileri Tarihi: Ahmet Câvid Bey'in Müntehabâtı (Istanbul, 2004), 442 ff. A later petition (BOA.C.TZ 6637) written by Vâsıf describes a prebend, probably the same, located near Afyonkarahisar in the sub-district of Bolvadin and village of Çay. It was valued at 38,734 akçe. While Sarıkaya says that he never received this zeamet (lxxii n. 2), Vâsıf said clearly (MEHÂSİN 5, 2: 232) that he took possession of it until the end of the war and used its income to meet his expenses.

[43] Abdürrezzâk was also accompanied by Süleyman Penâh Efendi, Ataullah Beyefendi, Mehmed Hayrî Efendi, translators, two other clerks from the correspondence office, and his son Ahmed Hamid Efendi. See MEHÂSİN 5, 2: 235–237; "Vekâyi'nüvis Enverî," 361–365; RESMÎ, 64 (trans.), 118 (text); and Fâik, 147. The Ottoman archives contain a later audit of their expenses (BOA.D.BŞM.d 4322), as well as instructions (BOA.MHM. d 171, p. 192) dated late B AH 1186 = late October 1772 to Dağıstânî Ali Paşa in Rusçuk.

in Istanbul, informed them that while Mustafa III privately felt peace to be in the empire's interest, he was ready to banish the members of the delegation to spare himself from public discontent. By springtime, Abdürrezzâk and his retinue began to despair. Despite their efforts and the army's support, the imperial council would not give its consent. The conference dissolved in failure on March 22, 1773, and the sultan again ordered the army back to war with the hope of winning a victorious peace.[44]

Like his colleagues, Vâsıf's thoughts at this period undoubtedly turned on the difficulties of peacemaking. More specifically, he must have struggled to square his own ideological commitments with the dynasty's need for a negotiated settlement – a dilemma, it should be noted, with an established discourse in late eighteenth-century intellectual life. Ottoman statesmen and thinkers had long argued the merits of peace. The author and moralist Ḥasan Kâfî al-Aqḥiṣârî (d. 1616), an early example, had ended the late sixteenth-century treatise *Precepts of Wisdom for the Order of the World* (*Uṣûl al-ḥikam fî niẓâm al-ʿâlam*) with a brief section on the topic. Aqḥiṣârî's was less a reasoned defense of peace than, as the title indicates, a series of axioms, prophetical wisdom, and scriptural quotations. He also insisted generally on honoring treaties or *pacta sunt servanda*.[45] More characteristic of Ottoman attitudes, however, was the defense of peace penned by the empire's first court historian, Mustafa Naîmâ Efendi. Naîmâ wrote in the aftermath of the War of the Holy League (1683–1699) and Peace of Karlowitz. At Karlowitz, the empire ceded large territories to European states for the first time, and Naîmâ used his work to support the treaty's architect, Grand Vizier Köprülü Amcazâde Hüseyin Paşa. His defense consisted of several parts likening Karlowitz to earlier Islamic treaties. After a descriptive title, Naîmâ told the story of Muhammad's famous capitulation to his Meccan enemies in the 628 Treaty of Ḥudaybiyya. The moral of this treaty as he explained it was simple: to act through "the means at hand." Naîmâ pointed out that while Muhammad was endowed with divine powers, he deliberately submitted to harsh terms to teach believers "to avail themselves of worldly

---

[44] MEHÂSİN 5, 2: 237–238, 241–246, 249–250; "Vekâyiʿnüvis Enverî," 365–366, 372–376; RESMÎ, 64–66 (trans.), 118–120 (text); and Şemdânîzâde, 2b: 91. See also Aksan, *Ottoman Statesman*, 159–162; Hammer-Purgstall, 3: 552; and Köse, 82–86.

[45] Ḥasan Kâfî al-Aqḥiṣârî, *Uṣûl al-ḥikam fî niẓâm al-ʿâlam: risâla fî al-fikr al-siyâsî al-islâmî*, ed. Iḥsân Ṣidḳî al-ʿAmad (Kuwait, 1987), 171–174. Aqḥiṣârî composed this work in Arabic during the Eğri Campaign of 1596 and later that year translated it into Ottoman Turkish. Mehmet İpşirli has published this translation and gloss as "Hasan Kâfî el-Akhisarî ve Devlet Düzenine Ait Eseri *Usûlü'l-Hikem fî Nizâmi'l-Âlem*," *Tarih Enstitüsü Dergisi* 10–11 (1979–1980): 239–278.

contingencies" and use all available means.[46] This lesson mattered insofar as all polities undergo hardship. After setting forth the Arab historian Ibn Khaldûn's dynastic life cycle, Naîmâ noted that wise rulers generally avoid war in the presence of serious disorder, including extended campaigns and disunity. In the course of history, many had therefore preferred peace to war and chose peace as the "lesser of two evils (*ehven-i şerreyn*)" to preserve their realms, such as the Ayyubid sultans Saladin and al-Kâmil, who respectively retook Jerusalem from Crusaders in 1187 and ceded it by treaty in 1229. In conclusion, Naîmâ turned his praise to Amcazâde Hüseyin Paşa. He wrote that the War of the Holy League led the empire to bankruptcy and crisis. Restoring order and the treasury depended on a period of peace, "so that it was necessary, through a truce, to sheath the vengeful sword," but leading jurists prolonged the conflict in the hope of winning a "victorious peace." Only when the Grand Vizier came to power was this opposition overcome and the empire saved.[47]

That peacemaking was a supremely delicate subject is shown by Naîmâ's care to reconcile Karlowitz with Ottoman militant ideals: as a temporary peace, a necessary lull in the empire's struggle with the infidel before resuming warfare. This he did quite shrewdly. First, Naîmâ demonstrated that unfavorable terms with non-Muslims had historical precedent in the Peace of Ḥudaybiyya and the surrender of Jerusalem, both of which were treaty models par excellence.[48] Second, he implied that the Peace of Karlowitz was strictly temporary. For, as his readers knew, both of these previous cases ended in renewed war after a short reprieve. Third and finally, Naîmâ suggested that a temporary truce would aid the dynasty and lead to the recovery of lost territory or to further conquests. Muhammad and the Ayyubids captured Mecca and Jerusalem, respectively, in the years following their treaties. This, too, Ottoman readers knew. Above all, however, Naîmâ was attempting to lessen the ideological dissonance caused by defeat. Karlowitz was a watershed that marked Ottoman agreement to a more or less permanent peace with Austria, Russia, Poland, and Venice. But to accept peace as permanent would be to admit defeat, and "the acceptance of defeat . . . would amount to a total

---

[46] Naîmâ, 1: 10–20. Thomas' "the means at hand" (69–73) does not quite capture the nuance of this phrase, which invokes a very specific intellectual discourse on causality.

[47] Naîmâ, 1: 21–30, 30–33, 45–48; and Thomas, 77–82.

[48] Wilson Bishai, "Negotiations and Peace Agreements Between Muslims and Non-Muslims in Islamic History," in *Medieval and Middle Eastern Studies in Honor of Aziz Suryal Atiya*, ed. Sami A. Hanna (Leiden, 1972), 56–58, 60–61; and Khadduri, 210–213. On Ḥudaybiyya see EI[2], s.v. "Al-Ḥudaybiya" and "Hudna"; DİA, s.v. "Hudeybiye Antlaşması."

abandonment of the ideological justification of the Ottoman state and would have led to the dissolution of the emotional bond this theory effected in the Ottoman social fabric."[49] The result for Naîmâ was a sort of make-believe.

It is highly significant that Naîmâ became a model for Vâsif's generation. Filled with events and terms carrying heavy intellectual baggage, all marshaled to vindicate Karlowitz, his treatment became a prototype for many late eighteenth-century defenses of peace. Its mention of "worldly contingencies" evoked heated contemporary debates over fate and human will; its historical examples recalled the triumphal career of early Islam and reminded readers that peace was a justifiable but temporary respite; and its reference to "the lesser of two evils" and to "victorious peace" introduced key arguments on the legal and moral merits of peace that, while not fully developed, would resurface frequently in later years. Vâsif too adopted this model. At least in the early stages of his career, he held that peace, such as it was, was a temporary expedient, but one the empire needed from time to time, delay being potentially fatal. It is not clear when he first read Naîmâ – perhaps at Bucharest or earlier – but the arguments were well-known in his circle. He was unquestionably familiar with them.[50] Vâsif and his peers were therefore understandably distraught by the collapse of the second round of negotiations. Ahmed Resmî blamed courtiers and ulema who, in his view, espoused a too rigid view of Tatar independence, sycophants like Osman Efendi who misled the sultan into thinking that peace could be won by force. Resmî had supported Abdürrezzâk's efforts and even presented him with an essay before the conference, a short work that rejected the idea of perpetual expansion in favor of stable interstate relations. His ideas were radically different from Naîmâ's, but bore little fruit; Bucharest was a heavy blow for him.[51] Vâsif for his own part felt betrayed by the empire's leadership. The breathing space they needed was legally defensible. He and his peers had done their duty and taken steps to end the war, but neither Mustafa III nor the Grand

---

[49] Abou-El-Haj, "Ottoman Attitudes," 136. My conclusions here draw on this article as well as the same author's "Ottoman Diplomacy at Karlowitz" and "The Formal Closure of the Ottoman Frontier in Europe, 1699–1703," *Journal of the American Oriental Society* 89 (1969): 467–475. See also Aksan, "Ottoman Political Writing, 1768–1808," in *Ottomans and Europeans: Contacts and Conflicts* (Istanbul, 2004), 32 n. 1.

[50] For example, MEHÂSİN 1, fols. 8b-10a, 85b-86b.

[51] RESMÎ, 65–66 (trans.), 119–120 (text). İsmet Parmaksızoğlu has published this essay as "Bir Türk Diplomatının Onsekizinci Yüzyıl Sonunda Devletler Arası İlişkilere Dair Görüşleri," *Belleten* 47 (1983): 527–535. I treat Resmî's radical thoughts on peace more fully in the next chapter.

Vizier would act. Vâsıf was especially incensed that Muhsinzâde, a mentor and patron, had refused to exert pressure on the delegation's behalf and deferred so timidly to Istanbul. This, to him, was cowardice.[52]

As spring turned to summer and the empire returned to a war footing, Vâsıf's frustrations could only simmer. His duties took precedence. In Şumnu, Muhsinzâde was preparing for a renewed Russian offensive, which, when it came, broke over Babadağı, Karasu, Silistre, and other points south of the Danube, and Vâsıf found himself involved in the army's day-to-day activities. Since at least 1772, he had been working parallel to his other functions as secretary to the left-wing cavalry (*gurebâ-yı yesâr kâtibi*) – one of the old corps of palace horse that traditionally guarded the army's camp, train, and sacred relic, the Prophet's banner. Possibly this was part of his service to Abdürrezzâk Efendi, who, though a bureaucrat, was being increasingly drawn into active command.[53] Vâsıf followed the summer's reports with emotion, at times alarm, at times joy. The Ottoman loss at Karasu was nothing less than a rout. However, late in the season, Silistre's outnumbered forces broke Rumiantsev's siege of the town to win a sudden and crushing victory. Vâsıf traveled there himself after the battle with the Grand Vizier's felicitations for Osman Paşa, the resident commander, and was awed by what he saw: a victory so total that cannons and munitions lay scattered everywhere, abandoned, the road nearly impassable from heaped Russian corpses. It seemed that there was fight in the empire yet.[54]

Nevertheless, by the fall, a Russian force had pushed its way to Pazarcık a mere sixty miles to the northeast of Şumnu and had repulsed all efforts to dislodge it. Muhsinzâde consulted with his ministers, the danger being, so it appeared, that they might march directly on the imperial camp. According to later accounts, Abdürrezzâk Efendi urged the Grand Vizier to move the army into a more defensible position outside of the city. If it pleased, he also offered to travel with his retinue to Yenipazar, a fifteen-mile march away, to rally the friendly forces at nearby Karasu and Pazarcık and turn them against the Russians. The council approved of his plan and in early November, he rode out with about five hundred men,

---

[52] MEHÂSİN 5, 2: 245, 280–281.

[53] The original date of this appointment is not known. It was reconfirmed on 8 Za AH 1186 (January 31, 1773), Vâsıf receiving his warrant of office and ceremonial robe in Bucharest. MEHÂSİN 5, 2: 240; and "Vekâyi'nüvis Enverî," 371. See also Afyoncu, "Tevcihat Kayıtları I," 125; and Karslızâde, 64.

[54] TESLIYETNÂME, fols. 4b-5a. Vâsıf claimed elsewhere (MEHÂSİN 6, fol. 22b) that he was in Silistre in early 1774 to announce the accession of Abdülhamid I. Mahmud Sâbit corroborates this fact in *Târîh-i Cedîd-i Silistre*, ÖN H.O. nr. 102b, fols. 61a-61b.

Vâsıf, as always, in train. In Yenipazar, the chief scribe assembled a motley group of several thousand soldiers, deserters, and other fit bodies, fortified the town, and sent three hundred horsemen to reconnoiter in nearby Kozluca, where they surprised and pursued a Russian column. Abdürrezzâk then traveled through Kozluca to Pazarcık. As he and his retinue neared the city, they were informed by patrols that the enemy had withdrawn, thinking that the full imperial army was on the move and mistaking them for outriders. Vâsıf judged from their disordered camp and from food half-cooked in kettles that the retreat had, for this reason, been hasty. He and his colleagues knew better.

Perhaps against better judgment, Abdürrezzâk Efendi decided to spend the night in Pazarcık. He and his men were understandably uneasy. Their force was small and vulnerable. The Russians would not long be deceived and it was no surprise when further patrols reported that the enemy had regrouped and could return as early as the next day. Abdürrezzâk and Vâsıf stayed up with the Filibe mufti Nasûhî Efendi to discuss a plan of action. Shortly after Nasûhî Efendi had retired, however, a man interrupted their lucubrations with a letter from the nearby Black Sea port of Varna. Abdürrezzâk read the message with concern and gave it to Vâsıf: Varna was heavily invested by the Russians and its inhabitants were begging for aid. The two men agreed that there was no way to relieve the port with the Russians so close by, unless they might somehow drive them back. Yet their doubts remained as ever with the rank and file. They decided that the men would likely desert if word of the siege got out, and with that, they parted until morning. That night, Vâsıf got little rest and was awoken – without warning – by a thunderous explosion. The whole town was soon roused and in an uproar, soldiers screaming that the Russians were attacking and mounting up and fleeing in all directions, some toward the imperial army, others aimlessly. Vâsıf had two of his aides ready the correspondence scribes' horses and went to check on Abdürrezzâk Efendi. "Stay calm. Let me see how the chief scribe is doing," he said. Since their lodgings were joined, it took Vâsıf little time to find the diminutive Abdürrezzâk standing atop a horse-block, ignored by attendants and winded from shouting for a mount. Vâsıf tried to calm his patron, who feared that the Russians were counterattacking. There had only been one blast, he pointed out. If this were a surprise attack, or if the Russians simply wanted to cause confusion, they would not stop at one salvo. "There is something behind this," he assured him. "We shall see what surfaces." Sure enough, shortly afterward, the message came that Pazarcık was not under attack. It seemed instead that the Russians had mined the dome of the town's mosque using slow match and that the terrific report – which caused such bedlam – had come from its detonation. This story was quickly confirmed. But the fact remained that much of Abdürrezzâk Efendi's party had fled. Although he was able to recover some of the men, many others reached the imperial army with rumors that the force had disintegrated wholesale in a surprise attack. Abdürrezzâk perforce wrote to the Grand Vizier to clarify. He and Vâsıf then made arrangements for Pazarcık's defense before heading back to Şumnu, where they found Muhsinzâde doubly pleased: by their return as well as by the good news out of Varna, where the Ottomans had won another victory.[55]

2.3 THE SHOCK OF DEFEAT, 1773–1774

By the autumn of 1773, the war had dragged on for five years. If Vâsıf celebrated these token successes, and there is no reason to doubt that he did, he must also have reflected on them from the wider vantage of his social and intellectual milieu. Vâsıf was a servant of the empire, an educated Muslim and Ottoman gentleman. The victories at Silistre and Varna were providential, to be sure, but neither he nor his colleagues could ignore the facts of a conflict that had been little short of ruinous. The war formed a paradox and faced him with hard questions, questions of a causal nature. What was happening to the empire? Why was it happening? Was there nothing that he and others could do about it? The death of Mustafa III that January lent these thoughts added impetus. Vâsıf mourned Mustafa as a master and patron and in spite of his failings, especially for his generous welcome in Istanbul three years prior. But he felt a less effable sense of loss, too. There was now an impassable gulf between the empire of his youth – the "feast days" of the sultan's early reign, a peaceful and prosperous time before the war's upheaval – and the present, a reality that others, too, acknowledged.[56] Those days seemed long ago. Was there nothing they could do? Were they all powerless?

---

[55] MEHÂSİN 5, 2: 272–275; "Vekâyi'nüvis Enverî," 419–422, 429–432; Şemdânîzâde, 2b: 109–110; and RESMÎ, 70–71 (trans.), 124–125 (text). Vâsıf and Abdürrezzâk left Şumnu on 19 Ş AH 1187 = November 5, 1773, and returned on 10 N = November 25. It is worth noting that Pazarcık – Dobrich in present-day Bulgaria – is more often called Hacıoğlu-Pazarcık or Hacıoğlu-Pazarı in Ottoman sources to differentiate it from a town of the same name to the west (Pazardzhik or Tatar Pazarcık). Kozluca is now Suvorovo, after the Russian commander. As a general rule, place names in this region have variants and have changed, sometimes several times, during the nineteenth and twentieth centuries.

[56] MEHÂSİN 5, 2: 279–280. Vâsıf traveled (MEHÂSİN 6, fol. 22b) at this juncture to Silistre to announce Abdülhamid I's accession to the throne. According to Mahmud Sâbit

These were by no means isolated sentiments for the time. While scholars are only beginning to study early modern Ottoman intellectual life, we
have indications that fate, free will, and causality were among the major
problems of Vâsıf's age. The issue was one of agency. How much control,
in other words, do we humans have over our actions and the wider world:
are we "masters of our fate or puppets moved from on high?"[57] Vâsıf and
his peers could draw in their search for answers on a very old theological
discourse, one which sought to reconcile God's absolute power with His
divine justice. This discourse had emerged early in Islamic history and, by
the eighth century, yielded two basic views. On the one hand, some
thinkers known as Fatalists or Predestinarians (*jabriyya* or *mujbira*)
asserted God's omnipotence and held that humans lack the will, choice,
and power to make decisions. Our actions must be the result of God's will
alone, they held, for He can have no rivals in power. On the other hand,
and against the Predestinarians, supporters of free will (*qadariyya*) replied
that God is all-just and must give humans some measure of agency – if He
did not, our religious duty and even moral right and wrong would be
illusions. This was the belief of later rationalists known as the Mu'tazila.

Three influential theologians, Abû al-Ḥasan al-Ash'arî (d. 935/36),
Abû Manṣûr al-Mâturîdî (d. 944), and al-Ghazâlî (d. 1111), later synthesized these views. Al-Ash'arî tried to preserve God's power through an
atomistic or occasionalist cosmology, in which God constantly "rear-
ranges all the atoms of this world and creates their accidents anew –
thus creating a new world every moment."[58] According to al-Ash'arî,
the universe is formed of bodies made from atoms and the accidents
which inhere in them. On earth, the lowest sublunary sphere, God at
every instant recreates these atoms according to His will and joins and
separates them in a process of generation and corruption (*kawn wa fasâd*,
Trk. *kevn ü fesâd*). While al-Ash'arî rejected the idea of a "natural law" or
causality outside of God as a curb on divine power, he acknowledged that
humans might "acquire (*kasb*)" and accept responsibility for actions
created by God. This view was opposed by al-Mâturîdî, who agreed that
God willed and created human acts, but argued that the choice belonged

---

(fols. 61a-61b), he read the proclamation in a large council and received a robe of honor
from the garrison commander Hasan Paşa. Sâbit dates this event to 13 Z AH 1187 =
February 25, 1774. However, given that he records Mustafa's death date as 7 Z rather
than the correct 7 Za (January 20), it may be that Vâsıf was actually in Silistre a month
earlier on 13 Za = January 26.

[57] I draw in what follows on Menchinger, "Free Will," 446–448.

[58] Frank Griffel, *Al-Ghazali's Philosophical Theology* (Oxford, 2009), 126.

to man, not to God. Al-Mâturîdî thus fell between the Mu'tazila and al-Ash'arî, whose theory of acquisition was called by some a "moderate fatalism." Al-Ghazâlî, meanwhile, often seen as al-Ash'arî's follower, was able to merge his occasionalistic outlook with Aristotelian causality to forge what in time became Sunni Islam's predominant theological orthodoxy. The key idea for him was "God's custom ('âdatullah, Trk. 'âdetüllah)." Al-Ghazâlî held that God is the only real agent in the universe, willing and creating everything, but that He chooses to act via secondary causes (or, at least, the appearance of causes). God is therefore the only true agent. He is the Primary Cause in the cosmos or, put differently, "the one who makes causes function as causes (musabbib al-asbâb)." However, al-Ghazâlî realized that this distinction did little in everyday life. God could break causality at any moment, it is true, but His custom in linking cause and effect meant that humans had to rely in day-to-day affairs on a sort of visible "natural law." Al-Ghazâlî thus made a key distinction between fate as a matter of theological doctrine and fatalism as an approach to life.[59]

There is no doubt that Ottomans wrote or thought about causality through the lens of these older ideas. Worldly causes (esbâb) for them were "secondary" and brought about by God the Primary Cause. During the eighteenth century, moreover, human agency gained importance as an intellectual problem to the extent that it was tied to issues like warfare, political reform, and the empire's supposed exceptionalism. For theologians and Sufis, this concern surfaced in tracts on free will, which flourished from the late sixteenth century to the nineteenth century, and in the popularization of a concept treated in the next chapter called "particular will (irâde-i cüziyye)." For statesmen and thinkers who dealt with the immediate ends of human agency, the question was more practically limited to whether or not to act through worldly causes. Still, late eighteenth-century Ottomans were divided. While many held the consensus view that mankind had free will in moral, civil, and political life, and that to deny free will's exercise was sinful, there are strong indications of a sentiment – how widespread is not known – of fatalism. Vâsıf knew

---

[59] Şerif Mardin notes that al-Ghazâlî distinguishes between a natural law that relies on God's will and one that is independent of the deity; or, per Thomas Aquinas, natura naturata as opposed to natura naturans: The Genesis of Young Ottoman Thought: A Study in the Modernization of Turkish Political Ideas (Syracuse, 2000), 86–94. Natural laws in Islamic thought are thus "due to habit and have no more than a juridical status" (See Seyyid Hossein Nasr, An Introduction to Islamic Cosmological Doctrines [Boulder, CO, 1978], 8–10), while miracles are an abrogation of this habit (khârq al-'âda).

that in his last days, Mustafa III had succumbed to fatalism and gloom, sickened, some said, by grief. And he could tell that others were reacting similarly, dismissing the war as hopeless, predestined, a function of God's will.[60] Vâsıf as an educated Ottoman could understand this position. Denying human agency was a logical, if extreme, assertion of the general Sunni belief that God creates all things and that believers have a duty to trust in Him fully. It was also comforting and politically expedient to blame the empire's plight on divine trial, rather than on any moral or material deficiency (or worse still, the enemy's superiority) that might require reform. Like other causal positions, fatalism was a way to answer the problem of theodicy, a way to reconcile calamities with a just and almighty God. Yet Vâsıf refused to accept this thinking. He would not resign himself to despair. His studies as a young man, particularly in speculative theology, had taught him to respect God's absolute power and goodness. He believed in fate as a point of doctrine and as part of the philosophical system of occasionalism, not in the facile, inert fatalism into which many of his peers were sinking. To Vâsıf fate was a force entwined with human will. The two were closely linked. As for the war, it surely contained some inscrutable divine wisdom, some hidden lesson in which he and his peers had a role to play. However, the difficulty lay not merely in discerning this wisdom, but in acting on it. Just how this might be done was far from clear; the precise relationship of the variables – fate and free will, knowledge and action – was something over which he would struggle in mind, in deed, and in writing for the rest of his life.

The remainder of the war meanwhile provided Vâsıf with little clarity. After another winter at Şumnu, now heavily fortified, on May 25, 1774, Muhsinzâde assembled his ministers to discuss the spring offensive ordered by the new sultan, Abdülhamid I, a council the scribe most likely attended. The Grand Vizier's goal was to craft a strategy. The council proposed to send three columns to attack Russian positions on the southern shore of the Danube, concentrating on the fortress of Hırsova, after which they would rally at Silistre, cross the river, and hopefully force a settlement. Although he did not like diverting manpower from the imperial army, Muhsinzâde Paşa accepted this proposal in its essentials. He then asked who should lead the main force. The council fell silent. When he gestured toward his steward Ahmed Resmî, Vâsıf, who knew

---

[60] MEHÂSİN 5, 2: 280–281. In his corpus at large, Vâsıf attributed fatalistic views to statesmen (e.g. İLGÜREL, 170, 197) as well as to members of the ulema (e.g. MEHÂSİN 2, fol. 196a).

Resmî's opinions on the war and army, saw his hesitation. The Grand Vizier repeated the question. "Please don't make me speak," Resmî finally said, and stirred the room into debate by airing his doubts on the campaign's feasibility. Vâsıf was unsurprised by Resmî's dissent; in fact, he admired it. Nevertheless, the council ultimately decided to proceed and named the Janissary Ağa Yeğen Mehmed Paşa as commander. Mehmed Paşa must have had doubts of his own, for he stalled by asking the Grand Vizier to guarantee his supplies and, no sooner than this was done, requested a second-in-command. At this juncture, and after more awkward silence, Abdürrezzâk Efendi stood and volunteered. "I have a life," he declared. "Let it be a sacrifice for my faith and country. I will go with him." Since it was highly unusual for a chief scribe to hold military command, Muhsinzâde tried to reason Abdürrezzâk into standing down. He refused. The Grand Vizier could only yield and the joint force left Şumnu a little more than two weeks later on its way north, Yeğen Mehmed Paşa commanding the infantry and Abdürrezzâk Efendi the cavalry.[61]

To Vâsıf, the spring campaign must have been akin to déjà vu. The force under the Janissary commander and chief scribe was much larger than the previous fall, numbering some 25,000 men, but once more he found himself in Abdürrezzâk's retinue on the Pazarcık road. He was ill at ease besides. His experience in battle up to this point had been uniformly dreadful. Years later, he recollected in hindsight that the operation had started poorly when a powder explosion in Şumnu killed a number of gunners, an accident that some interpreted as a bad omen. That Vâsıf then read anything sinister into the event is doubtful. One of his activities during this time was to draft a petition for his prebendal income in Anatolia, with which he was having trouble, and it is more likely that he was too busy putting his affairs in order to worry about omens and prognostications, though he may have rued his patron's impulsive streak.[62] The army reached Yenipazar two days out of

---

[61] MEHÂSİN 5, 2: 294–296; "Vekâyi'nüvis Enverî," 459–461; and RESMÎ, 71–72 (trans.), 126–127 (text). Şemdânîzâde (3: 5–6) and Fâik (109) concur that the appointment was irregular. Enverî declares elsewhere (432) that Abdürrezzâk's service as a commander was unprecedented for a chief scribe.

[62] The petition (BOA.C.TZ 6637) is dated 26 Ra AH 1188 = June 6, 1774, and requests a *zeamet* located in Afyonkarahisar. Vâsıf claimed that this prebend belonged to one İbrahim Hazine Efendi, who died without issue and left it vacant, and that he deserved it by virtue of his scribal service. However, an inquiry by the financial bureau found that İbrahim Hazine was not dead at all, but had been captured with the Crimean *serasker* İbrahim Paşa and sent to St. Petersburg. His prebend was then entrusted to Hacı Mehmed, formerly the Grand Vizier's steward, with the income used to support his family. The request was thus denied (see also Sarıkaya, lxxii n. 2). Whether this document refers to Vâsıf's earlier prebend or to another is not entirely clear. Still, it sheds some light

Şumnu; on the third day, they stopped at Kozluca, where scouts reported an enemy patrol three hours away in a valley called Uşanlı. Not knowing that the Russians had concealed forces in the nearby forest, Yeğen Mehmed Paşa and Abdürrezzâk Efendi assumed that they were concentrated at Pazarcık and sent a minor officer, Uzun Abdullah Paşa, with several thousand men to take control of the valley. It was an ambush. On June 20, the Russians emerged from cover and surprised Abdullah Paşa, who, under intense fire and his horse hampered by the wooded terrain, sent urgently for aid. Abdürrezzâk Efendi rode to his relief with several hundred cavalry and chanced on some Janissaries withdrawing on foot. An argument ensued. The Janissaries claimed that they were escorting the wounded to safety. When Abdürrezzâk ordered them to accompany him, demanding why they required so many men, they refused, protesting that he was mounted and would desert them if trouble arose. "God forbid that I should abandon you," he said. "If you like, I will go with you on foot." But at that, one of the Janissaries trained his gun on the chief scribe and fired, shouting, "What do you say to this?" The others followed suit. Abdürrezzâk managed, some-how, to spur his horse and flee the mutineers, but by the time he reached Uşanlı, the battle had turned. The Ottomans were falling back in full retreat. Vâsıf, meanwhile, had stayed behind in Kozluca and was writing to the Grand Vizier on Abdürrezzâk's behalf to apprise him of the situation. What he saw now must have gravely disconcerted him: soldiers "streaming like a torrent" through camp, paying no heed to the tents and moving in the direction of the imperial army. The telltale signs of a rout were soon confirmed when the Russians appeared on high ground over Kozluca, emplaced guns, and opened fire. Vâsıf and about one thousand others joined the exodus. Although their retreat was at first orderly – much of the artillery having been saved – the soldiers' panic increased and, within the hour, the infantry began to cut the reins of the draft horses, discarding the cannons to effect their escape. Thus, the army abandoned its camp and most of its ordnance.[63]

Yeğen Mehmed Paşa, Abdürrezzâk Efendi, and the remnants of the army straggled back to Şumnu to face the bleak prospect of a siege.

on his situation. For one, Vâsıf seems to have been concerned with his finances, and we know that he had been dismissed from his position as secretary to the left-wing cavalry on 6 L AH 1187 = December 21, 1773 (Afyoncu, 125). Second, his half-baked ignorance about İbrahim Hazine Efendi (unless we can accept it as a deliberate falsehood) strength-ens the theory that he was not part of the group captured in 1771.

[63] MEHÂSİN 5, 2: 297–299; "Vekâyi'nüvis Enverî," 463–467; Şemdânîzâde, 3: 7–9; and RESMÎ, 72–73 (trans.), 127–128 (text). The army left Şumnu on 5 R AH 1188 = June 15, 1774, and returned by 15 R = June 25 at the latest.

In days, the Russians advanced to Yenipazar, two hours away, and the statesmen made plans to strengthen the city's defenses as well as to fight outside of the entrenchments. Morale was on the verge of collapse. The campaign's utter failure produced no small anger toward its commanders, above all the Grand Vizier and Abdürrezzâk Efendi. It so happened, then, that when sentries caught two people trying to sneak past the city gate, one a woman in disguise, their rage turned to open mutiny. Knowing the chief scribe's fame, the fugitives tried to intimidate the growing crowd by claiming to be his servants – she his concubine. An armed mob more than one thousand strong then descended on Abdürrezzâk's tent. Only through sheer luck – including hiding in the Sacred Banner's pavilion – did he avoid a violent death, at which point the Grand Vizier's Albanian guard intervened and he was secreted away to Istanbul, relieved of office.[64] Though suppressed, this mutiny revealed serious grievances. The judge and chronicler Şemdânîzâde blamed it on soldiers' resentment of Abdürrezzâk's leadership, in violation of the long-held rule in Ottoman political thought against mixing professional spheres. Scribes had no business conducting war, he concluded.[65] That the Grand Vizier would allow it was therefore a damning indictment of his judgment and management of the war. Even Vâsıf wondered whether Abdürrezzâk Efendi had gone too far. Despite admiration for his patron, he thought that the chief scribe's severity with the rank and file was unwise. Indeed, it had been a near fatal error.[66]

It was in any event too late for regrets. The Russians tightened their grip on Şumnu and on June 30, repulsed the Grand Vizier's final sally, after which fleeing Ottoman forces plundered their own baggage-train. Many of the scribes headed south over the Balkan range. Those who remained were debating whether to join them or to venture toward Edirne when a sudden thunderstorm flooded the plains around the city, leaving them trapped. With retreat impossible, they had no choice but to man the stockades and await the final assault that began three days later. Survivors remembered an appalling siege. According to Vâsıf, who was evidently still in the city,[67] the Ottomans had obtained a letter from

---

[64] Vâsıf said (MEHÂSİN 5, 2: 299–301) that the man actually belonged to the household of a scribe named Nüzhet Efendi and that the woman was his wife. See also "Vekâyi'nüvis Enverî," 468–470; Şemdânîzâde, 3: 9–10; and Fâik, 109–110.

[65] Şemdânîzâde, 3: 6, 10.

[66] MEHÂSİN 5, 2: 299. Fâik repeats (109) that the chief scribe had made many enemies who were actively seeking his downfall.

[67] MEHÂSİN 5, 2: 303.

Marshal Rumiantsev several days before, but lacked interpreters to translate it. Now, on July 3, a Russian messenger revealed that the letter contained peace proposals. The Ottomans were desperate. They could neither escape nor hold out much longer and returned the messenger to Rumiantsev to request a truce. The Field Marshal refused, clearly in no mood to negotiate, and continued to press the siege. The surviving statesmen then determined at an emergency council to sue for peace, without a truce and at whatever cost, and agreed overwhelmingly to name delegates. When the new chief scribe İbrahim Münîb Efendi would not go alone, Ahmed Resmî Efendi was chosen to accompany him. The two received instructions to offer the Russians large concessions and made for Rumiantsev's headquarters at Küçük Kaynarca on July 12, the battle raging round Şumnu unabated. Nine days later – July 21, 1774 – they signed a twenty-eight article treaty. The war was at last over.[68]

[68] MEHÂSİN 5, 2: 301–307. Vâsıf relied heavily on Enverî's detailed account (471–489) of the same events, who was likewise an eyewitness. See also RESMÎ, 74–76 (trans.), 128–130 (text); and Aksan, *Ottoman Statesman*, 165–167.

3

Years of Faction and Reform (1774–1787)

Vâsıf's return to Istanbul in the late summer of 1774 was bittersweet. He had left Sivas six years earlier sure of his place in the world, a young man for whom Ottoman society had coherence, meaning, and historical destiny. That confidence was now shaken. The war had been a crucible for Ottoman élites, exposing the empire's frailty and raising ominous doubts for some about its exceptionalism. Vâsıf's own experience was this and more. He had seen the losses firsthand, but he had observed something too of the order, industry, and ingenuity of the Russian Empire and its agents. His violent confrontation with a civilization able to best his own was a shock he could no sooner undo than return to his old life in the Anatolian heartlands. What was more, Vâsıf no longer felt at ease in the capital. The Treaty of Kaynarca was not the peace for which he had hoped. He and his peers had paid a heavy price to save the imperial army – accepting harsh terms, a war indemnity, and Crimean independence – only to find that many in Abdülhamid I's circle deemed it too costly. Having helped to draft the terms, and having lost his patrons in the war's chaotic end, Abdürrezzâk Efendi to dismissal and exile and Muhsinzâde Paşa to illness shortly after the peace, Vâsıf was in an uncomfortable position.[1]

If the scribe had dreamt of a hero's welcome or even more modest honors on his arrival, he was quickly disabused of the notion. The army's homecoming was the beginning of a decade-long reckoning, a period of

---

[1] After the mutiny in Şumnu, Abdürrezzak was exiled to Bursa and then to Kütahya. Fâik, 110. Muhsinzâde Paşa had been gravely ill for some time and died on 26 Ca AH 1188 = August 4, 1774. HADÎKAT, supp. 3: 15.

bitter partisanship in which careers were made, unmade, and remade anew. The war had shaken the empire's statesmen. Peace now left them rudderless, unsure of how to proceed beyond the shifting of blame. In the administrative reshuffling that followed the army's return, Vâsıf failed to secure a chancery position. He also ran afoul of Muhsinzâde's wife Esma Sultan, Abdülhamid's younger sister, who claimed that the late Grand Vizier had promised her the income from Vâsıf's prebend in Anatolia. She accused him of stealing the grant, confiscated it, and transferred it to her own client. Because she was so close to the sultan, and perhaps because he now lacked influential patrons, he could find no one to intercede on his behalf and was left without a job or income.[2] Vâsıf's reception in the capital fed his growing disillusionment with Abdülhamid. Unlike Mustafa III, he saw few merits in the new ruler. A sultan ought to be magnanimous and reward those who are loyal; moreover, his generosity was a prerequisite for justice. To Vâsıf, Abdülhamid had failed to be magnanimous and therefore failed to be just. He later repined:

When the statesmen who had suffered for so many years in the imperial army returned to Istanbul, they hoped to remain in office and for kind reward. Instead they had to swallow the cup of dismissal, some of them on the road and some in Istanbul, and returned to their homes one after the other like so many nameless criminals, evoking the Arabic proverb, "I was happy to return even without booty." And both high and low thought this situation disagreeable and did nothing to help them.

Vâsıf contrasted his case with campaigners who, after the sixteenth-century conquest of Egypt, were richly rewarded by Selim I. Abdülhamid was no Selim, he implied, at least where justice and equity were concerned.[3]

---

[2] MEHÂSİN 5, 2: 232. Some biographical sources (Fâik, 147; Karslızâde, 64; and Schlechta-Wssehrd, 6) say that Vâsıf continued to serve in minor posts in the receiver's office after the war, but I have not found textual or archival support for this claim. There is also nothing to substantiate his complaints about Esma Sultan (d. 1788), who was a daughter of Sultan Ahmed III, tightfisted, and one of the sultan's closest confidants. See Fikret Sarıcaoğlu, *Kendi Kaleminden bir Padişahın Portresi: Sultan I. Abdülhamid (1774–1789)* (Istanbul, 2001), 157 ff. Still, Vâsıf obviously hoped for the prebend's restoration, as he monitored its passage through the hands of four different people in later years.

[3] MEHÂSİN 6, fols. 5a-6a. Vâsıf conveniently ignored the outcomes of the two wars. Selim I could afford to be generous, for the conquest of Egypt was a stunning Ottoman victory that solidified his pretensions as a world sovereign. Vâsıf's critique relies on the Ottoman moral tradition, derived ultimately from Aristotle's ethics, in which generosity was a lesser virtue related to the cardinal virtues of temperance and justice. See KINÂLIZÂDE, 104–106; and Marinos Sariyannis, "The Princely Virtues as Presented in Ottoman Political and Moral Literature," *Turcica* 43 (2011): 121–144.

FIG. 3.1: Abdülhamid I (reg. 1774–1789).

While it would be easy to dismiss these complaints as personal grievances – and they are certainly that – Vâsıf's words also reflect a changed atmosphere at court, notably in the factional realignments that followed Abdülhamid I to the throne. It had been Vâsıf's misfortune to ally himself with the wrong people at the wrong time. His patrons and their clients, like Abdürrezzâk Efendi, had been close to Mustafa III and were purged. Abdülhamid's retainers and hangers-on expected preferment and favor after his accession. He did not disappoint. An extreme representative of these men and their sense of entitlement was one of the sultan's creatures, the secretary to the chief black eunuch (*dârüssaade kâtibi*) Yazıcı Ahmed Efendi. Ahmed Efendi used his influence at the palace to amass great wealth. Late in the war, while the imperial army was still at Şumnu, he started an extortion racket that threatened statesmen and many of Vâsıf's superiors with reprisals unless they surrendered their valuables to him, ostensibly as "gifts" to the treasury. In nine months, this sort of blackmail had earned Ahmed Efendi over 1,000 purses of *akçe*. Vâsıf, then, knew how the system worked: obsequious bootlickers and backslappers could, with luck, remain in office. Those who spoke out only invited ruin.[4] Yet he and his peers were disadvantaged in another respect, namely their embarrassing connection to Kaynarca. It is no coincidence that most, if not all, of the men responsible for the unpopular treaty found themselves out of office or in exile in the new reign. Only the exceptional figure escaped with his career undamaged.[5]

In late 1774, Vâsıf's position therefore hung in the balance. The treaty had yet to be ratified, though factions in the Ottoman government and abroad were already expressing their opposition. That autumn, the Crimean Tatars sent a delegation to Istanbul asking the sultan to reinstate his name on coinage and in Friday noon prayers and to invest the Khan, Sahib Giray, according to old forms. As both of these acts broke Kaynarca's third article, which made the Crimea an independent state, the government risked angering the Russians or even reigniting the war in its reply. It consequently held a council to discuss the matter, a meeting that Vâsıf, it appears, joined with other statesmen and ulema. Although the council admitted that the requests violated the treaty, they decided

---

[4] MEHÂSİN 6, fols. 6a, 13a-14a. Yazıcı Ahmed targeted prominent men like Abdürrezzâk Efendi, Sırrı Selim Efendi, and the then-treasurer (*defterdâr*) Derviş Mehmed Efendi with letters demanding a list of all their possessions. Visitations and physical threats followed. Abdürrezzâk alone lost 10,000 *kuruş* and a family heirloom: a set of emerald, pearl-encrusted worry beads. Only some of these sums were restored when Yazıcı Ahmed fell from grace.

[5] According to Vâsıf, these casualties included Abdürrezzâk Efendi (exiled), Ahmed Resmî Efendi (dismissed), İzzet Mehmed Paşa (dismissed), Mustafa III's courtiers and intimates Mustafa Bey (exiled) and Süleyman Efendi (exiled and executed), Sırrı Selim Efendi (dismissed), and Râif İsmail Efendi (dismissed and exiled). See MEHÂSİN 1, fol. 112b; and MEHÂSİN 6, fols. 27b-28a, 35b-36a, 37b, 43a-43b, 60a. Sarıcaoğlu also describes (137–139) this factional realignment.

that there was no harm in approaching the Russians, at least insofar as they were obliged to do so by holy law. They would pursue the matter. They then proposed to send someone to Field Marshal Rumiantsev, who was camped at Jassy, to discuss the matter in its intricacies and to clarify phrasing in several other peace terms. Vâsıf's earlier duties served him in good stead. He was familiar from the Bucharest conference with the treaty's fine points and, just as importantly, he had already worked closely with Rumiantsev. Several statesmen recommended him, and the council approved.[6]

Vâsıf was aware that this appointment was of a highly sensitive nature. İzzet Mehmed Paşa, Muhsinzâde's replacement as Grand Vizier, gave him documents and oral instructions and he began making arrangements to travel overland to Moldavia. However, before his departure, the chief scribe Râif İsmail sent word that Yazıcı Ahmed Efendi would entrust him privately with some final orders. Vâsıf was appalled by what he heard from Ahmed Efendi. "In my meeting with the scribe," he wrote at a later period, "he tried to meddle in all of the peace terms and undermine every pillar of the treaty. He absurdly insisted that such and such article should be thus and that we must refuse Tatar independence in any form even if it meant a return to war." Ahmed Efendi also informed Vâsıf that he was to receive the large sum of 2,000 kuruş from the sultan over and above his travel expenses. Whatever the secretary's intent – whether he was acting on his own or for another, possibly the sultan, to scuttle the treaty – Vâsıf understood that the directions were as good as war. Astonished, he feigned agreement and went to report the affair to the chief scribe. Râif İsmail too was alarmed. Together, they took the "spurious orders" to the Grand Vizier, who concurred that they might easily provoke a disastrous Russian response. İzzet Paşa hence told Vâsıf to follow his original orders, but above all to act with prudence, and on October 23, 1774, he took to the road. Thirteen days later, on November 5, he had crossed the Danube and reached Jassy.

Rumiantsev greeted Vâsıf on that fall day in Jassy for the third time in as many years. After giving him a day to rest while documents were translated, he summoned the scribe to his quarters. "What are your state's oral instructions?" he asked. "What they propose in writing violates the treaty, does it not?" Vâsıf assured Rumiantsev that his government was

---

[6] MEHÂSİN 6, fols. 6a-6b. On these and contemporary developments in the Crimea, see Fisher, 58–63; Halim Giray, 188–189, 191–192; and RESMÎ, 77–80 (trans.), 131–133 (text). Gabriel Noradounghian provides the text of Kaynarca in French translation in *Recueil d'actes internationaux de l'Empire ottoman* (Paris, 1897/1902), 1: 319–333.

not trying to reopen the articles of peace. Rather, it wanted clarification. Kaynarca did not adequately define the sultan's role in the Crimea, he said, for if the sultan was to be the Tatars' religious head, as stipulated in the peace terms, his role in coinage, in the Friday noon prayer, and in the Khan's investment must be clear. This was no small matter; the Crimean ulema were already warning their people of dire consequences. Moreover, the Tatars feared for their security with the peninsula's fortresses in Russian hands. The Grand Vizier therefore kindly asked that the Russians consider surrendering some of them. Rumiantsev could tell, despite all of his protestations, that Vâsıf's orders were to renegotiate terms. He refused out of hand; neither Tatar independence nor the Crimean fortresses were open to discussion. The two men then moved to different articles – Article Eleven on free Black Sea navigation, Article Sixteen governing the Danubian Principalities, Article Twenty-five on prisoners of war, and Article Twenty-seven calling for an exchange of embassies to ratify the treaty. Over the next two days, Vâsıf extracted pledges from Rumiantsev on Ottoman sovereignty in the Principalities and, "appealing to his famous justice and foresight," on prisoners of war. But the Field Marshal was immovable on certain points. He particularly bristled at the Grand Vizier's attempts to dilute Tatar independence and Russian rights on the Black Sea. "It was in the hope of obtaining two things that we spent blood and treasure for so many years," he told Vâsıf, decisively. "One is Tatar independence, in order to spare ourselves the troubles they have caused us by their disorders. The second is to gain commercial benefits on the Black Sea like other states. I am not authorized to discuss these two matters further, and nothing would come of it even if I tried." With the meeting at an impasse, Vâsıf gave Rumiantsev money and clothes for the Ottoman captives in St. Petersburg, and set out the next day with the Field Marshal's reply.[7]

By most reasonable standards, the mission to Jassy was a success. There had been no cause to think that anyone could win a diplomatic coup or amend Kaynarca's main articles. Still, Vâsıf had managed without leverage to wrest several guarantees from the Russians; he thought he had done his best and therefore hoped to be repaid when he tendered his report in Istanbul in mid-November. That he was bitterly disappointed is only too evident from his later recollections. Vâsıf claimed that İzzet Mehmed Paşa

---

[7] MEHÂSİN 6, fols. 6b-11b. Vâsıf reached Jassy on 1 N AH 1188 (November 5, 1774) and stayed for three days, leaving on 4 N = November 8, 1774. The items he gave to Rumiantsev were for the Crimea *serasker* İbrahim Paşa, the Bender warden Abdülcelilzâde Mehmed Emin Paşa, and one other figure.

and others had congratulated him and promised him future reward. But he was not given a post that year. When the treaty was at last ratified in January 1775, meanwhile, he played no part in the formalities. The chief scribe, the Russian chargé d'affaires, the interpreters, and privy secretaries – all received recognition and ceremonial fur pelisses. Vâsıf felt cheated. "As the verse says," he wrote, "'One bears a fresh trial and one hopes for a fresh reward' ... Any intelligent man knows that while I, luckless, secured these amendments with the greatest of difficulty, they were credited to the chief scribe out of sycophancy and in order to win favors."[8] The blow to Vâsıf's amour-propre was severe. However, he faced a more acute problem in that his future prospects looked increasingly bleak; like many of his wartime colleagues, his career was falling into eclipse.

We know little about Vâsıf's whereabouts and activities over the next four or five years, as his name vanishes from records. As with others, the most well-known being Ahmed Resmî Efendi, the best explanation for his absence lies in the story of the empire's fractious politics. Kaynarca was deeply unpopular, its terms humiliating. Although discredited by the war, the empire's more reactionary voices found new strength in the issue of the Crimea and appealed to public opinion, the capital's religious authorities, and a large body of Tatar refugees to take back the peninsula. There was no place in post-war government for men like Vâsıf. He and his peers were too stained and divisive to hold office, and for him, the period was likely one of disgrace or enforced retirement. How he survived is unclear. It may be, as one biographer suggests, that he consoled himself in the capital with study; it may also be that he resumed menial work as a copyist to make ends meet. His own words refer to straitened circumstances and to vain attempts to find patrons.[9] Vâsıf was not without friends during these years, but those friends could not immediately ease his predicament. He had cordial, if remote, relations with Grand Vizier İzzet Mehmed Paşa as well as with Râif İsmail, his one-time patron, and likewise kept in touch with Abdürrezzâk Efendi, now far afield in Egypt studying with the traditionist and lexicographer Muḥammad Murtaḍâ al-Zabîdî. If these connections held out hope, however, they were of no use in the here and now. Vâsıf watched helplessly as the Grand Vizier and chief scribe were turned from office in 1775 and 1776. Moreover, the government's

---

[8] MEHÂSİN 6, fols. 11b-12b. See also Ahıshalı, 221 n. 338.

[9] Vâsıf declared (MEHÂSİN 5, 2: 232–233) that he struggled financially under Abdülhamid I, and complained in a later work (NEVÂBİG, fols. 2a-2b) about the lack of patronage and opportunity he encountered early in his reign. See also Schlechta-Wssehrd, 6.

increasingly brazen attempts to alter or repudiate the treaty struck him as inept and dangerous.[10]

Yet if the early years of Abdülhamid's reign tended to favor reactionaries, it was not on account of successful policy. Once in power, these forces quickly spent their credit. Having uselessly lobbied the ambassador Nikolai Repnin, who took their bribes but did nothing, the imperial council stood by in the fall of 1776 as Russian forces ousted their candidate for Khan and reoccupied the peninsula. In 1778 they sent two flotillas against the Crimean fort of Aktiar to aid Tatar rebels, one in March under Canikli Ali Paşa and a second in August under Canikli Ali and the Grand Admiral Gazi Hasan Paşa. Both failed. Some council members wept at the news; Vâsıf for his part was disturbed by the measures, for he worried that they threw good money after bad and only strengthened the enemy's position. Their failure in any event forced the government to negotiate and, after inconclusive results, to replace the chief scribe Ömer Vâhid Efendi with two men linked closely to Kaynarca – the former chief scribes İbrahim Münib Efendi and Abdürrezzâk Efendi, who had lately returned from Egypt. With help from the French ambassador the two resolved the crisis with a compromise: the 1779 Aynalıkavak Convention, which accepted the Russians' choice of Khan in return for their withdrawal from the peninsula and restoration of some territory.[11] Aynalıkavak marked a shift in the empire's political landscape as well as a turning point in Vâsıf's near-term fortunes. That the empire eschewed adventurism was a tacit admission that the Crimea could not be retaken, at least for

---

[10] Vâsıf largely admired (MEHÂSİN 6, fols. 27b-28a, 43a-43b) İzzet Paşa and Râif İsmail. Other contemporaries were not always as kind; some criticized Râif for having a drug addiction, probably to opium, which they said gave him delusions of grandeur. See RESMÎ, 78 (trans.), 132 (text). According to al-Jabarti, both Abdürrezzâk and İzzet Paşa went to Egypt in these years. With al-Zabîdî, Abdürrezzâk audited traditions (*hadith*) and privately read al-Harîrî's *Assemblies*; he also helped the scholar to petition İzzet Paşa, now governor, to restore a local dervish lodge: *'Ajâ'ib al-âthâr fî al-tarâjim wa'l-akhbâr* (Bulaq, 1879), 2: 200, 4: 188. See also Stefan Reichmuth, *The World of Murtaḍâ al-Zabîdî (1732–91): Life, Networks, and Writings* (Cambridge, 2009), 68 f. Peter Gran hints that Abdürrezzâk studied with several other noted scholars, including Aḥmad al-Dardîr (d. 1786): *The Islamic Roots of Capitalism: Egypt, 1760–1840* (Austin, TX, 1979), 39, 56, 62.

[11] On events leading to the Aynalıkavak Convention, see Aksan, *Ottoman Statesman*, 171–177; Fisher, esp. 58–111; and RESMÎ, 79–80 (trans.), 132–133 (text). Vâsıf thought (MEHÂSİN 6, fols. 41b-42a) that Repnin had duped "those ignorant in European affairs" and manipulated them into believing he could alter the treaty terms. He was likewise critical (ibid, fol. 94a) of the attacks on Aktiar, saying they were "of absolutely no benefit," cost the bankrupt empire money, and eased Russia's seizure of the Crimea. For the convention's text, see Noradounghian, 1: 338-334.

the time, and of the need for a more sober focus on affairs at home and conciliation abroad.[12] This development favored colleagues like Ahmed Resmî, who began to reemerge into public life. What was more, the convention rehabilitated Abdürrezzâk Efendi. Vâsıf saw his chance when the latter regained the post of chief scribe on April 28, 1779, to recognize his role in negotiations. He wrote Abdürrezzâk a chronogram for the occasion – "What cheer! The son of the *reis* became *reis*" – an adroitly crafted verse that used numerology to encode the appointment date.[13] The poem also served as a not-so-subtle hint. Vâsıf hoped to remind the chief scribe of his loyalty and consideration, which would ideally take the form of employment. Nor did he wait long for a reply. Before the summer was over, Abdürrezzâk had involved him in a new literary undertaking, one that would revive his career.

Abdürrezzâk Efendi's return to prominence was linked as much to contemporary factional politics as to his formidable diplomatic talents. In the late 1770s, a crop of new men had risen to power – the naval hero Gazi Hasan Paşa, the chancery scribe Halil Hamid Efendi, and the palace habitué Seyyid Mehmed Ağa – around whom rival groups coalesced. In forging relationships, one had to choose sides, which, as ever in court life, required a calculation of risk and benefit. The differences between these groups were less political than personal. Ottoman factions at the time pursued power, not coherent programs, and all three figures supported a similar foreign policy and some modicum of reform. Abdürrezzâk ultimately sided with Mehmed Ağa. As the palace sword-bearer (*silâhdar*), Mehmed Ağa was the sultan's confidant and had influence far beyond his official station or even the sitting Grand Vizier, for which reason Abdürrezzâk probably cultivated him. It was Mehmed Ağa who eased his appointment to Aynalıkavak and to the head of the chancery; it was likewise through his offices that the chief scribe advanced his own client, Vâsıf.[14] During their courtship, Abdürrezzâk dedicated

---

[12] On the relationship of factions and the empire's foreign affairs, see Christoph Neumann, "Decision Making without Decision Makers: Ottoman Foreign Policy Circa 1780," in *Decision Making and Change in the Ottoman Empire*, ed. Caesar Ferrah (Missouri, 1993), 29–38.

[13] MEHÂSİN 6, fols. 97b-98a. Ottoman poets used chronograms, a popular verse form in which each letter carries a numeric value, to celebrate important events. Here "son of the *reis*" refers to the fact that Abdürrezzâk's father, Tavukçubaşı Mustafa Efendi, had served as chief scribe a generation earlier.

[14] All three faction heads eventually served as Grand Vizier. On Mehmed Ağa, see HADÎKAT, supp. 3: 31–32; and DİA, s.v. "Karavezir Mehmed Paşa." İ.H. Uzunçarşılı has published studies of Gazi Hasan and Halil Hamid: "Cezayirli Gazi Hasan Paşa'ya

a short essay to Mehmed Ağa: an Arabic gloss on the twelfth-century Mu'tazilî scholar Jârullah al-Zamakhsharî's *Exceptional Aphorisms*, or *Nawâbigh al-kalim*, an anthology of proverbs with a long commentary tradition. Abdürrezzâk had begun the work years before, but set it aside during the war. Now he made a clean copy with the title *Rising Suns to Illuminate the Exceptional Obscurities (al-Shumûs al-bawâzigh fî idâ'at mushkilât al-nawâbigh)* and submitted it in the summer of 1779. One or two months later, on August 22, Mehmed Ağa fortuitously became Grand Vizier. Having enjoyed the commentary, and probably at Abdürrezzâk's urging, the now Mehmed Paşa decided to have the work translated into Turkish for wider circulation. This task he gave to Ahmed Vâsıf.[15]

Over the next months, Vâsıf worked feverishly on the commission. Most likely finished in October 1779, the result was not simply a translation, but an expanded Turkish gloss on Abdürrezzâk's commentary.[16] It was a showpiece, as well. Lettered Ottomans commonly used works of poetry and prose to gain appointments or cash reward. Vâsıf had not had regular employment in five years and wrote to overwhelm the reader with his ability, leading, ideally, to material support. He therefore put his classical learning on display in a rich, overwrought style. He anatomized

---

Dair," *Türkiyat Mecmuası* 7/8 (1942): 17–44; and "Sadrâzam Halil Hamid Paşa," *Türkiyat Mecmuası* 5 (1935): 213–268. Neumann lists ("Decision Making," 33) Abdürrezzâk Efendi under Gazi Hasan Paşa's faction. While I have found no evidence to this end, the sources make such relationships all but impossible to read, as in one episode (MEHÂSİN 6, fols. 99b-100a) where Abdürrezzâk was highly critical of the admiral, but also saved him from dismissal. In any event, both Fâik (110–112) and Vâsıf (MEHÂSİN 6, fol. 97b) explicitly credited Mehmed Ağa with Abdürrezzâk's rehabilitation.

15 NEVÂBİG, fols. 3a, 12b-14a. This work survives in copies from the 1760s under the title *al-Shumûs al-bawâzigh fî sharḥ al-nawâbigh*. Abdürrezzâk also copied a Persian work on literary figures, *Badâi' al-afkâr fî ṣanâi' al-ash'âr*, by the Timurid polymath Ḥusayn Vâ'iẓ Kâshifî. İsmet Parmaksızoğlu, ed., *Türkiye Yazmaları Toplu Kataloğu*, vol. 34/4 İstanbul *Süleymaniye Kütüphanesi: Mustafa Aşir Efendi Koleksiyonu* (Ankara, 1994), 525–526, 540–541. On al-Zamakhsharî, see Brockelmann, 1: 289–293.

16 NEVÂBİG survives in a single manuscript with a colophon date of R AH 1194 = April/May 1780. The text is badly abraded in places. As a commentary on a commentary, Vâsıf rubricated al-Zamakhsharî's original text and highlighted Abdürrezzâk's explanations in grey before adding his own gloss. Sarıkaya argues (ccxliv-ccxlv) that he must have completed the work sometime between May 1779 and May 1780. We can narrow this estimate further. For one, Vâsıf says that Seyyid Mehmed was Grand Vizier at the time of composition; he also lists himself without office. Based on these considerations and the fact that he angles for patronage, it seems most likely that Vâsıf finished the commentary between late August 1779 and his appointment as first fortifications officer or *büyük kale tezkirecisi* on October 15. At the very latest, it would have been finished before Abdürrezzâk's dismissal in Z AH 1193 = December 1779/January 1780.

for whom he would serve as a spokesman and plot his first thoughts on history, reform, and social order. Like others around him, Vâsıf needed to justify the government, and there is a tendentiousness and incoherence in his writing that is tempting to read as propaganda. To do so, though, at least entirely, affords an incomplete picture. Inconsistency may come from simple confusion. As an inquisitive, loyal Ottoman who had witnessed some of the war's worst moments, Vâsıf naturally wanted to understand the mechanisms of his empire's defeat and how and why it had fallen so low. If he was not always clear, we might think of his inconsistency not merely as a sign of political expedience but as a struggle to find order in the unfamiliar. Such, after all, is a hallmark of an intellectual mind.

In 1780, Vâsıf did not have the leisure or means to struggle, however, for he was toiling precariously in the treasury's lower levels. In December, he lost Abdürrezzâk Efendi, who fell out with Mehmed Paşa, forfeited his post, and died, the Grand Vizier following him shortly to the grave.[27] We sadly have no record of the scribe's emotions at his patron's death. Probably he was grief-stricken. Abdürrezzâk had done much to further his career and, being close to the same age, their bond was surely more filial than Vâsıf's earlier relationship with Gül Ahmedpaşazâde Ali. That they had become more closely tied as family is also a distinct possibility. There is circumstantial evidence that Vâsıf's wife, Ümmü Gülsûm Hanım, about whom we know next to nothing, was the chief scribe's sister, daughter, or other close relative. If Ali Paşa's death had been like losing a father, then, Abdürrezzâk's passing was like that of a brother and Vâsıf retained a close bond with his family for decades.[28] Vâsıf spent the next two years in limbo. Passed up for appointment in 1781, his posting the next fall was scarcely better than the last: director of the outer documentation office or

---

[27] Fâik alleges (111–112) that Mehmed Paşa wanted to dispose of the courtier Ahmed Nazif Efendi, whom he deemed a threat, and advised the sultan to make him governor of Aydın province. Abdürrezzâk warned Nazif, whose wife Ahiretlik Hanım, Abdülhamid's daughter, interceded on his behalf and had the order canceled. Mehmed Paşa then sent Abdürrezzâk in his place as retribution. However, why the chief scribe shielded Nazif Efendi is not clear. See also Neumann, "Decision Making," 38 n. 25.

[28] Sarıkaya unearthed (lxvi) Ümmü Gülsûm's name during his meticulous research. Her relation to this family does not seem resolvable. One possibility is that she was a sibling: in a 1787 letter, Abdürrezzâk's biological brother Ahmed Azmî refers to Vâsıf as his "brother," perhaps in the sense of brother-in-law. This would mean that Ümmü Gülsûm was their sister and that Vâsıf had at some point married into one of the empire's leading bureaucratic families. See John Rylands Library, Turkish MS nr. 51, letter 34, Ahmed Azmî to Franz von Dombay, an Austrian dragoman. The letter mentions Vâsıf's recent arrival in Spain and must therefore date to the summer or fall of 1787. It could also be that Ümmü Gülsûm was one of Abdürrezzâk's several unnamed daughters (Fâik, 110).

kâğıd-ı birûn emini. The documentation office supplied the treasury with writing materials – quite literally, paper-pushing – and dealt with petitions and the issuing and collecting of fees for patents of office. While its director held the rank of bureau chief, his prestige, like that of the fortifications officer, was low. For Vâsıf, the post was a welcome barrier against poverty, but whether it fulfilled his aspirations as a littérateur and scribe is quite a different matter.[29]

What finally secured Vâsıf's place in bureaucratic and intellectual circles was the rise of Halil Hamid Paşa, one of the eighteenth century's most charismatic ministers. Witty, cultured, and undeniably bold, Halil Paşa had risen through the chancery. Convinced that another war with Russia was inevitable, he began an ambitious reform program when named Grand Vizier in late 1782 and surrounded himself with like-minded allies, of whom Vâsıf was one. The prior link between the two, Grand Vizier and treasury scribe, is obscure. They almost certainly knew each other. The bureaucracy was a small world of some fifteen-hundred scribes and fifty bureau chiefs; not only did Halil Paşa and Vâsıf associate with the same people, Ahmed Resmî and Râif İsmail to name two, but they had both served in the receiver's office, possibly at the same time.[30] What is more certain is that the Grand Vizier recognized Vâsıf's verbal prowess and placed him where he might maximize this talent, as court historian or *vekâyi'nüvis.* As Vâsıf told it, his assignment to this job was largely happenstance. Halil Paşa discovered that the long-time historian Sadullah Enverî was overburdened with work. "When he saw that this great duty needed to be given to another," he said, boastfully, "he appointed me, Ahmed Vâsıf, unfit though I be, who have long sung my patrons' graces and excelled my peers in winning kind regards."[31] In all likelihood, Halil Paşa's aim was more specific: influencing opinion. By the 1780s, the office of court historian had existed for most of a century. Attached to the imperial council and under the chief scribe's oversight, it was a permanent position exempt from the bureaucracy's yearly cycle of appointments and drew its salary from other posts, real or honorary. The *vekâyi'nüvis'* main duty was to write the empire's history, which he

[29] Uzunçarşılı, *Osmanlı Devleti,* 381. Sarıkaya (xcv) has verified this appointment, which occurred on 3 I. AH 1196 = September 11, 1782, and lasted for one year.

[30] Findley (*Reform,* 56) estimates that the late eighteenth-century Ottoman civil bureaucracy numbered between 1,000 and 1,500 scribes in the treasury and chancery. See also EI², s.v. "Khwâdjegân-i Dîwân-i Humâyûn." On Halil Hamid Paşa's early life and career see Fâik, 119; HADÎKAT, supp. 3: 34; DİA, s.v. "Halil Hamîd Paşa"; and Uzunçarşılı, "Sadrâzam," 215–219.

[31] MEHÂSİN 1, fol. 4b.

generally did using a daybook and privileged access to chancery documents. Ceremonies, appointments and dismissals, council minutes, diplomatic and military affairs – the historian included them all in his work, which he arranged in chronicle form and submitted in yearly or biennial installments. There were also special commissions. The court historian, usually adept in poetry and prose, was expected to compose essays and occasional verse on demand, often for cash reward.[32] This does not necessarily mean that the Grand Vizier wanted Vâsıf to be a hack. Court historians could disagree or criticize within limits and might produce a sympathetic account without resorting to the cheaper forms of flattery; how each undertook the task thus says something about their character and pretensions. For Vâsıf, the appointment must have seemed like a godsend and the realization of his frustrated aspirations. Pleased with himself, he succeeded Enverî on November 2, 1783. He would monopolize the position for three and a half years.

The new historian gathered Enverî's notes, his orders being to resume where his predecessor had left off in mid-1782 and to update the chronicle accordingly.[33] He worked zealously, perhaps overly so, laboring over his style and extravagant in his praise of Halil Paşa. He was also highly didactic. Vâsıf and his peers subscribed to a view of history common to many pre-modern societies and with a long tradition in the Turco-Persianate world, namely that the past offers lessons to apply, by analogy, to present situations; that history is a moral field of knowledge.[34] He wrote in his preface:

[32] On this post and its duties, salary, and relationship with the imperial divan, see Robert Charles Bond, "The Office of the Ottoman Court Historian or Vak'anüvis (1714–1922): An Institutional and Prosopographic Study" (Ph.D. diss., Stanford University, 2004), esp. 35–51, 108–110; Mücteba İlgürel, "Vak'anüvislerin Taltiflerine Dâir," in Prof. Dr. Bekir Kütükoğlu'na Armağan (Istanbul, 1991), 183–192; Bekir Kütükoğlu, "Osmanlı Arşivleri ile Vak'anüvis Tarihleri Arasında Bağ," in Osmanlı Arşivleri ve Osmanlı Araştırmaları Sempozyumu (Istanbul, 1985), 123–125; and idem, "Vekâyi'nüvis," 103–111. Eighteenth-century court historians were institutionally distinct from earlier şehnâmecis. Most consider Mustafa Naîmâ to be the first vekâyi'nüvis in this newer sense, though Bond (e.g. 69) argues for Mehmed Râşid Efendi (d. 1735). Cf. Erhan Afyoncu, "Vekâyi'nüvis Tabirine Dair," Türklük Araştırmaları Dergisi 10 (2001): 7–19.

[33] Vâsıf alluded to these orders in MEHÂSİN 1, fols. 5a–5b, which is an author's copy, and in a later petition BOA.AE.Abd 532. He also added a marginal note (8b): "What follows are events of the auspicious year [1782], the secrets of the Sublime State and fateful events that Enverî Efendi failed to record. To make it easy for readers, I have written them without pretense to style and free from the trumperies of figure and metaphor." Kütükoğlu has shown ("Vekâyi'nüvis," 107) that it was normal practice for court historians to revise their predecessors' notes.

[34] Hagen and Menchinger, esp. 102–104.

Historiography is a science through which the affairs of peoples and their genealogies, crafts, events, and circumstances are known; its subject includes the conditions of past prophets, kings, philosophers, and others; its aim is knowledge of these events; and its benefit is admonition and good counsel ... Since, then, it upholds the good order of the realm and immaculately preserves past rulers' customs and practice, we see through proof of reason that historiography's judgments, by use of analogy, are a guiding principle, and that the comparison of predecessors' circumstances to our time yields great advantage.[35]

Vâsıf's definition of history as a useful field was by no means unique. In fact, he borrowed heavily in this passage from Kâtib Çelebi, who offered a nearly identical formulation in his Arabic bibliographical work the *Dispeller of Doubts* (*Kashf al-zunûn*) and who in turn lifted the definition from the sixteenth-century encyclopedist Taşköprüzâde (d. 1561). For Ottomans, history could teach readers much about life, moral, political, or otherwise. Kâtib Çelebi, again following Taşköprüzâde, even likened it to a "second life" with benefits akin to those of travel.[36]

The idea that history offers lessons draws on an epistemology – a theory of how we know things – which Vâsıf outlined in the same preface. As a philosophically-minded historian, he understood that historical knowledge is possible even though the past lies outside of our lived experience. People know things through senses like sight and sound, he recognized. But history can serve as an aid when sensory experience fails; namely, it can give proxy knowledge of the past which we might then apply to our own problems. This is precisely what Kâtib Çelebi and Taşköprüzâde meant when they called history a "second life." Yet Vâsıf delved deeper in this passage into the foundations of historical knowledge. "Scholars say that experience in affairs is without doubt to be reckoned one of mankind's virtues and that human judgment reaches maturity through experience," he continued. But how do we gain such experience? Vâsıf credited a so-called "experiential intellect":

Know that there are four levels of intellect. The first is the "material intellect," which is a sheer capacity to perceive noumena ... The second is the "habitual intellect" through which necessary knowledge is gained, and this is thought to be how we acquire discursive knowledge. The third, the "acquired intellect," is actualized in the discursive knowledge it perceives such that it becomes

---

[35] MEHÂSİN 1, fols. 3a-3b. This passage reappears in MEHÂSİN 6, fols. 3a-3b.

[36] Kâtib Çelebi, *Kashf al-zunûn 'an asâmî al-kutub wa'l-funûn* (Beirut, 2008), s.v. "'Ilm al-târîkh." Cf. Taşköprüzâde, *Mawsû'at muṣṭalaḥât miftâḥ al-sa'âda wa miṣbâḥ al-siyâda fî mawḍû'ât al-'ulûm* (Beirut, 1998), s.v. "'Ilm al-tawârîkh"; and Hagen and Menchinger, 93.

self-aware ... And the fourth is the "experiential intellect," which results from studying histories new and old and investigating the vicissitudes of fortune.

The experiential intellect is what, for Vâsıf, makes history beneficial. This sort of knowledge "leads latter-day men to distinguish between good and bad behavior ... versing them in affairs and making them sage counselors in public matters."[37]

Vâsıf's discussion of "intellect" involved him in an old discourse over knowledge and morality. In Islamic thought, the intellect, or *'aql*, refers to unaided reason and that part of the human soul which "knows" or "thinks." Following Aristotle and his commentators, philosophers held that the soul traversed different levels of intellect ranging from full potentiality to full actualization. Although they differed in naming these levels, they generally held that the soul's progress reflected interactions with an Active or Agent intellect, the least of the intelligences which in Aristotelian and Neoplatonic cosmology parallel the celestial spheres and emanate from the First Intellect or First Cause. The Active Intellect, they thought, was what impressed knowledge on the human mind.[38] Vâsıf applied this discourse to his own chronicle with an added level of experiential knowledge, an "intellect" not recognized in the classical tradition but current in some works of Persianate historical writing. The experiential intellect for him sat atop ever more complex forms of knowledge. The potential and habitual intellects furnish the mind with basic knowledge, the "primary intelligibles" that form all higher thought and allow us to make reasoned judgments and decisions. But while the acquired and experiential intellects are both discursive and work through logic and argument, the latter acts as a shortcut bypassing direct observation. By putting the experiential intellect at the top of his hierarchy, Vâsıf implied that knowledge gained through experience, and hence through history, crowns all knowledge. Second, and more importantly, he indicated that history-

---

[37] MEHÂSİN 1, fols. 2b-3a. Also in MEHÂSİN 6, fols. 2b-3a; and Hagen and Menchinger, 103. In a later work (GAZAVÂT, fols. 1b-2a), Vâsıf remarked that "wise men ... naturally incline to histories and, through much study, perfect their calling by acquiring the experiential intellect."

[38] Herbert Davidson introduces these theories in *Alfarabi, Avicenna, and Averroes on Intellect: Their Cosmologies, Theories of the Active Intellect, and Theories of Human Intellection* (Oxford, 1992). The usual stages are potential intellect (*'aql hayûlânî* or *intellectus potentialis/materialis*), habitual intellect (*'aql bi'l-malaka* or *intellectus in habitu*), actual intellect (*'aql bi'l-fi'l* or *intellectus in actu*), and acquired intellect (*'aql mustafâd* or *intellectus acquisitus*). See also EI², s.v. "'Akl"; and DİA, s.v. "Akıl." On the Aristotelian/Islamic cosmos, the heavenly spheres governed by celestial intelligences, and the sublunary world of generation and corruption, see Nasr, 132–133, 139–141, 236–251.

writing is instructive at its deepest level. For him, history consisted entirely and literally of exempla.[39]

It is important at this point to place Vâsıf's epistemology within a still larger complex of ideas, namely that of philosophy (*hikmet*), moral education (*edeb*), and the perfection of the soul. For the intellect is not morally neutral; there is a direct connection between it and right conduct. Islamic thinkers considered the intellect not just as a source of knowledge, but as a natural way of knowing what is right or wrong without the authority of revelation, a sort of "lumen naturale." What distinguishes man from animals, what gives his actions meaning, what makes him a responsible agent, is intellect.[40] The term *hikmet* is at the heart of this relationship. Usually translated as "philosophy" or "science," *hikmet* was in fact a more expansive concept. Ottomans like Kâtib Çelebi and the moralist Kınâlızâde Ali defined it as a field of knowledge examining all things in their essence, both in mind and substance, the end of which was the soul's perfection and felicity in the here and hereafter.[41] For philosophers, the way to this Good was twofold. One aspired to perfection in philosophy's "speculative" and "practical" spheres – in knowledge and action. Yet they also held that knowledge was a prerequisite for action. A soul could become perfect in deed only after progressing to the highest level of intellect and becoming perfect in thought. Only when a soul properly understood objects could it perceive God's attributes and sound belief; and only when it acquired a proper belief in God through speculative philosophy, and rid itself of error, could it come to distinguish good behavior from bad. What linked Vâsıf to this tradition was his emphasis on moral education. Moral formation was the bedrock of Ottoman and Persianate ethics, works of "practical philosophy" or *hikmet-i 'ameliyye* that fused personal morality, household economy, and politics. Vâsıf

---

[39] Hagen and Menchinger, 104. The "experiential intellect" does not appear in early schemas. Ibn Sînâ and al-Ghazâlî, for instance, deemed experience a form of cognition rather than an intellect in its own right (e.g. *Mi'yâr al-'ilm* [Egypt, 1961], 186–193). The concept can however be found in the Timurid historian Mîr Khvând's *Rauzat-us-safa, or Garden of Purity*, trans. E. Rehatsek (London, 1891), 1: 24–32. Textual parallels suggest that Vâsıf may have used Mîr Khvând as a source for this passage. Ibn Khaldûn also referred to it but in a distinctly subordinate role. See *Muqaddima Ibn Khaldûn, prolégomènes d'Ebn-Khaldoun, texte arabe*, ed. M. Quatremère (Paris, 1858), 2: 412–413, 417–419. My thanks to Deborah Black and Philip Bockholt for this information.

[40] G. E. von Grunebaum, "The Concept and Function of Reason in Islamic Ethics," *Oriens* 15 (1962): 4–5. See also Franz Rosenthal's classic study, *Knowledge Triumphant: The Concept of Knowledge in Medieval Islam* (Leiden, 1970).

[41] Kâtib Çelebi, *Kashf al-zunûn*, s.v. "'Ilm al-hikma"; and KINÂLIZÂDE, 41–42.

quite naturally assumed that the experiential intellect and history served practical philosophy, and so individual and political morality, and that his readers could use history to correct themselves or others. His words on education and knowledge demonstrate as much.[42] Like Naîmâ and Kınâlızâde's student Mustafa Âli, Vâsıf likewise used practical philosophy in his chronicle to draw explicit morals ranging from discourses on individual virtues and vices to counsel on justice and proper administration, making the work in some senses a handmaiden to ethics. To call Vâsıf's approach philosophical, then, is quite accurate. Historical knowledge for him was inextricably joined to moral education and practical philosophy and hence to philosophy's ultimate aims: fostering proper belief in God, knowledge of right and wrong, the perfection of the soul, and individual and communal salvation.[43]

Political reform also figures as a central concept in this earliest section of the chronicle, which Vâsıf began with an encomium to the Grand Vizier. Ottoman statesmen resented the treaty of Kaynarca and cherished hopes of retaking the Crimea, he wrote. However, while the late war revealed the empire's weakness and called for urgent attention, nothing, if we can believe him, was done. The viziers who served between 1774 and 1782 failed to make headway through stupidity and neglect, Abdülhamid I's wishes notwithstanding, so that the sultan appointed Halil Hamid Paşa "for the sake of the realm's order." We are informed that in his brief term the Grand Vizier had already recovered lapsed military prebends. He raised salaries through rational economies, brought market prices under control, stamped out venality, and reimposed sartorial laws the neglect of which had caused a great many "abominations." He also introduced a two thousand-man light artillery corps and new cannons "to match those of the enemy." Lastly, Halil Paşa restored the empire's martial vigor, issuing orders to drill and prepare for a possible war with Russia. Vâsıf's preface is unalloyed eulogy. Yet it also voiced an optimist's faith in the empire. "It is clear to those who study history," he declared,

---

[42] E.g. MEHÂSİN 3, fol. 215b; and MEHÂSİN 6, fols. 22a-22b. The Persian philosopher Naṣîr al-dîn Ṭûsî (d. 1274) was the touchstone of Ottoman ethics. His *Nasirean Ethics* defined practical philosophy as the study of voluntary action in a tripartite division adopted by Ottoman moralists: personal ethics (*ahlâk*), oikonomia (*tedbîr-i menzil*), and politics (*siyâset-i müdün*). See DİA, s.v. "Ahlâk"; Majid Fakhry, *Ethical Theories in Islam* (Leiden, 1991), 131–142; KINÂLIZÂDE, 44–46; Kâtib Çelebi, *Kashf al-ẓunûn*, s.v. "Akhlâq" and "'Ilm al-ḥikma"; and Taşköprüzâde, s.v. "'Ilm al-akhlâq."

[43] E.g. MEHÂSİN 2, fols. 2a-4a, 27b-29b, 78a-79b; MEHÂSİN 3, fols. 188a-189b; and MEHÂSİN 6, fols. 29a-29b. See also Fleischer, *Bureaucrat*, 42–43, 302; and Naîmâ, 1: 25, 4: 1891.

that while our sovereigns are subject to some of the civil turmoil that often affects Islamic dynasties, they have always managed to right the situation directly and have become even more powerful and mighty than before.[44]

The Grand Vizier would of course champion this renewal. Indeed, for Vâsıf, he was no less than the empire's savior: a centennial reformer, or "*sâhib-i mia*," referenced in a famous hadith, "the Lord God will send to this community at the turn of each century someone who will restore its religion."[45]

What exactly did reform mean to Vâsıf? What did it mean to contemporary Ottomans? As the historian and his peers expressed it, reform was a largely conservative notion tied to ideals of socio-political stability. The key phrase was *nizâm-ı 'âlem*, a formula that translates as "world order" and articulates the whole of the Ottoman moral universe. "World order" had its origins in a primeval, Hobbesian state of nature derived from Aristotle and later Arab philosophers. The idea, as they held, was that humans are social beings. Yet they are also susceptible to carnal desire. If left alone humans will disrupt society with violence, and only government (*siyâset*) and a ruler's administration of justice (*'adâlet*) can restrain the passions, keep people in their station, and make society function. The ideal "world order" was likewise rigidly compartmentalized. Social groups – usually soldiers, scribes, artisans, and farmers, the so-called "four pillars" – filled roles in a society that was seen as naturally hierarchical and unchanging. Movement could not be allowed, lest it disturb the order and the whole system fall into chaos, hence Ottomans expressed aversion to social mobility as well as to any change in the structure's legal and institutional underpinnings, or what they called "ancient practice (*kânûn-ı kadîm*)." We might then think of the ideal Ottoman order as a building. The structure itself is the "order of the world." Yet there are essential elements inside that form and prop up the structure. Hierarchical social groups, the "four pillars," provide support, encircling and sheltering which are the walls and framework of "ancient practice." Upholding the entire edifice is the keystone, justice, whose administration is dispensed by a virtuous ruler. This keystone sits above the structure, but is crucial to its integrity. It holds the pillars in place, in proper equilibrium, and prevents them from toppling into each other or perforating the walls. Without justice, indeed without any of these elements, the whole structure collapses. The upshot of *nizâm-ı*

---

[44] MEHÂSİN 1, fols. 5a–10a.

[45] MEHÂSİN 1, fol. 8b. Vâsıf cited this tradition from Jalâl al-dîn al-Suyûṭî's *al-Jâmi' al-ṣaghîr*, on which see Brockelmann, 2: 147.

'âlem is that it makes radical reform impossible. The order itself is not alterable. One can restore the status quo, but no more.[46]

"World order" pervaded early modern Ottoman thought and conditioned the way that statesmen and intellectuals thought about reform. Vâsıf and his peers did not strictly separate the political from the moral; political problems for them were signals of deeper ills and disorders in the empire's fabric. The bureaucrat Dürrî Mehmed Efendi (d. 1794), for example, offered a cautious assessment in his 1774 tract the *Choice Desire to Correct Disorder (Nuhbetü'l-Emel fî Tenkîhi'l-Fesâd ve'l-Halel).* Dürrî's main concern was disorder, notably among the military, subjects, treasury, and servitors that formed the realm's foundations, hence his solutions focused on the restoration of justice. The *Choice Desire* also shows a high level of what Cornell Fleischer once called "kanun-consciousness."[47] For Dürrî, the past was the proper template. "The way is to follow ancient practice," he said in one passage, "and for the military to serve sincerely and respect career paths and experts according to the model (*kânûn*) of the late Sultan Süleyman."[48] Canikli Ali Paşa's 1776 *Rare New Stratagem (Tedbîr-i Cedîd-i Nâdir)* took an even more guarded approach to *kânûn-ı kadîm*. "Today cannot be compared with yesteryear," he fretted. "Before there were honorable commanders, effective officers, and other leaders. Now there is a dearth of able men."[49] Ali felt that neither bravery nor adherence to ancient practice prevailed. He idealized the past, notably the reigns of Süleyman I and Mehmed II, and

---

[46] Surveys of this vast subject include Patricia Crone's *Medieval Islamic Political Thought* (Edinburgh, 2004); and Şerif Mardin's *Young Ottoman Thought*, esp. 81–106. Scholars have also written extensively on its major conceptual components. "World order" is ably interpreted by Gottfried Hagen in "Legitimacy and World Order," in *Legitimizing the Order: The Ottoman Rhetoric of State Power* (Leiden, 2005), 55–83; but also by Tahsin Görgün, "Osmanlı'da Nizâm-ı Âlem Fikri ve Kaynakları Üzerine Bazı Notlar," *İslâmî Araştırmalar Dergisi* 13 (2000): 180–188. On the concept of justice, see Boğaç Ergene's "On Ottoman Justice: Interpretations in Conflict (1600–1800)," *Islamic Law and Society* 8 (2001): 52–87; and Linda Darling, *A History of Social Justice and Political Power in the Middle East: The Circle of Justice from Mesopotamia to Globalization* (New York, 2013). For ancient practice, Mehmet Öz, "Kânûn-ı Kadîm: Osmanlı Gelenekçi Söyleminin Dayanağı mı, Islahat Girişimlerinin Meşrulaştırma Aracı Mı?" in *Nizâm-ı Kadîm'den Nizâm-ı Cedîd'e: III. Selim ve Dönemi*, ed. Seyfi Kenan (Istanbul, 2010), 59–77.

[47] E.g. Fleischer, *Bureaucrat*, 8, 102, 158.

[48] Dürrî, TSMK Hazine nr. 1438, fol. 287b. He further raised "ancient practice" on fols. 292b-293a, 294a. Atik describes this treatise with the author's biography in "Kayserili Devlet Adamı Dürrî Mehmed Efendi ve Layihası," in *II. Kayseri ve Yöresi Tarih Sempozyumu* (Kayseri, 1998), 69–74.

[49] Canikli Ali, ÖN H.O. nr. 104b, fol. 16b. Cf. Yücel Özkaya, "Canikli Ali Paşa'nın Risalesi 'Tedâbîrü'l-Gazavât,'" *AÜDTCF Araştırmaları Dergisi* 7/13–14 (1969): 144–145.

argued that the empire was more successful when its rulers took an active role in war, virtue, and learning. Ali wanted to restore proper order or *nizâm* and singled out the neglect of *kânûn* as the main cause of Ottoman defeats. He was especially disturbed by what he saw as an inexcusable blurring of social lines and the presence of "outsiders" in the military – long a focus of anxiety in Ottoman political thought.[50]

Vâsif's prescriptions were much the same. He too assumed the existence of a universal order and the need to reinforce social boundaries and ancient practice. We see this in his support of sartorial laws, intended to distinguish the realm's estates, and his belief that a breakdown in these laws led to "abominations." Vâsif held that "outsiders" had corrupted the sapper corps and provincial cavalry, as well. The empire needed these men in its sacred duty of jihad, he wrote in one chronicle entry, and supported them with crown-lands. Yet outsiders, subjects of non-military background, had usurped many of these prebends and were unable to serve, and he insisted that the grants be restored according to ancient practice.[51] The moral dimension of these views emerges especially where Vâsif placed piety, reform, and worldly success side by side. He for example endorsed public recitation of religious texts, or what he called "spiritual provisions," as a way of securing God's approval for material reforms.[52] But it is his use of the phrase *sâhib-i mia* that is most arresting. The centennial reformer or the "one who restores (*müceddid*)" calls up a very specific idea of reform as moral or ethical renewal. The *müceddid* was supposed to halt religious decay. His variety of reform, eliminating sinful innovations and restoring the practice of the early Muslim community, appealed to contemporary Ottoman anxieties over world order. That Vâsif gave this title to Halil Paşa expressed a hope, at least rhetorically, that the Grand Vizier would return the empire to proper practices and purer religion.[53]

---

[50] Canikli Ali, ÖN H.O. nr. 104b, fol. 60b. Cf. Özkaya, 167. See also Fleischer, *Bureaucrat*, 154 ff.

[51] İLGÜREL, 177, sub anno hegirae 1198 = 1783/4. Cf. MEHÂSİN 6, fols. 67b-68b.

[52] MEHÂSİN 1, fols. 42b-44a, sub anno hegirae 1198 = 1783/4.

[53] Many Ottomans appear to have shared Vâsif's hopes for a restorer or even messiah (*mahdi*). Halil Paşa proved a logical fit insofar as his term coincided with the turn of the thirteenth hijri century (AH 1197–1199), but later thinkers and poets also proclaimed Selim III and Mahmud II as restorers and saviors. See Cem Dilçin, "Şeyh Galip'in Şiirlerinde III. Selim ve Nizam-ı Cedit," *Türkoloji Dergisi* 11 (1993): 218; and Seyfettin Erşahin, "Westernization, Mahmud II, and the Islamic Virtue Tradition," *The American Journal of Islamic Social Sciences* 23 (2006): 46–47. On the wider tradition of "restorers," see Ella Landau-Tasseron's "The Cyclical Reform: A Study of the Mujaddid Tradition," *Studia Islamica* 70 (1989): 79–117.

The path to reform was nonetheless controversial. Some argued that a simple return to the old ways was enough. Others, like Dürrî Mehmed, cited Ibn Khaldûn and insisted that allowances must be made for the changing times. A central concept in this debate was *mukâbele bi'l-misl*, a "meeting like-for-like" or "reciprocation" that became increasingly important in eighteenth- and nineteenth-century intellectual life. Reciprocation meant to use an enemy's tactics and technology against him.[54] Canikli Ali put the problem quite lucidly by pointing out that warfare had changed since Süleyman I's day. The empire's enemies now fought with cannons and muskets rather than swords and lances and, this being the case, tactics and technology were a major reason for Ottoman defeats. He wrote:

The enemy does not fight as he once did but slowly adopts tactics, fighting not with lance or sword but cannon and mortar. This has occurred many times in warfare up to now, and many times have we matched the enemy. So I maintain that in this era we must use wiles against the enemy's wiles, cannon against his cannon, and mortar against his mortar.[55]

Reciprocation raised several thorny issues: how can human reason be applied to political problems? To what extent is innovation justified? Where does one draw the line between legitimate change and illicit innovation? While many Ottomans claimed leeway for this sort of reform, others were not as certain. Vâsıf largely agreed with Canikli Ali on reciprocation, for instance. Halil Paşa's artillery corps "met the enemy like-for-like," he said, "and it is a secondary cause of victory for every state to acquire weapons to match those of its enemy." Yet he felt that Ali's treatise did not go far enough and arrogated too much importance to the military, its proposals old fashioned.[56] Others, quite to the contrary, rejected innovations altogether and argued that the only legitimate reform was to return to the uncorrupted days of old. There was little consensus.[57]

---

[54] Uriel Heyd first brought attention to this concept in his article "The Ottoman 'Ulemâ and Westernization in the Time of Selim III and Maḥmûd II," in *Studies in Islamic History* (Jerusalem, 1961), esp. 74–77. Kahraman Şakul notes its role in eighteenth-century reform in "Nizâm-ı Cedid Düşüncesinde Batılılaşma ve İslami Modernleşme," *İlmî Araştırmalar* 19 (2005): esp. 118–121.

[55] Canikli Ali, ÖN H.O. nr. 104b, fols. 65b-66a; and Özkaya, 170.

[56] MEHÂSİN 1, fol. 7b. Vâsıf later derided (ibid, fol. 214a) Ali's treatise as overly antagonistic, "simplistic," and "out of step with the times."

[57] Reciprocation was part of a wider legal discussion of tradition (*sunna*), innovation (*bid'at*), and what constituted acceptable change in the Muslim community. Vâsıf and many others believed, as Heyd says ("Ottoman 'Ulemâ," 74–75), that "to learn from the infidel enemy would not constitute a religiously illicit innovation (*bid'at*) but would be an application of the legitimate maxim of *mukâbele bi'l-misl* or reciprocation, that is fighting the enemy with his own weapons." Fazlızâde Ali (fl. 1740), on the other hand, gave

Still, the prevailing discourse was unquestionably one of restoration. Ottomans looked to nebulous Golden Ages for models, either in the early Muslim community or in the empire's glorious past, and even the sultan and bureaucracy longed for a "long-lost Köprülü vizier" – a traditionalist reformer who would reestablish order, perpetuate *kânûn*, and put the empire to rights.[58]

3.3 THE "LESSER OF TWO EVILS," 1783–1784

The urgency of reform was soon underscored by an unfolding crisis on the northern frontier. On April 8, 1783, Russia formally annexed the Crimea, capping a nine-year struggle following Küçük Kaynarca. The next move was crucial. Most Ottomans had never fully accepted Crimean indepen-dence, hoping that the loss was temporary, but shied from committing the empire to open hostilities. Now they faced a choice: accept the annexation as a fait accompli or declare war. As recriminations dragged into the fall of that year, the mood in Istanbul was somber.[59]

In truth, Ottoman statesmen had feared this scenario for some time. Retaking the Crimea had been a key aim of each successive government after 1774, and they had spent the better part of a decade bickering over the prospect of another war. As they framed it, the question was insepar-able from wider issues of reform and the dynasty's exceptionalism. It was not a matter of abandoning the peninsula or the realm's martial ideals, or even of the merits of war and peace as such, but of how best to repair the empire's strength. Dürrî Mehmed took a typical stance. Both as a reform tract and justification of Kaynarca, his *Choice Desire* likened the empire to a body. Like men, states grow, mature, and decline, he said. If the youthful empire fought tirelessly against its enemies, it was only natural for it to need rest in adulthood. The dynasty could no longer wage continuous war nor face Russian military might. Yet Dürrî felt that this

a nearly unlimited scope to illicit innovation and argued that the only legitimate reform was to return to the uncorrupted practices of the early community. See Marlene Kurz, *Ways to Heaven, Gates to Hell: Fazlızâde 'Alî's Struggle with the Diversity of Ottoman Islam* (Berlin, 2011), esp. 98–100.

[58] MEHÂSİN 6, fol. 49b. The Köprülüs were a line of seventeenth-century strongmen who sought to restore institutions in accordance with *kânûn*. For Abdülhamid's views on tradition as well as his desire for a Köprülü-like reformer, see Sarıcaoğlu, 62–64, 155. On the "Golden Ageist" zeitgeist in general, see Kafadar's "Myth of the Golden Age," 37–48.

[59] On the Crimean crisis, see M.S. Anderson, "The Great Powers and the Russian Annexation of the Crimea, 1783–4," *The Slavonic and East European Review* 37 (1958): 17–41; and Fisher, 128–152.

condition was reversible. Statesmen had a duty to restore the empire to "the most preferable state of constant victory" and to purge defects in the body politic as so much bad blood, he argued. Intermittent peace ensured the realm's health, and so he prescribed five to ten years of appeasement and gradualist reform. Only then, after thorough rebuilding, might the government renounce Kaynarca, defeat the Russians, and retake the Crimea. We should note that Dürrî closely imitated Naîmâ in his position: peace was a temporary and necessary reprieve that had historical precedent and ultimately served the dynasty's welfare. For him peace was a necessary evil; "constant victory" remained the ideal.[60]

Ahmed Resmî was a more radical voice in the discussion. Resmî had signed Kaynarca at the cost of rank and reputation and his defense of the treaty in *A Summary of Admonitions* (*Hulâsatü'l-İ'tibâr*), composed around 1780, was highly personal. Resmî dissected the late war in this work, urging his peers to avoid the same mistakes. While his "admonitions" were often practical, his overriding concern was to critique the mindset of those who, in his view, had foolishly incited and prolonged the war. Resmî denied that warfare must be the basis of "world order." He instead stressed the need to pursue peace at all times, as a tenet of government policy justified by reason and sanctified by holy law. In his *Admonitions* and elsewhere, he called for peace, defined borders, and negotiation and diplomacy, and thereby repudiated two pillars of Ottoman ideology: militant exceptionalism and an ever-expanding state. Yet perhaps because he was radical, Resmî's arguments gained little momentum. As Dürrî's more restrained defense indicates, the 1768–1774 war convinced many of the empire's weakness, but failed to alter the basic terms of debate. Resmî himself was constrained by them, in fact. Although he presented peace as a universal good, he also carefully qualified it as "feigned friendship (*müdârâ*)" and implied that peaceable relations with non-Muslims could not be fully genuine. Not even Halil Hamid Paşa's circle was willing or able to endorse his style of pacifism.[61]

Ahmed Vâsıf began his chronicle in the midst of the Crimean crisis. He had suspected Russia's aims since his negotiation service years before and

---

[60] Dürrî, TSMK Hazine nr. 1438, fols. 283a-286a, 294b-296a. The similarities with Naîmâ cannot be coincidental. Dürrî's phrasing, use of the biological metaphor, and choice of historical examples (Saladin and Jerusalem) almost certainly mean that he took the historian as a model.

[61] Virginia Aksan has studied Resmî's views and originality at length in *Ottoman Statesman*, esp. 184 ff., and in "Ottoman Political Writing, 1768–1808," in *Contacts*, 32–36. See also RESMÎ, 15–18.

followed developments closely, with growing alarm. He also recorded them. Indeed, the historian spilled much ink to oppose an armed response. To depict Vâsıf or his allies as "peacemakers" would not be strictly correct, though. At least publicly, all Ottomans deemed Kaynarca a truce, a temporary break from hostilities, and differed on war and peace not in a Resmian sense, but only in the empire's readiness to wage war.[62] The statesmen's first reaction was to temporize. In the summer of 1783, the Grand Vizier held a council at the home of *şeyhülislâm* Dürrîzâde Mehmed Ataullah Efendi over lodging a formal protest, which, as Vâsıf had it, split the government. Halil Paşa warned against a protest on the grounds that his reforms were unfinished and that the Russians would read it as a declaration of war; he wished to buy time to the spring. However, he met firm opposition from the *şeyhülislâm* and from Grand Admiral Gazi Hasan Paşa, who led a rival faction. The dynasty's honor was at stake, they said. How could they stay silent when the Russians had so brazenly seized the Crimea? When the council voted to issue a protest, Halil Paşa countermanded the decision and delayed.[63]

How the opposing factions saw these events and why they disagreed emerges distinctly from Vâsıf's commentary. Many clearly thought it best in the situation to act assertively and to trust in God in case of war. In council over a subsequent ultimatum from Russia's ally, Austria, the Istanbul judge Müftîzâde Ahmed Efendi stood and implored his colleagues to reject their demands, as they were a pretext and against holy law. A "decisive response" was best. "And if by their own volition they break the treaty, then, following the verse, 'How oft by God's will hath a small force vanquished a big one,' the winds of victory shall blow to our armies and the dynasty's ill-wishers shall be confounded," he declared. All in attendance agreed. Müftîzâde repeated these sentiments in council on November 29, 1783. While he was willing to accept mediation with the Russians, he conceded, if war broke out, God would punish whoever had violated the treaty. Halil Paşa could continue his reforms thereafter.[64] Vâsıf, on the other hand, urged caution and means other than war, or in

---

[62] MEHÂSİN 1, fols. 8b–9a.

[63] MEHÂSİN 1, fols. 28a–30a. Aksan estimates (*Ottoman Statesman*, 180–181) that this meeting occurred in mid-1783 and summarizes from Vâsıf. See also Uzunçarşılı, "Sadrâzam," 228. A.I. Bağış gives the date as 29 Ş AH 1198 = July 30, 1783, in *Britain and the Struggle for the Integrity of the Ottoman Empire: Sir Robert Ainslie's Embassy to Istanbul, 1776–1794* (Istanbul, 1984), 12.

[64] MEHÂSİN 1, fols. 32b–36a, 53b. The Austrians demanded an indemnity for alleged losses to Ottoman piracy, paying which would have violated the law. See Panaite, 290–291. Müftîzâde quoted from the Quran 2:249.

his words, the "lesser of two evils (*ehven-i şerreyn*)." Austria was trying to provoke the empire, he observed, and while everyone favored action, the risk of war was too great. The empire needed time. He wrote:

Even if we suppose that the empire in capitulating chooses the lesser of two evils and unites under solemn oaths, we would still need at least several years, by God's grace, to stamp out our differences, properly order the army and ordnance, and meet all of our enemies by land and sea. If as before we are rash rather than prudent, then God forbid ... I need not say the infidel will increasingly covet Muslim lands. But if we are resolved and give total freedom to those who govern and implement reforms like the past year's efforts; if, dismissing jealous and malicious slander, we are firm, steadfast, and ignore sophistry even in the face of setbacks, it is not improbable that the Lord, God willing, will grant us the Crimea and many territories besides ...

Vâsıf then recited an Arabic verse: "Victory but by our own making is rare."[65]

The phrase "lesser of two evils" deserves some explanation. "Choosing the lesser of two evils," referenced earlier by Naîmâ, is a legal maxim and form of juristic preference based on necessity or duress (*zarûret*). Hanafi law at times permits jurists to make rulings more suitable, convenient, or conformable to a given case. Otherwise illegal acts can be lawful under duress, as expressed in another maxim, "Necessity permits what is prohibited." There are nevertheless limits to this rule, in that duress is a strictly temporary state and can relax the law only so long as it lasts. Nor can circumventing the law lead to greater harm or injury. To "choose the lesser of two evils," then, means to opt for the less onerous and damaging choice when forced to make an illicit decision.[66] We can derive two major insights from Vâsıf's use of this concept in his chronicle. One is that he and his opponents were disputing in legalistic terms. Austria had confronted the empire with an unpalatable ultimatum, but while Müftîzâde Ahmed and others argued the illegality of submission and felt it their duty to risk war, trusting in God, Vâsıf held that submission was not only justified, but preferable according to the law. That is, he deployed the term to defend otherwise illegal concessions. The second insight is that "choosing the lesser evil" is provisional by rule. The legal literature makes it clear that duress is

---

[65] MEHÂSİN 1, fols. 49b–50a.

[66] The precept is defined in Cevdet's nineteenth-century legal code *Mecelle-i Ahkâm-ı 'Adliyye* (Istanbul, 1882/83), 26, and by its commentators Ali Haydar and Salî Rustum Bâz al-Lubnânî. See, respectively, *Dürerü'l-hukkâm şerhu mecelleti'l-ahkâm*, ed. Raşit Gündoğdu and Osman Erdem (Istanbul, 2000), 1: 53–57; and *Sharḥ al-majalla* (Beirut, 1986), 32. Saim Kayadibi's *The Doctrine of Istihsân (Juristic Preference) in Islamic Law* (Ankara, 2007) is a good entry point to the topic. See also EI², s.v. "Ḍarûra" and "Istiḥsân."

a temporary condition whose legal exemptions expire therewith.[67] In this way, peace with Russia was to be borne only as long as necessity dictated. The Ottomans could resume their conquests and recapture the Crimea once the reforms took effect, as Vâsıf reminded us.

It is also important to note the causal dimensions of the dispute. Müftîzâde and others trusted in the justness of their cause and in God, who, they said, would take sides and grant them victory on the battlefield. In early December 1783, Müftîzâde bitterly complained to Gazi Hasan Paşa about Russia's seizure of the Crimea. As he considered the matter, compromise was impossible. What must happen if we respond firmly, he asked? Must we all simply acquiesce? We will trust in God and respond if the Russians declare war – that is quite the truth of it! Gazi Hasan Paşa sympathized, but pointed out that the empire faced two strong opponents and lacked all the means of war, including troops, treasure, and able command.[68] By way of contrast, around the same time, Halil Paşa privately solicited advice from his councilors. The remarks of one Bekir Paşazâde Süleyman Beyefendi embodied the activist approach of this circle. After suggesting that war wait several more years and listing the empire's many challenges, he reflected:

While I have no doubt that God is almighty and powerful and will help the weak and oppressed, it is undeniable that the divine custom is to create everything through causes. God alone has knowledge of future outcomes. To open the gates of war with such potent enemies while secondary causes are entirely lacking, relying on a supernatural victory, is like taking deadly poison and foolishly trusting that the antidote will work.[69]

This too had been the point of Vâsıf's earlier verse: to stress the recklessness of an anti-causal approach.

The debate over the Crimea came to a head on December 18, 1783. With the Russians awaiting a final decision and insisting that any further delay meant war, Abdülhamid I ordered Halil Paşa to call a general council "to decide on war or peace" and to reach a decision suiting the empire's situation and holy law. The minutes of this council, which Vâsıf inserted into his chronicle, are remarkably vivid and emotional. Halil Paşa first had the relevant documents read aloud and addressed the council. He reminded them that they served the empire and should say candidly whatever was best for the realm, war or peace. "Here your stature does

---

[67] Cevdet, *Mecelle*, 26; Haydar, 1: 53–55; al-Lubnânî, 30–31; and Kayadibi, 216–217.
[68] MEHÂSİN 1, fols. 70a-70b. See also Menchinger, "Free Will," 463–464.
[69] MEHÂSİN 1, fols. 73a-73b.

not matter," he said. "This council must end with a decision. Do we capitulate or wage war? It is not possible to delay or to give any answer other than one of these two choices." The Grand Vezir and *şeyhülislâm* met an initial hesitation with urgency: "Why are you silent? You must speak the truth, whatever it is!" Sâdık Molla Efendi, a member of the ulema, rose first and said that in the circumstances peace was preferable to war and the proper course. Müftîzâde Ahmed Efendi followed but suggested, rather, that the decision properly belonged to the sultan. Halil Paşa rebuked him. This was no advice at all, for the sultan had ordered that the matter be resolved in council. Certain voices next spoke in favor of peace. Gazi Hasan Paşa drew attention to the empire's weakness, signaling that he now stood with his rival the Grand Vizier, and said that war must occur through secondary causes, two of which, the army and treasury, were wanting. Another statesman, Süleyman Penâh Efendi, contrasted the situation with the late and disastrous war against Russia. Now the empire faced not one but two formidable powers, which Gazi Hasan surmised was actually three or four with minor allies. Penâh Efendi continued that the greatest danger lay in Istanbul's vulnerability and that peace was best. Halil Paşa too expressed his support of peace. "My own wish," he said, "is not to prevent a campaign or to shrink from war." Were the empire ready, he vowed that he would trust in God and act, but such was not the case. A campaign was premature. The chief accounting officer (*muhâsebe-i evvel*) then asked the ulema to rule on the matter's legality. Two, Müftîzâde and Tevfîk Efendi, replied that the legality of war and peace depended on knowing the realm's strength, of which they were ignorant. Halil Paşa castigated them; everything had been detailed item by item. But he pursued the point and a discussion followed on the army's readiness.

At this stage, the tide turned against war. The director of the imperial arsenal pointed out that even the most hawkish vizier, Gazi Hasan Paşa, was wary. Gazi Hasan agreed. "I cannot say that war is fitting at a time like this. It would end badly, heaven forfend. In this case there is nothing better for the empire than peace," he said. Halil Paşa again asked for a legal opinion. The *şeyhülislâm* consulted his peers and Müftîzâde Efendi responded that the law required they choose the lesser of two evils. Here, he continued, if the evil of a campaign surpassed the evil of peace, they must choose peace. A councilor reminded him that the dangers of war had been weighed. What were the dangers of capitulation? Müftîzâde answered that the Russians had broken a treaty and annexed a Muslim territory. To capitulate was to accept this injury as well as the subjection of Muslims. The council quickly moved to qualify their submission. Come what may, observed one member, the empire must continue its reform in case the Russians press their advantage. "You cannot consider this a permanent peace," he said. Halil Paşa also likened capitulation to a truce, as afterward, they might complete the reforms and launch a campaign. Returning to the point, the accounting officer prompted the ulema a third time. If the empire's weakness was thus, they agreed, peace was permitted by holy law. Müftîzâde concurred. The Grand Vezir then polled the council, who voted unanimously for peace but agreed that the decision must be kept secret. "God damn him who speaks of this meeting elsewhere," said one.[70]

Vâsıf's own assessment of these proceedings came in a coda to the text, where he again defended peace as the "lesser of two evils." The empire's defense normally relies on the treasury, army, provisions, and governmental unity, he wrote. Not only had the past decade's campaigns eroded state order and made resistance futile, but post-war leaders had furthered Russian aims by their failure to act. There was therefore no choice but to accept the annexation. "And so," he explained,

It was widely known that the empire was in grave danger and surrounded by enemies awaiting the least pretext. As a result, it was as if a cancer had stricken the realm's vulnerable body. If care were not immediately taken to excise it, with sound ministrations, it would metastasize and (God forbid) destroy the polity itself. Since a limb must as a rule be amputated for the health of others, this decision, which was permissible according to the law and unanimous, was under the circumstances a sort of "choosing the lesser of two evils."

It is well to add that Vâsıf's imagery in this passage recalls two further maxims – "Choose the limited injury to avert the general" and "Remove the greater injury with the lesser" – and encapsulates the entire legal argument from duress.[71] He nonetheless foresaw objections. We are told that certain people could not fathom the decision and protested, saying, "What need was there to accept this situation?" Vâsıf countered them with the now stock example of Ḥudaybiyya and the early community's submission to its enemies, taking care, of course, to distinguish the two

[70] MEHÂSİN 1, fols. 77a-85b. I have only outlined this very detailed narrative. Both Aksan (*Ottoman Statesman*, 181–184) and Uzunçarşılı ("Sadrâzam," 229–231) date the council to 4 M AH 1198 = November 28, 1783. According to Vâsıf, it took place on 23 M or December 18.

[71] MEHÂSİN 1, fols. 85b-86a. Cf. Cevdet, *Mecelle*, 26; Haydar, 1: 56–58; and Kayadibi, 216. The classic illustration of these precepts is the demolition of private houses to prevent a fire from spreading.

cases. The Prophet's hand had not been forced; he might have annihilated his enemies without drawing his sword and a mere coup d'oeil. Muhammad's inclination to peace was instead "instruction in a blessed matter to the community," as he necessarily had knowledge of what was and is to come. This passage unmistakably channels Naîmâ's defense of Karlowitz. Apart from citing Ḥudaybiyya, Vâsıf introduced a distinctly causal rationale for peace that supported his patron's reform efforts, and his inference, as in Naîmâ, was that peace is no more than a truce. Like Dürrî Mehmed, Vâsıf almost surely took Naîmâ as his model. The fact that he placed more weight on the legal grounds for peace as the "lesser of two evils" takes nothing away from his overarching point. This was to be a temporary peace.[72]

For Vâsıf and his peers, the Crimean crisis was a controversy over human reason and the law, and how these could or should contain warfare. The annexation was patently illegal. Yet Vâsıf knew and feared what might happen if the government acted overzealously, and he and his allies in effect made use of a legal loophole, a technicality. War and peace as such were not in dispute, then, at least not in official utterances. Peace remained an expedient within terms set in the late seventeenth century and not even the most liberal statesman could publicly forego militant rhetoric. An intellectual like Vâsıf, meanwhile, might draw on a literary model some eighty years old without, presumably, sacrificing for effect. Still, even a qualified peace was highly contentious. The empire's recognition of the annexation on January 8, 1784, provoked considerable backlash. The perception that the government had abdicated its duties was such that some ulema branded Halil Paşa an infidel and threatened the sultan with revolt and deposition. While Halil Paşa's circle had carried the argument, the loss of the Crimea stoked popular rage to a degree rarely seen and increased tensions in the capital, allowing belligerent voices to gain hold in council.[73] They would shortly reap a bitter harvest.

---

[72] MEHÂSİN 1, fols. 86a-86b. İLGÜREL (100) transcribes this passage incorrectly. Ahmed Cevdet later harshly criticized Vâsıf for what he considered his sophistry over the annexation. See Mücteba İlgürel, "Cevdet Paşa Tarihi'nin Kaynaklarından Vâsıf Tarihi," in *Ahmed Cevdet Paşa Semineri: 27–28 Mayıs 1985* (Istanbul, 1986), 119.

[73] Niyazi Berkes, *The Development of Secularism in Turkey* (Montreal, 1964), 67; and Kemal Beydilli, "Küçük Kaynarca'dan Tanzimât'a Islâhât Düşünceleri," *İlmî Araştırmalar* 8 (1999): 26. Abdülhamid (with good reason) went so far as to confer with scholars about how the empire might break its agreement: MEHÂSİN 1, fols. 93a-93b.

3.4 COLLAPSE OF THE REFORM FACTION, 1784–1787

In the aftermath of the annexation, the government's fissures came increasingly into the open. Halil Paşa had reached a key juncture. He had hired French officers and technicians, reopened a naval engineering school at the imperial arsenal, enlarged the light artillery corps, and established drills; his work on the mortar and sapper corps proceeded apace. But he faced staunch opposition. While the presence of foreigners in the capital was a source of muttered discontent, more immediately dangerous was his desire to reform the Janissary corps and to purge its rolls, for though the corps had become useless as a fighting unit, it retained powerful vested interests. He and his circle forged ahead slowly. Vâsıf for his part spent much of 1784 in a flurry of professional activity. His main task was to continue his chronicle, where he recorded the reforms with unstinting and at times fawning praise. Vâsıf defended the Grand Vizier's initiatives as "ancient practice" and the Janissary reform as a restoration of one of the teetering "four pillars."[74] He nonetheless signaled just how far the political tone had shifted that spring when the sultan commissioned him to prepare a short essay on European soldiers and their training. In March, Abdülhamid received a letter from *maréchal* Anne Charles Sigismond de Montmorency-Luxembourg, the Duke of Piney-Luxembourg, by leave of the French king. The Duke made an offer. Contending that the empire's losses stemmed from poor training, he proposed to lead a military mission to Crete or Rhodes to instruct Ottoman forces in fortification, mortars, and cannonry. Abdülhamid was intrigued, but before accepting, and as controversy swirled, he asked the historian to provide him with more details.[75]

In his essay, Vâsıf came out forcefully against the mission with a claim, tellingly, that European training was inherently at odds with Ottoman society and warfare. Europeans use force to levy men, he wrote. Their armies consist of orphans and conscript peasants, something utterly alien to the empire in its social and moral effects, while

[74] İLGÜREL, 155–160, 173–176, 177. In an addendum, Vâsıf lamented (165–167) that in his day, statesmen no longer cooperated or set aside their differences for the realm's greater welfare. He suggested that disunity had prevented the empire from facing its foes and forced it instead to "choose the lesser of two evils." See further Berkes, 61–65; and Uzunçarşılı, "Sadrâzam," 231–237.

[75] Vâsıf inserted the essay (MEHÂSİN 1, fols. 129a-130a) into his chronicle sub anno hegirae 1198. Its chronological position suggests that he composed it in mid- to late-May 1784. Cf. Cevdet, *Târih*, 3: 85. The Duke sent this letter via his son and aide-de-camp Charles Emmanuel. See Berkes, 65–66; Uzunçarşılı, "Sadrâzam," 235; and Virginia Aksan, "Choiseul-Gouffier at the Sublime Porte, 1784–1792," in *Contacts*, 59–65.

Ottoman soldiers are virtuous, united, and devoted to jihad. That they would triumph over the Europeans was for him unquestionable, nor, he added, should they stoop to learn enemy arts. Vâsıf's insistence on the dynasty's superiority led once again to the paradox: if God favored the empire and promised it victory, why did it fare so poorly in war? The historian interpreted this first and foremost as a divine trial. "Even if our men now face reverses and the infidel sometimes prevails on land or sea," he reasoned, "this is merely a result of *istidrâc*, born from their satanic efforts." For Vâsıf, *istidrâc* – a theological concept whereby God gives infidels success, making them prideful, in order to lure them to damnation and test believers – had led to recent defeats. Yet he vowed that *istidrâc* was short-lived. Enemy arms were no different than in the past and the realm would inevitably prevail. As for the French offer, Vâsıf concluded that it was needless in light of the Grand Vizier's reforms: "Ultimately there is still a way to address these concerns, which, praise God, we are gradually implementing," he said. The reforms would in time succeed.

It is worth noting that this essay differs substantially from Vâsıf's position of only a few months before. In fact, it is a shrewd piece of casuistry. While earlier he called for "reciprocation" and laid Ottoman failures on a lack of initiative, Vâsıf now denied that warfare had really changed. "The infidel's arms were no different when our armies were winning," he said. "We know what weapons they use today and if we assume they follow the rules of war, then all their maneuvers, formations, and shock tactics will come to naught on meeting our swords." He also tied victory and defeat to God's will. Citing cases when the empire had won while outmatched, "how," he asked, "can anyone credit victory to a refinement of the means of war and defeat to inadequate arms?" Yet Vâsıf brushed off all his reservations in the essay's conclusion. Nor did he go so far as to deny human will outright. It may be that he was constrained in what he could say or that he was trying to co-opt more conservative voices. For him, arms and tactics normally underwent historical change; in his body of work, reciprocation and imitation are the key mechanisms of reform. Still, some in the empire considered reciprocation illicit, and by removing it, Vâsıf could remove potential objections to the Grand Vizier's programs and present reform as a matter of simply upholding the old ways. God would see to the rest. Vâsıf knew as well that a French force in the Mediterranean raised suspicions, especially as their ambassador Choiseul-Gouffier had once advocated a French imperial presence in Greece, Egypt, and the Aegean. Critics had already assailed Halil Paşa for associating too closely with the infidel. The mission on balance simply posed too much risk.[76]

Vâsıf by now had reestablished himself in the bureaucracy and was enjoying a higher profile. In the summer, he began working as galley scribe or *kalyonlar kâtibi* in Galata, north of the Golden Horn, the site of a deepwater anchorage and the imperial arsenal. This was no honorary duty. The *kalyonlar kâtibi* kept ship records and ensured that the arsenal galleys were victualed and had a full complement of men. It was a busy but lucrative post.[77] With stable employment, the scribe and historian could at last assume a lifestyle more befitting his rank and to which, he felt, he was entitled. We do not know where he lived in Istanbul during this time, but he began to set up a large household, taking on a steward, groomsmen, musicians, librarians, cooks, and other servants, and had access to new luxuries. He and his wife, Ümmü Gülsûm, seem to have started a family, as well, and by mid-decade had a young son named Abdullah Lebîb.[78] Despite his still middling position in the bureaucracy, Vâsıf was hopeful. That autumn, he presented the Grand Vizier his chronicle for the hijri years 1196 to 1199 (AD 1782 to 1784) and, under orders to continue, began a new section with verse by his friend Mehmed Mekkî Efendi: "A year of God's blessing."[79]

---

[76] The essay's contradictions have led some to interpret it, incorrectly in my view, as advancing an arch-conservative and fatalistic position. I have elsewhere ("A Reformist Philosophy of History: The Case of Ahmed Vâsıf Efendi," *Journal of Ottoman Studies* 44 [2014]: 146–151) critiqued this view and reassessed its stance on reform and causality. Cevdet, too, (*Târih*, 3: 88–96) was highly critical and suspected Vâsıf of dissembling his true beliefs. See also Aksan, "Choiseul-Gouffier," 62 f.

[77] Vâsıf specified (İLGÜREL, 186) that the appointment took place on 5 L AH 1198 = August 22, 1784, and was to be "temporary." See also Fâik, 147; Fâtin, 432; and Sarıcaoğlu, 147. BOA.AE.Abd 9384 gives some sense of his daily activities and concerns the victualing of *Kaplan Yaşlı*, an imperial galley with a crew of fifty-five, and the purchase of four months of staples. The document bears Vâsıf's signature and seal. See further on the galley scribe in Uzunçarşılı, *Osmanlı Devleti*, 425, 430–431.

[78] A Spanish newspaper reported in 1787 that Vâsıf had a household in Istanbul of ninety-two people, including a tutor for his ten-year-old son. His retinue in Spain numbered forty-six. These sources require caution, however, as one also claimed he kept forty wives and concubines. See Aceituno, 35; and Kutlu, 108, 110. William Beckford in *The Journal of William Beckford in Portugal and Spain, 1787–1788*, ed. Boyd Alexander (Gloucestershire, 2006), 191–209 passim, corroborates the size of this retinue. BOA. AE.Abd 23342 records Vâsıf's allocation of summer ice on 5 Ş AH 1199 (June 12, 1785), a perquisite over and above his pay.

[79] MEHÂSİN 1, fols. 150a, 151a. Vâsıf added a chronogram of his own to Mekkî Efendi's from the Quran 5:52: "It may be that God will grant victory [= AH 1199]." On the writing of chronograms as part of palace New Year celebrations, see Cahit Telci, "Osmanlı Yönetiminin Yeni Yıl Kutlamalarından: İstanbul Tekkelerine Muharremiye Dağıtımı," *Sûfî Araştırmaları* 3 (2012): 1–6.

Not everything in life revolved around work and history, however. Vâsıf had involved himself in other intellectual ventures. In early 1784, he and the director of the imperial council (*beylikçi*), Râşid Mehmed Efendi, approached the Grand Vizier with a proposal. The empire's only Arabic-type press had been out of operation for decades. Founded by İbrahim Müteferrika in 1726, it had issued a total of seventeen titles in history, politics, geography, language, and science, but had proved a commercial failure. Vâsıf and Râşid wanted to revive it. While the historian may have owed his interest to the late Abdürrezzâk Efendi, who in 1779 tried to print Murtaḍâ al-Zabîdî's Arabic dictionary the *Crown of the Bride* (*Tâj al-'arûs*) after paying nine purses of *akçe* for a set, the project more generally addressed the empire's need for technical knowledge.[80] Vâsıf argued, plausibly, that copying was a slow and demanding task that led to errors, scarcity, and high prices. There was also an underlying motive: namely, rumors that the French wanted to buy the unused typeface and press. Vâsıf and Râşid privately discussed the matter, he said. They would purchase the press and run it jointly, paying down expenses with profits while donating the capital and a part of the income to the imperial mortmain. Halil Paşa presented their plan to Abdülhamid, who readily accepted. In late winter, he issued warrants and the two men began operations.[81] Râşid and Vâsıf bought the press and refurbished it. They then hired staff, including a brilliant type-setter named Gelenbevî İsmail Efendi, later the empire's foremost

---

[80] Orlin Sabev's *İbrahim Müteferrika ya da İlk Osmanlı Matbaa Serüveni (1726–1746)* (Istanbul, 2006) is the authoritative study of the press' early period. See also Kemal Beydilli, *Türk Bilim ve Matbaacılık Tarihinde Mühendishâne, Mühendishâne Matbaası ve Kütüphânesi (1776–1826)* (Istanbul, 1995), 99–100, 104; and Giambattista Toderini, *Letteratura Turchesca* (Venice, 1787), 3: 6 ff. The Englishman James Matra detailed efforts by the "Secretary of State" to restart the press in a July 3, 1779 letter. Richard Clogg, "An Attempt to Revive Turkish Printing in Istanbul in 1779," *IJMES* 10 (1979): 67–70.

[81] MEHÂSİN 1, fols. 114a–116a; Mehmed Subhî et al., *Târih-i Sâmî ve Şâkir ve Subhî* (Istanbul, 1784), unpaginated preface. The official petition (BOA.AE.Abd 1064) details this arrangement. Vâsıf and Râşid were to pay for the press, its premises, employees, and other expenses. The imperial trust would receive one *akçe* for each ten-quire section of a printed book and proportionally less for smaller sections. The books would be stamped after binding failing which they could not be sold. Vâsıf and Râşid also agreed to abide by the press' original mandate to print only histories, dictionaries, and other non-religious subject matter. Abdülhamid enthusiastically noted Müteferrika's printed histories: "Quite right, everyone has trouble getting them copied. But it is an easy thing when they are printed – extremely easy." Toderini includes (3: 210–222) a dragoman's transla-tion of the sultan's decree dated 18 Ra AH 1198 = February 10, 1784. Cf. D'Ohsson (3: 506–509), who dates the decree 18 R = March 11.

mathematician. According to the cleric Giambattista Toderini, who visited on May 4, the new printers set up shop in a suite of rooms in central Istanbul, near Çemberlitaş, and were soon making proofs. Besides Gelenbevî, Râşid and Vâsıf engaged two compositors from the press' early days as well as proofreaders. Toderini in his visit apparently met Vâsıf, who had assumed daily oversight and showed him plates from the original Müteferrika incunabula, and noted the group's activity.[82] The press was at work that very moment; it was producing a history. Perhaps to indulge the sultan's fondness for the subject, the imperial printers had chosen the 1730–1744 court chronicles of Mustafa Sâmî, Hüseyin Şâkir, and Mehmed Subhî for their first effort. They released it that fall in a folio edition resuming Müteferrika's series of print histories, to which Vâsıf added an exultant preface. He called the new book a prodigy – a historical event. "We started this operation with a free hand, trusting in God," he preened. "This was something that certain rich and artful men had long contemplated but thought could not be done ... Praise be to God, we succeeded in printing books more legible, more accurate, and better than ever before."[83] The public was less enamored. In truth, production had been plagued by error, over-expenditure, supply problems, and damaged type. Many of Müteferrika's original letters had become worn or misshapen through use. Râşid and Vâsıf made replacements with a poor alloy, softer and less attractive, and were then unable to recast the whole face. When Toderini visited again on November 4, the printers were short of paper and struggling to make headway on a sequel. Worse was to come.[84]

In spite of hints to the contrary, Vâsıf's recent professional stability had given him a false sense of assurance, an illusion of security. Now the bolt

---

[82] Toderini identifies (3: 223–224) this "overseer" as a Turk of rank. Franz Babinger in *Stambuler Buchwesen im 18. Jahrhundert* (Leipzig, 1919), 21–23, says that the press was close to the so-called "Burnt Column" of Constantine. See also Vâsıf's preface in Subhî; and Cevdet, *Târih*, 3: 120–121.

[83] Subhî, unpaginated preface; Toderini, 3: 226. In the preface to the 1785 edition of *Târih-i İzzî*, Vâsıf listed a Mustafa Efendi and an Adam Efendi as the work's proofers.

[84] Toderini, 3: 226–227. While Cevdet rated (in Sabev, 315) Râşid's and Vâsıf's books below those of Müteferrika, saying that they were less clean and accurate, the overall quality of early Ottoman printing was not high. Arabic letters were difficult to join cleanly and give these early editions a decidedly messy, disjointed appearance. See Rudi Lindner on some of their technical and aesthetic shortcomings, "Icon among Iconoclasts in the Renaissance," in *The Iconic Page in Manuscript, Print, and Digital Culture*, eds. George Bornstein and Theresa Tinkle (Ann Arbor, 1998), 89–107. Printing expenses were also prohibitive. Râşid wrote (in Beydilli, *Mühendishâne*, 104) that they spent over 4,000 *kuruş* to buy the press and about twice as much to make it operational – a small fortune.

FIG. 3.2: Gazi Hasan Paşa (d. 1790), war hero, Grand Vizier, and long-time Grand Admiral.

fell. In early 1785, the decade's factional struggles came to a dramatic and bloody climax. On March 29, Grand Vizier Halil Paşa began to disburse the Janissaries' yearly pay at the imperial palace according to custom, all signs suggesting that he retained the sultan's favor. Two nights later, he was roused from bed, stripped of his seal of office, exiled, and replaced in the interim by Gazi Hasan Paşa. Within a month, he was dead. On the same day, other members of his circle also fell. Râif İsmail and the former Janissary commander Yayha Ağa were removed and executed; the *şeyhülislâm* Dürrîzâde Ataullah Efendi was exiled and likely poisoned. Why did the reformist faction collapse so suddenly, so spectacularly? It appears that the root cause was Gazi Hasan Paşa's intense personal rivalry with the Grand Vizier. One theory has it that he and his allies notified Abdülhamid that the Grand Vizier, Râif İsmail, and the *şeyhülislâm* were plotting to replace him with his younger and more pliant nephew, prince Selim. According to another, they convinced him that Halil Paşa was deliberately provoking a Janissary revolt with his reforms. Some gossip even called the minister a freemason, likely for his links to the French. While we cannot know whether or not any of this was true, the rumors circulated and Gazi Hasan seems to have pressed the sultan to act. His task was made easier in that Halil Paşa had alienated many through his reforms and the loss of the Crimea. When his severed head arrived in Istanbul, it bore a placard reading, among other things, "a traitor to faith and country."[85]

Halil Paşa's fall left Vâsıf and other reformers in grave danger. He had again bet on the wrong side. Under the circumstances, his support for the vizier and at times fulsome praise looked not only suspect but incriminating, and it is not hyperbole to say that his life was in peril. If cowardly, then, Vâsıf's reaction was understandable. He distanced himself from the Grand Vizier, cynically denouncing the man he had once called the empire's savior. Vâsıf accused the disgraced minister of injustice and greed. Halil Paşa had been corrupted by power, he claimed, and abused his position to amass great wealth and property. He embezzled and took bribes, killed innocents, and so browbeat his peers that they equally feared to advise or to praise him. The historian made Halil Paşa into a moral archetype, a tyrant whom he and other statesmen had been powerless to challenge. Vâsıf was lucky that his hypocrisy was not readily detectable. His work's most damaging sections were not yet public and he played a double game, purging his drafts while ingratiating himself with the realm's new power holders, Grand Vizier Ali Şahin and *şeyhülislâm* İvazpaşazâde İbrahim Efendi, but more so Gazi Hasan, who had the sultan's ear.[86] Vâsıf managed to keep his arsenal post through the

---

[85] This event has been treated in many places. See for example Berkes, 67; DİA, s.v. "Halil Hamîd Paşa"; HADÎKAT, supp. 3: 35–36; Sarıcaoğlu, 148–153; and Uzunçarşılı, "Sadrâzam," 239 ff.

[86] MEHÂSİN 1, fols. 181a-184b. Vâsıf wrote in a medallion in the earliest part of his chronicle (fol. 1a) that, as it contained secret information, the sultan might withhold it

summer; he remained busy at court and wrote verse to congratulate Abdülhamid on the birth of a son and to comfort him on the loss of another.[87] He was also preparing a major installment of the dynastic chronicle. Vâsıf sent his version of the year's events to the şeyhülislâm, who was "extremely pleased," and then forwarded it to the sultan, who approved and directed him to add Râif İsmail's execution and the death of Dürrîzâde Ataullah. Vâsıf complied. He revised the work, bound it with two earlier years, and, probably that autumn, submitted it to the palace. In an accompanying letter, he claimed that the chronicle gave a "balanced judgment" on the hijri years 1197 to 1200 (AD 1783 to late 1785) that reflected well on the principal actors and offered guidance; adding that he had improved Sadullah Enverî's work, he begged to begin recording the next year. Abdülhamid was suitably pleased. And he softened whatever remorse Vâsıf felt in condemning old allies with a 500 kuruş reward and leave to begin a new year with verse that he, Vâsıf, had written.[88]

A mix of careerism, talent, and lack of scruples enabled the historian to cling to favor for the next year and a half. He did his utmost to please. Power was now in the hands of more aggressive personalities like Gazi Hasan and his protégé Koca Yusuf Paşa, who became Grand Vizier in January 1786 and actively sought confrontation with Russia. Although unsatisfied with his lot, Vâsıf was less troubled by living off

from the wider public. A palace document (TSMA.E 7028/261) states that this portion remained with the Grand Vizier, in whose estate it was discovered. Vâsıf then made deletions (e.g. MEHÂSİN 1, fols. 28a-28b, 36a, 38b, 41a-41b, 44b, 65b-66a) at a later date that softened his praise of Halil Paşa, as well as Dürrîzâde Ataullah and Mehmed Râşid. Cevdet quite rightly criticized him for being two-faced. See İlgürel, "Cevdet Paşa," 118; and Kütükoğlu, "Vekâyi'nüvis," 123–124.

[87] Vâsıf noted (MEHÂSİN 1, fol. 218a) in appointments on 3 L AH 1199 = August 9, 1785, that the post of galley scribe went to "the Grand Admiral's divan secretary." However, BOA.AE.Abd 9384 shows that he was active in this duty until at least Za AH 1199 or September 1785. It is not clear when his term in the arsenal ended. In July, Vâsıf meanwhile celebrated the birth of the future sultan Mahmud II with a verse: "This historian marked the date with a pearl / For Prince Mahmud, how graceful his just name [= AH 1199]." MEHÂSİN 1, fol. 216a. In October, he wrote another chronogram on Mehmed Nusret's death from smallpox: "Alas! Today a pure youth fled this mortal world / This historian marked his death year: he dwelleth in heaven [= AH 1199]." Ibid, fol. 225b.

[88] See BOA.AE.Abd 1487 for Abdülhamid's editorial requests. Vâsıf's letter (BOA.AE.Abd 532) says that he submitted his own volume along with two sections of Enverî's chronicle in his possession. The sultan's gloss orders the Grand Vizier to apprise him of any reward, which BOA.AE.Abd 414, written several days later, specifies as 500 kuruş. "That is enough," the sultan replied. According to another document (BOA.AE.Abd 25728) the historian then submitted two chronograms for a new section (AH 1200). The latter presupposes the sultan's orders to continue the chronicle and appears to date from early AH 1200. See also İLGÜREL, xlii; and Sarıcaoğlu, 65–66.

the avails of hypocrisy than by what he considered the sultan's caprice and partiality for Enverî, whom he had more richly rewarded in the past. Early that year, Abdülhamid commissioned Vâsıf to write a personal history of the long-time admiral Gazi Hasan, an extravagant eulogy he later admitted to be overdone and "dictated by time and circumstance."[89] Much of his income during this period also came through largesse. In the summer of 1786, Vâsıf received a total of 2,000 *kuruş* in gifts and in return for a new section of chronicle; he was also made temporary head of the suspended payments office or *mevkûfâtçı*, another post in the treasury.[90] Vâsıf's bad faith did not necessarily lead him to retreat from his intellectual positions, however. He still called for reform, if under new management, and stressed the need to restore order and to work through secondary causes. One of his more striking contributions from this time addressed the shuttering of two profitable bullion mines in Anatolia. Vâsıf supported these closures because the mine operators had forced nearby villages to work them, which he felt undermined social order and might provoke God's wrath. Yet he proposed a way to recoup their loss: alchemy. Drawing on Galenic humorism, Vâsıf explained to his superiors how all metals share the same essence, gold, and differ in other properties through climatic variation. He argued that it should therefore be possible to transmute base metal artificially, using fire and "imitating the processes of nature" to make silver and gold. This he likened favorably to medicine, agriculture, and other "artifices." While we do not know the result of the scheme, it opens a significant window on his world. For Vâsıf, God ruled over everything in creation; yet God also made the universe operate through regular, visible causes that humans could predict and, in some

---

[89] Vâsıf inserted this essay sub anno hegirae 1200 in his chronicle MEHÂSİN 1, fols. 250a–254b. He made the admission in a later work, MEHÂSİN 2, fol. 49a, after clarifying that the sultan had specially requested it. Although Vâsıf later complained about his lack of recognition under Abdülhamid I (e.g. MEHÂSİN 6, fol. 4b), Toderini's claim (3: 231) that he fell out of favor during the period is incorrect. Vâsıf was unhappy with his compensation. The 2,500 *kuruş* sum Enverî received for one submission, for instance, was far more than he ever saw from Abdülhamid. See Enverî, *Târih*, ÖN H.O. nr. 202, fol. 202a; and Filiz Çalışkan, "Vâsıf'ın Kaynaklarından Enverî Tarihi," in *Kütükoğlu*, 145.

[90] This appointment took place on 4 L AH 1200 = July 31, 1786, and was for a term of eight months. MEHÂSİN 1, fol. 274b. A document (BOA.C.MF 2478) dated 29 Ş AH 1200 = June 27, 1786, records a 1,000 *kuruş* payment to Vâsıf for a chronicle submission. A second (BOA.C.ML 29999) indicates that he received 1,000 *kuruş* more that same month as part of gifts disbursed from poll-tax monies. See also İlgürel, "Vaka'nüvislerin Taltifleri," 186–187. On the suspended payments office, see Uzunçarşılı, *Osmanlı Devleti*, 342, 357.

cases, manipulate. This outlook was at the heart, and perhaps *the* heart, of late eighteenth-century Ottoman reform.[91]

What finally pushed Vâsıf from favor came, as it happened, from an unexpected quarter. He and Mehmed Râşid had struggled to make a success of the imperial press, which they continued to operate after Halil Paşa's fall and execution. Tensions grew. In 1785, they released a second book after much labor, a large folio edition of Süleyman İzzi's 1744–1752 court chronicle. Vâsıf's preface was humble, even apologetic, and effectively admitted that they had failed to meet expectations. "We thus beg the pardon of gentlemen and learned enthusiasts if they should note certain typos," he said. "Remember us, your two humble servants, with good will." Perhaps in an effort to boost sales, the two also lowered their prices and offered both books together at a bargain.[92] The press' lack of success was not just a problem of commercial viability, however. It was one of personality. Râşid had originally entrusted Vâsıf with day-to-day operations in return for a share of income, perhaps due to his access to texts and long experience with collation and copying. Yet Vâsıf became territorial. According to one source, he bullied the typesetter Gelenbevî İsmail. More seriously, Râşid discovered that he was not fulfilling the legal terms of the partnership and had even embezzled a good deal of money. By 1786, their relationship was ruined. Râşid confronted an unrepentant Vâsıf and ousted him, taking control of the press and leaving lasting resentment on both sides.[93]

The story did not end so simply, though. Vâsıf let anger get the best of him and evidently began to slander his partner, who pursued the matter at

---

[91] MEHÂSİN 1, fols. 199a–200a, 226a–230b, 261b, 267b–269a. Vâsıf equally tried to explain phenomena like earthquakes and smallpox through natural causes, usually within the Arabo-Hellenic scientific tradition. Interested readers are directed to my dissertation for detail, esp. 80–84.

[92] Süleyman İzzi, *Târih-i İzzi* (Istanbul, 1785), unpaginated preface. According to the frontispiece, the book was finished during the vizierate of Ali Şahin Paşa in AH 1199, and therefore sometime between late April and November 1785. Toderini says (3: 226–228) that Vâsıf and Râşid had begun work on the history as early as late 1784. The price was set at fifteen *kuruş*; Toderini himself bought both the histories in May 1786 for twenty-five *kuruş*. Râşid later conceded (in Beydilli, *Mühendishâne*, 104) that the books cost some fifty to sixty purses of *akçe* to produce and that many did not sell.

[93] Vâsıf's ouster most likely occurred at some point in 1785. Toderini (3: 231–235) visited the press once again on January 13, 1786, and says that Râşid was by then sole proprietor. Later that year, he published a commentary in quarto on Ibn al-Ḥājib's work of Arabic syntax, al-Kâfiya (Güzelhisarî Zeynîzâde Hüseyin, *I'râb al-kâfiya fî al-naḥw* [Istanbul, 1786]), which must date between January and October and makes no mention whatsoever of the historian. Mehmed Emîn relates (*Dercü'l-Vekâyi'*, fol. 87a) the story of their falling out and says that he heard it directly from Râşid.

the highest levels at court. Led by Grand Vizier Yusuf Paşa, the empire by 1786 was again on the brink of war with Russia and searching for allies. Abdülhamid moved to strengthen ties with Morocco and Spain at the strategic head of the Mediterranean, with whom the empire had existing relations. He wished to prevent a repeat of 1770, when a Russian fleet had rounded Gibraltar and crushed the Ottoman fleet off the coast of Anatolia at Çeşme. He was seeking mid-level envoys. That Vâsıf knew much about either of these lands or expected to be an ambassador is unlikely. He thought of Spain as a great infidel sea power, mainly for its battles with the Barbary corsairs, and must have been surprised to learn of his assignment to its far-flung court. For this, he could thank Râşid. His former friend, now increasingly his enemy, had orchestrated the selection to have him removed from the capital; Vâsıf was therefore summoned to the Porte on December 28, 1786, where he and Ahmed Azmî, possibly his brother-in-law, received robes of honor and orders for a spring departure. We do not know how he took the news. The appointment was a sort of "honorable exile," a hardship post far from the capital where, despite all his craving for diplomatic laurels, he had little to gain and much to lose. Nevertheless, the embassy would prove pivotal in Vâsıf's larger intellectual formation. It would alter his views of Europe and of the empire itself.[94]

---

[94] On this appointment, see MEHÂSİN 1, fols. 292a-292b; and SEFÂRETNÂME, fol. 328a. The phrase "honorable exile" belongs to Mehmed Emîn, *Dercü'l-Vekâyi'*, fols. 86b-87a. For the embassy's background, see Unat, *Osmanlı Sefirleri*, 144; and Sarıcaoğlu, 215, 228–229.

4

"Honorable Exile": In Spain (1787–1788)

4.1 ON FOREIGN SHORES, 1787

On July 25, 1787, a French ship entered the harbor at Barcelona and signaled its arrival with a broadside. Eager to disembark, and running low on food and fresh water, the ship's crew hailed port authorities for permission to land. They waited a full day before being refused. Plague was about, an officer told them; the king, Charles III, had decreed that all ships from their port of origin of Istanbul must first pass through quarantine. Apologizing, the officials gave the vessel new orders to sail for quarantine on the island of Minorca. This news did not please the vessel's chief passenger, the ambassador Ahmed Vâsıf. After more than three weeks at sea, Vâsıf was in no mood to trifle and sent ashore a reply laden with protests, vituperations, and veiled threats. He had not made such careful preparations to be insulted, nor did he intend his mission to the Spanish court to start so inauspiciously.[1]

By rule and custom, the Ottoman Empire did not maintain regular diplomatic contact with other states, nor did it usually send representatives abroad. The basis for this practice – unilateralism – had to do with the particular way that the Ottomans viewed themselves against the outside world. Not only had the empire's statesmen and thinkers inherited a juristic tradition that divided the world between Muslim and infidel, between the "realm of Islam" and "realm of war," but they saw the empire as wholly

---

[1] SEFÂRETNÂME, fols. 328b-330a. This work is Vâsıf's official account of the embassy. The manuscript that I have used, kept in the Topkapı Palace library, is longer and more detailed than abridgments found elsewhere. See also Manuel Conrotte, *España y los países musulmanes durante el ministerio de Floridablanca* (Madrid, 1909), 89.

exceptional and superior to all others, Muslim and non-Muslim, past and present. Unilateralism was one expression of this superiority. The empire rarely sent envoys to foreign lands and, when it did so, made the host country aware that it was receiving a special favor. Embassies were therefore political, to be sure, but also a performance meant to impress the realm's grandeur. Or such, at least, had been the case for most of the early modern period. By Vâsıf's time, things had begun to change. Although they clung to the pretense of unilateralism, eighteenth-century Ottoman élites, conscious of their diminished military power, increasingly resorted to bi- or multilateral diplomacy and sent extraordinary embassies in ever larger numbers. These proved significant for a number of reasons. They were on one hand steps toward the empire's eventual integration into the concert of Europe, a so-called "Europeanization of Ottoman Diplomacy" that led in the 1790s to permanent diplomatic ties with Britain, France, Austria, and Russia. On the other hand, Ottoman embassies became significant points of exchange – technical, political, military, and intellectual – with the same powers to whom they were looking, tentatively, for models of reform. An eighteenth-century Ottoman ambassador was not simply a diplomat, then. He was equally a cultural and intellectual envoy sent to observe, to absorb, and to embody and uphold the empire's honor in a foreign land.[2]

The story of these embassies also shows a more pragmatic side to Ottoman statecraft, helping to soften the legalistic, martial overtones that we find in official statements. While highly visible, the rhetoric of "infidel" and jihad did not unduly shape Ottoman foreign relations in the eighteenth century and was often suborned to other goals. Yirmisekiz Çelebi Mehmed Efendi's 1720–1721 stay in Paris is one such example. Mehmed Efendi was sent to the French court in view of a shifting balance of power on the continent, especially the rise of Russia and Austria as major threats to the empire. The ambassador's official mandate was as

---

[2] These embassies are often studied primarily as vessels for "westernization" or "modernization": e.g. Fatma Müge Göçek, *East Encounters West: France and the Ottoman Empire in the Eighteenth Century* (New York, 1987); Norman Itzkowitz and Max Mote, eds., *Mubadele: An Ottoman–Russian Exchange of Ambassadors* (Chicago, 1970); and Mehmet Yalçınkaya, "Osmanlı Zihniyetindeki Değişimin Göstergesi Olarak Sefaretnamelerin Kaynak Defteri," *OTAM* 7 (1996): 319–338. Berrak Burçak critiques this approach in "The Institution of the Ottoman Embassy and Eighteenth-century Ottoman History: An Alternative to Göçek," *International Journal of Turkish Studies* 13 (2007): 147–151. See also Hurewitz's classic "The Europeanization of Ottoman Diplomacy: The Conversion from Unilateralism to Reciprocity in the Nineteenth Century," *Belleten* 25 (1961): 455–466.

a messenger – to inform the French that the sultan would allow them to repair the Church of the Holy Sepulchre in Jerusalem. In truth, however, the holy sites were a pretext; Mehmed Efendi had a fact-finding mission. The French and Ottomans shared friendly diplomatic and commercial ties going back to the sixteenth century and, at the time, had the same enemies. Mehmed Efendi's main objective seems to have been a formal alliance with the French against the Austrians, though he proved unsuccessful in this regard. But more lasting fruit came from the ambassador's orders to observe and record French society, "to visit the fortresses, factories, and the works of French civilization generally and report on those which might be applicable" in the empire. Mehmed Efendi visited the city's hospitals, zoos, parks, libraries, operas, and theaters; he met with the astronomer Jacques Cassini at the Paris observatory and described French manners, dress, and military accomplishments. The duc de Saint-Simon, the courtier and diarist, wrote that Mehmed Efendi

Observed with taste and discernment all that Paris could offer him in curiosities and royal houses roundabout, where he was magnificently entertained and received. He seemed to understand machines and manufacturing especially coins and the press. He seemed to know a great deal and have great knowledge of history and good books. He ... intended on his return to Constantinople to establish there a printing press and a library.[3]

Mehmed Efendi's son, Çelebizâde Mehmed Said Efendi (d. 1761), would indeed establish this press in Istanbul with İbrahim Müteferrika, a cultural borrowing of no small value.

The embassies of Ahmed Resmî to Vienna (1757–1758) and Berlin (1763–1764) offer more proof of how the empire balanced its diplomatic needs, on one hand, with ideological and legal ideals on the other. By mid-century, Europe's political gravity shifted more and more to the east, away from France to Prussia and Russia. Prussia's rising power under Frederick II shook up old alliances and led to a string of conflicts. The War of Austrian Succession (1740–1748), the Seven Years' War (1756–1763), France's 1756 entente with Austria, the partitions of Poland – Ottoman élites followed these events closely, as they not only embroiled the continent in war but stood to expose the realm to its northern enemy's ambitions. These currents would also in time draw the empire into the 1768–1774 war and set the terms for the "Eastern Question" of the next century. While neutral, then, the Ottomans looked for potential allies and began a long dalliance with Prussia. Resmî's travels took place in this

---

[3] Quoted in Berkes, 33–35. See also Göçek, 3–81.

context. Prussia was at war with Austria during the ambassador's stay in Vienna and secretly pursuing a defensive alliance in the Ottoman capital. Resmî's admiring reports on Frederick suited the mood in Istanbul, where one could hear cries of "Brandenburg, Brandenburg!" in the streets and coffeehouses after Prussian victories. The 1763 embassy to Berlin meant to finalize this pact – unsuccessfully, as it happened. Resmî met with Frederick, who pressed the advantages of an alliance and whose character he, the ambassador, made the subject of a detailed study. Yet Resmî also returned with a better grasp of European politics, becoming perhaps the first Ottoman to appreciate the idea of a "balance of power" and the collective efforts of European monarchs to prevent one state's hegemony over others.[4] In any event, these embassies show the willingness of eighteenth-century Ottomans to engage with their non-Muslim neighbors. This does not mean that older categories had disappeared or that religion no longer colored foreign relations; it only means that élites now recognized they could ill afford to act alone and would seek allies in their more direct conflict with Russia.

Vâsıf's own mission to Spain occurred in the waning days of this Ottoman unilateralism. Although he had been outside of the empire before, in St. Petersburg, we possess much fuller information for his time in Spain both in its everyday detail and in its impact on his intellectual outlook. As a foreigner abroad, he could not help but feel certain incongruities. The Spain of Goya and Boccherini had a cosmopolitanism, a brilliance which he had never before encountered, yet he soon learned to dislike its inhabitants for what he saw as their vanity and deceit. More to the point, Vâsıf was attracted yet also repelled by the political reality on the ground. Bourbon Spain was in the midst of a revival guided by the rationalizing, centralizing policies of Charles III and his first minister José Moñino y Redondo, conde de Floridablanca. The scope and success of these projects intrigued the ambassador, pushing him toward a more comprehensive view of reform, but at the same time, led him to reflect melancholically on his empire. Here, after all, was the storied realm of al-Andalus; here, a powerful Muslim civilization like his own had once flourished. Seeing the relics of this greatness in a Christian land posed a lesson and warning from which he and his colleagues ought to learn. Certainly, they could not ignore it.

---

[4] See Aksan, *Ottoman Statesman*, 34–99, 195–198. Beydilli treats these relations in his study *Büyük Freidrich ve Osmanlılar: XVIII. Yüzyılda Osmanlı-Prusya Münâsebetleri* (Istanbul, 1985).

FIG. 4.1: José Moñino y Redondo (d. 1808), conde de Floridablanca and chief minister of Charles III of Spain.

Vâsıf had spent a good deal of energy in planning the voyage after his appointment the previous winter. He studied Spain's geography as well as earlier embassy records, noting expenses and the valuables they had borrowed from the treasury. It was typical, for instance, for an Ottoman envoy to take things like jeweled blades and caparisons to enhance his gravity while abroad. These researches were complete by mid-March, at which time he was granted a travel allowance of 12,500 *kuruş*.[5] The matter of gifts was of an even higher order. In May, the imperial council established a group to find items for the Spanish king with a working budget of 26,800 *kuruş*. The task was to identify which gifts might be taken directly from the palace treasury and which would have to be bought, and then to make arrangements accordingly. The group largely finished its work by late June, though not without challenges. One of these was financing. While the total value of gifts was immense – some 143,700 *kuruş* – the council had avoided costs by relying heavily on items in the treasury, some of which had to be repaired or remade, and its actual expenditure of 25,000 *kuruş* was less than the initial budget.[6] Even Vâsıf's stipend was a hardship. It was the same amount given to ambassadors thirty or forty years earlier, indeed substantially less in real terms, and due to the treasury's embarrassment, had to be siphoned off from other earmarked funds.[7] Vâsıf's spring had thus been inordinately busy.

---

[5] Vâsıf inquired about the said valuables and was given records for two embassies: those of Mustafa Hattî Efendi to Vienna in 1748, and Numan Bey to Poland in 1777. He requested a jeweled sword, dagger, and two scabbards as well as two boxes, a diamond seal, and four sets of caparisons: see BOA.AE.Abd 762; and TSMA.d 10363, dated 12 C AH 1201 = March 2, 1787. Two financial documents (BOA.C.HR 2938 and 5748) record his stipend, with the respective dates 20 Ca = March 10 and 5 C = March 25. Further details are found in TSMA.d 2057, fols. 3b-4a (Ca = February/March 1787). Vâsıf also studied (SEFÂRETNÂME, fol. 349a) Spanish topography and history in a work called *Coğrafyâ-yı Kebîr*. This was likely the Turkish translation of Blaeu's *Atlas Maior*, a copy of which was kept in the palace library. See DİA, s.v. "Ebû Bekir b. Behrâm" for more on its translator and various names.

[6] The group's procurements are documented in BOA.D.BŞM.d 5486. This binder includes a list of gifts signed and sealed by Vâsıf and dated 7 N AH 1201 = June 23, 1787. A series of decrees (BOA.AE.Abd 884, 1216, and 8795) also traces their activities, the last detailing the treasury steward's requests for more time in order to craft replacement items and the sultan's insistence on the original deadline of 1 N. See further Mücteba İlgürel, "Vakanüvis Ahmed Vâsıf Efendi'nin İspanya Elçiliği ve Götürdüğü Hediyeler," *İÜEF Tarih Dergisi* 46 (2007): 29 ff.

[7] BOA.C.HR 5748. Cf. BOA.C.HR 2938, which specifies that Mustafa Hattî and Ahmed Resmî had identical sums in 1748 and 1763. See also Azmi Süslü, "Un aperçu sur les ambassadeurs ottomans et leurs sefaretname," *AÜDTCF Tarih Araştırmaları Dergisi* 14 (1981): 235–236; and Unat, *Osmanlı Sefirleri*, 19–28.

In addition to official preparations, he remained in his usual posts and made provisions for his own burgeoning household. He corresponded with the Spanish ambassador in Istanbul, Juan Bouligny y Paret, from whom he obtained quarantine orders, and with Choiseul-Gouffier, who furnished papers and may have helped him to hire a ship; in mid-June, he received a brevet appointment as head of the Anatolian accounting office or *anadolu muhâsebecisi*, a promotion to match his new diplomatic rank.[8] Vâsıf also continued to chronicle during this time. Abdülhamid had ordered him to update his work until departure, when a temporary appointee would step in. That Vâsıf fully expected to resume the chronicle after returning from Spain is indicated both by his own words and by the author's copy, which ends abruptly and is, quite clearly, unrevised. Indeed, its last entry dates from less than a month before he sailed on July 1, 1787, bearing gifts and greetings for the Most Catholic King.[9]

Vâsıf had not foreseen such a cold reception in Barcelona, however. Having been promised quarantine on the mainland, in the city, he stood firm and sent ashore his papers from Bouligny, as well as the French ambassador's bill of health. To these documents he added a threat: that he would return to Istanbul if not allowed to land. "Consider the repercussions and give us a definite answer," he said. The authorities took several hours to consult the city's captain general, Francisco González de Bassecourt, conde del Asalto, before relenting and welcoming the ambassador ashore two days later with other civic leaders, to whom he complained vociferously. Vâsıf and his party then entered quarantine. The following twenty-seven days must have been tedious. They were also stressful in that the city had warmed to him and hundreds of spectators peered continually over the stockades, gawking at the Ottoman entourage as if they were exotic animals. To pass the time, Vâsıf asked his guards to organize music, which they did in well-attended concerts that his own men joined. Although he later derided European music as "an insufferable din," contemporaries reported that Vâsıf thoroughly enjoyed these performances. Indeed, he would attend the opera four days running after finally entering Barcelona on August 23, including stagings of

[8] SEFÂRETNÂME, fols. 329b-330a. According to BOA.C.HR 2938, the French ship was hired on 11 Ş AH 1201 = May 29, 1787, for 4,500 *kuruş*. It was important as a matter of protocol that Vâsıf's bureaucratic rank should match his status as an *orta elçi*, the equivalent of minister plenipotentiary. His promotion on 30 Ş = June 17 did just this, on which see BOA.A.RSK.d 1623, p. 37; and Afyoncu, "Tevcihat Kayıtları I," 124.

[9] MEHÂSİN 1, fol. 292b; and MEHÂSİN 2, fol. 4b. Vâsıf wrote (SEFÂRETNÂME, fol. 328b) that he and his retinue sailed from Tophane on 15 N = July 1. This date is corroborated by Ahmed Câvid, *Hadîka-i Vekâyi'*, ed. Adnan Baycar (Ankara, 1998), 158.

El mágico catalán (*The Magic of Cataluña*) in the Baroque genre of *comedia de magia*, and *La villanella rapita* (*The Abducted Country Girl*), an opera buffa in two acts. Vâsıf might have owed such musical enthusiasm to his months in Russia; in any case, it reminds us that official statements do not always match true feelings.[10]

Vâsıf's few days in Barcelona were filled with official visits, gift exchanges, and formal and informal receptions, a schedule that, along with the city's novelty, drained the newly arrived ambassador. The presence of an Ottoman dignitary – the first ever in Spain – had excited popular curiosity. Not only were he and his suite mobbed by large crowds, but they also inspired music and poems, including, of those that survive, a *corrido* by a local balladeer and a song presented to them by the maestro of the royal chapel, "Canción anacreóntica":

> Heaven grant you peace, exalted minister,
> Who came from the sublime Porte
> To make peace between the Turkish empire
> And the vast realm of Spain.
> Let all Spain rejoice and Cataluña
> Above all acclaim you,
> For behold! It first saw in its lands
> The Turkish empire's great hero!

From this period too dates a rare image of Vâsıf: an engraving of him in furs and turban bearing the legend, "Exmo. Sr. Ahamet Vaciff Effendi." Our only known credible likeness, it shows a fine-featured man with an aquiline nose and confident, slightly haughty expression. Never in his life had Vâsıf received such attention. Yet its charm must have worn thin as the unremitting physical and emotional rigors of travel took their toll. Though a vain man, and though he played his role with exactitude, Vâsıf soon complained in irritation about the constant public exposure and tried to escape it when he could. At one dinner held in his honor by the conde del Asalto, in whose palace he and his men stayed, he left the table

---

[10] SEFÂRETNÂME, fols. 329b-331b, 345b; and Conrotte, 89. According to the *Diaro de Madrid*, the quarantine station's Swiss guards held a concert every two days, including one on August 9 to an audience of 16,000. Vâsıf himself requested these, citing a "fancy" for European music. On the evening of August 25, he attended a dress rehearsal of an opera and went again the next afternoon and following two days to different productions. The *Diario* also noted his frequent gallantries toward the city's ladies. Quoted in M. Helena Sánchez Ortega, "Las relaciones hispano-turcos en el siglo XVIII," *Hispania* 49 (1989): 187–195. Also in Aceituno, 34–37.

after the first course to rest and doze, returning only a long while later for dessert.[11]

Over and above these distractions remained the more important diplomatic mission, nonetheless. In late August, the embassy set out for its rendezvous with the Spanish court nearly 400 miles inland at La Granja de San Ildefonso, the king's summer residence north of Madrid. Vâsıf was eager to see to his duties; and he felt, or perhaps just idly boasted, that the king was equally impatient to receive him. He and his train moved down the coast through Tortosa and Valencia, where he was able to compose his thoughts. The landscape pleased him. Places about which he had only ever read – cities, rivers, mountains, names – resonated from a distant past that, while long effaced, he took the time to record. But Vâsıf made room for pragmatic observations, too. He carefully noted major fortifications, for example, along with local industry and production. He above all seems to have been impressed by the country's large population, which formed a source of wonder and annoyance; the roads, he wrote in pique, were choked with throngs of spectators coming from afield and who in Valencia delayed him and even had to be forcibly restrained. The embassy pressed on. From Valencia, they turned northwest into Castile, passing through Cuenca and Valdemoro. Circling Madrid, past Las Rozas, on the evening of September 24 they reached La Granja and were put up in a lodging half a mile from town.[12]

The appearance of the ambassador and his entourage in La Granja was sheer, calculated spectacle. Ottoman embassies sought to project the empire's might, to overawe their hosts with size and splendor. Although Vâsıf was under financial constraint, he made the most of his limited resources and put on a good show. The court surely took notice. One figure who we know watched closely, if for slightly different reasons, was

---

[11] Vâsıf grumbled in SEFÂRETNÂME, fol. 331b, that crowds impeded his entry into the city, for example. On his time in Barcelona, as well as the text of Canción anacreóntica, see Aceituno, 36–37; and Conrotte, 89–90 and Appendix XI. Francisco Burguete, a local balladeer, composed a verse "romance" about Vâsıf from his arrival to his departure for Valencia, published as Relación nueva en la que se describe el arribo y desembarco, que ha hecho en el ciudad de Barcelona el dia 28. de julio de este año de 1787. El Exc.ᴹᴼ Señor enviado de la Sublime Puerta Otomana ... (Valencia, 1787). On this work see further Kutlu; and Ertuğrul Önalp, "La crónica de Ahmet Vasıf Efendi, primer embajador turco en la corte española (1787–88)," OTAM 10 (1999): 175–191. The engraving survives in the Biblioteca Nacional de España, Material gráfico, Sala Goya/Bellas Artes IV/8 (shown in image one).

[12] SEFÂRETNÂME, fols. 331b-333b. See also Aceituno, 37; and Conrotte, 91. Vâsıf said that the trip took a total of twenty-six days. This means that he and his men left Barcelona around August 30, 1787.

Floridablanca. First secretary of state since 1776, Floridablanca led a cadre of ministers who had effectively transformed Spain through the principles of Enlightened governance and political economy. Not only did he and his peers seek to consolidate royal authority, curbing traditional privileges of the nobility and Church, but they tried concertedly to encourage trade and industry, improve agriculture, and reform the administration of Spain's overseas colonies. Ties with the Ottomans fit this agenda both economically and diplomatically. In 1782, the two sides had signed a twenty-one article commercial treaty, and only after much dithering had the empire deigned to send a representative, Vâsıf, to signal its friendship and to confirm the agreement. The Spanish were naturally keen to cement their trade privileges. Just as pressing, however, was the chance for a quid pro quo. Floridablanca knew that the Ottomans needed his cooperation in case of war with Russia to blockade the Strait of Gibraltar or for any other support. In return, he could pressure them to rein in the Barbary corsairs, whose activities had long plagued the kingdom's coastal waters and damaged fishing and trade. Such an understanding does appear to have been in play. For while Vâsıf's stated mission was to present the sultan's gifts and salutations, his colleague Ahmed Azmî in Morocco indicated that he was actually seeking some kind of alliance.[13]

The embassy's first order of business was to deliver the sultan's gifts and letter to Charles and, in turn, to be received by him at court. The days preceding the audience were contentious. When visited by the master of ceremonies, Vâsıf dismissed his instructions regarding Spanish protocol. "That is your affair and we need not concern ourselves with it," he told him imperiously. "At the audience we shall behave cordially according to our own protocol." He refused to see Floridablanca before the king on the same grounds, though he ultimately agreed to a meeting if it were strictly informal. Vâsıf also protested about the respect shown to his rank. Although an *orta elçi*, or minister plenipotentiary, he demanded to be treated as a full ambassador and hence as the equal of other European

---

[13] In Nazire Karaçay Türkal, "18. Yüzyılın İkinci Yarısında Osmanlı-Fas İlişkileri: Seyyid İsmail ve Ahmed Azmi Efendilerin Fas Elçilikleri (1785–1787)" (master's thesis, Karadeniz Teknik University, 2004), 67–68. Azmî was kept apprised by an Austrian dragoman in Spain: see John Rylands Library, Turkish MS nr. 51, letter 34. The sultan's official letter (BOA.A.DVNS.NMH.d 9, pp. 206–207) by contrast says nothing of a military agreement. Floridablanca for his own part had contacted (in Conrotte, 87 ff.) his ambassadors in Paris, Vienna, and Istanbul about Ottoman diplomatic practice and how to treat their dignitary. On the intellectual climate of Spanish reform, see Gabriel Paquette, *Enlightenment, Governance, and Reform in Spain and its Empire, 1759–1808* (London, 2011).

ministers resident. Why this surprising belligerence? Granted it was real and not a later embellishment, it may be possible to appreciate Vâsıf's behavior if we consider that his position had changed markedly in only a few weeks of travel. Ottoman–Russian relations had reached a nadir during the summer of 1787. With the influential Gazi Hasan Paşa on expedition in Egypt, war hawks gained ground in Istanbul and Grand Vizier Yusuf Paşa, acting with a free hand, pressured the sultan to make escalating demands on the Russians. On August 14, the imperial council voted for war and issued an ultimatum for Russia's immediate withdrawal from the Crimea and other territories. By September, there were clashes. Vâsıf must have learned at some point after his arrival that the empire was at war, probably through the same diplomatic channels that allowed him to communicate with Azmî, and thought about how best to proceed. Securing Spain's help was now more urgent, but complicated by the presence of a hostile Russian ambassador. Some might have chosen delicacy; not so Vâsıf. Rightly or wrongly, he saw cabals everywhere and responded by bullying his hosts, insisting on rights to which he was not entitled, and trying to upstage his rival. Later, he would accuse the Russian ambassador of undermining his standing with the Spanish. He likewise claimed that a court faction had tried to blackmail him and to block his audience with the king unless he bribed them. Presumably bluffing, he threatened to call off the embassy altogether.[14]

The king received Vâsıf on September 30, 1787, a Sunday, in a lavish prearranged ceremony. From their lodgings, the Ottomans processed on horse, riding slowly, and at the royal palace, the ambassador and his train advanced through crowds and ranks of guardsmen to the accompaniment of fife and drum. Preceding all was the sultan's letter, held aloft by a steward. In the palace foyer, Vâsıf was greeted by uniformed nobles and a general who conducted him into the throne room. Charles was standing; to his right was Floridablanca and to his left the West Indies minister and other officials. Vâsıf was struck by the seventy-one-year-old king's frailty, but took the imperial letter, kissed it thrice and touched it to his forehead, and moved forward to address him. "I set towards the king with a mild, majestic air," he wrote later.

---

[14] SEFÂRETNÂME, fols. 333b-335b, 339a-340b. Conrotte (89–92) writes that Vâsıf resisted protocol on some occasions. But he adds that, in general, "his behavior caused no complaints." On the war with Russia, see Teşrifâtî Hasan, *Târih*, ÖN H.O. nr. 230, fols. 11a-16b; and Stanford Shaw, *Between Old and New: The Ottoman Empire under Sultan Selim III, 1789–1807* (Cambridge, MA, 1971), 21–27.

I said before him in a lofty voice that this was the gracious imperial letter of His Majesty Our Lord Sultan Abdülhamid Khan, and that he had deigned to appoint me as envoy with his letter and imperial gifts in order to confirm the peace which Spain had previously sought and to strengthen the bonds of friendship between us.

As Floridablanca took the letter, Charles expressed his thanks and friendship for the sultan and, the brief formalities over, had Vâsıf withdraw to meet privately with the Prince of Asturias and other *infantes*. That evening, Floridablanca fêted him. Seated at the head of table, surrounded by gold and silver settings and commanding the court's attention, Vâsıf may have reflected that he was in a very different place indeed.[15]

4.2 OBSERVING AN ENLIGHTENED COURT, 1787–1788

In the months following the royal reception Vâsıf had time to build upon his observations of Spain as well as to work toward a military accommodation. There was much to see and do. With the king's permission, he visited the Alcázar in Segovia, two hours from La Granja, where was housed the Royal Artillery College, or what he called a "military school (*talîmhâne*)." He was suitably impressed. "The school is not only filled with mathematical instruments," he remarked,

But its walls are hung with diagrams of sieges, assaults, troop formations, and mustering. Youths and others interested in artillery were busy here and there studying with teachers, and I was told that the students are supported by the king. Most of them are sons of the nobility. To demonstrate their proficiency, they drilled outside of the school with cannon and mortar and detonated mines that they had dug a month before in the field. As the weather was hot they could not complete the drills. Yet their skill was obvious.

In Segovia, Vâsıf admired the city's fortifications and textile industry – namely its high-quality but high-priced broadcloth – which Charles had recently tried to revive through royal corporation. He also made a short trip to the imposing Escorial.[16]

In early October, the court moved for the winter to Madrid, where the ambassador and his entourage lodged in the frescoed palace of Buen

---

[15] SEFÂRETNÂME, fols. 335b-339a. See also Conrotte, 91, citing a letter from one Don Jerónimo Caballero to Floridablanca on October 1, 1787, and an account in the *Gaceta de Madrid* from the twelfth of the same month.

[16] SEFÂRETNÂME, fols. 341b-342b. Vâsıf wrote that he left La Granja for the Escorial on 17 Z AH 1201 = September 30, 1787 and that he had a second audience three days later. This does not appear to be correct, since Spanish sources all attest that on September 30, he was received by the king.

Retiro and where he made diplomatic and social rounds. Vâsıf made little headway with Floridablanca on Gibraltar, though we do not know why. According to Ahmed Azmî, the Spanish agreed to close their ports if a Russian fleet appeared, but would not commit to defending the strait; he advised that the empire work instead with Britain. Floridablanca for his part called on the Ottoman envoy at least three times and wrote to Bouligny in Istanbul that "he has said nothing of business, though he and his people keep us quite busy."[17] Vâsıf was nonetheless active in the capital's social circles and, it would seem, a much sought-after guest. One figure who made his acquaintance during this period was the young English littérateur, eccentric, and pedophile William Beckford. Best known for the Oriental fantasy *Vathek*, Beckford was in Portugal and Spain to escape a scandal involving a seventeen-year-old boy. He wrote in his journal that December that he met Vâsıf during an outing to Buen Retiro, speaking through an interpreter:

Never was I more delighted than upon entering a stately saloon, spread with the richest carpets and perfumed with the fragrance of wood of aloes. In a corner of the apartment sat the Ambassador, wrapped up in a pelisse … I began asking many questions concerning Constantinople and the state of modern Turkish literature and received the most satisfactory answers indeed. I could not have addressed myself to a person better calculated to give me information, the Ambassador being one of the first scholars in the Empire and commissioned by the Sultan to write the history of his ancestors.

Within days, the two were dining and attending the opera together. Beckford took to sending Vâsıf brioche each morning and claimed that he had "quite won his heart."[18] What Vâsıf made of the young man – a quixotic foreigner who could declaim Ottoman and Persian poetry by heart – is not clear. He never mentioned the relationship. However, Beckford's journal reveals a side to Vâsıf's time in Madrid that is quite at odds with his own somber account. For the month in which he appears in the journal, Vâsıf frequented the opera, joined in a biweekly ladies' salon held by one Mme. Badaan, and attended nightly balls, dinners, and concerts. The maestro Boccherini made an appearance at one of the latter, held on December 29, at which Beckford evidently (and to the ambassador's mirth) danced a wild fandango. In January, the two went "a-cavalcading,"

---

[17] Ahmed Azmî in Türkal, 67–69. Cf. Ortega, 181. William Beckford claimed that Vâsıf's rooms in Buen Retiro had once belonged to the famed castrato Farinelli (d. 1782). See *Italy; with Sketches of Spain and Portugal* (London, 1835), 2: 306.

[18] Beckford, *Journal*, 191–193, 196. Entries for 14, 18, and 23 December 1787.

FIG. 4.2: William Beckford (d. 1844), littérateur and eccentric known for the Gothic tale *Vathek*. Reproduced by kind permission of the National Portrait Gallery, London.

picnicking and racing horses. But while he relished Madrid's social life, Vâsıf did not entirely neglect his work. Beckford also recorded his meeting the envoy of Tripoli, with whose twelve-year-old brother he, Beckford, was smitten.[19]

---

[19] Beckford's journal must be carefully differentiated from his *Sketches*, a later work based on the journal that is heavily edited and alternately omits or interpolates material, sometimes as pure fabrication. His fandango, which purportedly outraged Boccherini, may be one of these inventions. The *Journal* mentions Vâsıf (197–208) in entries for 14, 18, 22, 23, 26, and 29 December 1787 and for 1, 3, 5, 8, 9, 11, 12, 14, and 19 January 1788. Cf. idem, *Sketches*, 2: 306–309, 330–334, 339, 358, 363–364. See also Malcolm Jack, *William Beckford: An English Hidalgo* (New York, 1996).

It is fair at this point to ask how Vâsıf's time in Spain affected him intellectually. Did it leave a lasting impression? Did it shape his later thinking on politics or reform? This is a question that we cannot fully answer for the reason that he did not express his opinions on the matter. That Spain was a Christian kingdom did not pose insuperable obstacles. Ottoman intellectuals long recognized a basic division between divine and human political authority and held that régimes might rule through revealed law (siyâset-i ilâhiyye), human reason (siyâset-i 'akliyye), or some combination thereof. The relationship between revelation and reason was a classic problem for Islamic thinkers. While humans were "political beings" capable of reason and political organization, they held, or in Aristotle's terms zoon politikon, human reason was inferior to divine wisdom and needed guidance in the form of a revealed prophetic law. This fact did not necessarily preclude human legislation or even rational inquiry. Revelation and reason could and did aspire to a similar aim: happiness. The question, then, had to do with the respective spheres of divine and man-made law in the polity. While Ottomans agreed that revealed law was always the best basis for government, some admitted, though not without controversy, that if human reason could not guarantee salvation, it might at least offer models for worldly order and prosperity.[20] Vâsıf himself could not help but notice the effects of Bourbon Spain's centralizing, rationalizing policies. The building of new roads, canals, and infrastructure; the curbing of privileges and consolidation of regal power; the establishment of crown corporations; the promotion of trade and industry – the fruits of reform were all around him. In many cases, he recorded them; in some, he expressed admiration. Still, Vâsıf neither openly engaged with these specific concepts nor adopted any new ideas wholesale. If anything, he and other Ottomans who traveled abroad were apt to fit what they saw in Europe into their own frameworks. That is to say, they did not simply absorb novelties, but tried to harmonize them, selectively, with what they already knew.

We would thus be unwise to read Vâsıf's account of Spain or the words of any eighteenth-century Ottoman visitor to Europe for clear signs of

---

[20] Human law might provide good order, material prosperity, and perhaps even justice, but only a state ruled in accordance with divinely revealed law (sharî'a) could ensure subjects salvation in the hereafter. For example, Ibn Khaldûn argued in the fourteenth century that there were three types of polity: religious nomocracy (siyâsa dîniyya), the state based on reason (siyâsa'aqliyya), and the "Virtuous City" of Plato's Republic (siyâsa madaniyya). See Crone, 259 ff.; and E. Rosenthal, Political Thought in Medieval Islam: An Introductory Outline (Cambridge, 1962), 84–109. The Ottomans drew directly on this philosophical inheritance: see Hagen, "Legitimacy and World Order," 67–71.

"Western impact." After all, such encounters were highly conflicted. The idea that early modern Ottomans inevitably absorbed European influence while abroad, as if by osmosis, ignores some major practical and intellectual hurdles.[21] Ottoman envoys rarely spoke foreign languages before the nineteenth century, for example. Vâsıf knew little or no Spanish. He had limited contact with locals and relied in his interactions on interpreters, without whom he was effectively deaf and dumb. Vâsıf also had an unflagging faith in the empire and its institutions, laws, and cultural and moral superiority. It was a great struggle for him to digest the realm's late defeats, much less to accept the fact that the non-Muslim world now exceeded his own in military and economic power. What could a middling kingdom like Spain teach his civilization? We should not downplay the mental barriers that he and others faced. An Ottoman ambassador might at times explore a host culture and its customs, but this interest was usually personal and of much less weight than geopolitical goals. Vâsıf had a political mission. He also had a keen desire to help his empire and to restore its greatness. It should come as no surprise, then, that he filtered his observations accordingly and that his view of Spain was, at best, ambivalent.

Vâsıf certainly continued to scrutinize the structure of Spanish society and government that fall and winter. He marveled at the canals near Madrid, for example, which linked the city to the ocean, facilitated industry, and reminded him of those about which he had read in France. He came to appreciate the size of Spain's navy and overseas empire in Africa, Asia, and the Americas as well as the immense revenues these colonies produced. If he deplored the state of agriculture or high prices, or the character of Spaniards themselves, his political evaluation of the kingdom was on the whole positive.[22] Vâsıf was likewise interested in how the realm was governed. He soon understood. Charles, who in his opinion was a shrewd monarch, effectively delegated power to a council of state that Floridablanca had established and over which he presided. This was the so-called *Junta Suprema de Estado*. "The king delegates his affairs to ministers and assigns one to each of the following fields: the West Indies, the naval shipyards, legal suits, the arsenal, military mobilization, and domestic and foreign affairs," he remarked.

None may interfere with another. The first minister quite clearly oversees foreign affairs and is charged with reporting news from abroad. He privately watches the

---

[21] Burçak, 147 ff.   [22] SEFÂRETNÂME, fols. 346a-346b, 349a, 350b-351b.

other ministers' doings; and no matter how they may plead with or even petition the king, they will get no hearing if they do not toe his line.

The king thus maintained some indirect control through Floridablanca, even though he spent most of his time hunting. To Vâsıf, such an arrangement was familiar. Being concerned with reform and factionalism in his own realm, he furthermore saw how the council disciplined wayward voices and allowed the government to form concerted policy.[23]

There may be hints that Spain shaped Vâsıf's ideas at a still more basic and conceptual level. Consider, for one, his words on political relations with non-Muslims. Vâsıf wrote on the Christian powers of Europe extensively and seems to betray a shift in tone after the embassy, as seen in his treatment of a memorable 1774 event. In July 1771, Austria entered into a secret pact with the empire with promises of diplomatic and military aid against Russia, an agreement that it soon vacated. After Kaynarca, however, Austria exploited the realm's weakness and annexed the territory of Bukovina in Moldavia for its troubles as an "ally."[24] Vâsıf first noted this episode in his chronicle in 1783–1784. "It is in no way licit to trust Christian countries," the historian said, "and absurd to think that infidels will aid Islam in wartime."

Yet under Mustafa III the villainous Austrians duped our empire and agreed in return for some considerations to check the Muscovite by force of arms or diplomacy. They even sent troops into Poland and made as if ready for war. However, the lands they conspired to annex with Russia in the partition of Poland did not satisfy and they pressed for more gains, claiming great expenses and demanding the agreed part of Moldavia from our empire in lieu of cash ... No matter how much the late Grand Vezir İzzet Mehmed Paşa, chief scribe İsmail Paşa, and other statesmen resisted – arguing the Austrians had not kept their side of the deal – it was in vain. Peace had just been made with Russia and a refusal would have meant war. They thus complied according to the adage, "Choose the lesser of two evils."[25]

This same event took a markedly different cast, nevertheless, when in a later work, Vâsıf framed "Austria's perfidy" in terms of human nature, a shared balance of power, and the failure of other states to intervene. Balance is a respected concept in politics, he wrote, so that it is customary for states to unite against an aggressor and take action. Yet some had now abandoned this practice:

---

[23] Ibid, fols. 342b-343a.   [24] Aksan, *Ottoman Statesman*, 155–157; and Köse, 56–57.
[25] İLGÜREL, 166–167, sub anno hegirae 1198 = 1783/84. Vâsıf expressed (MEHÂSİN 1, fols. 39a, 74b; and İLGÜREL, 169) these sentiments elsewhere in the chronicle with a hadith, "Unbelief is a nation unto itself." Cf. D'Ohsson, 1: 40–41.

Men are prone to evil and vice by nature, hence they fawn and constantly seek to gain advantages ... In this campaign, then, the Austrians secretly agreed to enter the war as needed to help us against the Russian enemy; they even acted as if they would honor this provision by sending men to the frontier. Yet we saw no trace of their promised aid or a declaration of war – and they not only indemnified the empire for so-called expenses but also annexed nine districts of territory from Moldavia. Those who are privy to our era's secrets know that the empire, exhausted by its six-year war with Russia, bore this injury perforce.[26]

While Vâsıf blamed Austria's betrayal in the first instance, in the 1780s, on the innate enmity of non-Muslims – using legal and religious key-words – by the 1790s, he had begun to stress political calculation and a balance of power that included both Christians and Ottomans. The Austrians wagered, correctly, that fellow states "would look the other way at their opportunism" and took full advantage. The Ottomans were thus left helpless, by no small fault of their own.

It is hard to say what role, if any, Vâsıf's time abroad played in these shifts in rhetoric. His service as an ambassador may well have proved a real lesson, offering a deeper insight into diplomacy and teaching him the practical value of cooperation with neighbors, Muslim or no. It may also be that the experience opened Vâsıf's eyes to the wider world, breaking down some of his ingrained cultural and intellectual prejudices. We should not forget social context, however. Vâsıf wrote as a courtier. He dedicated his chronicle and other works to an imperial master, and as such tried to suit both his patron's views and the prevailing mood in Istanbul. The change in his attitude toward "infidel" powers may not reflect his own views at all or, at least, may signal a general shift at court to active foreign engagement. Perhaps not by coincidence did Vâsıf begin using the idea of a "balance of power" in the 1790s, when Sultan Selim III sought to forge more lasting diplomatic ties and to enter fully the concert of Europe. As is often the case in biography, we cannot hope to tell what Vâsıf truly believed or to distinguish the private man from his public guise as courtier and statesman. The two, in fact, are likely inseparable. The most that we can do here is take note – and, for foreign relations, the shift is unmistakable.

Let us also briefly consider reform. The intellectual currents to which Vâsıf and fellow Ottomans were exposed while abroad, directly or indirectly, were very different from their existing views. The notion of a primordial world order that so dominated pre-modern Ottoman political writing and restricted the scope of reform was, in many ways,

[26] MEHÂSİN 5, 2: 307–308.

absolutely alien to Enlightenment concepts like historical progress and the perfectibility of man. That reason could be widely applied to political problems – not only in the limited military sphere, but in administration, finances, the economy, and even social order – is something that the historian increasingly asserted after 1788, however. For example, Ottomans regarded economics as a branch of Aristotelian practical philosophy and the proper management of the household or *oikonomia*. In this sense, it is hard to speak of Ottoman economic thought at all outside of how they applied such principles to the sultan's household in its widest sense, that of the realm. They had no abstract concept of an "economy."[27] Yet Vâsıf saw very different premises in Spain. He became familiar with political economy, the principles of which were widely popular among the Bourbon reformers. By the early 1790s, he also began to speak more generally about commerce as a subject "worth consideration" and adopted a stridently mercantilist position, stressing the empire's need to maintain a positive flow of specie and to intervene directly in concerns like manufacturing and trade in order to compete with other states. To be clear, we cannot simply credit these developments to Vâsıf's time abroad. Ottomans had been aware of mercantilist arguments since at least the late seventeenth century. Nor were his efforts to widen the scope of reform especially revolutionary; they merely fed an ongoing debate over human law and how reason could, or should, solve political problems. It is nonetheless true that the embassy marks a distinct change in how Vâsıf spoke about reform. Whether from personal experience or zeitgeist, his growing calls for economic and social intervention began to stretch older concepts like world order to the breaking point. The embassy played a role in this, albeit an unclear one.[28]

Vâsıf's psychological state was more obviously affected by the voyage. For him, Spain's present was not easily uncoupled from its history as

---

[27] See Fatih Ermiş, *A History of Ottoman Economic Thought: Developments Before the Nineteenth Century* (London, 2014), esp. 81–110. This work must be used with caution.

[28] Vâsıf assumed that the world had a finite amount of wealth and that the empire had to protect its balance of trade, lest other countries, Russia and India above all, siphon off its wealth. For examples, see MEHÂSİN 2, fols. 160b-162b; and MEHÂSİN 4, fols. 183a-183b. Among his practical suggestions was to have wealthy statesmen invest in trading ventures (MEHÂSİN 2, fols. 165a-166b) and to force children and the unemployed into trade schools on the example of European states (ibid, fols. 169b-170a). This last scheme advocates total employment, an idea that Paquette highlights (40–45) in contemporary works of Spanish political economy. However, Ottomans observed similar situations elsewhere in Europe. Yeşil offers an instructive example in Ebubekir Râtib (esp. 142–144, 214–230), who came under the influence of German cameralism in Vienna. See also Ermiş, 121–162.

a formerly Muslim land and, for all that he admired in the kingdom's military and economic power, he reflected on what had been lost. Vâsıf knew the history of al-Andalus and the Reconquista, a summary of which he added to his report. He took careful note of ruins, landmarks, and the hometowns of famous scholars. At the Escorial, he visited the royal library and even became quite emotional on seeing its Arabic manuscripts. "When the Christians seized al-Andalus they gathered Islamic books and deposited them in two collections," he recalled.

One of these burned. The other they moved to this library ... I saw some ten Qurans in the collection and a great many works of jurisprudence, traditions, and theology, some of them written in Egyptian script and some in Maghrebi. Grief and sadness overcame me.[29]

Vâsıf's musings were not unconnected to his own situation, of course. There were parallels and lessons to be had from the past. That he blamed al-Andalus' fall on misrule, stupidity, and infighting in his historical précis to some extent reflected his own anxieties. Were the Ottomans not on a similar path? The empire was far from united; the factionalism that he so abhorred but participated in was a mortal danger, doubly so in wartime, and threatened the realm with further disintegration. In Madrid, Vâsıf had encountered Muslims from Spanish-controlled Oran. Why did they live under an infidel king, he demanded? Their answer – that they preferred Spanish rule – was a stinging rebuke.[30] Vâsıf on the other hand applauded the Barbary corsairs, whose success against the Spanish was something to be emulated. The Algerians acted with strength and impunity despite having signed a treaty, he observed:

One day I asked an Algerian who had come to Madrid for trade and who visited me from time to time, "Why did you make peace when your livelihood comes from the Spanish?" He replied that it was all to their advantage. The peace would last three years at most and they had lost none of their earlier gains. They had enough from the Spanish to last two or three years; there was no harm whatsoever for them.

---

[29] SEFÂRETNÂME, fols. 344a-345a. Vâsıf acquired a two-volume catalog of this collection, which he described as being in Latin and Hebrew. He also left notes throughout his report on cities and landmarks: e.g. on Barcelona as the home of "a great many scholars and pious men" (fol. 332b); on the name of Madrid under Muslim rule (fol. 346a); and on Murcia as the birthplace of Ibn al-'Arabî (fol. 347a).

[30] Vâsıf's capsule history of al-Andalus (SEFÂRETNÂME, fols. 349a-350b) attributes its collapse to the fourth Almohad ruler Muḥammad al-Nâṣir (d. 1213), whose "idiocy and misrule" fractured the realm and led to the disastrous 1212 defeat at Las Navas de Tolosa (al-'Iqâb). He cited the said Muslim subjects of Spain in MEHÂSİN 2, fol. 132b, as a warning against misrule.

Yet an ostensible peace did not stop the Algerians from continuing to prey on shipping or from forcing the Spanish to pay ransoms. Indeed, Vâsıf praised their "unity, steadfast faith, and devotion to jihad." For him, they exemplified those qualities which the empire most needed but, sadly, most lacked.[31]

Nor did the news from home quiet the ambassador's anxieties. The empire had declared war in haste, late in the season, and despite a few engagements on the Black Sea, the front had remained quiet. There would perforce be a spring campaign. But Koca Yusuf Paşa's highhandedness had strained his relations with Gazi Hasan Paşa. Now returned from Egypt, Gazi Hasan criticized the war's timing and management and bickered openly with the Grand Vizier, a quarrel causing further delays. We do not know exactly where Vâsıf sided in this particular dispute. He too hoped that the Crimea would one day be restored to the empire, by force if need be, but judging from his earlier and later words, he likely agreed with Gazi Hasan that the realm was not ready to face the Russian army without further reform. It was certainly not ready for a two-front war. When Austria joined Russia against the empire in late February, then, the situation appeared to be very serious and Vâsıf had no more reason to tarry in Spain. He was needed in Istanbul.[32]

In early March, Charles III summoned Vâsıf to the Escorial for the last time to give an official reply to the sultan. Vâsıf then took his leave. The embassy traveled southeast via Murcia to the Mediterranean port of Cartagena, where they met dignitaries and exchanged gifts and farewells. Vâsıf noted the city's large naval arsenal, bustling quays, and facilities for sailcloth and rope.[33] There he also met Don Federico Gravina y Nápoli, captain of the thirty-four-gun frigate *Santa Rosa* that would carry him home and with whom he sailed on April 1, 1788. The winds were initially fair; proceeding northeast, in three days the *Santa Rosa* passed Majorca and Minorca. Upon entering the Gulf of León, however, the ship weathered a storm that shredded the topsails and forced it to stop for three days in La Valletta, Malta, for repairs. Ruled by the Knights of St. John, a crusading order that raided Muslim shipping, Malta had long been

---

[31] SEFÂRETNÂME, fols. 351b-353b.

[32] According to Taylesanizâde Hâfız Abdullah (*İstanbul'un Uzun Dört Yılı (1785–1789)*, ed. Feridun Emecen [Istanbul, 2003], 1: 289), Vâsıf informed the court of his pending return in March or April 1788. Shaw presumes (e.g. *Old and New*, 34) that Yusuf Paşa and Gazi Hasan led rival factions, but, in fact, the latter had been Yusuf's long-time patron and ally. Cf. DİA, s.v. "Yusûf Paşa, Koca."

[33] SEFÂRETNÂME, fols. 347a-348a. See also Aceituno, 38, citing the *Gaceta de Madrid* from March 7, 1788; and Conrotte, 92.

FIG. 4.3: Federico Gravina y Nápoli (d. 1806), naval officer and captain of the ship that returned Vâsıf to Istanbul. Reproduced by kind permission of the Biblioteca Nacional de España.

a concern for the empire and before resuming the voyage, Vâsıf used his unexpected shore leave to gather information on the island as well as to liberate seven Muslim prisoners. The *Santa Rosa* then returned to sea. Forced ashore again, briefly, at Sigri on the island of Lesbos, Vâsıf and his party entered the Dardanelles several weeks later on May 3 and anchored at Çanakkale. Gravina had been warned in Malta that the Ottomans were keeping foreign vessels out of Istanbul. He could not in any case enter the straits in an unauthorized warship and they waited six days for permission and a favorable wind. At last, on May 12, the *Santa Rosa* entered the Golden Horn in Istanbul and Vâsıf, thanking Gravina for his courtesies, set foot on Muslim territory. He had been gone for ten months and twelve days.[34]

Like any returning envoy, Vâsıf's most immediate task was to report to the sultan and court in a memo called an embassy report or *sefâretnâme*. By the late eighteenth century, such reports had become standard. Highly formal and conventional, indeed a distinct literary genre, the *sefâretnâme* gave fellow bureaucrats an account of the ambassador's itinerary as well as of the host country and its people and culture. Lengths could vary; some were brief, while still others numbered hundreds of pages. But if these reports offered readers a glimpse into the unknown, they also allowed the author to present his time abroad to best advantage. It is almost certain that Vâsıf had considered how to write his own embassy report. He was familiar with the genre and more especially with the popular models of Yirmisekiz Çelebi Mehmed and Ahmed Resmî – landmarks in the genre's development and in Ottoman awareness of Europe – which had perhaps formed part of his reading the spring before. Vâsıf may even have started to write before landfall. The result was a carefully structured narrative, composed, he said, "in simple and unlabored prose" and giving an up-to-date account of Spanish affairs, geography, and history along with intelligence on Malta and North Africa.[35] However, what is most

---

[34] SEFÂRETNÂME, fols. 348a-349a. Vâsıf wrote (MEHÂSİN 5, 1: 82–83) that the *Santa Rosa* anchored at Sigri to weather a spell of rough weather and to take on provisions. As the warship was flying foreign colors, he had to send a messenger ashore to calm the garrison. Gravina's records furnish further details on the voyage. The captain received his sailing orders in January 1788 and arrived in Cartagena in mid-February to make preparations. His log notes the exact itinerary, though certain place names are now hard to establish. The *Santa Rosa*, as best we can tell, rounded the Morea after its repairs in Malta and entered the Aegean islands, passing "Cerico (Serifos?)," Chios, Lesbos, and Tenedos. According to Gravina and the ambassador Bouligny, it reached Istanbul on May 12, 1788, at two o'clock in the afternoon. José Sánchez Molledo, "El viaje de Federico Gravina a Constantinopla en 1788," *Arbor* 180 (2005): 732–734. However, contemporary Ottoman sources date its arrival a day earlier to May 11, 1788 (= 5 Ş AH 1202). Ali Osman Çınar, ed., "Mehmed Emin Edîb Efendi'nin Hayatı ve Târîhi" (Ph.D. diss., Marmara University, 1999), 18.

[35] SEFÂRETNÂME, fol. 328a. Vâsıf had likely read about French canals in Yirmisekiz Mehmed Çelebi's 1721 embassy report, namely the Canal du Midi. Cf. Göçek, 20–23. He also later praised and included Resmî's two reports in MEHÂSİN 5, 1: 120–132,

striking about the report is not so much the content as the tone. Although he privately assured Bouligny of his gratitude and vowed that "Spain is a great power and close friend of the Porte," Vâsıf took every opportunity in the embassy report to disparage his hosts, minimizing his interactions with the Spanish, belittling their culture and morés, and playing up his own petty triumphs. He complained bitterly about their stinginess – they neither gave him gifts nor adequately covered his expenses, he claimed – though this was untrue. Vâsıf had in fact received very valuable gifts like a diamond ring worth 14,000 reals, a pink diamond worth 2,770 reals, a gold box, and bales of fabric. The Spanish had also provided generously for his interpreter and servants. His comments were at best mean-spirited and at worst deliberate falsehoods.[36]

What are we to make of Vâsıf's report? Some scholars have attributed its pettiness and bombast to a closed, unreceptive mind, one even dismissing it outright as "a valuable lesson in the limitations of the genre."[37] This is a misreading. Vâsıf was highly intelligent and not normally close-minded. Yet he was self-serving enough to lie when it worked to his benefit. It is better to assume instead that he crafted the whole of the report quite deliberately. More specifically, it is likely that he let serious professional and economic concerns color his account. While undoubtedly happy to be home, Vâsıf discovered on arrival that his position in Istanbul had changed for the worse. He returned with little to show his superiors, having failed to secure an alliance or even an informal understanding with the Spanish, and evidently without much of an attempt to do so. Scapegoating his hosts and

239–262. On the genre itself, see Kemal Beydilli, "Sefaret ve Sefaretnâme Hakkında Yeni Bir Değerlendirme," *Journal of Ottoman Studies* 30 (2007): 9–30; Michael Bonner and Gottfried Hagen, "Muslim Accounts of the *dâr al-ḥarb*," in *The New Cambridge History of Islam*, ed. Robert Irwin (Cambridge, 2010), 4: 482 f; and DİA, s.v. "Sefâretnâme."

[36] Vâsıf claimed (SEFÂRETNÂME, fols. 341a, 346b-347a) among other things that the Spanish presented him with 3,500 reals when he arrived in lieu of other gifts, which they later held against the cost of his food and supplies. He also said that they gave nothing to his interpreter, as a result of which he was forced to pay 600 *kuruş* out of pocket. It is obvious from Vâsıf's own estimate of the exchange rate (one real = 2.5 *kuruş*) that these gifts were hugely valuable, worth at least 40,000 *kuruş*. Cf. Ortega, 182; and Conrotte, 92, who says that Vâsıf's dragoman and suite received a lump sum of 2,050 piasters and who alternately values the ring at 90,000 reals. In mid-May, Juan Bouligny wrote (quoted in Molledo, 735) to Floridablanca: "As for Vâsıf Efendi, he continues for now to praise the kindness, generosity, and grandeur of His Majesty and our court in the most appreciative terms, assuring me that Spain is a great power and a close friend of the Porte."

[37] Aksan, *Ottoman Statesman*, 36. This impression is due partly to the fact that scholars have relied on an incomplete and much expurgated version found in Cevdet, *Târih*, 4: 348–358. These excisions must have occurred at a very early date, for they appear in the report as copied by the contemporary court historian Mehmed Edîb Efendi (18–32).

focusing on trifles was an easy remedy. The need to show some sort of victory, however small, was also imperative in that Vâsıf was facing unemployment. The year before, he had been promised his post as court historian – or so he believed. The government had named a replacement, a low-level scribe named Teşrifâtî Hasan Efendi, with the tacit understanding that Vâsıf would resume his duties in the following year; the fact that the embassy was little better than exile did not, consequently, stop him from hoping to regain his footing in the bureaucracy and to once again take up his chronicle and his work in the financial section. But the war changed everything. By the time the *Santa Rosa* docked in Istanbul, the Ottoman army had taken to the field with the Grand Vizier and much of the reshuffled bureaucracy. Vâsıf learned that his old post now belonged to two others: Sadullah Enverî and Mehmed Edîb, who were recording events in the army and capital, respectively. He later recalled:

While I was, of course, sorely tried by my embassy, the sultan had expressly ordered that the said position be given to a proxy till my return. However, the imperial army had already marched by the time I finished my duties and reached Istanbul. As it is old custom for court historians to accompany the army, Enverî Efendi was reappointed *in propria persona*.[38]

Vâsıf had lost out. The fact that he brought with him from Spain a small fortune in gifts does not appear to have calmed his worries over the post's lost prestige and income. With his job in the suspended payments office also reassigned and his brevet appointment set to expire, his near-term prospects were dim. He therefore tried his best to salvage the situation and hurriedly submitted his report along with letters from Charles III and Floridablanca. All he could do then was wait.[39]

---

[38] MEHÂSİN 5, fol. 4b. Kütükoğlu dates ("Vekâyi'nüvis," 118) Enverî's appointment to 24 N AH 1201 = July 10, 1787. This is too early in that it falls before the Ottoman declaration of war. Teşrifâtî Hasan's work ends (ÖN H.O. nr. 230, fol. 18b) with the army's departure from Istanbul on 9 C AH 1202 = March 17, 1788. Enverî himself wrote (*Târih*, ÖN H.O. nr. 105, fols. 3b, 6b) that his appointment began "the day that the imperial army left the plains of Davud Paşa" or 11 C = March 19. Edîb for his part began (3) chronicling on 9 C or March 17.

[39] SEFÂRETNÂME, fol. 328a. See also Cevdet, *Târih*, 4: 39, 51–52. Vâsıf was dismissed in absentia as *mevkûfâtçı* on 1 R AH 1202 = January 10, 1788. See BOA.A.RSK.d 1623, p. 37; and Afyoncu, "Tevcihat Kayıtları I," 124. Interestingly, on May 15, 1788, Bouligny wrote (quoted in Molledo, 735) as follows: "The day before yesterday I congratulated [Vâsıf] on his safe arrival. He in turn sent me His Majesty's letters to the sultan and Grand Vizier as well as Your Excellency's [Floridablanca] to the latter and the Grand Admiral, begging for a French translation to better read and submit them to the sultan and etc. I immediately obliged him." It is not at all clear why Vâsıf made this request.

5

At War (1788–1792)

5.1 WARTIME ISTANBUL, 1788–1791

Vâsıf was nearly fifty-three years old when he returned to Istanbul in the spring of 1788. Approaching old age, he no longer had the luxury of time and could see that his career was in serious jeopardy. That he had staked relationships and standing for private gain was not a mortal sin by the standards of Ottoman bureaucracy – indeed, his punishment was mild and the embassy gave him the chance to save face – nor was it probably something that he regretted. But reentering professional life was hard. For one thing, Vâsıf had fewer friends than before. He was gaining an unsavory reputation for greed and hypocrisy and had made powerful enemies, men like Mehmed Râşid, who during his absence had become chief scribe and head of the bureaucracy as a whole.[1] Vâsıf also could not hide his failings as an ambassador, try as he might through rhetoric or bombast. When his report did not yield a new post, he was forced like any jobless scribe to wait two months for the bureaucracy's yearly round of dismissals and appointments. He was still a bureau chief and could hope

---

[1] We gain some idea of Vâsıf's reputation from a manuscript of his history in Berlin (Ms.or. quart nr. 1116, fol. 93a), where, beside a moralizing passage on a greedy minister, one reader wrote: "In fairness, O historian, was your behavior any better in being made ambassador to Spain?" Mehmed Râşid replaced Feyzî Süleyman Efendi as chief scribe on 12 Ra AH 1202 = December 22, 1787. Afyoncu, "Tevcihat Kayıtları I," 139. As Fâik and Edîb explain (130 and 84, respectively), Râşid initially left on campaign with the imperial army, but was recalled to Istanbul when his proxy, Mehmed Nahîfî Efendi, died. He returned to manage the capital's scribal affairs in the fall of 1788. Vâsıf later wrote (MEHÂSİN 3, fol. 182a) that while Râşid was thereafter only the proxy chief scribe, he in fact retained full control of the bureaucracy for two and a half years.

for placement, but there was a real prospect that he would never regain his old prominence as a statesmen and historian.

It was cold comfort to Vâsıf when general appointments at last took place that July. Although he secured a job, his new title as head of the poll-tax accounting office, or *cizye muhâsebecisi*, was at the same level as his earlier positions and a distinct demotion from those he had held in Spain. The poll-tax office handled the special tax, or *cizye*, levied on non-Muslims. One of twenty-two offices in the lowest level of the treasury, it prepared receipts for the tax's collection and kept the names of district guarantors, which it turned over to the courts for inspection every year in the lunar month of Muharrem.[2] There were of course advantages in the post. Namely, it was a paid position in Istanbul that did not require his presence at the front. Vâsıf was certainly not eager to join the army and had no qualms whatsoever with remaining behind, in comfort and in safety, in the capital. But the post was a step back in terms of prestige. So too did it keep him stuck at the bottom of the treasury and far from his ideal seat in the scribal corps. It may well be that the assignment was a deliberate slight. Early biographers claim that Vâsıf's enemies, notably those around the chief scribe, conspired at this time to deprive him of all but the most poorly paid offices and to reduce him to poverty. It is plausible that he faced open hostility in reviving his career in addition to a poor reputation and lack of patrons. Given his pecuniary habits, however, it seems unlikely that Vâsıf was ever as poor as he led on. To colleagues, he was merely playing a pauper. Not only was he sanctimonious and untrustworthy, they held, but continually after handouts – in the words of Âsım, "a sweet-talker as grasping as an importunate beggar."[3]

The war's first year brought a mix of excitement and hardship to Istanbul. As Vâsıf worked in the treasury, reports filtered in announcing the losses of Khotin and Jassy to the Austrians and the rout of the Ottoman Black Sea fleet; in early September, the Russians invested the key fortress of Özü. Such setbacks were to be expected in a two-front war,

---

[2] This appointment occurred on 4 L AH 1202 = July 8, 1788. See BOA.A.RSK.d 1623, p. 37; Afyoncu, "Tevcihat Kayıtları I," 124; and Schlechta-Wssehrd, 6. On the post itself, see Uzunçarşılı, *Osmanlı Devleti*, 348, 357.

[3] Fâik, Fâtin, and Karslızâde (pp. 147, 432, and 64, respectively) all accept this rumor. Âsım contrasts (1: 256–257, 259) Vâsıf's offices during this time with those before and after, adding that "the best way is the middle way." He also accuses him of habitually petitioning the palace and other grandees for financial aid. Cf. TSMA.d 4819 in Uzunçarşılı, "III. Sultan Selim Zamanında Yazılmış Dış Ruznâmesinden 1206/1791 ve 1207/1792 Senelerine Âit Vekayi," *Belleten* 37 (1973): 611.

especially against better equipped adversaries. Less foreseeable was the Grand Vizier's brilliant success on the Danube, where he drove into the Banat, took the strategic town of Mehadiye, and, at Slatina on September 20, defeated the main Austrian army. Koca Yusuf then pressed his advantage early the next spring, threatening to break out over the Carpathian Mountains into the Austrian rear.[4] While Vâsıf surely celebrated these victories with the capital's inhabitants, not all was well. The winter was severe. Prices rose sharply and the government took measures to blunt food shortages and illegal hoarding. In late December, a fire also gutted the government offices at the Sublime Porte (*Bâb-ı Âli*), though damage to official records was minimal. But the most stunning news of all came the morning of April 7, 1789: the sultan was dead. Abdülhamid I had passed away in his sixty-eighth year, felled by a stroke.[5]

The crown prince Selim, Abdülhamid's successor, came to the throne that April amid widespread hope that he would not only lead the empire to victory, but restore its past glories. Such hopes were not entirely unwarranted. The son of Mustafa III, Selim was youthful, cultured, and appeared to have the makings of a fine ruler. Born in 1761, he had enjoyed under his father a freedom and education quite uncommon for an Ottoman prince, attending the imperial council and observing the late sultan's military reforms. He read extensively, loved music, and wrote poetry under the name İlhâmî, "the divinely-inspired." Selim also harbored well-known reformist sympathies. Kept to the palace by his uncle Abdülhamid, Selim had been part of a rumored plot by Grand Vizier Halil Paşa who, it was said, wished to replace the sultan with a more amenable figure. He similarly corresponded with the French king Louis XVI, courting him for future military and technical aid. It is incorrect to see Selim III as an "enlightened monarch," however, at least as far as his premises and motivations were concerned. Selim's interest in reform came from the same beliefs that drove earlier Ottoman thinkers rather than from any philosophical program of rationalism or benevolent absolutism – it came, namely, from a conviction that the empire needed to restore "world order" and thus its old greatness. This view had shaped the prince from

---

[4] These campaigns are detailed in Enverî, ÖN H.O. nr. 105; and in Mehmed Sâdık Zaîmzâde, *Vak'a-ı Hamîdiyye* (Istanbul, 1872). See also Shaw, *Old and New*, 29–32.

[5] Edîb, 89–91, 102. The fire occurred on 24 Ra AH 1203 = December 23, 1788. According to Edîb, Abdülhamid took ill on 10 B AH 1203 (April 6, 1788) and died before sunrise the following morning. Cf. Enverî, H.O. nr. 105, fols. 98b-99a, who records his death date as April 9. Used or owned by Vâsıf, this manuscript contains a marginal note in his hand (fol. 99a) sharply correcting Enverî. See also Sarıcaoğlu, 34–35.

The Grand Seignior.

FIG. 5.1: Selim III (reg. 1789–1807).

an early age. Palace astrologers declared him a "world conqueror" at birth, for which reason he was named after his forebear Selim I, conqueror of the Holy Cities, the Levant, and Egypt. Selim III sincerely thought that he was destined by God to restore the empire and, more to the point, to avenge its recent humiliation and territorial losses. Though not single-minded, this belief guided much of his activity as monarch.[6]

Vâsıf too entertained high hopes for the sultan. As a bureau chief, he would have attended Selim's formal enthronement, or *cülûs*, at the palace and gone afterwards to the Porte, where he and other dignitaries received robes of honor from the Grand Vizier's proxy, Sâlih Paşa. He may also have been in the royal audience chamber the next day to hear Mehmed Râşid read aloud the sultan's first decree, in which he confirmed Yusuf Paşa as his Grand Vizier and vowed to fight the war "until we have revenge on the enemies of our faith, the Russian and Austrian infidels."[7] But besides being a time of pomp and celebration, Selim's accession was a distinct opportunity for Vâsıf. The reign promised to open new doors. Vâsıf did not mourn Abdülhamid, who, he felt, had never properly appreciated his genius. His position might fast improve if Selim proved to be wise and generous or if he could attach himself to one of the favorites who stood to influence the new reign. Ebubekir Râtib Efendi, Mustafa Reşîd Efendi, Küçük Hüseyin Ağa, Tatarcık Abdullah Efendi – these men and others like them were key. Most had known Selim as a prince. They shared his vision for the empire and soon acquired top posts or acted behind the scenes as a camarilla. There was little doubt that such "new men" would welcome Vâsıf's views. Yet Vâsıf's future depended as much on establishing good relations with them as on his prior reformist credentials. Although the sultan made his intent to reform the empire clear only a month after coming to the throne, at a council in the palace's Revan Pavilion, connections were what mattered most in patrimonial Ottoman society. Vâsıf himself had learned too well not to overvalue things like principle.[8]

Selim moved with great energy during his first months in power. He began by removing members of the old guard like the still Grand Admiral Gazi Hasan Paşa and by installing his own men in their stead; he similarly gained the military's support by granting a bonus and issuing wages in

---

[6] On Selim III's birth and upbringing, see DİA, s.v. "Selim III"; Ahmet Cevat Eren, *Selim III'ün Biografyası* (Istanbul, 1964), 5–12; and Âsım, 1: 347–349. On his music and poetry, see Necati Elgin, *Üçüncü Sultan Selim (İlhâmî)* (Konya, 1959). Cf. Beydilli, "III. Selim: Aydınlanmış Hükümdar," in *III. Selim ve Dönemi*, 27–57.

[7] Edîb, 122 ff. See also Uzunçarşılı, "Sultan III. Selim ve Koca Yusuf Paşa," *Belleten* 39 (1975): 237.

[8] Over two hundred members of the élite attended the Revan council on May 16, 1789. We do not know whether Vâsıf was present, but he was certainly aware of the event: MEHÂSİN 2, fols. 12b-14a. Cf. Edîb, 132–134. On Selim's cadre of reformers, see Shaw, *Old and New*, 86–91.

advance. Selim was eager to build on the past year's success. Spurning diplomatic overtures from Spain, France, and Prussia, he ordered the army back into the field and even, if briefly, contemplated taking active command. The summer campaign did not go as well as he hoped, however. After Selim dismissed Koca Yusuf Paşa for failing to repeat his victories against the Austrians, the new Grand Vizier, one Hasan Paşa, led the realm into a series of stunning routs – at Foksani in July and in September on the Rimnik or Boze river – which decimated the army as a fighting force. In October, Belgrade fell to an Austrian siege, followed by the forts of Bender and Akkirman. As the realm's defenses crumbled, Selim scrambled to raise more men.[9] While the Ottomans and Austrians had reached a stalemate by mid-1790 and signed a nine-month truce with plans for talks at Sistova, a town on the Danube, on the basis of *status quo ante bellum*, Selim refused to negotiate with the Russians. He preferred to fight for better terms or what he called a "victorious peace." But the army was in no condition to fight. The fall of another fortress in December 1790 – this time İsmail, after a bloody siege – set off riots in Istanbul, and to restore calm, Selim had the Grand Vizier shot and replaced with Koca Yusuf, whom he ordered to prepare once again for a new campaign.[10]

There are, in truth, few sources for Vâsıf's activities and sentiments during this period in wartime Istanbul. Whether he struggled like others with prices, food shortages, mounting debts, and the capital's growing insecurity is something that we simply do not know. He never wrote about it. Yet Vâsıf was affected by the news from the front. The defeat at Foksani struck him as a terrible waste, a blunder in which the Ottomans were caught unawares by a joint Austrian and Russian attack. Just as at Kartal in 1770, a battle which he had survived, Vâsıf blamed the rank and file's sin and lack of devotion. "How can a force win," he asked, "when it is unruly, depraved, and, being oblivious of the enemy's whereabouts, flees shamelessly the instant that he appears?" Vâsıf was also galled that the Ottoman command had failed to scout ahead. How was it that they had not seen the enemy? How did the Russians follow their movements at a distance of forty hours but they, two hours away, could not detect the Russians? "It is only logical that if one group can strategize, so can another," he declared.[11] The news from the Boze was still worse for

<hr/>

[9] Shaw, *Old and New*, 33–39.
[10] Shaw, *Old and New*, 51–60. See also MEHÂSİN 2, fols. 47b, 62a-62b, 74b-76b; Edîb, 180–181; and Uzunçarşılı, "III. Selim," 243.
[11] MEHÂSİN 2, fols. 25a-26a, 27a. Cf. Enverî, ÖN H.O. nr. 105, fols. 144b-147a.

Vâsıf, for this second loss not only shattered the main army, but added personal grief to public disaster. During the retreat, a group of Ottomans had tried to cross the river on horseback and, in their confusion, fell and drowned. One of the dead was Mehmed Hayrî Efendi, a three-time chief scribe and friend with whom the historian had served at Bucharest and whose poetry he would later compile in memoriam. Words failed Vâsıf. He felt that the army had shown itself wholly unable to match the infidel and that it had betrayed the faith by fleeing battle. Hayrî's death – a sacrifice that ensured his eternal reward – served to underscore this failure. "The greatest efforts could not have saved him," he wrote. "He was struck down by Providence and joined the righteous dead, drowning in the said river and gaining true martyrdom: Think not that Death took him / But bid him, truly, to martyrdom."[12]

We can say rather more about how Vâsıf renegotiated his career in the early days of the new reign. He had links to a number of influential figures. He was friends with Feyzî Süleyman Paşa, for example, a two-time chief scribe turned vizier, and was on good terms with the religious scholars Tatarcık Abdullah Efendi and Mehmed Mekkî Efendi, who was briefly şeyhülislâm in 1787. Vâsıf likewise knew Mustafa Âşir Efendi, the army judge advocate and future şeyhülislâm who was Abürrezzâk Efendi's brother and possibly his own relative through marriage.[13] These men were not necessarily mutual friends or even living in Istanbul. Feyzî Süleyman and Mustafa Âşir were far off in the imperial army. Given this, and pitted against equally strong enemies, Vâsıf must have relied to some extent on his stock-in-trade of flattery and cast a wide net for patrons. The results were positive; in June 1789, Vâsıf became temporary head of the Anatolian accounting office, an appointment that cannot be regarded as anything but a promotion. The *anadolu muhâsebecisi* was one of the top figures in the treasury after the chief accounting officer (*baş muhâsebeci*), the keeper of the daily ledger (*büyük rûznâmçe*), and the treasurer (*defterdâr*). Indeed, he was a second level bureau chief. His office, meanwhile, issued receipts and permits to holders of tax farms, pious foundations, and customs dues, and during the late eighteenth century allocated funds for soldiers and pensioners in the Aegean. Vâsıf had held this office in Spain, though in name only. His appointment now was a significant advance. Although the post was to be in proxy in Istanbul

---

[12] MEHÂSİN 2, fols. 31b-33b, 35b. See also Hasan Şener, ed., "Hayrî: Hayatı, Edebi Şahsiyeti, Dîvânı'nın Tenkitli Metni" (Ph.D. diss., Fırat University, 1999), 325. Cf. Enverî, ÖN H.O. nr. 105, fols. 171b-176b.

[13] MEHÂSİN 3, fols. 3a-4a, 168b-169a; Âsım, 1: 256; and Schlechta-Wssehrd, 7.

and carried a modest salary, only 2,000 *kuruş* per year, it promised a high level of prestige and commanded a staff of 150 men in the treasury. Just as importantly, it would keep him safely out of harm's way.[14]

Vâsıf's good fortune in gaining a promotion, his first in years, was matched by his success in winning new commissions. In the winter or spring of 1790 the Grand Vizier's proxy, Ağa Hasan Paşa, summoned the scribe to appear before him. Hasan Paşa had lately heard from Selim, who sent him a number of old chronicles with orders to have them revised and assembled in one volume with more recent events. The sultan desired a history of his and the previous reign. The problem, as Vâsıf learned, was that the court historian Edîb had been dispatched to Kütahya in Anatolia to levy soldiers and was neither in Istanbul nor able to bring the records up to date. For this reason, and in light of his prior experience in history, Hasan Paşa was giving the task to him. Vâsıf took possession of the chronicles. He recognized them: two were parts of his own unfinished history from the decade before; the other two had been written by Enverî Efendi.[15] Vâsıf began to revise his own work while drafting what had occurred since Selim's accession, where Edîb had left off. Although these

[14] MEHÂSİN 2, fol. 21a; Edîb, 149; and Enverî, ÖN H.O. nr. 105, fol. 135b. The appointment took place on 4 L AH 1203 or June 28, 1789. It is listed without date in BOA.A.RSK.d 1623, p. 37; and Afyoncu, "Tevcihat Kayıtları I," 124. An imperial decree from early 1791 (BOA.HAT 11579) states that Vâsıf's yearly income as proxy *anadolu muhâsebecisi* was less than what the full holder in the imperial army earned. On the post in general, see Uzunçarşılı, *Osmanlı Devleti*, 69, 337, 347, 355–356. A further source (Taylesanizâde, 1: 396–397) lists an "Ahmed Vâsıf, the steward of Hatice Sultan," as receiving the directorship of Istanbul tax farms (*İstanbul mukâta'acılığı*) at the same time. This is likely an error. The name appears elsewhere as Ahmed Rifat, and we do not know Vâsıf to have held the position or to have had any connection with Hatice Sultan, Selim III's sister. Following Taylesanizâde, 1: 416, his post in the accounts office became permanent on 28 Z AH 1203 = September 19, 1789.

[15] MEHÂSİN 2, fol. 4b. The details of this event are confusing. The commission itself and the reasons behind Vâsıf's selection are outlined in three archival documents (BOA.HAT 11082, 11187, 5747/5) which date from ca. Ş AH 1205 = April 1791. As Ağa Hasan Paşa refers to making the appointment "last year," we can infer that it occurred at some point in AH 1204 and probably, given the nature of Edîb's absence, in the winter or spring before the campaign season. By noting his own "reappointment" the following year, Edîb implies (118) that Vâsıf also received the title of proxy court historian. Vâsıf held this position until his second term as full court historian began in B AH 1205 = March 1791. See also BOA.C.MF 8581; Cevdet, *Târih*, 5: 115–116; and Kütükoğlu, "Vekâyi'nüvis," 118–119. Cf. Sarıkaya, lxxvi, who has confused the chronology. The two volumes by Enverî may have been his chronicles of the years 1768–1775 and 1774–1783, respectively. It is also possible that they were sections of the latter, which he divided into two parts at the year 1779 (Enverî, ÖN H.O. nr. 202, fol. 182a). It is clear in either case that Selim had a large project in mind.

notes do not survive, their shape is evident from later chronicles that incorporated them. Vâsıf took down major ceremonies surrounding the accession – Selim's enthronement, the oath of fealty (bî'at), the customary girding of the sword (taklîd-i seyf) – as well as appointments, dismissals, events in the capital, and news from abroad.[16] The act of reading his old history against unfolding events must also have spurred his mind to larger questions. Had Halil Paşa's reforms worked? Was the empire on sounder footing? Had it been ready for war? The army's recent showing suggested not. Having seen European military tactics and training up close, Vâsıf was starting to see that the realm needed more than just weapons and matériel to match its enemies. Reciprocation would require thorough-going change.

It took Vâsıf most of a year to polish up his old work for submission. By early 1791, he had a clean copy and was ready to start on Enverî's two volumes, hopefully for goodly reward, and he had reason to be optimistic. Vâsıf had been in Istanbul for nearly three years. He enjoyed seniority in the treasury and was making good, if slow, progress on a royal commission, whose delays, in any case, reflected a growing indispensability at court and consequent demands on his time. Or so he thought. In March, aghast, Vâsıf found that he had been called up for the spring campaign. He asked colleagues for help, claiming poverty, and appealed to Ağa Hasan Paşa to intercede lest his work on the dynastic history suffer, but the pleas fell on deaf ears. Rather than reverse the order, Selim halted Vâsıf's historical revisions altogether and transferred him to the army as full court historian and anadolu muhâsebecisi. Vâsıf was not pleased. He swore that the assignment was a cabal hatched by his enemies: "A list arrived summoning several men from Istanbul to serve in the army," he wrote several years after.

Certain degenerates, wishing me ruin, plotted to add my name to the list along with the rest, and while well-wishers came to my aid and petitioned the Porte several times on my behalf, on account of my great poverty, it was to no use. Ultimately I despaired. And I was not only forced to make dear purchases but to leave for the imperial army with heavy debts and much upheaval.

---

[16] BOA.HAT 11082 indicates that Edîb used Vâsıf's notes after his reappointment as historian in 1791, presumably as the basis for the years 1789–1790. Vâsıf also referred to this usage in MEHÂSİN 2, fol. 4b. However, the link between the two accounts is not entirely clear insofar as Vâsıf returned to the work in 1793 and revised it, making comparison difficult. Overall, the texts share a common structure and subheadings, but differ in wording. One verbatim overlap is the appointment of Ahmed Azmî as ambassador to Prussia: MEHÂSİN 2, fols. 63a–64b. Cf. Edîb, 170–172.

Vâsıf thus made ready for the journey. He tendered his work to the palace in its various stages of completion – the revised and unrevised histories along with his partial notes – before leaving Istanbul in late March.[17]

5.2 THE DANUBIAN FRONT, 1791

The first sight of Şumnu, the Ottoman army's winter camp, comes as one descends the north slope of the Balkans toward the Danube. For Vâsıf, it evoked hard memories. He had last seen the city seventeen years earlier, when he, the late Muhsinzâde Mehmed Paşa, and others had endured a brutal Russian siege before their surrender at Kaynarca. Şumnu was a large settlement, but loomed still larger in the scribe's mind through its ties to death, hardship, and humiliation, and his renewed acquaintance, suffice it to say, was not by choice. In camp, Vâsıf could immediately sense the army's unreadiness. Koca Yusuf Paşa had raised a large number of men and spent the winter trying vainly to put them in fighting order, his efforts hampered by inadequate supplies and the soldiers' poor discipline, training, and morale. When the scribe arrived, Yusuf Paşa was in the nearby port of Varna to inspect its defenses in case of attack. Shortly after his return, on April 13, 1791, the army moved out of its barracks and onto the plains around the city.[18]

Şumnu probably gave the historian his first real look at the fruits of the late military reforms. The Ottomans had spent more than a decade to plan

---

[17] MEHÂSİN 2, fols. 4b, 81a. This call-up occurred in late B AH 1205 = late March 1791. While Vâsıf provided no date, he marked off a passage in Enverî (ÖN H.O. nr. 105, fol. 287b-288a) as the start of his account at the army – the notes of which Enverî later appropriated. The passage contains the date 27 B = April 1. One archival document, BOA.C.MF 8581, records Vâsıf's receipt of five quires of writing paper, perhaps supplies for his journey. It is dated 22 B AH 1205 (March 27) and refers to him as full court historian and head of the Anatolian accounting office. Two more archival documents (BOA.HAT 10467, 11579) discuss his treasury replacement in Istanbul and note that he is "leaving tomorrow, on Monday." They are undated; however, March 28 was a Monday. According to BOA.HAT 11187, Vâsıf submitted the clean copy of his revised history before departure, along with the original copies and the unrevised volumes of Enverî's history. Selim approved, but we do not know whether he issued any reward. In a final follow-up document (BOA.HAT 11082), Ağa Hasan Paşa indicated that Vâsıf had left behind his historical notes and offered to provide them to Edîb. See also Cevdet, who criticizes (Târih, 5: 115) Vâsıf for preferring to stay in Istanbul.

[18] MEHÂSİN 2, fols. 85b-86b, 87a. Cf. Enverî, ÖN H.O. nr. 105, fols. 292b-294a, 295a. Koca Yusuf Paşa made a five-day trip to Varna from 26 B to 30 B AH 1205 (March 31 to April 4, 1791). The army camped on the plains outside of Şumnu on 9 Ş = April 14. Vâsıf described this city, its inhabitants, and its environs in MEHÂSİN 5, 2: 210–211. See also Shaw, Old and New, 61–62.

for this second act against Russia but now seemed, outwardly, no better equipped or prepared. What had happened? What went wrong? As we have seen, the central bureaucracy in Istanbul did in fact implement a range of measures and new policies in the years after Kaynarca. Some of these focused on special units, often with aid from French technicians. The Ottomans had taken steps since 1774 to improve their artillery, for instance, hiring officers like Baron François de Tott (d. 1793), founding a rapid-fire corps, and upgrading the imperial foundry. De Tott had also set up an artillery school, which, like his rapid-fire corps, survived in various guises in the capital into the 1780s. Reform targeted other areas, too. The Frenchmen André-Joseph Lafitte-Clavé (d. 1794), Joseph-Gabriel Monnier de Courtois (d. 1818), and Antoine-Charles Aubert (b. 1745) helped the government strengthen forts along the Danube and Dardanelles; Gazi Hasan Paşa used foreign shipwrights and carpenters to build twenty-two new ships of the line and more than a dozen frigates for the navy, lighter and more maneuverable than before. Nor did the Ottomans rely only on outsiders. The gadgets of one vizier, İsmail Zihnî Paşa, including a volley gun, boded well for homegrown technical genius and caught the eyes of both the Grand Vizier and Abdülhamid I.[19]

The problem was that these measures failed to address, much less solve, the deeper issues of finance, training, and supply. Military reform faced systemic barriers. By the mid-eighteenth century, the empire fielded a largely mercenary army and contracted the work of recruitment, provisioning, and mobilization to notables, or a'yân, in the provinces. It is true, as scholars note, that this system proved to be flexible. Yet it also had drawbacks. The empire's privatized supply chain, for example, run by "military entrepreneurs," was prone to abuse and rife with corruption, waste, and profiteering. There are many cases of agents hoarding, stealing from stores, cutting flour with dirt or sand, and even distributing thirty-year-old biscuit to cut corners. The quality of men gathered – more likely impressed – by these local contractors was also suspect. Levied troops of the period as well as the Janissaries resembled local militias rather than a professional army, being raw, untrained, and not normally subject to military discipline. Abdülhamid I and Selim III tried in vain to remedy this situation, the former struggling in the 1770s to quash irregular local

---

[19] See Virginia Aksan, "Breaking the Spell of the Baron de Tott," in *Contacts and Conflicts*, 111–137; Kahraman Şakul, "Military Engineering in the Ottoman Empire," in *Military Engineers and the Development of the Early-Modern European State* (Dundee, UK, 2013), 195–197; idem, "Hattat İsmail Zihni Paşa: Life and Death of an Ottoman Statesman and an Inventor," *Journal of Ottoman Studies* 44 (2014): 67–98; and Sarıcaoğlu, 188 ff.

(*levend*) forces. Selim, for his part, derided his troops in 1791/92 as an unreliable "rabble."[20]

A top-down solution had to contend with two major issues, however. One was funding. Early modern warfare cost huge amounts of money, sums the realm could not spare. Russia had forced an indemnity of 7.5 million *kuruş* on the empire in the Treaty of Kaynarca, about half the yearly budget, and the government tried to tackle shrinking revenues and rising costs by taking out loans and voiding lifetime freehold (*mâlikâne*) grants, both of which failed. Istanbul found that it could not rescind freehold; it had no way to collect agricultural taxes without contractors. Attempts in the 1770s and 1780s to reform the empire's prebends, or *timâr*, which once supported provincial cavalrymen, were equally futile. The army no longer relied on cavalry, while the fiefs now largely served as sinecures for grandees, absentee élites, and other members of the dynasty; the fact that scribes like Vâsıf held such grants indicates that, as a tool for funding the military, the *timâr* was obsolete.[21] The second issue was closely linked to this type of enrichment. Simply too many people had an interest in the system. The once crack Janissaries had morphed over a century from a standing army into something more akin to a socio-military guild, a vast supply of manpower on paper, but useless as a fighting force. The corps drew migrants, tradesmen, and urban gentry, whose place on the muster rolls granted them tax and legal immunities as well as chits (*esâme*) for monthly pay and rations. By our period, the Janissaries in and around Istanbul numbered 100,000 men. The total number of chits in the empire reached some 400,000, of which maybe only ten percent paid battle-ready soldiers. Yet try as they might, would-be reformers could not purge the rolls. While vitiated and a drain on resources, the corps profited its members and the bureaucracy as a whole through a brisk trade in these chits – commerce that went all the way to the top, including one Grand Vizier, Çelebi Mehmed Paşa, who fell from grace in 1778 with the revelation that he held pay chits for more than 600 soldiers. The Ottoman military had begun to shift from an early

---

[20] Kahraman Şakul, "The Evolution of Ottoman Military Logistical Systems in the Later Eighteenth Century: The Rise of a New Class of Military Entrepreneur," in *War, Entrepreneurs, and the State in Europe and the Mediterranean, 1300–1800* (Leiden, 2014), 312–320, 322–326. See also Virginia Aksan, *Ottoman Wars, 1700–1870: An Empire Besieged* (Harlow, UK, 2007), 72–75, 130–135, 147–160; and idem, "Ottoman Military Recruitment Strategies in the Late Eighteenth Century," in *Contacts and Conflicts*, 196–202.

[21] Ali Yaycıoğlu, *Partners of the Empire: The Crisis of the Ottoman Order in the Age of Revolutions* (Stanford, 2016), 26–30, 35–38; and Sarıcaoğlu, 189–190.

modern system of state-funded militias to what, by the nineteenth century, would be a conscript army. This change was painful, however. Reform threatened too many people's prestige and livelihoods; it is thus no surprise that efforts tended to be ad hoc.[22]

If Vâsıf felt nervous about the coming campaign, his fears were realized that April when a force led by Nikolai Repnin crossed the Danube and stormed the town of Maçin, forcing its Ottoman garrison to retreat to Hırsova. As Maçin controlled the road to the Danube fortress İbrail, its fall threatened to cut off a key link in the empire's defenses. Yusuf Paşa decided to counter this danger by sending fresh men and supplies to his commander in Silistre, Karahisarî Ahmed Paşa, with orders to relieve Hırsova and march against the Russians. He needed a courier for the task – he chose Vâsıf. The Grand Vizier entrusted Vâsıf with his instructions as well as with Ahmed Paşa's patent of office, robe of honor, and 20,000 kuruş for his needs. The scribe then made his way from Şumnu to Silistre, some seventy miles to the north. What he found there unsettled him: Ahmed Paşa refused to cooperate and indeed made every effort to avoid the appointment. "His Excellency knew the situation and was afraid," he later remarked.

He faked illness, then argued, and then forgot his earlier claims and contradicted himself. He at last protested his situation and said that he could not go – for he was a warden and had no equipage for the field – and began to make demands that the empire could not meet. Clearly his aim was to make excuses in order to shirk duty.

Vâsıf managed to talk Ahmed Paşa out of his obstinacy. He reported the vizier's lack of supplies and in a few days, men, munitions, and coin began to arrive from camp to quiet any objections. However, as Vâsıf outfitted this force over ten days, distributing liberal bribes, word came that a second Russian force had moved south from Galatz to invest İbrail by land. Koca Yusuf Paşa and his retinue rushed to Silistre. Meeting with Ahmed Paşa, the Grand Vizier sent him to Hırsova with most of the new levies and an added 15,000 kuruş; he then loaded the rest of the men onto boats and sent them downriver to relieve the fortress while a separate column marched on Maçin from Babadağı. These maneuvers thankfully worked. The Russians broke their siege and withdrew quietly to Galatz, while the Grand Vizier reinforced Silistre before returning to imperial camp, Vâsıf in train.[23]

---

[22] Aksan, "Ottoman Military Recruitment," 193–195; and Yaycıoğlu, 30–32.

[23] MEHÂSİN 2, fols. 87a-89a, 144b-145a. Cf. Enverî, ÖN H.O. nr. 105, fols. 295a-297b. Judging by its placement in the chronicle, this episode took place in mid- to late-Ş AH

Vâsıf's actions at Silistre gained him Yusuf Paşa's trust. The Grand Vizier increasingly had him oversee supplies, requisitions, inspections, and like matters as they waited on the plains at Şumnu. He also named the scribe to a new position, head of the general accounts office, or *baş muhâsebeci*, when the army finally struck camp in early June. This was one of the highest posts in the treasury. The fact that Vâsıf was a stand-in for one İbrahim Efendi, who was too ill to join the campaign, did nothing to lessen the honor or diminish the role he was to play in the field. The episode gave him pause, however. The Ottomans were by no means ready to face Repnin and had so far succeeded through deft gambits, there being no direct confrontation between the two sides. A battle might prove disastrous, for morale at camp was low and it was doubtful that the Ottomans could wage a campaign without putting themselves at risk.[24] When the imperial army marched for Kozluca on June 10, then, it did so less of its own will than to fulfill the sultan's orders. The Grand Vizier told his commanders to proceed to Pazarcık before turning toward Hırsova and Maçin, where he hoped to engage Repnin, while he himself struck north to tour his defenses with Vâsıf and a small retinue, planning to rejoin the army in a few days. The party stopped first at Rusçuk. There, among other things, they inspected the Danube flotilla, sent it to Silistre to provide support, and crossed to Giurgevo to view a badly damaged fortress. Yusuf Paşa, Vâsıf, and the others then returned to Rusçuk and took boats downriver to Tutrakan and Silistre, picking up munitions on the way; they passed the night and set off overland for Pazarcık the next morning. This lightning tour lasted five days. As Vâsıf learned, however, the army in that time had only come halfway, or scarcely sixty miles. They had encountered problems with the water supply. What was more, a violent quarrel had erupted between the Janissaries and the Albanian soldiers at Kozluca. His presence needed, Yusuf Paşa packed up his retinue and hurried south to the army.[25]

1205, the next date given being 26 Ş or April 30. Vâsıf specified that he remained behind in Silistre and returned to Şumnu with the Grand Vizier.

[24] MEHÂSİN 2, fol. 92b. Vâsıf wrote (fols. 91a-92b) that the arrival of an orderly contingent that spring greatly lifted spirits at camp, for they had not seen such a sight in a long while. On his appointment, see also Hammer-Purgstall, 3: 553; and Zaîmzâde, 119.

[25] MEHÂSİN 2, fols. 93a-94b. Cf. Enverî, ÖN H.O. nr. 105, fols. 301a-303b. The imperial army and Grand Vizier both left Şumnu on 8 L AH 1205 = June 10, 1791. According to Vâsıf's account, the latter reached Rusçuk that same evening along with himself, the master of ceremonies Mustafa Efendi, and twenty-five others. The next day (9 L = June 11), they inspected the town and Giurgevo, left by boat, and spent the night anchored at Tutrakan, where they discovered munitions and had these sent away in

It is hard to ignore the uncanny parallels between the campaign of 1774 and the Ottoman army's situation that spring. Nor were the similarities lost on Vâsıf. He was again with an army that could barely function and that had little sound intelligence, much less any idea of how to act on it. He was again serving a Grand Vizier who, despite his better judgment, was being pushed into battle by Istanbul politics and his master's elusive hope for a "victorious peace." Even the names were the same. Şumnu, Uşanlı, Pazarcık, Hırsova – for the scribe, these places evoked fearful memories of times past and colleagues long dead. The imperial army was now at Kozluca, where Vâsıf and Abdürrezzâk Efendi had once narrowly escaped with their lives. The leadership could not decide how to proceed. Word came on June 14 that the Russians were moving against Tulça, a major bastion on the Danube, followed several days later by reports that they had turned south toward Babadağı. It was not clear where Repnin was headed. Some said Maçin; others suggested that he would double back to Tulça. Be what may, Yusuf Paşa ordered the imperial army north and by late June, when they had reached Hırsova, it was obvious that the Russians were again targeting Maçin. A decisive battle was at hand. That the Grand Vizier still doubted his men is nevertheless evident from a request that he made of Vâsıf to draft a speech for the occasion, under the watch of his steward Mustafa Reşîd Efendi, with which he could unite them. On July 6, at Hırsova, Yusuf Paşa addressed his officers with these words and prevailed on their honor, binding them with oaths.[26]

The text of this speech is found in one of Vâsıf's later chronicles under the misleading title, "an extempore address." It is in fact carefully worded. Aiming to motivate, the speech is part exhortation, part censure, and part appeal to the proto-patriotism of late eighteenth-century Ottoman "faith and country" or dîn ü devlet. As a ghostwriter, Vâsıf portrayed the war as part of an older and ongoing struggle. "Our old enemy the Muscovite has

requisitioned wagons and boats for use at Giurgevo and Silistre. The following dawn (10 L = June 12) the party moved on, reached Silistre in the afternoon, inspected its fortress and armory, and lodged in town. They set off for Pazarcık on 11 L or June 13 to rendezvous with the army, but were waylaid on the road by more requisitions and did not arrive until nightfall. They presumably set out for Kozluca on the following day, 12 L = June 14. See also Cevdet, Târih, 5: 121.

26 MEHÂSİN 2, fols. 95a-96b. Cf. Enverî, ÖN H.O. nr. 105, fols. 303b-306b. The army left Kozluca for Pazarcık on 19 L AH 1205 = June 21, 1791. They continued on 25 L or June 27 through the towns of Musabey, Kurnalı Dere, Karasu (Negru Vodă?), and Boğazköy (Cernavodă), arriving at Hırsova on 29 L = July 1, a Friday. See also Cevdet, Târih, 5: 121–123; and Zaîmzâde, 116 ff. Vâsıf wrote later (MEHÂSİN 2, fols. 102a-103a) that Yusuf Paşa sensed sedition in the army and would have preferred to avoid battle, but was pressured by the sultan and his own advisors.

long coveted the empire's lands," he wrote, "but till the year 1768 he had failed in his design, with mixed results." The war that year was mismanaged and marred by the army's disorder, as everybody knew, and the Russians took the Crimea, expelled the Tatars, and annexed the peninsula. But the Crimea did not satisfy them, Vâsıf continued. They usurped trade in the Mediterranean and Black Sea and gained more power by eroding the privileges of Ottoman subjects. Russia also lacked agriculture. While they could scarcely make ends meet with their own realm and Poland, now with the Crimea they exported grain and were slowly bankrupting the empire, siphoning off its specie. Such an enemy would stop at nothing and must be opposed. Calling on his listeners' pride and sense of duty, the solution that Vâsıf urged was for the army to fulfill its obligation of jihad and to fight:

God, be He exalted, made us believers by nature and told us that we shall gain paradise through jihad. But though our swords are keen and our steeds are swift, the sword does not cut or the horse charge on its own. We are fleeing the enemy! Fearing cowards, our men scatter before their laughable tactics and firecracker-volleys!

Vâsıf claimed that the Ottomans were terrified by cheap Russian tricks and pyrotechnics. So too did they scorn divine commands and succumb to envy and malice, so that God allowed "the meanest of Christians" to humiliate them as punishment – a clear reference to *istidrâc*. Did the Christians not call the empire "a walking corpse?" Did the least infidel not insult them? In such circumstances, they must fight; as the empire was exhausted and the viziers could no more ask the sultan for money or aid, Vâsıf implored his listeners to serve God and the realm. "What day is zeal for?" he asked.

Is it not time to prove ourselves as Muslims? How can we live with such disgrace? These lands were conquered with much spilt blood and the conquerors were men like us. Yet we – we cannot even keep what we have, much less capture other realms ... If we repent our disobedience with a pure heart, if we unite, if we firmly face the enemy for several hours, then all his order will inevitably fail. God has enjoined us in scripture to jihad and promised that if we stand fast in battle, we shall surely defeat the infidel. How can we expect victory without unity and resolve?

With sincere effort, Vâsıf concluded that the Ottomans would not only prevail, but have revenge, regain lost territories, and win fame and eternal reward. Would his listeners swear to it? Would they include their own men in the oath? Anyone who did not wish it should remain behind, he said, and there could be no compulsion. But they must decide, "for this is the last chance."[27]

Moved to duty or shame, Yusuf Paşa's men warmed to the speech, took the oath, and prepared to move northward. In early July, the Janissary corps left Hırsova for Maçin. The Grand Vizier followed them with a large force, but left behind his financial officials and scribes to give the illusion that the main army remained at camp. Vâsıf, too, seems to have stayed at Hırsova. As the Ottoman army was on the road, they heard from the Maçin garrison that Repnin had suddenly crossed the Danube and, failing in his first assault, would attack again the next day. Yusuf Paşa hurried his men; the Janissaries reached the town at dawn on July 8 and dug in. What happened next resembled so many battles of the previous quarter century. The assault began at seven o'clock that morning and enemy troops advanced from three sides on the stockades. The Ottomans at first resisted, returning fire for about two hours and even making an odd sortie, until the Russians trained their mortar on the horse. When the cavalry predictably scattered, Repnin ordered his men into the stockades and met only minor opposition from a few hundred Janissaries. The rest panicked and fled. The Ottoman commanders were powerless to stop them and abandoned their posts in retreat. Outside of the town, the Grand Vizier heard cannon fire and hastened ahead only to find men fleeing heedlessly south. He was unable to stem the tide, and his own men became infected with panic, cut the draught horses, and grabbed what they could of powder, munitions, and provisions before joining the march toward Hırsova and Karasu. Yusuf Paşa at this point could merely try to form an orderly retreat. The oaths had failed; his army was shattered. He had also lost most of the ordnance which he had spent the last year in gathering. Maçin had been an utter catastrophe.[28]

Back in Hırsova, the Grand Vizier vainly regrouped. He gathered what men and supplies he could and within several days was again on the march toward Maçin, where he and the rest of the Ottoman army encamped

[27] MEHÂSİN 2, fols. 96b-99b. Also found in Enverî, ÖN H.O. nr. 105, fols. 306b-309b; and Cevdet, Târih, 5: 124-126. The versions differ in only minor ways. On the import of "faith and country" in the eighteenth century, see Aksan, "Ottoman Political Writing," 43-44; and Şakul, "Nizâm-ı Cedid," 119-120. Vâsıf's phrase "walking corpse" echoes the idea of the empire as a "sick man." He also groused that Europeans likened the realm to a domestic fowl or dîk: most likely a turkey (dîk-i hindî).

[28] MEHÂSİN 2, fols. 99b-102a; Enverî, ÖN H.O. nr. 105, fols. 309b-314a; and Zaîmzâde, 116 f. Vâsıf relied heavily on informants in his version of the battle, suggesting that he was not actually present. Cf. Enverî, who claims (fol. 313b) to have been an eyewitness in the Grand Vizier's entourage. See also Shaw, Old and New, 61-62.

on July 21, the Russians having withdrawn across the Danube. Yusuf Paşa vented his frustration. He had sensed the mood in the army and avoided battle for as long as possible. Fearing he would be routed and forced into unfavorable terms, he had shared his thoughts beforehand with Mustafa Reşîd, his steward, proposing to negotiate. Reşîd and others had deterred him. Selim wanted some sort of victory, they said, and to make peace without fighting was cowardly and would greatly displease him. Yusuf Paşa now regretted heeding this advice. "Look here, *you* caused this situation," he said. "None of this would have happened had you listened to me. We might have upheld the empire's honor and even secured suitable terms."[29] As it was, the Ottoman army had been effectively destroyed and could barely hold together, much less mount an offensive, and when the Grand Vizier again raised the idea of negotiating with Repnin, his ministers agreed. They sent a letter to the general in Galatz. They had reached Maçin with a great force, they wrote, but as the outcome of another battle was uncertain, they were equally ready to make peace. What were his terms? Repnin sent them three conditions: that Kaynarca and later treaties should remain in force; that the occupied principalities of Moldavia and Wallachia be restored to the Ottomans with certain stipulations; and that the Dniester should mark the two empires' new border. The Grand Vizier and the statesmen discussed these in council. Repnin's terms were unfair, but it was clear that he would not budge. What was more, the sultan had at last sent them his permission to begin peace negotiations. What should they do? The council decided that under the circumstances, they had no choice but to seek a truce. Because of his prior experience, and perhaps because Yusuf Paşa trusted him, the council chose to send Vâsıf as their delegate.[30]

The mission to Galatz was a risky one for Vâsıf. He neither had room to negotiate nor any guarantee that the terms would prove acceptable in the

[29] MEHÂSİN 2, fols. 102a-103a, 107a-108a; Enverî, ÖN H.O. nr. 105, fols. 314a-315b. Yusuf Paşa dispatched a force from Hırsova on 16 Za AH 1205 = July 17, 1791, but its commander "took ill, fell from his horse, and died" after several minutes' travel. The whole army marched the next day and reached Maçin on 20 Za = July 21. They camped on the plain outside of the city three days later, on 23 Za or July 24. Vâsıf also learned on his trip to Galatz (fols. 102a-102b) that the Russians had been very vulnerable before the battle, their bridge having disintegrated, and that they had forced Ottoman prisoners to rebuild it. See also Cevdet, *Târih*, 5: 157-158.

[30] MEHÂSİN 2, fols. 108a-109a; and Enverî, ÖN H.O. nr. 105, fols. 316b-317b. Cevdet, *Târih*, 5: 158-159, follows these accounts. Zaîmzâde writes (118-119) that Vâsıf was chosen in view of his earlier service at Bucharest and in the belief that he could, given such experience, secure a good result.

Нис. Илашкевичъ   Print par Ivachkewitch

Князь Николаи Васильевичъ   Le Prince Nicolas Vassiliewitch
        Репнинъ,   Repnine,
        1734 — 1801   1734 — 1801

FIG. 5.2: Nikolai Repnin (d. 1801), Russian general, diplomat, and victor of Maçin.

army or, more importantly, in Istanbul. That Selim had allowed them to speak with Repnin did not mean he would accept the results, and certainly he would not if they smacked of dictation. Satisfying the empire's honor (*şân-ı devlet*) was a key issue in any settlement; Yusuf Paşa thus supplied Vâsıf with a letter to Repnin, but also with ample money and orders to use it liberally to the empire's advantage. Vâsıf kept his task in strict secrecy. Leaving Maçin on August 1 with a handful of men, he crossed the Danube to İbrail in order, officially, to convey orders to the Ottoman garrison commander. He then stole north to Galatz.[31]

Nikolai Repnin received Vâsıf coolly and left him to wait for a day while the Grand Vizier's letter was translated. The historian's opinion of the general was already quite poor. Unlike Rumiantsev, Vâsıf felt no warmth or respect for the victor of Maçin, whose high-handed behavior he recalled from nearly two decades earlier in Istanbul. "Repnin was an ill-tempered, self-satisfied man proud of all the evil that he had committed on campaign," he later wrote. "He was a rogue, a liar, and a haughty man who fancied himself second to none in solving great affairs."[32] Nor did their meeting change these perceptions. Repnin summoned Vâsıf the next day to his lodgings. He first asked that the Ottomans notify their fleet of the potential truce in order to prevent any mutual injury. Vâsıf agreed. "What is the catch?" he said. "Draft a letter and I shall send it to the Grand Vizier. He will forward it if he approves." They then began ten days of contentious negotiation. It quickly became clear that Repnin was not willing to offer any compromise on his initial three terms. Vâsıf, for example, objected to the Russian proposal for Moldavia and Wallachia and charged the general with using vague language that he could and would reinterpret. "What is the aim of this passage? Doesn't the addition of such vague statutes contradict the claim that you are restoring the territories freely?" Repnin for his part insisted on the wording, accusing the Ottomans of bad faith and of failing to honor prior agreements over the Principalities. He at last made it known that he would not discuss matters further and gave Vâsıf an ultimatum. If the envoy did not produce a sealed voucher from Ottoman command agreeing to all the terms, Repnin said, as originally proposed, he would call off the truce completely. This ultimatum pushed Vâsıf to act. He sent word to the Grand Vizier and advised him to choose whatever alternative – war or peace – was more beneficial to the realm, knowing, of course, that there could be no real prospect of a return to war. The reply and sealed voucher were thus soon in coming. Yusuf Paşa held a council at Maçin to discuss the truce with the army, who urged him, in light of their hardships, to choose the "lesser of two evils" and accept Repnin's terms. The Grand Vizier drew up the

---

[31] MEHÂSİN 2, fol. 109a; Enverî, ÖN H.O. nr. 105, fol. 317b; and Uzunçarşılı, "Dış Ruznâmesi," 611.

[32] MEHÂSİN 6, fols. 31a, 41b. Repnin had been Catherine II's ambassador in Istanbul in 1775/76 as part of the ratification of Küçük Kaynarca. Cf. his behavior as recounted in his 1777 embassy report in *Mubadele*, 125–203. See also MERSH, s.v. "Repnin, Nikolai Vasilevich."

document and sent it to Galatz, where Vâsıf submitted it on August 10, 1791, in exchange for an eight-month truce and a future peace conference. The next day, he returned to the army.[33]

We cannot know Vâsıf's thoughts or exact state of mind when he entered the imperial camp at Maçin. He had secured a truce and potentially saved the army, but only at some cost to the empire. He had endorsed Repnin's terms without wringing from him the slightest concession and had even accepted a loss of territory between the Bug and Dniester rivers. Vâsıf may have felt that he had had no choice or that the terms, on balance, were worthwhile. Yet if he worried about the risk to his person and reputation, it was surely some consolation that the Grand Vizier and army had also staked their honor on the decision. What is sure is that Vâsıf could not have expected to find himself at the center of a new crisis over war and peace.

5.3 THE MAÇIN BOYCOTT, 1791

The army was in fact in an uproar when Vâsıf returned. Only the day before had he exchanged sureties with Repnin and declared an eight-month truce as the first step toward lasting peace. Hostilities were at an end; the war was supposed to be over. Yet Selim had now changed his mind, unaware of these events. The sultan had always wanted a "victorious peace" and, on reviewing the terms in Istanbul, especially that the Dniester form the empire's new border, he had withdrawn his leave to negotiate and ordered the Grand Vizier to break off talks. The army was to fight for better terms, he said.[34]

Selim's change of heart put Yusuf Paşa and his army in a hopeless position. Although he desired peace, and though he had just formalized the truce, the Grand Vizier could not disobey his master's express will

---

[33] MEHÂSİN 2, fols. 109b-110b; MEHÂSİN 6, fols. 70b-71a; and Enverî, ÖN H.O. nr. 105, fols. 317b-318a. See also Fâik, 147; Karslızâde, 64; Schlechta-Wssehrd, 6; and Hammer-Purgstall, 3: 553. Vâsıf later discovered that the letter for the fleet never left Maçin, as some in the imperial camp argued that they could win a naval encounter with the Russians and so protect the realm's honor. In fact, the Ottomans lost an ensuing battle on the Black Sea.

[34] Sema Arıkan, ed., *III. Selim'in Sırkâtibi Ahmed Efendi Tarafından Tutulan Rûznâme* (Ankara, 1993), 31–32. See also Âsım, 1: 25; Abdullah Altun, ed., "Said b. Halil İbrahim'in 'Tarih-i Sefer-i Rusya' Adlı Eseri: Transkripsiyon ve Değerlendirme," (master's thesis, Erciyes University, 2006), 87; and Ahmet Özcan, ed., "Kethüda Said Efendi Tarihi ve Değerlendirmesi" (master's thesis, Kırıkkale University, 1999), 57–58. These last three sources are all based on the same account.

without putting his life in peril. But neither could he give battle. Indeed, he could not hope to fight Repnin without risking the army's final collapse and a Russian advance across the Danube into the Ottoman heartlands. The reverse also angered many in the ranks and fed an increasingly explosive atmosphere at camp. To fight meant to lose and to tarnish the realm's honor, or perhaps something much worse, while to refuse meant open mutiny in the field. Such a thing was unprecedented in the empire's history. It was also incredibly dangerous. In this mood, the Janissary Ağa and his subordinates visited Yusuf Paşa and prevailed on him to disobey the new orders. "We had more than 120,000 soldiers in the last engagement," they said, with exaggeration, "but the Muscovites crossed the Danube with 8,000 men, attacked, and completely routed us all. We cannot match the infidel's trained soldiers with our unruly men. Make peace now if you intend to do so, for we shall never win while our soldiers are ignorant of modern military tactics!" Yusuf Paşa acted as if stunned by their words and asked them, frankly, "How can I possibly lay these points before the sultan?" The officers replied that they would draft a petition themselves. As Vâsıf later recalled, they enlisted his help to put their refusal into words. "They in fact had me draw up the petition," he said. "They then submitted it to the Grand Vizier, who in turn sent it to the sultan so that he might not expect to succeed with such men in the future."[35]

The Maçin petition is internally dated to August 11, 1791, the day that Vâsıf returned from Galatz, and carefully spells out the army's justification for the boycott.[36] On that day, the document begins, a number of viziers, officials, and Janissary officers gathered in the steward Mustafa Reşîd's tent. The Grand Vizier had received word from Istanbul and was reconsidering peace, he informed them:

Today our prosperous lord wants to know whether you favor war or peace. His majesty the sultan has ordered by decree that we fight, take revenge on the enemy, and so have an honorable peace (şânlû musâlaha). Our lord says he shall therefore fight and cannot act otherwise. He desires an answer. Discuss what is best here and then apprise the Grand Vizier, be what may.

[35] HULÂSAT, 61–62. See also Esad Efendi, *Üss-i Zafer (Yeniçeriliğin Kaldırılmasına Dair)*, ed. Mehmet Arslan (Istanbul, 2005), 119–120. Vâsıf's authorship of this petition has been a point of contention. I discuss this problem in detail in the Appendix.

[36] For the petition, see Edîb, 239–247. The text is dated 11 Z AH 1205 = August 11, 1791. Âsım records (1: 25–29) a meeting, clearly the same one, on 5 Z or August 5, yet this appears to be an error as all other sources corroborate the document's internal dating. For example, otherwise identical accounts by Said b. Halil İbrahim (87–90) and Kethüda Said (58) give the date as 11 Z = August 11. See also Cevdet, *Târih*, 5: 160–165.

Much discussion followed. The officers spoke of the army's plight, raised various concerns, and recalled the soldiers' lack of mettle and how they deserted at the least pretext. They confessed that it was impossible to wage war with such an army and, according to the petition, all preferred peace: "We will swear to it here and in our lord's presence – in a word, in both the here and hereafter. We have nothing else to say." The officials were next summoned to the Grand Vizier's pavilion where he addressed them:

Earlier I submitted the peace terms from General Repnin to the sultan along with my other dispatches. But according to the sultan's latest decree and my proxy's letters, to make peace with the enemy without battle must dishonor the empire. How can peace be in the empire's interest? What difference is there in having the Dniester as the border rather than the Danube? Immediately weigh war on one hand and peace on the other – let us win a victory, by God's grace, and may it lead to an honorable peace. We are accused of not doing enough to fight and are told to take revenge, with God's aid, on the enemy. So, you see, the decree's contents are thus. I am ordered to war by the sultan. I cannot favor peace now. What say you?

After clarifying Selim's will, Yusuf Paşa concluded, "We will prepare immediately and return to battle tomorrow. All of you go, rouse your men and make ready, trusting in God. I am of no other mind or resolution."

Despite this bald injunction, Vâsıf made it clear that those present still refused to follow orders. They swore obedience but asked, once more, to broach the situation. Nothing would be better than to win a victory in the realm's defense, they said, and were it up to them, they would forfeit their lives. Yet one must consider the great peril that the empire and its subjects faced. What was more, the army was in no condition to fight. It was one thing to talk of returning to war, they observed, but between desertion and the enemy's strong position, a field battle was out of the question. They predicted that the army would disintegrate if the Russians offered battle, with no one but officers and a few other men remaining:

At present we cannot conceive of any remedy better than peace. And however unfavorable this peace may be, since we are standing our ground against the enemy the empire's honor – God be praised – will be secure. But if we give battle and are put to rout, what will the enemy do? They will issue heavy demands and force us to make peace under the shame of defeat.

All those in council, then, said that they favored a voluntary peace as the best course of action. With God's grace, they could put the realm in order, reform the troops, arrange everything as necessary, and in five to ten years seek revenge and retake what had been lost. "It is impossible otherwise," they said.

According to Vâsıf, Yusuf Paşa replied that he too agonized over how to defeat the Russians and manage the army. Nothing had worked and he had inclined to peace to salvage the realm's honor. But now the sultan ordered him to war. He could not disobey. The officials answered in unison:

The damage and disgrace of this will redound upon the empire! What can weaklings like us do? If the army does not fight, must we not defend the fortresses remaining here and particularly İbrail? If the imperial army moves hence we have no doubt İbrail will fall to the enemy and that even greater humiliations will follow. We therefore favor this peace.

Yusuf Paşa told them that he could not send such an answer to the sultan. "You write out the proper course among yourselves and make your decision; you are responsible." The Grand Vizier next produced the voucher that had been approved, by correspondence with Vâsıf, as the basis for the truce. "Now look here, the empire will opt for peace with the Russians on these terms," he told them.

Consider this carefully. Should we approve the voucher or not? Should we give battle or not? You must decide today and give me an answer. I am of no mind but to fight. I have allowed all of you to speak truly and in the future hold you responsible before God. No matter what sort of reckoning you give on Judgment Day, do not mince words here but answer and speak the truth.

In the end, all voted to approve the voucher, choose peace, and have their decision recorded in a sealed petition. The meeting ended with a promise to defer to the sultan, but also a plea for haste, as the Russians were unaware of their difficulty: "We consider this a blessing for both faith and country ... We have chosen what will save the empire's honor and what is beneficial for our religion."

The Maçin petition is not Vâsıf's own view of the boycott as such. The document reads like council minutes and is more likely based on real exchanges, offering up an array of justifications for peace. Yet we can assume that Vâsıf accepted these arguments just as he put them to paper. His later work may say nothing about the boycott and indeed avoid the topic, probably out of concern for his complicity and safety, but it still depicts peace in the 1787–1792 war as an opportunity, the "lesser of two evils," and "a pure blessing." As his role in negotiating the truce and in drafting the petition further attests, Vâsıf actively supported peacemaking.[37] The linchpin of the petition's defense is again the idea of

[37] E.g., MEHÂSİN 2, fols. 62a, 89a, 102a-103a, 110a. Vâsıf also added a marginal note (110b) to his account to stress the correctness of peace. When the truce was finalized at Galatz, he wrote, Repnin had some hundred cannons fired in a show of celebration and

peace as the "lesser of two evils." The officials framed their refusal to fight in terms of the realm's integrity and security. Their lives were immaterial, they said, but the army's weakened state presented too great a risk and defeat might bring deeper peril and heavier Russian demands. They therefore advocated peace as a reprieve; the empire could try its luck again after another round of reform. Peace in the petition, then, is still a largely conservative one: a temporary measure guided by duress and the whole edifice of legal reasoning used earlier by Naîmâ, Dürrî Mehmed, and Vâsıf himself. Another central point of argument in the debate is the nature of an "honorable peace." Such a concern was not new. Preserving the empire's honor and avoiding a dictated settlement had been issues throughout the eighteenth century at Karlowitz, Passarowitz, and Küçük Kaynarca. The honor and dignity of the empire required tangible concessions because the Ottoman view of war and peace, based on *force majeure*, made anything else unacceptable.[38] Selim III's orders to fight were hence based on a belief that submitting to negotiation damaged the empire's honor. To save face, he wanted to gain some sort of victory – an honorable peace for him was a "victorious peace." The army officers, conversely, argued that in the circumstances, a "voluntary peace" was enough. They had already done the realm credit by facing the Russians, and to risk battle was to risk that honor. The empire might then be forced to make peace "under the shame of defeat." Of course, the idea that the army willingly made peace is at odds with the total rout at Maçin and everything else that they claimed about the army's debility, an incredible imposture in view of their dire situation. The issue must certainly have been important to go to such lengths.

Vâsıf's treatment of peace in the early 1790s – in the Maçin petition and elsewhere – shows a debate among the Ottoman élite that was still within traditional limits. One could not publicly depict peace as anything more than an interlude or justify it on any but the most constrained terms. Selim's conflation of honor and victory also shows that the link between the empire's military fortune and "honor" in peace persisted to the end of the century. In this view, peace was neither permanent nor based on

thanksgiving. However, the noise spooked the Ottoman troops in nearby İbrail, who mistook it for an attack, panicked, and fled their posts. Word of an attack then reached the soldiers in Maçin with a similar effect. Vâsıf alleged that this event convinced the Janissary commanders that their forces could never match the Russians in battle.

[38] Naîmâ criticized (1: 45–46) some jurists after the War of the Holy League (1683–1699) for holding back peace efforts in the hope of a "victorious peace through a brave attack." Murphey mentions similar attitudes at Passarowitz in "The Politics of Peacemaking," 80–81, 90 n. 11.

anything like "commonweal," but prescriptive and wedded to a militant ethos. This would only begin to change at the turn of the century.

5.4 "BLACKGUARD" IN THE PROVINCES, 1791–1792

The effects of the Maçin boycott were not immediately felt in camp or in Istanbul. There were no purges or recriminations; Yusuf Paşa remained in office and, for the time being, kept the sultan's confidence as Grand Vizier. The army was preparing to move south to Şumnu, where it would over-winter and await the result of negotiations with the Russians, and there was good reason to be hopeful. Word of a favorable peace with Austria arrived in mid-August, a fourteen-article treaty that restored the prewar status quo and that, for small concessions, returned all of the fortresses and lands lost by the Ottomans. This happy result came through British and Prussian mediation. While the policy had been controversial in London, where Prime Minister Pitt clashed with the likes of Edmund Burke and Charles Fox over his support for "the Turk," the European powers pushed the empire to a compromise to preserve a united front against France's new revolutionary régime. The Ottomans got a good bargain in return for an amnesty, promises of free trade and travel to Austrian subjects, and guarantees for Austria's shipping against the Barbary corsairs. Vâsıf too received a reward for his service, or in spite of his role in the mutiny. On August 29, Yusuf Paşa confirmed him as the head of the general accounts office, making his temporary appointment permanent. Vâsıf marched three days later with the rest of the army, undoubtedly pleased, reaching Şumnu in late September.[39]

Reaction to the truce in Istanbul proved more vexed, colored by rumor, wishful thinking, and divisions in the government. Selim stated his own position quite clearly and especially his displeasure with the third term: "That blackguard Vâsıf has acted in haste and signed away the Dniester as our border!" he wrote in pique to the Grand Vizier. The sultan's opposition stemmed from the fact that the territory between the Bug and

---

[39] Vâsıf wrote (MEHÂSİN 2, fols. 116a, 121a) that the posting took place according to normal promotion patterns after İbrahim Efendi retired to Istanbul due to illness: "I was seen fit for the post because of my seniority and personal precedence; the said directorship thus fell to me as a matter of course in late Zilhicce." Enverî specifies (ÖN H.O. nr. 105, fol. 320a) the date as 29 Z AH 1205 = August 29, 1791. The army then left Maçin on 2 M AH 1206 (September 1) and halted at Hırsova and Silistre before proceeding to Şumnu on 17 M or September 16. Ibid, fols. 320a–320b, 322a, 326b. On the Treaty of Sistova and its articles, see Edîb, 208–225; DİA, s.v. "Ziştovi Antlaşması"; and Shaw, *Old and New*, 61–64. Noradounghian, 2: 6–16, gives the text in French.

Dniester rivers contained major fortresses like Özü and Bender. While he could not undo it, Selim rejected the truce in principle and ordered Yusuf Paşa to be ready for a spring campaign if the Russians would not lower their demands. His refusal to accept defeat fell heavily on his advisers – among them Mehmed Râşid, Tatarcık Abdullah, and Yusuf Ağa – who questioned the army's ability to fight. So too did a popular and incredible rumor that the Ottomans had not lost at all; that they had somehow recaptured the Crimea and forced the Russians to sue for peace. When faced with such claims in council, Râşid had no choice but to produce the petition itself and read it aloud, an act that shocked his listeners into silence and tacitly cast doubt on the sultan's judgment. Selim's advisers did not wish to cross him, but they also did not believe in his chimerical plans. The war was lost. "My lord, this matter is settled," one counselor replied. "God save His Majesty from error!"[40]

Although the boycott's major actors escaped with their lives and careers intact, at least for the time, Vâsıf soon sensed that he was being turned into a scapegoat. Selim made it known that the historian had given up too much at the negotiating table and that he held him personally responsible for the truce's terms. This, of course, was unfair. Vâsıf had tried to act in the empire's interest. It was not his fault that Repnin refused to bargain or that the Ottoman army lay in ruins, destroyed, in part, by the sultan's stubborn quest for victory. The task had been thankless. Vâsıf was thus stung to learn in September that Selim had approved his transfer to the hinterlands, to Belgrade, to carry out the empire's treaty terms with Austria. Earlier, one Ebubekir Paşa had been sent to the city with an adjutant named Çelebi Mehmed Efendi, a former accounts director who, following the treaty's fourth and sixth articles, was to help the vizier oversee, inspect, and record the surrender of arms and munitions there, at Šabac, and elsewhere on the Balkan frontier. Vâsıf was now given Çelebi Mehmed's task. Selim had judged the latter unfit and ordered the historian to join Ebubekir Paşa without delay, making clear that he expected care and dispatch.[41] Although he rankled at the idea of a journey hundreds of

---

[40] According to Edîb (239–242, 246–247) this council occurred on 19 S AH 1206 = October 18, 1791. The rumor, he says, was initially spread by deserters in order to explain their presence in Istanbul and to avoid punishment. They not only boasted and claimed to have so badly beaten the Russians that they were allowed to return home, but even threatened doubters, accusing them of being "apostates." Certain "idiot dotards" then repeated these views in the council. See also Arıkan, 36; and Uzunçarşılı, "Dış Ruznâmesi," 610.

[41] Vâsıf's orders are contained in BOA.C.HR 1285 and are dated to mid-Muharrem AH 1206 or mid-September 1791. He, Ebubekir Paşa, and Çelebi Mehmed Efendi each

miles to the west, wanting only to go home, Vâsıf could not afford to disobey and put his affairs in order. Probably by late September, he was on the road. "I was staggered by one diversion after another," he resentfully remembered. "For following the verse, 'Again fate casts him quietly aside / Again fortune sends him afar.'"[42]

While we do not and cannot know what really caused Vâsıf's transfer to the provinces that fall, Selim's displeasure evidently left him at the mercy of those who were keen to exploit his weakness. This, at least, is what he claimed a few years later. Vâsıf alleged that courtiers began to poison the sultan against him, targeting his new post in the accounts office:

Certain jealous and spiteful men, naturally hating the learned and urbane, warned that this post would increase my standing and suggest a tacit approval of the truce terms. Therefore, despite the distinct injustice of it, they advised that I be given some pressing duty as a way to further the realm's affairs yet still safeguard its honor, lest the Russians catch on and make more demands of us. The sultan knew that they were plotting out of envy and pure malice. Yet under the circumstances he was forced to go along and decided that I should demarcate the border in Bosnia or settle some matters in Belgrade. He then issued a decree to this effect.

Vâsıf wrote that the sultan gave him a choice: join the Ottoman–Austrian border commission in Bosnia or oversee the return of fortresses and munitions in Belgrade, following articles four and six of the treaty. With some trepidation, he chose the latter, he said. He then set out for Belgrade.[43] It remains unclear how far we can trust this version of events, however, for a very different story emerges from a daybook in the imperial palace archives. According to this source, Vâsıf, far from being a victim, offended Yusuf Paşa shortly after his return to the army and was sent away "in exile." It seems that a Russian general named Sergei Lashkarev came to camp and all but asked the Grand Vizier for a bribe, complaining about the historian's stinginess in Galatz. "We all know how Vâsıf is," he added. "He's always penniless." As Yusuf Paşa had provided a good deal

---

received a copy of the document. Ebubekir's appointment as Belgrade warden (MEHÂSİN 2, fols. 115a-115b) meanwhile occurred in mid-Zilhicce AH 1205 = mid-August 1791. Sarıkaya, lxxxvi, has confused the dating.

[42] MEHÂSİN 2, fol. 4b.

[43] MEHÂSİN 2, fols. 121a-121b. Vâsıf expressed vague misgivings about working with the border commission, though he did not explain what his concerns were. The commission was to make minor changes in the frontier as set out in a special convention signed on the same day as Sistova. The border protocols are also contained in a lengthy dossier in the Ottoman archives: BOA.KK.d 57. Some biographies of Vâsıf agree that his appointment was a means to remove him, i.e. Fâik, 147; Karslızâde, 64; Schlechta-Wssehrd, 6–7; and Hammer-Purgstall, 3: 553.

of gold for just this purpose, money which was now gone, the daybook claims that he became angry and curtly dismissed Vâsıf to Belgrade. It may be that Vâsıf actually did embezzle the money and invented a "plot" to gain sympathy or to efface the whole embarrassing episode. It may also be that Lashkarev was settling a score.[44] He and Vâsıf had crossed paths decades earlier in Jassy and seem to have been on bad terms; true or not, his imputation was believable and struck home because it played on Vâsıf's well-known cupidity. But Vâsıf's complaints may still hold some grain of truth. Events would show that he not only had rivals who coveted his post, but who attacked him when down.

If there was indeed a cabal, it worked quickly to deprive Vâsıf of his newfound directorship in the treasury. Selim had made no provision for this in his original orders. He addressed Vâsıf by title, *baş muhâsebeci*, and said that he was merely making him a special adjutant or *mübâşir* to the Belgrade warden. But by early October, the situation had changed. Reaching the town of Niş, Vâsıf discovered that he had been turned out of office and that his post had been given to one Sivâsî Hasan Efendi, a former accounts director who was lately his direct subordinate as *anadolu muhâsebecisi*. Sadullah Enverî, again, replaced him as court historian. Vâsıf was enraged. "The sultan's decree had *not* reassigned the position," he maintained.

Yet Sivâsî Hasan Efendi – lowlife scum whom everyone considers inept and stupid – conspired with a likeminded ogre and pushed the change with his allies in breach of its word and spirit, stealing the directorship on the day that I reached Niş . . . Struck by disaster, I entered Belgrade in utter despair, carried out my duties, and hoped for the noble sultan's favor.

There are hints that Sivâsî Hasan's alleged accomplice (Vâsıf's "ogre") was a scribe who had served in a string of senior posts during the war and as a courier between the capital and army, Mehmed Hakkı Bey. Mehmed might

---

[44] The daybook (TSMA.d 4819, published in Uzunçarşılı, "Dış Ruznâmesi," 611) views matters from the capital and lags by days or weeks for outside events. This report is dated 20 S AH 1206 = October 19, 1791. It lists two places of exile, Tenedos (Bozcaada) and Belgrade, though orthographic error may account for the discrepancy. Called "Serço" by Ottomans, Sergei Lazarevich Lashkarev (d. 1814) was Georgian by birth and served as a dragoman in Istanbul for many years. Vâsıf lodged a complaint against him in 1774 with Rumiantsev, claiming the "cretinous Georgian" was treating fellow Georgian slaves as prisoners of war and demanding their freedom. He noted (MEHÂSİN 6, fols. 10b-11a) that Lashkarev came to Jassy in person to dispute the charges. On Lashkarev and the prisoner exchange, see Will Smiley, "Let Whose People Go: Subjecthood, Sovereignty, Liberation, and Legalism in Eighteenth-century Russo–Ottoman Relations," *Turkish Historical Review* 3 (2012): 208 ff.

have used his access at court to influence the sultan. Selim surely needed no great coaxing to demote a "blackguard" and let him stew for a spell in the provinces; he urged Yusuf Paşa in an undated decree to send the "knave" to one of the agreed sites at once, repeating his anger and fear that the general accounts directorship would be viewed as a reward. To Vâsıf, however, the affair smacked of envy, pure envy of his good fortune and personal acumen. As he swore defiantly in verse, "It was from envy of the steed of my own nature / If an ignorant ass or two bade me ride on."[45]

Vâsıf's journey from Şumnu to Belgrade led him overland through the provinces. In his youth, the historian had traveled the eastern marches; now, as a much older man, he could see the realm's westernmost frontier. We can imagine Vâsıf noting certain parallels between the two regions, namely the weakness of central authority and the rise of local strongmen. Notable dynasties had ruled parts of the empire's east for years. Yet the growth of autonomous power centers here, so close to the capital, struck members of the imperial administration as a new and disturbing trend. The wars of the past twenty-five years had ravaged the lands along the Danube, once the empire's breadbasket but increasingly overrun by bandits, demobilized irregular troops, and warlords. A reliance on local contractors, entrepreneurs, and grandees forced the government to work with these actors, whose interests and loyalties at times aligned with its own but who also exerted leverage to carve out personal fiefdoms. Irregular militias only made things worse, filling the countryside with armed, shiftless men. Vâsıf and his peers could see that provincial militias represented a rich source of manpower, but also a real threat to order – especially in peacetime when they disbanded, came home, and either took to banditry or entered the private armies of the a'yân.[46]

---

[45] MEHÂSİN 2, fol. 121b. Vâsıf added two more couplets on the themes of envy and fortune to the margin of this account: "If we are not so much as an atom in this world / The trouble is that our envy is more than an atom," and "Fortune is the ancient enemy of the urbane / If one has obtained happiness, it humbles him." Cf. Enverî, ÖN H.O. nr. 105, fol. 325a, who does not mention any irregularities in the dismissal and who says that it occurred on 6 S AH 1206 = October 5, 1791. Enverî not only replaced Vâsıf as court historian, but took Sivâsî Hasan's place as head of the Anatolian accounts office. The dismissal is also recorded in BOA.A.RSK.d 1623, p. 37, and Afyoncu, "Tevcihat Kayıtları I," 124, but without date. According to Cevdet (Târih, 5: 232–233), notes in several copies of Vâsıf's chronicle name Mehmed Hakkı as the said "likeminded ogre." On Mehmed Hakkı see SO, 2: 562–563; Said b. Halil İbrahim, 87; and Kethüda Said, 58. Selim's decree is preserved in TSMA.E 356. My thanks to Aysel Yıldız for sharing this document.

[46] Aksan, "Ottoman Military Recruitment," 197–198; and Robert Zens, "In the Name of the Sultan: Hacı Mustafa Pasha of Belgrade and Ottoman Provincial Rule in the Late Eighteenth Century," IJMES 44 (2012): 129–146.

Vâsıf and his retinue first skirted the territory of a notable near Rusçuk, Tirsiniklioğlu İsmail Ağa. Born to a family of notables, İsmail Ağa had recently fled execution, joined a group of bandits, and begun to prey on the countryside. It is possible Vâsıf saw some of his handiwork up-close. İsmail Ağa would eventually return to Rusçuk, vowing to reform, but instead built up a personal army, expanded his powerbase along the Danube, and by the late 1790s, forced Istanbul to confirm his position.[47] The historian then made his way toward Sofia and Niş, keeping to the Balkan range and avoiding the city of Vidin, where one Pazvantoğlu was also growing in power. Pazvantoğlu Osman had been a Janissary chief at Vidin and fought in the war as a volunteer. In the early 1790s, like İsmail Ağa, he came home, started a second career as a bandit chief and warlord, and launched raids into both Serbia and Wallachia. Pazvantoğlu defied Istanbul's efforts to bring him to heel. He became a focus for discontent with the régime – attracting unemployed irregulars and Janissaries – and by 1795, openly declared his independence. If Pazvantoğlu Osman ultimately accepted a place in the imperial hierarchy, however, as governor of Vidin, he did not cede power and even conducted a secret foreign policy with the empire's enemies. For this, he was beloved as a local hero and celebrated in song and verse. As Vâsıf passed Niş, he and his men turned north on the Belgrade road and may have reflected on these provincial troubles. Scholars have rightly pointed out the complex relations between Istanbul and the provincial a'yân, especially the role of notables as brokers between center and hinterland and the blurred lines between loyalty and revolt. To Vâsıf, however, as to many in the capital, these notables were either rebels or leaders of so-called "mountain bandits." The rise of provincial power centers for them signaled a fragmented rather than a more flexible empire; they were a threat that had to be suppressed.[48]

Vâsıf's work in Belgrade and its environs took some six months to complete. He arrived to find the city in good order thanks to the governor, Ebubekir Paşa, who shot his predecessor and caused much of the mutinous Janissary garrison to flee to Pazvantoğlu in Vidin. In October, Vâsıf and the rest of the task force started to take over the citadels and munition

---

[47] DİA, s.v. "Tirsiniklioğlu İsmâil Ağa"; Shaw, Old and New, 236–237; and Yaycıoğlu, 92–94.

[48] Shaw, Old and New, 236–237; Yaycıoğlu, 103–106; and Robert Zens, "Pasvanoğlu Osman Paşa and the Paşalık of Belgrade, 1791–1807," International Journal of Turkish Studies 8 (2002): 89–104. See also Vâsıf's words on the so-called "mountain bandits" in MEHÂSİN 4, fols. 35b, 243b–245b, 301a–303b; and HULÂSAT, 64–65.

stores at Šabac, Smederevo, and Belgrade itself, three key strongholds on the Danube and Sava rivers and, thus, on the Ottoman–Austrian border. Ebubekir Paşa saw to Belgrade and Smederevo; one Şehsuvar Abdi Paşa to Šabac some miles to the west. Proceeding through the winter, Vâsıf assisted these transfers and recorded in type and amount the arms and other supplies surrendered by the Austrians.[49] His stay was not wholly dull, though. He found in Ebubekir Paşa a deeply learned and cultured man and a vizier of good pedigree, going back at least three generations. Ebubekir Sâmî had studied the rational and transmitted sciences with eminent scholars, including Gelenbevî İsmail Efendi, Vâsıf's old coworker at the imperial press. He was a skilled poet, stylist, and calligrapher and had much to share in civilized conversation. Vâsıf took to Ebubekir. He praised his learning and calligraphy, claiming it would please the master Ibn Muqla (d. 940) himself. He also said that the vizier's odes could be an eighth "Hanging Ode (mu'allaqât)," referring to seven famed pre-Islamic Arabic poems, and that he made other poets look foolish. Like Hayrî's work, Vâsıf in later years would collect and anthologize Ebubekir Sâmî's poetry.[50]

Things seemed to bode well when Selim at last summoned Vâsıf to Istanbul in early April 1792, as his task wound down, and the historian must have been hopeful. He had been away from his home and family for a year. He was also surely eager to strike a blow at the rivals who, he felt, had deprived him of his rightful due. Vâsıf prepared a report for the sultan upon arriving in the capital, submitting his final figures along with deeds that certified the fortresses' return. He waited in vain for a word from court; none came. As weeks and months passed, it became increasingly clear that Selim was in no hurry to forgive, and Vâsıf turned inward. His alienation from political life came at an unlucky juncture, a moment in the realm's history when his erudition, historical insight, and long years in the scribal bureaucracy would have proved useful and intellectually provocative. For with the war over, Ottoman élites stood at the verge of a great experiment – a new era in political reform and in the empire's governance was about to begin.

---

[49] MEHÂSİN 2, fols. 121b-122a. Sarıkaya, lxxxvii, has located more documents on Vâsıf's time in Belgrade. These include an archival register (BOA.MHM.d 197, pp. 65, 594–597) that provides details on the proceedings, dates Vâsıf's recall to Istanbul to mid-Ş AH 1206 = early April 1792, and contains a copy of his final report to Selim, dated 15 L AH 1206 or June 6, 1792. See also Zens, "Hacı Mustafa Pasha of Belgrade," 132–133.

[50] Ebubekir Sâmî, Divân, İÜ TY nr. 2836, fols. 1b-4b. On this vizier, see SO, 5: 1478–1479.

6

Vâsıf and the New Order (1792–1800)

6.1 THE VIEW FROM OUTSIDE, 1792–1793

In 1792, Vâsıf found himself on the outside of a defining event of his time, shut out from the boldest reforms in the empire's history. Selim III had long contemplated reform. His statements as a prince and new ruler left little doubt of his wish to restore the empire, and now, with the war over, he saw his chance. While most scholarship dates the so-called "New Order," or *nizâm-ı cedîd*, reforms to 1792, we should not minimize the role of the war and especially the Maçin boycott and its aftermath. The Janissaries had publicly sworn that their forces were ineffective; they gave the sultan proof of the military's collapse and of the need for systematic change, testimony that he used as leverage. This is not to say Selim and his men had a coherent vision. Nor did they intend to radically remake Ottoman society. Instead, the reforms moved from the same initial premises as earlier Ottoman efforts – restoring "world order" and, it followed, the empire's glory. The sultan's modest wartime measures support this idea. Laws expelling transients from Istanbul or re-imposing clothing restrictions, for example, sought to quiet "social ferment," but also mend what, to Ottoman minds, were serious ruptures in socio-political order. These same ideas continued to guide the government's approach in peacetime, at least at first.[1]

---

[1] The New Order is one of the most studied periods in Ottoman history, although, as will be clear from this chapter, it is still far from fully understood. Shaw's *Old and New* remains the most accessible study in English and is invaluable for its description of the reforms themselves (e.g. pp. 75–85 on Selim's wartime reforms). See further DİA, s.v. "Nizâm-ı Cedîd"; Yüksel Çelik, "Nizâm-ı Cedîd'in Niteliği ve III. Selim ile II. Mahmud Devri Askerî Reformlarına Dair Tespitler (1789–1839)," in *III. Selim ve Dönemi*, 565–590; and

Selim began to lay groundwork for his reforms once peace was secure, asking for proposals from members of the ulema and scribal corps. The essays that he received came from twenty-two of the empire's leading men, from jurists like Mustafa Âşir and Salihzâde Ahmed Esad Efendi (both future şeyhülislâms) to military men like Yusuf Paşa, scribes like Mehmed Râşid and Çelebi Mustafa Reşîd, and two foreign advisers. They were a veritable blue book for the court and its factions. If Vâsıf did not contribute himself, he knew those who did as friend and foe alike – for every Tatarcık Abdullah was an enemy like Râşid, or rivals like Sadullah Enverî and Mehmed Hakkı Bey, who he felt had stolen his last posts. While diverse, the essays also set out an ambitious agenda for military as well as economic, administrative, fiscal, and educational reform. Selim eventually acted on many of their ideas. The following years saw laws set to improve efficiency in the bureaucracy and discipline in the military. More significantly, they saw Selim try to undermine the Janissaries' power with a parallel army, one drilled in European style, armed with modern weapons, and funded with excise taxes from a special treasury. Taken together, these formed the so-called Ottoman "New Order."[2]

To understand the significance of these reforms, we must first try to grasp what they meant to Ottoman élites. How was the "New Order" new? Past thinkers had worked within an unchanging, unchangeable order. They sought answers from inside the system because, in their mind, they already had a successful template in the "ancient practice" that supported nizâm-ı 'âlem, which in turn ensured the empire's survival. Ottoman élites for the same reason saw their problems as largely internal rather than as proof of superior European power or method. Indeed, the ruling ideology could not allow Europe's superiority in any real sense, or any change in the underlying order. The focus instead was on how best to repair perceived disorders and restore the realm's exceptionalism, with

Fatih Yeşil, "Nizâm-ı Cedîd," in *III. Selim: İki Asrın Dönemecinde İstanbul*, ed. Coşkun Yılmaz (Istanbul, 2010), 103–121.

[2] These essays have attracted much study. Enver Ziya Karal published a précis of them in *Tarih Vesikaları* 1/2 (1941–1943) under the title "Nizâm-ı Cedîd'e Dâir Lâyihalar." Full texts have also appeared as theses, articles, and books: Ergin Çağman published ten in *III. Selim'e Sunulan Islahat Lâyihaları* (Istanbul, 2010), using the same Topkapı Palace manuscript as Ahmet Öğreten's thesis, "Nizam–ı Cedid'e Dair Islahat Layihaları" (Istanbul University, 1989). Essays by Mehmed Şerif Efendi and Tatarcık Abdullah have been published, respectively, as Çağman, "III. Selim'e Sunulan Bir Islahat Raporu: Mehmed Şerif Efendi Layihası," *İlmî Araştırmalar* 7 (1999): 217–233; and "Sultan Selim-i Sâlis Devrinde Nizâm-ı Devlet Hakkında Mütâlaat," *TOEM* 7/8: 74–88; 7/41: 321–346; 8/43: 15–34. Shaw lists and analyzes their contents in some detail in *Old and New*, 91–111.

two main points at stake: the precise nature and value of "ancient practice" and, very closely related, the extent to which human reason could solve political problems.[3] Selim's efforts drew on an existing strain in this discourse. Earlier writers like İbrahim Müteferrika and Ahmed Resmî – both widely read in the period – had argued for activism and a muted emphasis on the past. Müteferrika, for example, seems to have eschewed "ancient practice" entirely. To him, the art of war had changed; the old ways were obsolete and the only way to revive the empire was to emulate Christian powers. Such ideas were highly popular in Selim's circle. Elaborating on the activism of previous decades, reformers began to admit the novelty of modern warfare and took reciprocation to new lengths. In the same vein, many placed less stock in ancient practice. There are even hints of a willingness to experiment with the "four pillars" and the components of world order itself.[4]

Tracing the intellectual lineage of Selim's program does still not explain how or why it was new to Ottomans. There were of course innovations. The reforms targeted not just the army but, increasingly, new spheres like the economy, administration, and treasury. One also sees a shift in the tone of debate, at once more rancorous, as partisans tried to make reform the only legitimate discourse and to brand opponents as idiots, boors, and traitors.[5] But the New Order was no sudden break. Ottomans had yet to question the metaphysical order and remained wedded to the idea of reform as

---

[3] The idea that Ottoman reform remained confidently inward-looking until the late eighteenth century is not new. As Kafadar says in his reappraisal of Ottoman decline ("Question of Ottoman Decline," 43), there was no "*crise de conscience*." His "Myth of the Golden Age" is also instructive. See further Ali Akyıldız, "Osmanlı Bürokratik Geleneğinin Yenileşme Süreci: Yenileşmeyi Zorunlu Kılan Nedenler," in *İslâm, Gelenek ve Yenileşme* (Istanbul, 1996), 129–131; Edhem Eldem, "18. Yüzyıl ve Değişim," *Cogito* 19 (1999): 190–192, 195–197; and İlber Ortaylı, "Osmanlı'da 18. Yüzyıl Düşünce Dünyasına Dair Notlar," in *Osmanlı Düşünce Dünyası ve Tarihyazımı* (Istanbul, 2007), 95–96.

[4] I have argued this in my dissertation, esp. 214–262. Müteferrika exerted an enormous influence on Selimian reformers, notably in his work on military reform, i.e. *Usûlü'l-Hikem fî Nizâmi'l-Ümem*, ed. Adil Şen (Ankara, 1995). See also his preface to *Târih-i Na'îmâ*, 4: 1894–1899. Similar sentiments are found in an anonymous treatise usually dated to the early eighteenth century and published by Faik Unat, "Ahmet III Devrine Ait Bir Islahat Takriri: Muhayyel Bir Mülâkatın Zabıtları," *Tarih Vesikaları* 1 (1941): 107–121. While some venture that Müteferrika wrote or directly inspired this piece (e.g. Berkes, 30 ff.; and Unat, 107 n. 3), internal evidence may point to a composition in the late eighteenth or early nineteenth centuries (oral communication from Marinos Sariyannis, 2015).

[5] E.g. Beydilli, "Islâhât Düşünceleri," 25–30; DİA, s.v. "Nizâm-ı Cedîd"; and Şakul ("Nizâm-ı Cedîd," 118–124, 129, 149–150), who claims reformers tried to turn the New Order into a "social movement."

restoration. It was not, in other words, a new universal order to replace the old. Part of the difficulty lies in the ambiguity of the word *nizâm*. In Turkish, this term has several meanings. Although its main sense is "order," it can refer more concretely to a system or method, hence a régime, military corps, or set of laws. It is even problematic in the sense of "order" and can take both metaphysical (*nizâm-ı 'âlem*) or strictly worldly and political connotations.[6] The idea that "New Order" stood for order in a worldly sense – the order of the dynasty or realm (*nizâm-ı devlet* or *nizâm-ı mülk*) – and eventually attached to the reform program is worth our consideration. Textually, this sense is found early on. Müteferrika seems to have used it in this fashion, as a rational way of arranging the empire's political and military affairs unrelated to or within the overarching metaphysical order. In the *Rational Bases for the Ordering of States* (*Usûlü'l-Hikem fî Nizâmi'l-Ümem*), he described how Europeans relied purely on reason to develop new tactics, strategy, and weaponry that represented a "new military order (*nizâm-ı cedîd-i ceyşiyye*)." With these innovations, warfare had changed. Henceforth, any ruler who used the new art would prevail; any ruler who ignored it would lose. Vâsıf and peers like Süleyman Penâh and Ebubekir Râtib Efendi later couched reform in these terms, too.[7]

That Ottomans were prepared to innovate but not to break from the past is clear from the 1792 reform proposals, which show, if anything,

[6] See Hagen, "Legitimacy and World Order," 58. Görgün argues (187–188) that we must look to the term's intellectual history to understand why reformers described the program as new. For example, a cursory look through dictionaries hints that *nizâm* slowly took on more concrete meaning. Older Arabic seems to focus more on an abstracted concept of order than Persian, Turkish, and modern Arabic definitions. See Edward Lane, *An Arabic-English Lexicon* (New York, 2011), 8: 3034. Cf. Hans Wehr, *A Dictionary of Modern Written Arabic* (Urbana, IL, 1994), 1147; and F. Steingass, *A Comprehensive Persian-English Dictionary* (Springfield, VA, 2010), 1409–1410. If Meninski and Sâmî reflect seventeenth- and nineteenth-century Ottoman usage, respectively, one sees a similar contrast between abstract and concrete: Meninski, *Thesaurus Linguarum Orientalium Turcicae-Arabicae-Persicae* (Istanbul, 2000), 3: 5203; cf. Sâmî, *Kâmûs-ı Türkî* (Istanbul, 1899/1900), 1463.

[7] Beydilli has traced (DİA, s.v. "Nizâm-ı Cedîd") the phrase "new order" back as far as the late seventeenth century, meaning that Müteferrika's usage (e.g. *Usûlü'l-Hikem*, 146–148, 151–152) was not wholly isolated or unique. In the 1770s, Süleyman Penâh urged reform of the Janissary corps as a "new order," in Aziz Berker, ed., "Mora İhtilâli Tarihçesi veya Penah Efendi Mecmuası," *Tarih Vesikaları* 2 (1942–1943): 228. Râtib meanwhile used the term for rationalizing, enlightened reform in the Austrian empire: Yeşil, *Ebubekir Râtib*, 233. See also Enver Ziya Karal, *Selim III'ün Hatt-ı Hümayunları: Nizam-ı Cedit, 1789–1807* (Ankara, 1946), 29–30. Fatih Yeşil comes closest to the likely spirit of the New Order in "Nizâm-ı Cedîd," 103, calling it "a state of orderliness or new laws/regulations that would ensure the order of civil life, which is subject to reconstruction." I have also explored this question in my dissertation, esp. "The Meaning of Nizâm-ı Cedîd," 235–239.

uncertainty about how to proceed. Although Selim's allies repeated what Müteferrika had advised in creating a European-style corps to counterbalance the Janissaries, who refused to accept modern drill, they could not agree on an approach.[8] Much of their disagreement concerned "ancient practice" and its value for reform. Vâsıf's friend and colleague Tatarcık Abdullâh Mollâ, for example, took a cautious tack and advocated appealing to the old corps through *kânûn-ı kadîm*. The Europeans had a technical advantage in warfare, he argued, as opposed to the Janissaries whose disorder arose from their disregard of the old ways. He advised that the corps be pressed to accept drill and encouraged that in doing so, they would respect proprieties, regaining their old glory.[9] The implication is that Abdullah considered ancient practice to be a part of reciprocation. To him, it was valuable, at least so long as it could serve Selim's policies. Still other proposals argued for ancient practice only when it met the needs of the day. If not, it could be partially or entirely replaced. According to Mustafa Râsih Efendi, a former steward to the Grand Vizier and later ambassador to Russia, the Janissaries ought to be returned to ancient practice through their officers. However, he added that "those methods that are ancient practice and still valid should be strengthened. Other regulations might have worked when first instituted, but they should, due to changing times, be reformed to suit today's needs."[10] Çelebi Mustafa Reşîd then brought Râsih's argument to its logical end, asserting that ancient practice was wholly obsolete. Reşîd wrote that the realm's institutions had "decayed" over time and needed to be rebuilt from the ground up. "In view of our current troubles we must reform *kânûn* anew," he concluded. "The empire needs a new order [*nizâm-ı cedîd*]."[11] As it happens, Reşîd's words support the notion of the New Order as a purely rational reorganization of the empire's affairs.

To Vâsıf, however, these debates remained in the abstract. Left on the outside, without post or preferment, he could do no more than watch them unfold. There is little doubt that the historian fervently hoped to regain the sultan's favor and to join in the doings at court, but the question was how. Vâsıf's personal situation certainly did not lend itself to an easy solution.

---

[8] On close inspection, we see that the authors did not share a "conscious and clearly articulated agenda for positive change" (Kadir Üstün, "The New Order and its Enemies: Opposition to Military Reform in the Ottoman Empire, 1789–1807," [Ph.D. diss., Columbia University, 2013] 149), but disagreed over minor and major points. Cf. Yaycıoğlu, 38–47.

[9] Öz, "Kânûn-ı Kadîm," 75; and Karal, "Nizâm-ı Cedîd," 1 (1941–1942): 417–420.

[10] Öz, "Kânûn-ı Kadîm," 75. Cf. Karal, "Nizâm-ı Cedîd," 2 (1942–1943): 107–108.

[11] Öz, "Kânûn-ı Kadîm," 76. Cf. Karal, "Nizâm-ı Cedîd," 2 (1942–1943): 104–105.

He later wrote that he found himself in financial turmoil upon returning to Istanbul and had to take on heavy debts, having no savings or income. While it is not clear whether this was really true, he, like other statesmen, could only sustain a fitting lifestyle at great cost. God's grace alone spared his household, he said.[12] Vâsıf absorbed other blows to his prospects at this time, as well. In late 1792 or early 1793, he learned that his erstwhile rivals Mehmed Edîb and Sadullah Enverî had presented new chronicles to Selim, a fact that did not disturb him as much as how they had done so. Not only had each made use of his unfinished notes from Istanbul and the battlefront, respectively, but they had, in fact, added them wholesale to their work. Vâsıf was deeply angered. While Ottomans had a flexible idea of intellectual property, and while Vâsıf drew liberally from others in his own work, he felt that a line had somehow been crossed. To him, it was plagiarism. "The events that I recorded in the army and during the imperial accession in Istanbul became stock-in-trade, nay capital, to others. They put them verbatim into their histories, which they then submitted to the sultan for reward," he complained. We can probably guess the reasons for this proprietary attitude. Being unpublished, Vâsıf may have considered the notes to be off-limits. Still more galling was the fact that Edîb and Enverî had been rewarded and had thus, he felt, stolen credit for his accomplishments. For the unemployed historian, this was maddening and unforgivable. He gave rein to his despair in verse:

> The trials I bore night and day
>> Served to profit another.
> 'Twas me who planted the tree of knowledge,
>> Gave over days to the pages of time,
> Yet when the time came, with labor given,
>> My grief fit their melody ill:
> The honeyed abuse of my rivals.[13]

---

[12] MEHÂSİN 2, fol. 122a. See also Schlechta-Wssehrd, 7.

[13] MEHÂSİN 2, fol. 4a. Cf. ibid, Millet Kütüphanesi, Ali Emiri nr. 608, fol. 3b. Fâtin includes (431) this poem in his anthology as a sample of Vâsıf's verse. We have no reason to believe that Edîb and Enverî acted in bad faith by using these notes in their work, as it was common practice for court historians to "inherit" their predecessor's drafts. Vâsıf's charges of plagiarism are also rare for Ottomans generally, who often borrowed or quoted without acknowledgment. See Hagen and Menchinger, 105, on the idea of intellectual property. Vâsıf left further marginal notes in a copy of Enverî's history (ÖN H.O. nr. 105, fols. 287b, 326b) repeating his insinuation of plagiarism. Edîb's chronicle for this period ends on 26 M AH 1207 = September 13, 1792, and Enverî's on 9 Ş = March 22, 1793. Vâsıf was aware of their contents by mid-1793 at the latest, when he began his second chronicle.

Vâsıf's activity at this period is rather harder to reconstruct. By his own account, he spent a full year in scholarly pursuits: "I passed the time by devoting myself to study and disputation, as is my wont," he wrote.[14] Although the object of this study was outwardly far from politics, being mainly literary in nature, it surely had the political motive of securing patronage. One task that Vâsıf very likely undertook was a lexicon. He had always excelled at language; now, in a way, in turning to lexicography, he was returning to his early roots as a littérateur. Vâsıf looked to tackle the classic but notoriously obscure Persian history of Shihâb al-Dîn ʿAbd Allah b. Faḍl Allah Shîrâzî (fl. 1300), better known as Vaṣṣâf, a figure whose style he greatly admired and emulated. Once again, he was joining a tradition. Vaṣṣâf's florid prose and use of Turkish, Mongol, and Persian terms challenged even the most learned Ottomans, and, as with al-Zamakhsharî, the lexicon followed a long line of Turkish glosses and translations dating back several centuries. Vâsıf focused on Vaṣṣâf's first volume. Compiling material from two earlier scholars – one Behcet Ali Efendi and the late poet and court historian Hıfzî Mehmed Efendi – he wrote the book macaronically, defining and glossing in Arabic, Persian, or Turkish, depending on the word's origin and using a range of linguistic and historical sources. When finished, he dubbed it *Perplexities in Vaṣṣâf's Vocabulary*, or *Müşkilât-ı Lugat-ı Vassâf*.[15]

Vâsıf did not limit himself to his idol Vaṣṣâf's finer points, though. He also extended his efforts into poetry and, perhaps surprisingly, revived his testy relationship with the chief scribe Mehmed Râşid Efendi. In 1792 or 1793, Râşid asked him to gather and edit the late Hayrî Efendi's poems in an anthology or *divân*. Hayrî's untimely death on the Boze three years prior had been tragic; so too did it consign his skilled but unpublished verse to a likely oblivion. Vâsıf acted on Râşid's orders, knowing that the chief scribe, who was himself a poet, wished to prevent this end. He first

---

[14] MEHÂSİN 2, fol. 122a.

[15] This work exists in a single copy (TSMK Hazine nr. 1448) at the Topkapı Palace in Istanbul, the flyleaf of which bears a note identifying Vâsıf as the author along with the date 22 B AH 1207 = March 5, 1793. Behcet Ali and Hıfzî Mehmed died in 1777 and 1751, respectively: SO, 2: 363, 667. Although these dates admittedly yield a wide time frame, some sixteen years, I have placed the composition at this stage because it best fits Vâsıf's professional arc. So too does its presence in the palace suggest his search for patronage. However, it may also date to his first period of extended unemployment from 1774 to 1779. Only part of the manuscript being available to me, I have relied in this section on Sarıkaya's description, ccxlv–ccxlvii. See also Fehmi Edhem Karatay, *Topkapı Sarayı Müzesi Kütüphanesi Türkçe Yazmalar Kataloğu* (Istanbul, 1961), 2: 33; and DİA, s.v. "Vassâf."

gathered the poems from Hayrî's papers and arranged them by language and form – Turkish and Persian odes (kasîde), parallels (nazîre), strophes (kıt‘a), ghazels, chronograms (târih), and quatrains (rubâî) – omitting only his immature work. To this, he added a glowing preface and biography of Hayrî, whom he called "the leading poet of the age" and whose verse he likened to "an incomparable pearl." The anthology, then, was partly a memorial. Vâsıf praised poetry as "the best of arts." As such, he said, it was wrong to let posterity forget an accomplished poet after his death: "The poet's verse is his intellectual coin, indeed his life's income. To immortalize his works and revive his name is thus a way for us to obtain God's mercy." Still, Vâsıf did not miss this chance to flatter and curry favor with Râşid, crediting the project to the latter's keen perception and abasing himself as "Ahmed Vâsıf, who begs crumbs from the learned and bows before the refined."[16]

The collection of Hayrî Efendi's verse was not the historian's only foray into the Ottoman literary world at the time, but reflected his growing interest in poetry. Vâsıf had always been known as a stylist – a prose stylist – and was fiercely proud of his reputation. Poetry nonetheless had a special cachet in the empire as a vehicle for learned culture. Ottoman court poetry drew on the Persian literary canon for form, vocabulary, syntax, symbol, and metaphor and formed a rich if somewhat rigid medium. Anyone who was anyone wrote poetry. In fact, as an intellectual exercise, it was highly élitist. The poet's aim was not to create a mimetic image of the world or even to express emotion, but rather to craft ingenious, self-referential, musical verse within existing forms. To write poetry required a knowledge of Turkish, Persian, and Arabic; it demanded a deep reading in the masters and a long study of formal prosody and rhetoric. It should come as no surprise that verse was a pastime especially for scribes, then, who studied the language, used metered and rhymed chancery speech, and whose training coupled fluency in prose with poetry (şiir ü inşâ). Court poetry also grew in new and contentious ways in the eighteenth century. Some poets like Nedîm (d. 1730) developed a "natural" style with concrete imagery and fewer words of Persianate origin, building on the "simple Turkish (türkî-i

---

[16] Hayrî, esp. 318–326. While Şener does not try to date the collection, we can assign it with some confidence to 1792 or 1793 based on two considerations: Râşid was serving as chief scribe during this time (1792–1794) and Vâsıf, who lists himself without position, was jobless from mid-1792 to May 1793 and seeking patronage. Hayrî's death in September 1790 naturally forms the terminus post quem. See Fâtin, 87, 112, for samples of Hayrî's and Râşid's poetry. Mustafa Aslan has also published selections from the latter's divân in "Kayserili Raşit Mehmet Efendi ve Divançesi," Türkoloji Araştırmaları 2/3 (2007): 40–58.

basît)" movement of earlier centuries, and broke formal convention by drawing on Turkish folk poetry. This challenge did not go unmet, however. The great Sünbülzâde Vehbî (d. 1809) railed against innovators in the 1780s in verse for Halil Hamid Paşa, for one, calling them untutored and claiming that their style made poetry "a beggar's gate."[17]

The Ottoman poetic scene remained lively under Selim III, who tried his hand at music and verse and patronized figures like Enderûnî Fâzıl (d. 1810) and Gâlib Dede (d. 1799), one a follower of Nedîm and the other the author of an allegorical epic, *Beauty and Love (Hüsn ü Aşk)*, and the last great representative of the classical tradition. Vâsıf might have turned to verse out of real interest or to better sell himself at court. In any case, his efforts became more visible in the new reign. We know that he continued to write *pièces d'occasion* and that by the early 1790s, his work had gained enough notice to be the subject of parallels or *nazîre*, including one by the poet and *şeyhülislâm* Yahyâ Tevfîk Efendi. The historian voiced his growing confidence in a 1794 poem, saying "I am the lord of prose / Nor shall poets traduce my rights."[18] Vâsıf may also have begun to assemble his own poetry album, a work, unfortunately, either abandoned or mostly lost. This incomplete work exists in a single manuscript and contains only nine full poems, all ghazels, yet offers us a fleeting glimpse into his style. Vâsıf wrote on typical themes like fate, love, suffering, and separation. Yet while he used conventional form and later disparaged "Turkish and simple verse," his work shows the imprint of naturalizing poets like Nedîm in its syntax and vocabulary. The poems balance Persian and Turkish words and particles and, in some cases, approach a one-to-one ratio, as in a ghazel that begins "My heart bears legions of wounds from your glance / Do not think

---

[17] On Ottoman poetry in the eighteenth century, see Kemal Silay, *Nedim and the Poetics of the Ottoman Court: Medieval Inheritance and the Need for Change* (Bloomington, 1994), esp. 128–136; and George W. Gawrych, "Şeyh Galib and Selim III: Mevlevism and the Nizam-ı Cedid," *International Journal of Turkish Studies* 4 (1987): 91–114.

[18] Vâsıf, Millet Kütüphanesi nr. 608, fol. 166a; and Mustafa L. Bilge, "Vâsıf Tarihinin Üç Muteber Zeyli," in *Prof. Dr. Şevki Nezihi Aykut Armağanı*, eds. Niyazi Çiçek et al. (Istanbul, 2011), 42. Vâsıf also included (MEHÂSİN 2, fol. 80a) one of his poems, a ghazel, in a biography of Tevfîk Efendi sub anno hegirae 1205 = 1791. It begins: "He marred your beauty, O heart-ravishing lord / Forcibly he enamored you, lord." Tevfîk replied with a parallel ending in the couplet, "'Tis impossible to mimic such verse and prose / For in quality [*vâsıfen*] he made you the state's wordsmith, the Lord." This verse plays on "wordsmith (*vassâf*)" to compliment Vâsıf, likening him to the historian Vaṣṣâf. Vâsıf also wrote (see ibid, fols. 157b-158a, 160a) a double-chronogram in 1793 to congratulate the late Râif İsmail's son, İsmet İbrahim Beyefendi, on a judicial posting, and the next year sent verse to Selim.

there is a medical cure."[19] The reason that Vâsıf's poems did not survive is less clear. It may be that he failed as a poet or that, for some reason, his work did not suit contemporary tastes. At least one peer, Ahmed Âsım, hinted as much in a devastating critique of the man and his work. "Vâsıf was without a whit of subtlety or grace," he wrote early in the nineteenth century.

Whenever he read his work to those attending his salon, it was his habit to become drunk on their admiration and to torment anyone who kept silent or dared to question a word, putting on wounded airs. And while he sometimes wrote poetry, the truth is that it had neither beauty nor taste and would, indeed, invite satirical parody and lampoon. I have thus avoided the humiliation of offering examples.[20]

While certainly partisan, this passage fits well with what we know of Vâsıf's character. The inordinately vain historian craved validation and praise. If he truly hoped to be a great poet, he might simply have given up when the psychological and material rewards failed to appear.

Yet even if these literary works won few accolades, they still helped the historian gain small victories and ease his way back to court. Poet manqué or no, Vâsıf used both the lexicon and poetry in his search for patronage and employment; that he succeeded in this more modest aim was shown clearly, in mid-1793, by an abrupt change in his fortunes. In May, Vâsıf learned that he had been named to his old post in the Anatolian accounts office.[21] It was most likely Râşid who acted on his behalf. The two had patched over their quarrel and at least outwardly resumed cordial, if not friendly, relations. Vâsıf felt immense relief. He was returning to work in the treasury and could now reckon on a fixed salary. With the stress of joblessness gone, he was, however, not fully satisfied. What would happen to his position in the future? Would he be able to support his household? "Unless your star be in the ascendant / You shan't feed your household on yearly office," he wrote, in a worried couplet from the period. Vâsıf still prayed that the sultan would favor his scholarly pursuits. As it happened, again with aid from Râşid, these hopes were realized less than two months later when the Grand Vizier called him to the Porte to present him with

[19] Vâsıf, Divân, İÜ İbnülemin nr. 3692, fols. 19a, 22a-22b, 24a, 33a, 37a, 39a. Cf. MEHÂSİN 6, fol. 4a. See also Sarıkaya, cclxxiii–cclxxviii.

[20] Âsım, 1: 258. Modern opinion on Vâsıf's poetry has not been much kinder. Babinger deemed it (GOW, 336) "mediocre," while Schlechta-Wssehrd derided it (7) as "completely worthless." Cf. Bilge's recent attempt at a reevaluation, 42–44.

[21] MEHÂSİN 2, fols. 122a, 159b. This appointment took place on 5 L AH 1207 or May 16, 1793. See BOA.A.RSK.d 1623, p. 37; and Afyoncu, "Tevcihat Kayıtları I," 124–125. It is also mentioned in Fâik, 147; and Karslızâde, 64.

a robe of honor. Selim had dismissed Enverî, he said. Vâsıf would be court historian for a third term.[22]

6.2 "CHARMS AND TRUTHS," 1793–1794

With the realm more settled, Selim had at last revisited his wish for a comprehensive history of his reign. The task would be daunting. Vâsıf was to compile the existing records back to the imperial accession; in essence, he would have to rewrite and combine everything that he, Enverî, and Edîb had written in the past four years into one narrative. After this, and only after this, could he bring the court chronicle up to date. Vâsıf threw himself into revisions that summer and began to pare Enverî and Edîb, partly purging, partly redoing, and partly supplementing their work with new material. He was keenly aware of weak spots. Neither rival being his equal in rhetoric or prosody, a fact that he made much of, Vâsıf carefully smoothed their wordy or ungainly passages with his own "delicate phrasing." So too did he stress their "failures" by adding moral and political lessons, grist for his own brand of didactic historiography. By early September, the historian had brought the work to late 1790. This he sent to the palace as a sample for a newly planned chronicle, a volume that he would add to his first and call the *Charms and Truths of Relics and Annals* or *Mehâsinü'l-Âsâr ve Hakâikü'l-Ahbâr*. The preface to this sample praised Selim as both a ruler and patron and gave rein to Vâsıf's hubris. In the empire and in every dynasty, he wrote, sovereigns choose a "genius" and "rare stylist" to immortalize their reign and to give counsel. Vâsıf himself had served the dynasty for almost twenty-five years; he had spent five as its court historian. Yet while his first volume had impressed readers with its accuracy, fluency, and insight – some even comparing him to Vaṣṣâf – he had gradually fallen on hard times, his work forgotten and even stolen. Only by the sultan's mercy was he

---

[22] MEHÂSİN 2, fol. 122a. Vâsıf also revealed (ibid, fol. 5a) his anxiety when he wrote: "I prayed God that the base coin of my learning and skill should circulate in this sovereign's reign. But following the saying, 'Kings are inspired,' he now showered me with his royal mercies." While we do not have firm evidence for how Vâsıf was renamed court historian at this time, Râşid, who as chief scribe controlled his access to documents, must have played a key role. A note on the appointment (BOA.C.DH 2546) dated 13 Za AH 1207 = June 22, 1793, offers some context by praising Vâsıf's learning and talent. It adds: "As he therefore deserves favor, he has, out of royal munificence, been made court historian in order to record events." See also Âsım, 1: 256; Fâik, 147; Fâtin, 432; Karslızâde, 64; and Kütükoğlu, "Vekâyi'nüvis," 105–107, 119.

restored. Vâsıf then promised, if the work pleased, to finish his revisions and move to more recent events.[23]

The preface and sample established a number of motifs that would occupy Vâsıf in the new reign, and in fact for the rest of his life. One of these was ethics. His submission reflected a wide reading in the great works of Ottoman moral philosophy and especially Kınâlızâde's classic *Sublime Ethics*. Like many lettered Ottomans, Vâsıf based his view of morality on the understanding of the human soul (*nefs*) in Aristotelian practical philosophy. Hellenic tradition divided the soul into three parts – the vegetative or concupiscent soul, the animal or irascible soul, and the rational soul – each with differing moral tendencies.[24] Vice occurred whenever these led to a dearth or excess in behavior; virtue followed, by contrast, from moderation. The soul in this view was the seat of moral action. Given to base appetites, thinkers argued that it could and should be tamed through the knowledge and virtue taught by philosophy. For Vâsıf and authorities like Kınâlızâde, Taşköprüzâde, and Kâtib Çelebi, then, ethics not only instructed readers about virtue and vice, but also about how to achieve a wholesome moderation in action.[25] Still, Ottoman

---

[23] MEHÂSİN 2, fols. 1b-5a. Cevdet says (*Târih*, 6: 90) that Vâsıf presented this preface with a history from the imperial accession to AH 1205 or 1790/91, and quotes Selim's pleased reply. A note in Vâsıf's drafts (BOA.Y.EE 90, p. 42) clarifies that the submission consisted of seven parts (*cüz*) ending in Safer AH 1205 = October or November 1790. That Vâsıf considered the work to be a new volume is shown by his plan (MEHÂSİN 2, fol. 5a) to revise Enverî up to 1789 and to add this to his own "first volume." He would bring the revisions to the date of his appointment in June 1793 with new events thereafter. "By my life," he concluded, "this history is fit to be called the *Charms and Truths of Relics and Annals*." See also Kütükoğlu, "Vekâyi'nüvis," 119–120. Vâsıf made a similar complaint about his early work's neglect in MEHÂSİN 6, fol. 4b.

[24] On the soul, see KINÂLIZÂDE, esp. 62–70, 79–88; EI², s.v. "Nafs"; DİA, s.v. "Nefis"; Nasr, 248–250; and Fakhry, 64–66, 132–133. In this tradition, the vegetative or concupiscent soul (*nefs-i nebâtî/behîmî*) was concerned with growth, reproduction, and appetite; the animal or irascible soul (*nefs-i hayvânî/sebû'î*) with sense, locomotion, and defense; and the rational soul (*nefs-i nâtıka*) with speech and higher thought. While the concupiscent soul continually urged evil, the irascible soul vacillated between carnal appetites and remorse and the rational soul was free from sensual appetites. A threefold Quranic division roughly matched the philosophical: the carnal mind when fully dominant (*nefs-i emmâre*); the carnal mind when resisted but unsubdued (*nefs-i levvâme*); and the carnal mind when fully conquered (*nefs-i mutmainne*).

[25] E.g. KINÂLIZÂDE, 42–43, 93–107; Taşköprüzâde, s.v. "'Ilm al-akhlâq"; and Kâtib Çelebi, *Kashf al-zunûn*, s.v. "'Ilm al-akhlâq" and "'Ilm al-ḥikma." See also DİA, s.v. "'Âdalet" and "Ahlâk"; Fakhry, 111–112; and Majid Khadduri, *The Islamic Conception of Justice* (Baltimore, 1984), 106–134. Three cardinal virtues attached to the soul's three parts: temperance, bravery, and wisdom. Bravery, for instance, held a golden mean between the excess of recklessness (*tehevvür*) and the dearth of cowardice (*cübn*). A fourth virtue, justice, emerged only in souls that had developed the other three.

ethics did not limit itself to the individual soul. As part of practical philosophy, it formed the basis of economics and statecraft and informed politics as theory informs practice. Hence, the just ruler was supposed to be a "perfect man" – someone who had gained virtue in mind and deed – and had a duty to guide his subjects accordingly. On him depended the whole edifice of world order, a point Kınâlızâde made in urging kings to cultivate wisdom and justice:

> For as the body reaches its ideal through nature, nature through the soul, and the soul through the intellect, so the realm reaches its ideal through the king, the king through the administration of justice, and the administration of justice through wisdom. When wisdom is known in the realm and holy law in the king, there is order and subjects gain all possible perfection. But holy law shall be forsaken if wisdom is abandoned; and when the law is forsaken the king's majesty shall disappear, disorders arise, and blessings be obliterated.[26]

Vâsıf's turn to philosophy shows, for one, a deepening concern for ethics within history. For Ottomans, history was always a highly personal affair. What shaped the course of events more than anything, and certainly more than sociological forces, were powerful men and the moral choices that they made. Increasingly, this too was the historian's view. Not only did he highlight simple virtues and vices, but he integrated these – greed, envy, ignorance, desire – into larger moral themes than in his early work. For instance, Vâsıf warned in his sample against vanity, fickle fortune, and the corrupting nature of power. His main point was that the uncontrolled passions can lead to destruction. The world of generation and corruption, "the world of conceit," as he called it, is ever trying to ensnare us:

> Climbing high on fortune's wheel, men purge the fear of God from their hearts, amass wealth, confuse right and wrong, devote themselves to profit and gain, and fall headlong into perdition. They thus give themselves over to worldly pleasures and ... as wise men have seen countless times, are remanded to divine justice.[27]

For Vâsıf, the answer to this danger was simple. Restraint, self-control, personal reform – in a word, moral education. By the same token, though, he felt that history and practical philosophy should work together toward this end. History was no better than a tall tale without the sort of lessons

---

Ottoman moralists did not always agree on the soul's composition or its propensity for reform, however. I have treated these debates at length in my dissertation, esp. 178–183.

[26] KINÂLIZÂDE, 488.

[27] MEHÂSİN 2, fol. 11a. For other examples see fols. 15a, 77b, 78a-78b, 149a. Also ibid, TSMK nr. 1638, fol. 13b.

given by practical philosophy, after all, and useless unless it could improve readers.[28]

The new sample also borrowed heavily from the ethical tradition in its political ideals. One must recall that Ottomans made no clear distinction between the moral and the political. The idea of a moral order upheld by a just ruler was, in fact, central to how many eighteenth-century thinkers understood the empire. Kınâlızâde had once compared the king to a doctor; in order to govern, he had to study the realm's moral health, learn to diagnose its illnesses, and know the right cure. To be politically just, in other words, he had to be personally just.[29] Vâsıf too voiced this in his preface when he called for a "perfect being (*bir vücûd-ı kâmil*)" to rule and uphold order. He began the work with a view of socio-political order and how it must be maintained. "Know," he wrote, "that for man the ordering of faith, justice, and righteousness occur through a diversity of occupation and temperament and the survival of the species through mutual aid."

For were not some men base and others noble, and if the lowly had no need of the noble, there must be equality and, owing to conflicting desires, two opinions on a single matter. Thus there would everywhere be chaos and strife; the common people would rush to destroy each other and the order of the world and creation would come utterly undone – "Were men equal they would all be destroyed." It is therefore needful that in every era there be a perfect being to adeptly administer the law, ruling such varied people according to their merits and "keeping them in their proper place" through the scales of justice that order all creation.[30]

Vâsıf next explained how the ruler ought to support this order, drawing on the Neoplatonic model of the "Virtuous City" and Kınâlızâde's *Sublime Ethics*. Practical philosophy shows us that political rule is of two sorts, he said: virtuous and vicious. Virtuous rule (*siyâset-i fâzıla*) brings justice, strengthens the faith, promotes integrity and belief, and governs and nurtures the realm and its subjects. A virtuous ruler is called "Commander of the Faithful." By contrast, vicious rule (*siyâset-i nâkısa*) seeks sensual pleasures and lusts, wields injustice, seizes property, and enslaves its subjects. This sort of rule is also known as "tyranny." Virtuous rulers, he added, cleave to faith and wisdom:

---

[28] Vâsıf wrote on the occasion (MEHÂSİN 2, fol. 4a) that one purpose of history was "to improve public morals." He also drew special attention in the work (ibid, fol. 27b) and in an accompanying letter (BOA.Y.EE 90, p. 42) to his use of practical philosophy. Hagen and Menchinger, 97–98, note the personal dimension of Ottoman historical thought.

[29] KINÂLIZÂDE, 473. Crone, 161, says that "moral perfection was a key desideratum in a ruler in that virtue was required for justice."

[30] MEHÂSİN 2, fols. 2a-2b. Vâsıf quoted from a hadith in this passage.

Mastering their passions and nature, they treat subjects kindly, rule with justice, integrity, and benevolence, and have as their basic aim happiness and the perfection of morals. They are thus fit to be called "Shadow of God" and "Master." Yet vicious rulers incline to iniquity and spurn justice and moderation. Through force, the tyrant considers his subjects as so many slaves while he himself is enslaved to concupiscence and fills his realm with fear, suffering, discord, enmity, and ruin.[31]

Vâsıf's aim in treating rulership in this way is clear. He meant to imply that Selim III was the ideal sovereign, the "perfect being" of philosophy who would right the balance of *nizâm-ı 'âlem* and restore the realm. Beyond political virtue, though, the preface served to flatter and optimistically assert the empire's special role in history. "Religion and kingship are twins," Vâsıf declared, quoting a well-known adage. "One cannot be achieved without the other." Religion therefore acts as the realm's foundation and kingship its support – for a foundation is useless without support and a baseless support is toppled – and it is for this reason that rulers like the Prophet spread justice into the non-Islamic world. Vâsıf claimed that the Ottoman sultans too had served the faith in this way and revived Islam after a period of turmoil. Exceptionally blessed with God's aid and great wisdom, they ruled virtuously, enforced holy law, and lavished their subjects with kindness. With extravagant praise, he then added Selim to their number. The sultan had ruled virtuously from his accession. He was innately good and wise and wanted nothing more than to guard the realm, to rid it of injustice. Vâsıf thus prayed that his master's fortune would grow ever stronger and enable him to take revenge on his enemies. God willing, they would be crushed and the realm made prosperous.[32]

Vâsıf's concern with ethics is easier to pinpoint if we look more closely at his metaphysics. As before, one of the new work's biggest aims was to explain why the empire fared so poorly against Christian powers. What was causing these losses? Vâsıf had dwelled on free will at length in his earlier writing and now returned to the subject with renewed urgency, using the empire's late war as a sort of historical laboratory. To him, the problem was essentially moral. He blamed the rout on the Boze on the army's sins, for example, for the sinner betrays the faith and the traitor is a coward by nature. "It is for this reason," he vowed, "that our armies do

---

[31] MEHÂSİN 2, fols. 2b-3a. Cf. KINÂLIZÂDE, 455–457. On the "Virtuous City," see Taşköprüzâde, s.v. "'Ilm al-siyâsa"; Fakhry, 136–140; and Charles Butterworth, "Early Thought," in *A Companion to Muslim Ethics*, ed. Amyn Sajoo (London, 2010), 31–51.

[32] MEHÂSİN 2, fols. 3a-4a.

not hold fast on the battlefield."[33] Yet Vâsıf also faulted the empire for what he considered its sinful lack of readiness. Having seen European weapons and tactics first hand, in Spain and on the Danube, he criticized the government for failing to keep abreast of innovation. Warfare changes over time and a disobedient mass of soldiers cannot beat the new-style soldier fielded by Russia and Austria, he said. Nor can they expect God to hand them victory. Vâsıf thus moved away from his 1784 essay and instead directed readers to "secondary causes," which "encompass warfare and the arts of combat. In other words, the new military organization that is part of the mathematical sciences." Victory was not just a matter of bravery or trust in God, then. The Ottomans had to plan, strategize, and use good judgment because God acts in the world through causes. This idea Vâsıf justified theologically: "According to the philosophers, everything is contingent; what is contingent admits influence; and what admits influence cannot be without cause," he wrote.

The Sunnis say that although everything issues un-contingent from God and while man's deeds have absolutely no effect or influence on causes or the ability to influence the course of events, it is God's custom to create everything as an outcome of secondary causes. All sects therefore deem it necessary when they must undertake a matter to first secure the secondary causes and other needful things. Only then, following the sense of "Hobble your camel and trust in God," may they hope and pray for God's victory.[34]

For Vâsıf, morality and action went hand-in-hand and he increasingly saw human initiative as a duty equal to or greater than piety, zeal, or obedience. If the empire depended foremost on God, then, it needed a leader like Selim to guide it in virtue and action. Only then, only when they "observed Islamic practice and secured the necessary causes," would the Ottomans prevail.[35]

The sample played well with its royal audience. Shortly after its submission, Selim returned the work to Vâsıf "to continue in the very same manner" and with orders for a reward: 5,000 kuruş from the imperial mint. This was a goodly sum. It was more than Vâsıf had ever earned from Abdülhamid and more than what other chroniclers usually received.[36]

---

[33] Ibid, fol. 33a.

[34] MEHÂSİN 2, fols. 26a-27a, again quoting a hadith: G.W.F. Freytag, *Arabum proverbia, vocalibus instruxit, latine vertit, commentario illustravit et sumtibus suis editit* (Bonn, 1838–1843), 2: 112.

[35] MEHÂSİN 2, fol. 33a. See also Menchinger, "Reformist Philosophy," 151–154.

[36] MEHÂSİN 2, fols. 172b-173a; and Cevdet, *Târih*, 6: 90. One archival document (BOA. C.MF 939) dated Ş AH 1211 or early 1797 indicates that, by contrast, the court historian

Freed from financial worry, and no doubt elated by his success, the historian set about reworking the rest of Enverî's and Edîb's accounts of the war and expanding the work with new installments. He added morals and lessons; he likewise stressed his role as original author – for his rivals, after all, had merely stolen his notes. He even seems to have turned to his first chronicle with a plan, using Enverî as a bridge, to create a continuous work from 1783 to the present, though this remained unrealized. Vâsıf kept busy through the fall of 1793 and the following winter. While he failed to secure a post that May, he continued to write and compose occasional poetry as court historian. We also see him cultivating patrons like Selim's confidant and Grand Admiral, the powerful Küçük Hüseyin Paşa.[37]

With his chronicle accepted, furthermore, Vâsıf could finally join the partisan intellectual debates at court. Selim was moving ahead with his reforms. In 1793, he founded a second treasury, the "new revenue," or *irâd-ı cedîd*, and imposed a number of taxes and economies to fund his model army. Breaking with tradition, he also sent a scribe named Yusuf Agâh to London as the first resident Ottoman envoy. Vâsıf took pains to portray these actions as practical and fully in line with tradition, the basic concept, again, being reciprocation. Selim needed money to train and field a force on the new European lines, he wrote, just as he needed permanent embassies to study foreign crafts and trades and to gain intelligence. The formation of a merchant marine too was a way to check the empire's rivals. Vâsıf argued that Christian states had gained control of the seas through their greed, which led them to sail as far as America and China and to take great risks for profit. The danger for him was that this created an unfavorable balance of trade. Using the logic of political economy, perhaps learned in Spain, he warned that foreign merchants would soon siphon off the realm's specie unless the sultan could get wealthy statesmen

Halil Nûrî Bey received only 3,000 *kuruş* for a submission. See also Kütükoğlu, "Vekâyi'nüvis," 110.

[37] See MEHÂSİN 2, fols. 5a, 142b, 157b-158a. According to a document (BOA.HAT 13135), Vâsıf submitted his revisions in three volumes to the sultan, who ordered him to continue the work. TSMK nr. 1638 is the last section of this chronicle; BnF Supplément turc nr. 508 contains deletions and changes in a hand like Vâsıf's and is perhaps an author's copy. Vâsıf also wrote in a marginal note in Enverî, ÖN H.O. nr. 105, fol. 326b that "the events I recorded at the imperial army were put verbatim in this work and thus plagiarized. I have now added them with slight changes to the new history that I have composed." Some copies end with a fulsome eulogy to Küçük Hüseyin Paşa, whom Vâsıf credited with his appointment. See Millet Kütüphanesi nr. 608, fol. 166a; and Bilge, 42–43.

to build ships and invest in trade. But Vâsıf was equally quick to abuse would-be critics. Selim's new excise taxes were not illegal novelties, but had precedent in the sixteenth century under Sultan Murad III, he wrote. Those who claimed otherwise were either ignorant or "fanatical." So too were the unnamed "liars" who tried to dissuade the sultan with their "frigid asceticism and perverse fanaticism."[38]

Vâsıf's posturing is of interest in that it hints at an early pushback to the reforms. The New Order posed a threat to many Ottoman élites because it aimed to rebalance power in favor of the sultan and central government in Istanbul, away from the likes of the Janissaries, provincial notables, and others. We can better appreciate the broad basis for this opposition if we keep in mind that Selim sought a military revival, but also a top-down transformation of Ottoman society. The stakes were high. One item that galvanized opponents was the so-called "new revenue." As scholars have pointed out, Selim and his men essentially rewired the empire's financial nexus by diverting funds from rural tax-farms, fiefs, and benefices to the treasury; they targeted lapsed freehold, confiscated vacant tax-farms, and abolished other leases, transferring the fiscal units to central managers or cooperative rural actors. The new revenue treasury thus struck at the economic power of many élites, especially the a'yân, and forged new partnerships between Selim's reformers and sympathetic provincials. Those outside of the game faced political marginalization and even economic ruin. Along with the Janissary corps, with its widely coveted privileges and pay chits, the New Order menaced the vested interests of thousands in the capital and hinterlands. It is no surprise, then, to see its opponents resort to the charged language of "illegal innovation."[39]

In fact, there is some truth to these claims. Despite all efforts, Selim and his allies could not convincingly defend the reforms as traditional when they increasingly broke the basic tenets of Ottoman statecraft. In one sense, we can see Vâsıf's second chronicle as a return to the old. His ethical focus, his lessons, his philosophical framework – all of these were ways to lead readers back to the concept of nizâm-ı 'âlem. His vision of society still rested on the "four pillars," the compartmentalized bastions of social order. Vâsıf stated this openly in the work:

---

[38] MEHÂSİN 2, fols. 110b, 133b, 155a, 160b-164a, 165a-166b, 168b-169a. In several places, Vâsıf rebutted such real or imagined criticism with long marginal notes.

[39] Yaycıoğlu, 53–63; and Aysel Yıldız, "Vaka-yı Selimiyye or the Selimiyye Incident: A Study of the May 1807 Rebellion" (Ph.D. diss., Sabancı University, 2008), 194–202.

Islamic philosophers divide rational people into four estates: they are either soldiers, craftsmen and merchants, scribes, or farmers. To leave anyone outside of this scheme is improper and they should be forced into one of the estates. Some philosophers say that anyone who refuses to join one of the said groups ought to be killed, lest they trouble the people. Likewise, according to the saying, "Keeping each group to its own occupation orders the realm and vice versa," no class should be forced into the occupation of another class, as when merchants or producers are sent to war, for this causes chaos.[40]

Yet if Vâsıf tried to reassert old ideas of moral order, he was more than willing in the new work to tinker and at times even alter its elements for the sake of reform. Take for example his ideas on the merchant marine. Vâsıf wanted rich statesmen to buy ships and found trading concerns. He did not mention that this activity blurred two professional spheres, soldiers and merchants, nor that past thinkers had, for this reason, opposed such schemes.[41]

That reciprocation was starting to trump world order for Vâsıf emerges from a favorable aside on Christian social practice. Europeans occupy their children with a suitable trade, he wrote. No one in their countries is idle. Rather, beggars do not exist and must support themselves. When Europeans reach adolescence, they are moreover sent to schools called "academies," where they study mathematics and geography and learn about the habitable world. Yet Vâsıf said that it was not enough for them to know the names of seas, rivers, and countries; they also travel and campaign to gain firsthand experience and, having gained this knowledge, can lead troops, build fortresses, and increase the state's income. Infidels thus acquire useful trades through compulsion and training. Vâsıf then opined that, as Ottoman subjects had no wish to learn such skills, the European model might be imported:

In this way, God willing, mathematics and industrial methods would spread throughout our realm according to the sense of "The believer's persevering quest is wisdom, which he seizeth wherever he findeth." And we should expect that trained and able Muslims will not only learn all the European crafts but make a great many fine inventions.[42]

---

[40] MEHÂSİN 2, fols. 169a-169b. Cf. KINÂLIZÂDE, 451–453, who lists five estates (scholars, orators, administrators, warriors, and merchants) and five types of "outsiders."

[41] Metin Kunt notes that such activity broke with the Ottoman ethical tradition as well as the theories of Ibn Khaldûn: "Derviş Mehmed Paşa, Vezir and Entrepreneur: A Study in Ottoman Political-Economic Theory and Practice," Turcica 9 (1977): esp. 209–211.

[42] MEHÂSİN 2, fols. 169b-170a. Mardin alludes to this passage's significance in "The Mind of the Turkish Reformer, 1700–1900," in Arab Socialism: A Documentary Survey (Salt Lake City, 1969), 32. For the proverb, see Freytag, 1: 385.

This passage shows just how ready Vâsıf was to compromise "world order." While his 1784 essay had warned against conscription and "outsiders," what he now proposed was nothing short of social engineering. Vâsıf was advising the "dragooning" of subjects – orphans, beggars, and whomever else – into military academies for compulsory training. The source of these subjects was immaterial as was any danger of undesirable social mixing. Vâsıf was pushing the notion of an immutable universal order to the breaking point and even intimating that Ottomans might freely diverge from it, like the Europeans, in order to produce trained experts. In this passage, the edifice of *nizâm-ı 'âlem* seems on the verge of collapse. Indeed, the strain is nearly audible.

6.3 FROM EXILE TO CONSOLATION, 1794–1798

At the height of summer 1794, royal agents called on the court historian without warning and with orders for his summary dismissal and exile. For an Ottoman scribe, this sort of visit was a lurking fear, a sword of Damocles that hung unseen over his head, and it was with good reason that the moral literature of the day warned against fickle fortune. We can imagine Vâsıf being taken at home or at his workplace just as we can imagine his terror. Why was he being taken? What would become of him? The fall of an eighteenth-century statesman typically led to one or more unpleasant ends – death, confiscation, exile – and while Vâsıf's fate was to be the latter, he would have been in real fear for his life. Stripped of office and honors, he learned from the men that he had only days to prepare for a journey to the island of Lesbos. His crime? He did not know.[43]

What happened to Vâsıf that August, while not wholly clear, was the result of larger power struggles at court involving his friend Tatarcık Abdullah and his erstwhile ally, the chief scribe Mehmed Râşid Efendi. It seems that Abdullah and Râşid had fallen out during talks they were holding with a European envoy. According to Vâsıf, Râşid refused to believe that one of his translators had leaked details of the negotiations while drunk and, growing paranoid, denounced Abdullah Efendi to the

---

[43] Vâsıf wrote (MEHÂSİN 3, fols. 3b-4a) that he was exiled in the first ten days of M AH 1209, or between July 29 and August 7, 1794. Halil Nûrî's contemporary account (*Târih*, Beyazıt Devlet Kütüphanesi nr. 3369, fol. 3a) agrees with this dating. Two archival documents (BOA.C.DH 1563 and BOA.HAT 8283) contain orders on the place and manner of his exile, the first bearing the date mid-M AH 1209, or between 8 and 17 August 1794. See also Âsım, 1: 256–257; Cevdet, *Târih*, 6: 125–127; Fâik, 147–148; Fâtin, 432; Karslızâde, 64–65; Hammer-Purgstall, 3: 553; and Schlechta-Wssehrd, 7.

sultan. The accusation opened a rift between the two. Abdullah and Râşid began to trade veiled threats until, at last, the former sent an angry letter to a "high station" to complain of Râşid and urge his removal. Vâsıf claimed that his own role in the affair was purely incidental. It was clear that Râşid had many allies and would win, he said some years later, and thus one evening he and a group of colleagues went to Üsküdar to pay their respects to Tatarcık Abdullah at the house of the judge Şemseddin Efendi. The men dined together. Vâsıf wrote that they also spent some hours discussing science and collating books before returning home. When Râşid heard of their meeting, however, he reported it to Selim in the worst possible terms – as a subversive gathering – and not only secured the exile of Abdullah, but also of Vâsıf and two others named Keçecizâde Sâlih Mehmed and Seyyid Mehmed Efendi. In all this, the historian professed innocence. "I was wronged," he said. "I did not speak out of place but was accused by dint of association."[44] That Vâsıf was so blameless in the affair, no more than a victim of slander, is however called into question by a near-contemporary source. The historian Âsım wrote that he had in fact offended Râşid and his allies. Vâsıf at some point had written a letter to the former chief scribe and Aleppo governor Feyzî Süleyman Paşa, his friend, in which he fulminated against Râşid, the queen mother's steward Yusuf Ağa, and others. After Feyzî's death in 1794, this letter found its way to Yusuf Ağa via the mufti of Aleppo and enraged Râşid and his circle. Âsım's story makes a good deal of sense and is in keeping with Vâsıf's character. In the first moments of confusion that summer, when confronted by the sultan's men, he may well have recalled what he had written to Feyzî Paşa. In fairness, though, it was not merely the contents of the letter that led the chief scribe to target Vâsıf. Âsım also noted that Abdullah Efendi had publically rebuked Râşid, the şeyhülislâm, and the Grand Vizier over negotiations in which, he alleged, they profited at the state's expense. The fact that Vâsıf was Abdullah's friend only sharpened their anger; and Râşid must have felt doubly betrayed in that he had lately

---

[44] Vâsıf recounted this story some six years later in MEHÂSİN 3, fols. 3a-4a. That he and others were involved in some sort of plot seems to have been taken quite seriously. For example, Selim accused Seyyid Mehmed in BOA.C.DH 1563 of "words and deeds critical of the affairs of my empire," and said he therefore "must be made an example." According to Fâik (147–148) and Karslızâde (64–65), Râşid told the sultan that the men were speaking critically of state affairs and certain statesmen and were thus provoking sedition. Nûrî too indicated (fol. 3a) that they had somehow displeased Selim. On the teacher and judge Keçecizâde Sâlih Mehmed, see SO, 5: 1468–1469. Şemseddin Efendi was possibly Çavuşzâde Şemseddin Ahmed Efendi (d. 1809), also a teacher and judge: SO, 5: 1577.

helped the historian back to his feet, giving him patronage and a second chance. It seems likely, then, that a mix of personal and factional motives lay behind the exile and that the affair in Üsküdar was, indeed, a pretext.[45]

Once again, Vâsıf had played Râşid falsely and lost. He now faced no "honorable exile," but a true banishment to a remote Aegean island. Selim had decided that each of the four exiles should be sent to a different place: Tatarcık Abdullah to his estate in Aydın, Keçecizâde to Gallipoli, Seyyid Mehmed to Tenedos, and Vâsıf to Lesbos. Sorrowful, the historian made ready and set out some time in August by boat. The terms of his exile were strict. Vâsıf was to be under guard during the journey and was not allowed to travel elsewhere; while he received 3,000 kuruş to defray costs, this sum had to last months or years and he would perforce live in poverty.[46] Vâsıf probably stayed some three or four months on Lesbos. Although we lack details, we know that Selim changed his mind later that year and, in December 1794, issued pardons for all four men. The claim by some sources that Vâsıf never reached the island is thus, given the time that had passed, highly unlikely. Conditions had changed. Vâsıf found that his old post was in the hands of a new figure, Halil Nûrî Bey, who had become court historian after the death of Sadullah Enverî that fall. Râşid too had been ousted and power at court was shifting. Vâsıf exploited this on his return, visiting his old enemy and gleefully mocking him. "Wonders never cease!" he said. "No one but you could so soon punish and reward – a sword in one hand and a balm in the other!"[47]

---

[45] According to Âsım (1: 256–257), Tatarcık Abdullah and Râşid had fought over talks involving Wallachia and Moldavia and 2,000 purses of akçe. When Abdullah lost the argument, he rebuked şeyhülislâm Dürrîzâde Mehmed Ârif and Grand Vizier Melek Mehmed Paşa, who had both pocketed 50,000 kuruş of the original sum. "Is it right of us to adopt a plan that harms the empire?" he supposedly asked them. Abdullah then visited Râşid and accused him of perfidy and extravagance. He ended with a threat: "By God, you'll soon get what's coming to you." Two or three days later, he was exiled. See also Cevdet, Târih, 6: 136–137. Feyzî Süleyman was a chancery product who had been chief scribe twice (1779–1781, 1787–1788) before "turning paşa." He died in Aleppo on 3 N AH 1208 = April 4, 1794: Vâsıf, TSMK nr. 1638, fols. 7b-8a; and Fâik, 120–122.

[46] MEHÂSİN 3, fols. 3b-4a. See also BOA.C.DH 1563 and BOA.HAT 8283. Fâik (148) and Karslızâde (65) both say that Selim gave Vâsıf a 3,000 kuruş travel allowance.

[47] Vâsıf gave (MEHÂSİN 3, fol. 11a) the date of his pardon as mid-Ca AH 1209 or mid-December 1794. Nûrî, fol. 12b, specifies that the four men were pardoned from early Ca to late in the same month at intervals of several days. According to Fâik, 148, Vâsıf never reached Lesbos at all, but was freed while his ship was still inside the Dardanelles. Cf. Âsım, 1: 257, who says that he "spent a period of time drinking the bitter draught of exile." Enverî became court historian after Vâsıf's dismissal. However, BOA.HAT 8283 indicates that he was already seriously ill and, when he died on 13 R AH 1209 = November 7, 1794, Halil Nûrî Bey took his place. See also MEHÂSİN 3, fols. 2b, 9a-9b; Nûrî, fols. 2b, 10a-10b; Kütükoğlu, "Vekâyi'nüvis," 120–121; and Schlechta-Wssehrd, 4, 7, 9.

Being back in the capital restored some normalcy to Vâsıf's life. The next few years in fact proved to be a quiet and largely fallow period as far as his intellectual efforts were concerned. This does not mean he was idle, though. Vâsıf soon resumed work as director of the Anatolian accounts office, a post that he received in April 1795, and rotated for several years between that position and head of the general accounts office, or *baş muhâsebeci*, in the treasury's top rank.[48] The tasks and routines were familiar. From his inside position, Vâsıf could also watch as Selim's military, administrative, and fiscal reforms took root. In 1793, the sultan had founded a military corps and barracks outside of Istanbul in Levend Çiftlik – his new model army. Needing to fund the force, he began to transfer income to the new treasury from excises on wool, cotton, and certain alcoholic drinks as well as from tax farms, customs duties, and lapsed military fiefs (*timâr*). These measures raised more than 60,000 purses of *akçe* per year. Vâsıf in his official capacity was highly involved in the work. The accounts office oversaw most of the state's income and expenditure, from tax farms and imposts to expropriated estates, and he was in a position to reallocate such revenue to the new treasury. "You see," as Vâsıf explained in 1803, "no one – Muslim or non-Muslim, rich or poor – will give a cent to the treasury as a war levy while our finances are so straitened."

Nor does anyone go to war at his own cost to please God or for love of the Prophet or sultan. Gathering troops and ordnance to match the enemy, then, depends not on idle words but on money ... and we gathered the funds from the realm's own estates and resources so that nothing was based on chance or taken by force.

These resources, Vâsıf said, were then made over to the new army: "When an impost that rightfully belonged to the treasury fell vacant, it was no longer farmed out for a small sum, but was taken over and farmed by the government for the new treasury." He also pointed out that this practice was fully lawful.[49]

---

[48] Vâsıf directed the Anatolian accounts office from 4 L AH 1209 to 3 L 1210 (April 24, 1795, to April 11, 1796). He served as head of the general accounts office from 4 L AH 1211 to 4 L 1212 (April 2, 1797 to March 22, 1798) before being renamed to the Anatolian accounts office on 4 L AH 1213 or March 11, 1799. On these postings, see MEHÂSİN 3, fols. 152b, 218a; BOA.A.RSK.d 1593, p. 60 and 1623, p. 37; and Afyoncu, "Tevcihat Kayıtları I," 124–125.

[49] HULÂSAT, 93–95. We can infer some of Vâsıf's duties as *baş muhâsebeci* from a series of documents that are dated to the year 1797 and carry his seal: BOA.AE.Slm 4889 (dated 29 Ca AH 1212 = November 19), 5710 (6 Za 1211 = May 3), 9428 (2 S 1212 = July 27), 11250 (20 Ca 1212 = November 10), 12590 (2 M 1212 = June 27), 12688 (19 M 1212 = July 14), 14812 (9 M 1212 = July 4), and 15409 (12 Ra 1212 = September 4). We also find

By the late 1790s, Vâsıf was some sixty years old and had come to value stability. He would never again risk exile for petty career squabbles, a fact no doubt helped by his fairly comfortable place in the treasury and Mehmed Râşid's death in 1797. There was also a modest-sized family to tend. While his son Abdullah Lebîb came of age and married in 1795 or 1796, starting a career of his own as a teacher and judge, Vâsıf had at least three daughters who needed husbands: Hanîfe, Ayşe, and his eldest Züleyhâ. He and his wife in time matched the girls with local judges and bureaucrats. Züleyhâ and Ayşe wed a judge and a diplomat named Seyyidâ Efendi and Sâlih Bey, though it is not clear who married whom; Hanîfe's husband was a minor scribe named Ahmed Feyâzî Efendi.[50] The domestic pretensions of an Ottoman grandee were hard to maintain. Vâsıf was now residing in a stately residence in the old Istanbul neighborhood of Yerebatan, near the Sublime Porte and imperial palace and close to other scribal officials like the privy purse steward (hazîne kethüdâsı), who lived next door. It appears that the area was quite upscale. If Vâsıf's ambitions remained the same, meanwhile, as is likely, it is easy to suppose that he kept a household at least as big as in years past. His senior rank in the treasury, if not his own ego, would have encouraged this.[51]

But how can we explain Vâsıf's lack of advancement? He had never really wanted a career in the treasury. To his own mind, his skills were better suited to the chancery or diplomatic tasks than to the thankless

that as *anadolu muhâsebecisi*, he wrote a memo on organizing Istanbul's plasterers and pen makers guilds for the city prefect, or *şehremîni*, Ahmed Câvid Bey: TSMA.E.201/1–3 (dated 1–2 Ş AH 1212 = January 19–20, 1798). See also DİA, s.v. "Nizâm-ı Cedîd"; and Uzunçarşılı, *Osmanlı Devleti*, 346–347, 354–355.

[50] According to Sarıkaya (lxvi–lxvii), Abdullah Lebîb taught after 1798/99 and later held a number of judicial posts. The poet Antepli Aynî wrote a chronogram for his marriage that gives a date of anno hegirae 1210: "A morsel for a feast, Aynî marked the date / Lebîb got married auspiciously." For the full poem, see *Antepli Aynî Divanı*, ed. Mehmet Arslan (Istanbul, 2004), 454. Sarıkaya also uncovered the identity of Ayşe Hanım. Vâsıf's children appear in an estate inventory compiled after his death (BOA.BŞM.d 7370), which calls Züleyhâ his "elder" and Hanîfe his "younger" daughters but does not include Ayşe. They and their spouses also appear in later documents: BOA.C.HR 140 (on Sâlih Bey's 1808 appointment to negotiation service); BOA.C.ML 23317 (on Hanîfe's 1849 request for a pension after her husband's death); BOA.HAT 35 (on Lebîb's 1827 appointment as Jerusalem judge); and BOA.İ.DH 2002 (on Züleyhâ's 1841 petition for money to make the pilgrimage to Mecca). See also Mehmed Atâullah Şânîzâde, *Târih-i Şânîzâde*, ed. Ziya Yılmazer (Istanbul, 2008), 1: 560. I treat Züleyhâ's exile after a public scandal in the epilogue.

[51] MEHÂSİN 4, fol. 57b; and Arıkan, 348. Vâsıf wrote that his house abutted that of the *hazîne kethüdâsı ağa* and later the court chamberlain, or *mabeynci*, Ahmed Efendi, the son of Halil Hamid Paşa and a confidant to Selim. It was also close to the former mansion of one Bekir Paşa.

bookkeeping of the accounts office. Nor was the self-styled prodigy working on any literary pieces or commissions; he had been replaced as court
historian by a markedly lesser talent. There is a sense of stagnation about
this period of Vâsıf's career, the most likely causes of which were two.
Vâsıf was quite simply an unpleasant person. His peers had seen over and
over that he was smug, selfish, and conniving and accepted that his proven
gifts, however impressive or useful they might be, did not redeem these
faults. The second reason, related to the first, was a want of patronage.
Likability aside, Vâsıf's exile may have left him untouchable for a time and
even distanced him from friends and allies. It is not surprising, then, that
he began to look elsewhere for links. We know that Vâsıf ingratiated
himself inside of the palace with Ahmed Fâiz Efendi and Mabeynci
Ahmed Efendi, Selim's long-time privy secretary (sırkâtibi) and court
chamberlain, respectively. Early biographical sources state that one or
both of these Ahmeds aided the historian in securing later promotions,
and Mabeynci Ahmed moved next door to him for a time. Both men had
the sultan's ear. They were physically or emotionally close to him and,
along with Küçük Hüseyin Paşa, gave Vâsıf indirect access and influence
at the highest level. He had not sunk into apathy after all.[52]

As it happened, the events that spurred Vâsıf back to favor originated
abroad with the French Revolution. On July 1, 1798, a French fleet from
Toulon landed at Alexandria in Egypt, under Napoléon, crushing the local
Mamluks and taking control of Cairo and the province's rich delta. While
primarily meant to help French trade and threaten British access to India, the
invasion was clearly an act of war against the Ottomans. The court was
shocked. The French had been traditional if somewhat fickle allies since the
reign of Süleyman I in the sixteenth century. How could they attack the
empire? That Selim and his statesmen could not answer this question only
showed how deeply they had misjudged the 1789 Revolution.[53] Most
Ottomans had at first been indifferent, considering it a purely domestic or
European affair, and the officially neutral empire showed a certain sympathy

---

[52] Âsım, 1: 257; Fâik, 148; Karslızâde, 65; and Schlechta-Wssehrd, 7. Mabeynci Ahmed and
Ahmed Fâiz were part of Selim's inner circle. Likely as a result, both were murdered
on May 29, 1807, in the rebellion that overthrew him. See Yıldız, 819 f.

[53] Shaw, Old and New, 193–199, 247–256; İsmail Soysal, Fransız İhtilâli ve Türk-Fransız
Diplomasi Münasebetleri (1789–1802) (Ankara, 1964), 217–254; and Azmi Süslü,
"Rapports diplomatiques ottomano-français, 1798–1807," Belleten 47 (1983):
237–279. See on French propaganda activities L. Lagarde, "Note sur les journaux
français de Constantinople à l'époque révolutionnaire," Journal Asiatique 236 (1948):
271–276; and Richard Clogg, "A Further Note on the French Newspapers of Istanbul
during the Revolutionary Period," Belleten 39 (1975): 483–490.

to the new régime's agents in Istanbul by tolerating their symbols and propaganda. Selim only grew wary after formally recognizing the Republic in 1795 and seeing its ambitions turn outward. But he did not think that Egypt was a possible target. His envoy in Paris, Moralı Ali Efendi, had even assured him several months earlier that the fleet at Toulon was not a threat. The invasion was thus a rude awakening. Selim, not unfairly livid, felt the loss as a failure on the part of his ministers and reacted on August 30 with a swift purge, exiling Grand Vizier İzzet Mehmed Paşa and şeyhülislâm Dürrîzâde Ârif and terrorizing the rest of his circle with violent moods.[54]

It is easy to see how some Ottomans misread the Revolution if we look more closely at their ideas of political morality as well as at how they classified European states. To Ottomans, the empire's political morality differed in very basic ways from that of its non-Muslim rivals. Europeans pursued amoral and changeable politics; they were opportunists who could not be trusted. Vâsıf wrote in his second chronicle that such men were led by "satanic insight," a sort of Mephistophelian reason that led them to expand their borders, increase their income and population, and make their realms prosper through dubious means. Europeans would happily sacrifice treasure or kin for trifling gains or put politics before religion, he added.[55] There appears to have been a popular association with reason – cold, calculating, Machiavellian – that opposed the Ottomans' ingenuous self-perceptions, a feeling which only became stronger with the rise of European political concepts late in the century. One of Vâsıf's peers, Mehmed Emin Behiç, called "politics" or *politika*, "a European term that in our time means to act through trickery and deceit, but whose original meaning is *umûr-ı siyâsiyye* or *tedbîr-i müdün*." He thus contrasted the politics of Ottoman practical philosophy with European politicking – one ethical, one no better than trickery or ruse.[56]

In the Ottoman moral tradition, Christian régimes were imperfect and fell under the rubric of "vicious cities (*medîne-i gayr-i fâzıla*)."

---

[54] Yüksel Çelik, "Siyaset-Nasihat Literatürümüzde Nadir bir Tür: Mısır'ın İşgali Üzerine III. Selim'e Sunulan Tesliyet-Nâme," *Türk Kültürü İncelemeler Dergisi* 22 (2010): 88–95. See also HADÎKAT, supp. 3: 49; MEHÂSİN 3, fols. 188a-189b; and Nûrî, fol. 357b ff.

[55] MEHÂSİN 2, fol. 63a.

[56] Ali Osman Çınar, ed., "Es-seyyid Mehmed Emîn Behiç'in *Sevânihü'l-Levâyih*'i ve Değerlendirmesi" (master's thesis, Marmara University, 1992), 37 n. 14. Beydilli notes these competing views of politics in an excellent but undercited article: "Dış Politika ve Ahlâk," *İlmî Araştırmalar* 7 (1999): 47–56. Yeşil says (*Ebubekir Râtib*, 220–225) that Râtib Efendi, though heavily influenced by European thought, also at times used *politika* in a pejorative sense.

Being non-Muslim, they could not access holy law or ensure their subjects twofold felicity. Kınâlızâde had grouped such polities by characteristic vice as "ignorant," "vicious," or "erring." Each of these categories also had a number of subtypes.[57] Yet while it is true that Christian kings could use human law and reason to give subjects stability, material prosperity, and even justice, reason without revealed religion and morality was hollow, as Vâsıf held, little more than cheap trickery. Frederick II of Prussia embodied this sort of politics for the historian, who was familiar with his personality, style of rule, and foreign policy from sources like Ahmed Resmî's 1763–1764 embassy report. Vâsıf viewed Frederick with veiled awe and noted that he had won glory and territory, excelled in mathematics and war, and bested his neighbors. Yet Vâsıf disapproved of his methods. We are told that Frederick cared only to defeat his enemies and even claimed he might break treaties whenever it suited him, as treaties were only to be observed in commerce.[58] Catherine II, the Ottoman nemesis of the late eighteenth century, was a more sinister type. Vâsıf was well-informed about the Russian empress from his time in St. Petersburg. He knew that she had overthrown her husband Peter III in a palace coup and had seized power for herself. He also gave a sound account of the Pugachev rebellion. Not surprisingly, however, his portrayal was wholly negative and contained nothing like his awe for Frederick: Catherine was immoral, enslaved by passions, and took lovers; she was depraved and corrupted her son, the crown prince, to keep him from rule; and she was unnatural, a female usurper and regicide. Catherine in short was a paragon of evil and her success, at least to Vâsıf, came not from justice or human reason, but from God's intervention alone – a divine trial. Where Prussia might have been "ignorant" or "erring," then, Catherinean Russia more probably qualified as a "vicious" polity.[59]

---

[57] KINÂLIZÂDE, 445 ff., who drew on the concept of the "Virtuous City." For example, "ignorant cities" held incorrect beliefs, "vicious cities" had right beliefs but incorrect actions, and "erring cities" seemed outwardly like virtuous cities but had corrupt, and thus wrong, beliefs. See further DİA, s.v. "Ahlâk"; Fakhry, 139–140; and E. Rosenthal, 137–138.

[58] MEHÂSİN 1, fols. 287a-287b; and MEHÂSİN 4, fol. 199a. Vâsıf may have read Resmî's report on the Prussian court during his own 1787 embassy preparations. The work in any event circulated widely and he later added it, with warm words, to MEHÂSİN 5, 1: 239–262. See also Virginia Aksan, "An Ottoman Portrait of Frederick the Great," in Contacts and Conflicts, 67–80.

[59] Vâsıf dealt with Catherine II's personal history and character in MEHÂSİN 3, fols. 146b-147a; and MEHÂSİN 5, 1: 238, 2: 286–288.

As the great upheaval of the day, the French Revolution and its ideas of political liberty confronted Vâsıf and his peers with a different order of régime entirely. Ottomans at first did not know what to make of the Revolution or how to classify it. If some welcomed the event as a possible blessing, like Ahmed Fâiz Efendi, who prayed that it might "spread like syphilis" in Europe, others slowly realized that revolutionary ideology posed a threat to the empire's faith and sovereignty. In the early 1790s, Ebubekir Râtib Efendi worried about Jacobin propaganda and the prospect of a general European war. In 1798, the chief scribe Ahmed Âtıf blamed the Revolution on "materialists" and "atheists" and pointedly warned against its irreligion – for him, law without religion was clearly not enough to guarantee public order and tranquility. The invasion of Egypt that year ended any ambiguity. What was once strange or even curious had become a mortal threat, a tyranny worse than the most malicious Christian kingdom. The Ottoman declaration of war charged the French with spreading sedition across Europe, unjustly seizing property, and loosing basic human bonds with their "freedom." Like Edmund Burke, Vâsıf's colleagues had come to fear and revile the revolutionary government not only for its deeds but for what it represented. For them, absolute rule was imperative and political "freedom," such as it was under the Republic, a complete perversion of the natural order.[60]

Vâsıf expressed this view a few years later in his own chronicle. Although some claim that Ottomans were most shocked by the Revolution's secularism, Vâsıf could well envision régimes based on some mixture of revealed and human law and was more alarmed by threats to the empire's underlying social order. The Republic posed a danger to him because it had neither ruler nor law. It was quite literally lawless. This also explains how Vâsıf justified his later Francophile leanings, as he was less repelled by Napoléon, who, he felt, had restored

---

[60] MEHÂSİN 4, fols. 200a-200b. The largest study of these views is Wajda Sendesni's *Regard de l'historiographie ottomane sur la révolution française et l'expédition d'Égypte* (Istanbul, 2003). See also Zeki Arıkan, "Fransız İhtilâli ve Osmanlı Tarihçiliği," in *De la Révolution française à la Turquie d'Atatürk: la modernisation politique et sociale. Les lettres, les sciences et les arts* (Istanbul, 1990), 85–100; Faruk Bilici, "La Révolution française dans l'historiographie turque (1789–1927)," *Annales historiques de la Révolution française* (1991): 539–549; Zafer Gölen, "Reisülküttap Raşid Efendi'ye Göre İhtilal Sonrasında Fransa'nın Politik Yaklaşımları," *Toplumsal Tarih* 14 (2000): 12–15; Bernard Lewis, "The Impact of the French Revolution on Turkey: Some Notes on the Transmission of Ideas," *Journal of World History* 1 (1953): 105–125; Yeşil, *Ebubekir Râtib*, 167–175, 195–196; and idem, "Looking at the French Revolution through Ottoman Eyes: Ebubekir Ratib Efendi's Observations," *Bulletin of the School of Oriental and African Studies* 70 (2007): 283–304.

stability and monarchical authority to France.[61] The historian prefaced his account of the Revolution – which "plunged the world into chaos" – by observing that it had been sparked by Britain's colonies in the New World. The Americans inspired the French, who "brashly discussed the merits of freedom without rulers" and trusted that liberty and equality would ease their lives. They did not think of the benefits of absolute rule, he said, but instead chose "tyranny" and "anarchy." These ideas slowly took root. Thus, when the kingdom, bankrupt, took on loans and economies that some felt were unjust, they called the estates together in a parliament and formed a new government to curb the French king Louis' authority. The king at first capitulated. Yet, Vâsıf continued, "neither dynastic honor nor the pride of absolutism would brook shared rule" and Louis, fleeing to Vienna, was captured and killed. The rebels then took full control, turned their gaze outward, and began to spread their doctrines through Europe by force. To stress the Revolution's complete perversity and immorality in terms that an Ottoman reader could grasp, Vâsıf also added a marginal note comparing the republicans to the ancient Persian cult of Mazdak. "The false sect that the French have created is like that of the perverted philosopher Mazdak, which arose in the reign of Kayqubâd b. Fîrûz b. Yazdajird," he claimed. Mazdak too had preached a belief in radical equality and gained many converts, including Kayqubâd, who drove his subjects into error and cruelly tortured objectors. It was Kayqubâd's son who finally broke the spell. When the king ordered him to conform, the crown prince explained that the common ownership of goods and women confused lineages and undercut inheritance claims. It in fact made the pillars of law and order, rulership and the administration of justice, impossible. Kayqubâd at last saw the truth of his son's words and executed Mazdak. Any of Vâsıf's peers would have agreed that this was a wise course of action.[62]

It was unfortunate that the Ottomans could not so easily quash the French. The news from Egypt only worsened after the initial shock, with the French routing the Mamluks at the Battle of the Pyramids and seizing Cairo, and despite the loss of his fleet at Abûqîr, Napoléon by summer's end had consolidated his position and seemed to have control of the province. Selim, meanwhile, despaired. His moods were ever more fragile

---

[61] MEHÂSİN 4, fols. 269a–270b. Cf. Lewis, "Impact of the French Revolution," 123.

[62] MEHÂSİN 3, fols. 196a–197b; ibid, İÜ TY nr. 6012, fols. 4b–6b; and BOA.Y.EE 90, p. 33. In the *Shahname*, a Zoroastrian priest presents these arguments rather than the crown prince: Abolqasem Ferdowsi, *Shahnameh: The Persian Book of Kings*, trans. Dick Davis (New York, 2006), 679–683.

and erratic and frightened his ministers. It was at this point, then, most likely in the late summer or early fall of 1798, that certain statesmen invited Vâsıf to the Sublime Porte in the hope that he might bring calm. If not easy, their request was at least straightforward; they wanted him to draft an essay to sooth the sultan, a work that became known to posterity as his *Letter of Consolation*, or *Tesliyetnâme*.[63] As Vâsıf wrote in the finished manuscript, "when the enemy landed at Alexandria and invaded Egypt, the government asked me to compose a piece for the sultan to console and encourage him. So I quickly compiled some events, simply phrased, and submitted it to the Porte." Fourteen years later, in 1812, Vâsıf's son Lebîb recalled the story in somewhat more detail:

When the statesmen saw how the invasion had troubled the late Sultan Selim, they immediately bade to the Porte my father, the former chief scribe Ahmed Vâsıf Efendi, and hastened him to write an essay to console and admonish others. And he at once put together this essay of consolation in a few folios, from books of history and biography that were at hand.

It is most likely that Vâsıf's commission came from the new Grand Vizier, Yusuf Ziyâ Paşa, or from Küçük Hüseyin Paşa or the chief scribe Ahmed Âtıf. The late Abdürrezzâk Efendi's brother, Mustafa Âşir, also might have played a role, for he was now *şeyhülislâm* and remained close to the historian, who wrote a chronogram for his appointment.[64] In any case, the fact that Vâsıf wrote the essay rather than the sitting court chronicler Nûrî Bey must be seen as an admission of his superior talent. However much they disliked him personally, or however much he had repeatedly exhausted their goodwill, Vâsıf's peers chose at this difficult time to entrust him with the task.

At first glance, the *Letter of Consolation* appears to be an exercise in a rare epistolary form. Ottoman scribes learned to write letters for all occasions by

---

[63] This essay survives in two copies. In the likely presentation manuscript, Vâsıf shortly recounted (TESLİYETNÂME, fol. 1b) the history of the text and its commission in a marginal note. The second copy, Süleymaniye Kütüphanesi, Serez nr. 1890, was commissioned by Abdullah Lebîb from a copyist named Abdülmecîd al-Moravî and bears a colophon date of 1 Z AH 1227 = December 6, 1812. It also features extra poetry by Vâsıf (fol. 1a), a short introduction by Lebîb (fols. 1b-2a), and an excursus on Ottoman exceptionalism (fols. 7a-8b) from MEHÂSİN 5, 1: 7–10. Çelik has published an edited text in "Tesliyet-Nâme," 115–125.

[64] Vâsıf only included (MEHÂSİN 3, fol. 189b) a fragment of this poem in his chronicle entry on the promotion; Ayıntâbî Münîb's biographical compendium quotes it in full: "The angels gathered with longing to describe [*vâsıf*] / And marked his appointment date: the faultless *şeyhülislâm* [=AH 1213]." *Devḥatü'l-Meşâyiḫ: Einleitung und Edition*, ed. Barbara Kellner-Heinkele, in *Verzeichnis der orientalische Handschriften in Deutschland*, vol. 27, no. 2 (Stuttgart, 2005), 2: 415–416.

studying models in manuals or *münşeat*, examples of which included those of Mustafa Âli, Ferîdûn Ahmed Bey, and the eighteenth-century Grand Vizier Koca Râgıb Paşa. While these typically featured letters of a professional or personal nature, they could also contain copies of treaties, decrees, petitions, or other worthy literary specimens. Letters of consolation – called *tesliyetnâme* or *tâziyetnâme* – were but one form and usually written to comfort a friend or superior in a time of need. Vâsıf as a scribe would have been well-versed in their content.[65] Yet his *Letter* is much more. It is principally a historical essay, skillfully using fourteen examples to treat the French invasion in comparative terms and, thus, giving insight into how he saw causation, historical change, and the universe at large. It is also a full-fledged theodicy; that is to say, it is a vindication of God's power and goodness in spite of the existence of evil.[66] Although Vâsıf's earlier work had contained seeds of theodicy, the *Letter* marked his first defense of Ottoman exceptionalism in these terms as well as his first experiment with a coherent historical framework. By likening the invasion to other setbacks in Islamic history, Vâsıf offered a sweeping vindication of God's benevolence and of the empire's regenerative ability. It was, in a word, history as theodicy – a vision that he would increasingly apply to his output in later years.

Vâsıf began the *Letter* by declaring that the invasion, while serious, was certainly no cause for despair. Although they had taken Alexandria, the French held a weak and ultimately doomed position. They had betrayed in the empire a friendly and generous power and had been made haughty by divinely ordained success (*istidrâc*); both their pride and scripture confirmed they would suffer God's wrath. Vâsıf thus invoked in *istidrâc* the same divine providence as in his 1784 essay. As a further comfort, however, he reassured the sultan that misfortunes must occur because the universe is naturally variable. "This world," he wrote, "is the world of generation and corruption (*'âlem-i kevn ü fesâd*)":

The rule of change and instability in the sublunary sphere leads inevitably to accidents, and it is not natural for realms' affairs to be fixed or wholly free from political mishap. Yet, if various providential aspects of the cosmos at times seem vile, holy scripture attests that they lead to great good and benefit.

---

[65] Josef Matuz covers these manuals in "Über die Epistolographie und Inšâ-Literatur der Osmanen," *Zeitschrift der Deutschen Morgenländischen Gesellschaft* supp. 1 (1968): 574–594. On their role in Ottoman scribal training, see Aksan, *Ottoman Statesman*, 5–9; Çelik, "Tesliyet-Nâme," 96–99; and Bekir Kütükoğlu, "Münşeat Mecmuaların Osmanlı Diplomatiği Bakımından Ehemmiyeti," in *Vekayi'nüvis Makaleler*, 219–221.

[66] Eric L. Ormsby treats this problem in earlier Islamic philosophy in *Theodicy in Islamic Thought: The Dispute over Ghazâlî's "Best of All Possible Worlds"* (Princeton, 1984).

Vâsıf then looked to prove his thesis: that disasters have occurred "from the beginning of the world and the empire till our own day" but lead, ultimately, to the good.[67]

The *Letter*'s historical examples number fourteen and are drawn from Ayyubid, Mamluk, European, and Ottoman history. Generally, these episodes show the hand of providence or a fortuitous Muslim victory. During the Fifth Crusade, for example, crusaders landed in Egypt and took Alexandria and Damietta in turn before marching south on the town of al-Manṣûra. In the course of the siege, the Nile flooded, cutting off their path of retreat, and forced them to negotiate with the Ayyubids and surrender Damietta in exchange for safe conduct. In another example, the Andalusian ruler Abû al-Walîd Ismaʿîl met a huge Christian army outside Granada with only 5,000 men, but slaughtered over 50,000.[68] Vâsıf even added an anecdote of his own. During the 1768–1774 campaign, he related, the Russians besieged Silistre with 70,000 men and routed two Ottoman commanders. The city was hopelessly surrounded. In the final assault, however, 6,000 Ottomans made a sally "like a speck of white on a black cow" and with God's aid, smashed the Russians to break the siege. Vâsıf himself passed through Silistre after the battle. He claimed that the defeat was total and described a scene of almost unbelievable carnage.[69] Vâsıf's examples serve on one hand to show that all polities, in all ages, are subject to flux. "You see," he wrote, "this chaos is not unique to our age. Were I to detail the above accounts, the wars, and the riches thereby squandered it would form a weighty and instructive tome. Rulership is never without its cares or rulers without their enemies."[70] On the other hand, the same events confirmed God's solicitude for believers. According to the *Letter*, God would protect the empire until Judgment Day and in spite of reverses, as history and scripture attest. Vâsıf therefore urged Selim to take action against the French. "The remedy now is to trust in God and, asking aid from the Prophet, to purify our hearts, bestir ourselves, and make every effort to prepare secondary causes before time is lost," he said. "For it is ever the Lord's custom to aid His believers and to annihilate perfidious, oath-breaking infidels." Vâsıf also ended the essay by suggesting certain administrative and military reforms should the sultan succeed in regaining Egypt, including dividing it into three provinces, transferring

[67] TESLİYETNÂME, fols. 1b-2b. See also Menchinger, "Reformist Philosophy," 155–158.
[68] TESLİYETNÂME, fols. 2b-3a, 4b, respectively.
[69] TESLİYETNÂME, fols. 4b-5a. Cf. MEHÂSİN 6, fol. 22b; and Sâbit, fols. 61a-61b.
[70] TESLİYETNÂME, fol. 4a.

Mamluk posts to loyal men for three-year terms, and stationing a flotilla at Alexandria.[71]

The *Letter of Consolation* tackles many of the same problems as Vâsıf's 1784 essay and 1789–1794 chronicle. Most pressing to the historian and his peers was to reconcile Ottoman exceptionalism with the reality of defeat, which he did here, most outstandingly, by theodicy. As in earlier work, Vâsıf interpreted defeat as a miraculous divine trial. However, he also claimed that accidents were universal. The world was one of constant change, of atomistic "generation and corruption" through which God realized His perfect cosmic plan and where apparent evils were in fact good.[72] These two premises are not entirely congruent, but do not necessarily contradict each other. So too did Vâsıf's argument rationalize French power while still upholding the semblance of exceptionalism. His parallels suggested that the Ottomans, and believers more generally, experienced peaks and valleys, times of good fortune and ill, but that history and their role within it still progressed toward God's ordained end. Everything changes, as it were, while nothing really changes at all. The French invasion was no different.

In terms of causality, meanwhile, Vâsıf again had to address man's power to affect historical outcomes. In the *Letter*, he made change a fixed principle in the universe, through which God, the Primary Cause, reveals His will. Humans are powerless in this universe's larger revolutions. Victory follows defeat by God's grace, as Vâsıf illustrated, and believers to a certain degree must simply remain faithful. It is well to recall that this view is not "fatalistic" and that Ottoman thinkers had a complex understanding of the relationship between the worldly and the divine. Since God allows humans to act, at least in some cases, Vâsıf held that action (here administrative and military) complemented faith as a solution. What is instead novel about the essay is its focus on instability, an aspect of Vâsıf's metaphysics that became ever more visible in his later years. There seems to be a link between this idea and the historian's awareness of his own world's volatility. His experience in two wars had robbed him of certainties. His historical vision from the mid-1790s on was therefore tinged by anxiety and doubt as he came to see the empire's plight and the chaos of Napoléonic Europe as part of a universal, and perhaps inevitable,

---

[71] Ibid, fols. 5a-6a.

[72] This type of theodicy holds that suffering masks divine wisdom: that evils are really good or act as the instrument of good, so that the good would come to naught were the evil removed. The reverse can also be true, with apparent blessings working evil. Ormsby, 255–257, calls this explanation "apparent evil, real good." See also Griffel, 225–231.

breakdown in order. The fact that Vâsıf was forging these ideas into an interpretive framework thus gives us an important glimpse at his psychological state. If the question was still what had gone wrong, and what to do about it, the *Letter of Consolation* offered answers. Its theodicy was not only a guide to readers, but a vindication of Selim's reforms and compelling proof of the empire's exceptionalism.

6.4 NEW WARS, NEW REWARDS, 1798–1800

Vâsıf proved to be right, at least in a sense, about the French invasion's destabilizing effects. In a few short months, Napoléon overturned the ties that had guided Ottoman diplomacy for much of the eighteenth century and forced the empire to make common cause with an old enemy, Russia, against its traditional ally of France. These realignments took time. While Selim declared war on September 9, he was unable to formalize alliances with Russia and Great Britain or to mount a campaign until the new year, apart from sending two squadrons to the Mediterranean. The treaties that he eventually signed required the Ottomans to raise an army and to work closely with the British and Russian fleets off Egypt and in the Adriatic; their forces would also include a body of the new model troops, in action for perhaps the first time. In April, Selim reshuffled his bureaucracy to prepare. Vâsıf, having only returned to the Anatolian accounts office a month before, now found his name listed among the snap appointments. He had been made keeper of the daily ledger, or *büyük rûznâmçe*. It was his first promotion in four years. It was also a blessing in that he was to remain behind, safely, in Istanbul.[73]

The new post signaled an end to Vâsıf's purgatory in the treasury. The keeper of the ledger was a figure who ranked below only the treasurer himself, overseeing income from the poll-tax, tax farms, and mortmain trusts, as well as paying out certain kinds of pensions. His office also kept records on expenditures and receipts, which it summarized in yearly or biannual reports. We know that this promotion could not have resulted directly from the *Letter of Consolation*, which Selim, in fact, had not seen.

---

[73] MEHÂSİN 3, fols. 217b-218a, 223a-223b. These appointments fell, respectively, on 4 L AH 1213 = March 11, 1799, and 8 Za = April 13. Vâsıf also received a 100 *kuruş* gift on the first occasion (Sarıkaya, xcvii n. 5). See also Nûrî, fols. 398a-399a; Fâtin, 432; and Hammer-Purgstall, 3: 553. A register in the Ottoman archives (BOA.A.RSK.d 1623, p. 37; published by Afyoncu, "Tevcihat Kayıtları I," 124) dates his appointment to the daily ledger three days later to 11 Za = April 16. On the political situation, see Shaw, *Old and New*, 257–271; Soysal, 255–277; and Süslü, 240–242.

Vâsıf by his own admission submitted the essay during a turnover at the Porte and it "fell through the cracks," unread.[74] More probably, his reassignment was the work of figures acting on his behalf in the palace and elsewhere, like Mabeynci Ahmed, Ahmed Fâiz, or Mustafa Âşir. The *Letter* might have also won Vâsıf sympathy in governing circles, for he had, after all, acquitted himself well in the work. This theory is strengthened by the fact that with Halil Nûrî's death in May, as the army prepared to depart for Egypt, Ziyâ Paşa detained Vâsıf in his pavilion in Üsküdar to name him court historian for a fourth and final time. Vâsıf was overjoyed, and probably a bit stunned.[75] He had again met with one of those dizzying turns that characterized early modern Ottoman scribal careers. In a matter of weeks, he had gone from unemployment, with limited near-term prospects, to a top post in the treasury and a potentially lucrative sideline in chronicling. In all of this, perversely, he had a war with the French to thank.

By May 1799, Vâsıf was already quite busy preparing for the looming campaign in Egypt. It fell to him as keeper of the ledger to keep track of spending on victuals and supplies and to distribute the army's pay, for example. He also found himself in the odd position, on one occasion, of asking for funds on behalf of the Russian ambassador for an allied vessel operating near Istanbul. On the whole, Vâsıf felt his post to be prestigious. He would later boast in a short institutional history that the *rûznâmçe* office "oversees and audits all offices and finances." The fact that it kept accounts in Arabic and did not seal documents, he said, unlike other scribal offices, was still more proof of its stature and of the

---

[74] Vâsıf wrote in a marginal note (TESLİYETNÂME, fol. 1b) that he originally sent the work to the Porte, but found that it went unread due to administrative turnover. He resubmitted it at a later date to preface a separate work on the Egypt campaign, an effort which will be discussed below. On the keeper of the daily ledger, see Uzunçarşılı, *Osmanlı Devleti*, 338–339, 353 f.

[75] There are questions concerning the date of this appointment. Vâsıf wrote (MEHÂSİN 3, fols. 2b, 227a-228b) that it occurred on 15 Z AH 1213 or May 20, 1799, when he was in Üsküdar with other statesmen to see off the imperial army and pay his respects to the Grand Vizier. However, an archival document (BOA.A.RSK.d 1623, p. 37; Afyoncu, "Tevcihat Kayıtları I," 124) dates it to 22 Z = May 27. Part of the problem is that we do not know exactly when Halil Nûrî Bey died. Given that the latest event in his chronicle falls on 19 Za = April 24 (on this problem see Kütükoğlu, "Vekâyi'nüvis," 121 n. 113), Vâsıf's version is at least plausible. It may be that Ziyâ Paşa decided to invest Vâsıf informally, before leaving Istanbul, and that the position was only ratified some days later. Âsım (1: 257), Fâik (147), and Karslızâde (65) all link his new appointments to the intercession of Mabeynci Ahmed and Ahmed Fâiz. Selim also advised (BOA.HAT 13957) Ziyâ Paşa to "study Vâsıf's history" before he left to avoid the errors of past campaigns. Cf. Karal, *Selim III'ün Hatt-ı Hümayunları* (Ankara, 1942), 1: 64.

FIG. 6.1: Grand Vizier Yusuf Ziyâ Paşa (center) and the Ottoman army cross the desert into Egypt to face the French.

implicit trust that its staff enjoyed.[76] But Vâsıf's main ambition lay in his future as court historian. His return to the position after so many years was at least partly due to Selim's fondness for his work, but also to his ability to craft an intellectually lucid account of the reign. Consciously or no, the sultan recognized the historian's gift for systematization. Although Halil Nûrî had held the post for five years, Selim was clearly unhappy with his six-volume chronicle and ordered Vâsıf to rewrite it more or less immediately; like Enverî and Edîb, he directed the historian to revise, pare, and update the work and even sent specific materials to

---

[76] MEHÂSİN 4, fols. 211b-212b. Vâsıf's duties in the first two months of his term can be judged from a series of documents, all with his seal: BOA.AE.Slm 11729 (dated 15 Z AH 1213 = May 20, 1799), 11733 (17 Z 1213 = May 22), 12874 (20 Z 1213 = May 25), 14913 (24 Z 1213 = May 29), 14924 (5 M 1214 = June 9), and 14932 (26 Z 1213 = May 31).

include.[77] To have such an interested patron was a godsend. Vâsif, who recalled his earlier frustration with Abdülhamid, set to work that summer knowing the sultan would likely be generous if the results pleased. He hoped eagerly for a rich reward, not only in largesse but in lasting fame.

The revision of Nûrî's work took most of the year, in which time Vâsif followed his usual themes and played to Selim's love of self-consciously moralizing history. He knew that the sultan valued the past for its lessons. Selim had even lately reformed the office of the historian, ordering that, in the interest of keeping useful accounts, the *vekâyi'nüvis* should have full access to sensitive documents.[78] For Vâsif, the new installment was a natural sequel and second volume to *Charms and Truths*, and he did his best to praise history's many "sovereign benefits." He added that Selim, guided by the past, had both learned to deduce the course of the present and, from the present, where the future might lead. He was thus "full of pearls of wisdom." Vâsif truly thought his version to be superior. He was rather too dismissive of Nûrî, whose work he called "an attempt at writing," but tempered his criticism as Nûrî had been the son-in-law of Mustafa Âşir Efendi. He also drove himself hard. By the fall of 1799, in September, Vâsif had not only finished the revisions, but updated the chronicle with news from Egypt. These he submitted to the Porte in two volumes along with a florid covering letter.[79]

Not surprisingly, one of the new work's emphases was the sultan's reform program. Vâsif devoted space to decrees governing the navy, artillery corps, and system of military fiefs or *timâr* and to changes in the number of governors and the operation of a powder mill. He even inserted abstracts of the codes at the behest of the imperial council "so that their original sense should not be corrupted."[80] Yet in all this, his vision of

---

[77] MEHÂSİN 3, fols. 2b-3a. According to an imperial decree (BOA.HAT 15595), Selim sent reports belonging to Halil Nûrî to the Porte and ordered that they be given to Vâsif, so that he could integrate them into the chronicle. See also Kütükoğlu, "Vekâyi'nüvis," 121 f.

[78] Selim undertook this reform in AH 1210 or 1795/96 at the urging of Halil Nûrî, whose work contains (fols. 91a-93a) a copy of his petition and the subsequent decrees. See also Kütükoğlu, "Vekâyi'nüvis," 107–108. Characteristically, Vâsif noted the reform (MEHÂSİN 3, fols. 41a-41b) without crediting his predecessor.

[79] MEHÂSİN 3, fols. 2a-2b. Vâsif's covering letter (BOA.HAT 52143) identifies him as "still keeper of the daily ledger," a position that he held until 4 L AH 1214 = March 1, 1800. Another document (BOA.AE.Slm 9539) clarifies that he submitted the work in mid-R AH 1214 or mid-September 1799. On the relationship between Nûrî and Mustafa Âşir, see Münîb, *Devḥatü'l-Meşâyiḫ*, 2: 415.

[80] E.g. MEHÂSİN 3, fols. 29b-32a, 38a-40b, 43a-52b, 55b-65a, 72b-80b, 80b-131a, 193a-194a.

reform remained largely conservative. We often see code words in Vâsıf's treatment, allusions to older concepts of Ottoman socio-political order like the "outsiders" who had infiltrated the navy and *timâr* system and who should be purged, or to the need to keep farmers from settling in Istanbul. The underlying justification was a moral one – that of restoring "world order." So too did Vâsıf spend a good deal of time on ethics, usually in lessons on virtue or statecraft. It would of course be easy to dismiss this moralizing as insincere, given his history. Did Vâsıf use such discussions to please Selim? Was it hypocrisy or maybe an admission of personal weakness, a sign of interest in his own self-reform? We simply do not know.[81]

Vâsıf also used the new volume to refine his views on reciprocation, which he was coming to see as a central feature of reform and of Ottoman history as such – a kind of motor or historical principle. The historian had begun to interpret the empire's "decline" in terms of *mukâbele bi'l-misl*. While Christian Europe moved ahead, he argued, the Ottomans fell behind by neglecting math, geography, and other sciences and by failing to innovate. Vâsıf explained exactly how this process worked in a few digressions on the so-called "new science of war." The Europeans had always been powerless against Muslim arms and strove to invent a "new style of warfare," he wrote. Inspired by the Greeks and Byzantines, but also by Satan, they adapted their battle order, siege warfare, and tactics to the rules of geometry and learned how to fight in tight but adaptable formations, becoming virtually unbeatable. One key invention in this regard was gunpowder. Vâsıf pointed out that humans use tools to obtain food and defend themselves; they make weapons in lieu of physical limbs, following Galen, like spears for claws or swords for teeth. The Europeans in this way used gunpowder – invented in 660 by an Egyptian philosopher – to make up for their natural cowardice, for it gave them a means to neutralize human bravery from a distance. They researched its technologies because they could not withstand the strength of Muslim armies, Vâsıf said, and learned how to mitigate personal bravery through the shock and awe and range of their weapons. Gunpowder then spread everywhere. The Ottomans too adopted it, but failed to keep up. The empire, then, faced a most daunting foe. Its military was unable to match Christian firearms and tactics and scattered at the first volley. Weakness beset the army, the greatest of the realm's four pillars, which could no longer protect the realm. But reciprocation was universally valid. The empire needed only to look to its enemies for

---

[81] E.g. ibid, fols. 43a-44b, 54a-54b, 55b-56a, 188a-189b, 222a.

models, Vâsıf claimed, which sultans before Selim had failed to do. He therefore praised the sultan for his reforms and for founding the new model army, whose methods suited the Ottomans' bravery and "zeal for Islam" and presaged victory over the French.[82]

A second passage repeated and elaborated these views. Speaking of the late invasion, Vâsıf declared that the empire's plight was not unique or even limited to Muslim domains. The French Revolution had spread near and far to affect all realms, and for that, everyone suffered. Yet the Ottomans could prevail if only they accepted discipline, for their zeal was demonstrably better than the enemy's cowardice and false creed. Vâsıf said that while Muslims had beaten infidels absolutely until the year 1591–1592, the Islamic millennium, they had grown idle and battles afterward followed the adage, "War is unpredictable in its outcome." The empire weakened while the Christians developed a new order (bir tarz-ı cedîd) based on mathematics and reason that led them to victory. They produced firearms, became expert in defense, and began to best the empire's forces in field battles and sieges. Vâsıf maintained that the Ottomans should have matched the enemy on equal terms, but as no one took action, they "were forced by sophistry into a battle order that had long since grown obsolete." Their forces could not match the enemy's discipline and serious defeats ensued. Yet for all this, Vâsıf still insisted that the empire would last until Judgment Day. To revive the realm, God granted the throne to Selim, who since his accession had spent great energy on rational economies and reform. For close to thirty years, the empire had been diseased and the order of the world undone, yet the sultan was committed to its restoration: this was "absolute power based on divine support," Vâsıf said.[83]

What, if anything, might we consider new or significant about this work? Its ideas are not overly innovative. Ottomans from Mustafa Naîmâ and Dürrî Mehmed to more conservative voices like Fazlızâde Ali and Saçaklızâde Mehmed had all projected the empire's "decline" back to the thousandth hijri year, albeit for different reasons. While the former held the millennium to mark a transition to Ibn Khaldûn's "age of stasis," Fazlızâde associated it with the infiltration of Persian texts into the empire – heretical philosophical texts, to be precise. He and Saçaklızâde

---

[82] MEHÂSİN 3, fols. 5a–6a, 38a–39a. Vâsıf cited the Arabic translation of Galen's De usu partium corporis humani, called Kitâb fî manâfi' al-a'ḍa (On the Usefulness of the Parts). Brockelmann attributes (supp. 2: 417) the translation to 'A. b. 'Îsâ b. 'A. al-Mu'tamid (AH 256–79/AD 870–92).

[83] MEHÂSİN 3, fols. 215a–217a. Vâsıf expressed similar views in HULÂSAT, 35.

thought that Ottoman weakness was a result of sheer impiety.[84] If we can say anything for certain about Vâsıf's views in this period, it is that they were heavily indebted to İbrahim Müteferrika. In the treatise *Rational Bases*, Müteferrika built an argument for reform around the concept of reciprocation, his aim being, he said, to examine Ottoman weakness and explain the new weapons and military principles of Christendom. For him, European power came from the development of a new warfare based on reason, mathematics, and geography. Müteferrika argued that war had changed, that old methods were obsolete, indeed dangerous, and that the dynasty ought to inform itself of the enemy's "new military order," as well as to cultivate the sciences and work through causes. For ultimately, he claimed, Christians lacked the innate bravery of Muslims and had to rely on reason. This worked to Ottoman advantage, as they might combine the new military arts with their natural courage to bring the enemy to his knees. Reciprocation, a focus on worldly causes, Ottoman neglect of geography and mathematics, and the combination of innate Muslim bravery with rational reform – the main elements of Vâsıf's views were present decades earlier in Müteferrika's work.[85]

What is instead novel is how Vâsıf managed to join these pieces together. We are able for perhaps the first time to discern a system in his thought, an intellectual framework that could explain the empire's historical trajectory and the case, even the necessity, for reform. Selim had wanted a narrative. This he got. Following a logic that was suggested by Müteferrika and others, Vâsıf turned reciprocation from a legal rule into a principle that might drive military, governmental, social, and cultural change. It was universal, a law of proto-historical progress that

---

[84] Kurz, 51–54, 199–200. See also el-Rouayheb, *Intellectual History*, 21–22; and idem, "Myth," 203–205. Cf. the respective positions of Naîmâ and Dürrî on the empire's decline in Naîmâ, 1: 21–30, 44; and Dürrî, TSMK Hazine nr. 1438, fols. 284b-285b. The topic is treated more generally by Kafadar in his "Question of Ottoman Decline" and "Myth of the Golden Age."

[85] E.g. Müteferrika, *Usûlü'l-Hikem*, 128–148, 151–152, 160–162, 170–172, 191. No passage better illustrates the link between the two than the anecdote of the "Frankish king." As Vâsıf told it (MEHÂSİN 5, 2: 187), the Franks once fought the Goths and were routed seven times in seven years, losing many men and supplies. The king's men discussed his commander-in-chief's ill fortune and each year called for his dismissal. However, the king was a prudent and philosophical man; he ignored them and reconfirmed the commander, who in the eighth year crushed the enemy, broke their power, and forced them to make peace. The king then addressed his people. He declared that each year the commander had learned the enemy's strategies and acquired the means (*esbâb*) of overcoming them in the future. Now they had triumphed. Vâsıf took this story, which is unabashed in its activism and promotion of reciprocation, nearly ad verbum from Müteferrika's *Usûlü'l-Hikem*, 177–178.

could alter the course of Muslim and non-Muslim civilization and that justified a host of reforms. Here was something useful for Selim, whose circle pushed the concept aggressively.[86] Vâsıf also grafted reciprocation to the philosophical base of his *Letter of Consolation*, parts of which he added awkwardly to the chronicle to stress the world's instability. "As creation is naturally changing and unstable," he wrote, "it is a precept of philosophy for there to be upheavals in the world and, at times, peace and tranquility. Nor is this unique to any era. In other words, it is not natural for realms' affairs to be fixed or wholly free from political mishap."[87] There is nevertheless something unsatisfying in the way that these ideas cohere, or do not cohere. Where were the limits of free will in Vâsıf's ever-changing world? What must we accept as God's will or natural chaos and what can we change? If evil does in fact lead to good, what need is there for us to act in the world at all? These are questions he never addressed.

While it failed to form a cogent whole, the mixture of ideas – human effort and reciprocation on one hand, cosmic flux on the other – still led Vâsıf down a number of interesting paths. For one thing, an uncertain world naturally posed challenges to rulers and put a premium on deliberation. Vâsıf saw this clearly, arguing in the early nineteenth century that the application of reason and policy was preferable to violence:

It is a precept of philosophy from the beginning of the world to now that chaos should at times appear on the face of the earth, always through a cause. We know from experience that worldly disorder is removed now through bloodshed and now through the policies of soldiers and scribes; and it is written in books of ancient philosophy that settling a matter through judgment is, where possible, better than wasting lives and that one must avoid risk, for proper discernment in the vital affairs of government is hard.[88]

In a later work dedicated to Küçük Hüseyin Paşa, one of the leaders of the Egypt campaign, Vâsıf likewise praised cautious military command. Hüseyin Paşa was aware that "war is uncertain" and used prudence, he said, so that while the Ottomans lost certain skirmishes, the admiral's vigilance led to a final victory.[89] Of course, from such sentiments it was

---

[86] Seyyid Mustafa Efendi used a similar line of argument in his 1803 *Diatribe de l'ingénieur Séid Moustapha sur l'état actuel de l'art militaire, du génie et des sciences à Constantinople* (reprinted in Paris, 1810); so did Dihkânîzâde Ubeydullah Kuşmânî in the tract *Zebîre-i Kuşmânî fî Tarîf-i Nizâm-ı İlhâmî*, written in the early 1800s but never published. See Şakul, "Nizâm-ı Cedîd," 127–131, 135–140. I will discuss these works in more detail in Chapter 7.

[87] MEHÂSİN 3, fols. 213a–215a.   [88] MEHÂSİN 4, fol. 274b.

[89] GAZAVÂT, fols. 8b–10a.

but a small step to the revaluation of war itself. In his work on Nûrî's chronicle, Vâsıf first voiced a more pensive view on warfare that reflected the empire's changing diplomatic needs as much as it did the metaphysics he had developed in his *Letter*. After 1793, Vâsıf abandoned the phrase "lesser of two evils" for those expressing war's uncertainty and variability. Most often this was the Arabic saying "War is unpredictable in its outcome (*al-ḥarb sijâl*)" or paraphrases thereof.[90] No longer did he describe peace as a necessary evil, for war, as anything else in the "world of generation and corruption," had become inherently risky. The empire could not depend on it as in the past. While this may sound like a minor rhetorical shift, the result was that Vâsıf loosened his earlier legalistic justifications for peace based on an unchanging enmity with the *dâr al-ḥarb*. God, he now argued, ordained times of war and peace rather than a perpetual state of hostility and no one, believer or unbeliever, was immune to fortune. Stressing the need to control warfare and its outcome, Vâsıf's later work put peace and war in human hands and was ultimately a more philosophical position – both a major step forward in his own thought and in the intellectual history of Ottoman reform.

Vâsıf waited impatiently for a reply to his submission, convinced of its quality and expecting to earn a reward from the palace or some other token of goodwill. Word eventually came from his old friend from Belgrade, Ebubekir Sâmî Paşa, who was now the Grand Vizier's proxy and whose poems Vâsıf had lately collected in an anthology.[91] Ebubekir invited him to the Porte. Selim had quite enjoyed the chronicle, he said. The sultan had suggested only small changes and would now have the whole work made into one volume, a clean copy of which he wanted in three to five months. The historian was taken aback. That Ebubekir made no mention at all of a reward startled and offended him. He had worked too hard and too long to be put off, he felt, and he knew his own value. Vâsıf seems to have remonstrated with Ebubekir Paşa and had him press the sultan, audaciously, for a monetary award. Ebubekir did so, apologetic and aware of the request's impropriety. He reminded Selim of Vâsıf's

---

[90] This Arabic saying is evidently quite old. See Freytag, 1: 384: "Bellum est situla"; and Lane, s.v. "S-J-L." It often appears with Turkish variants in Vâsıf's work after 1792: e.g. MEHÂSİN 3, fol. 215b; MEHÂSİN 4, fols. 35b, 290b; and MEHÂSİN 5, 2: 114.

[91] Vâsıf wrote in a preface (*Divân*, İÜ TY nr. 2836, fols. 1b-4b) that he undertook this task while Ebubekir was the Grand Vizier's proxy and he was court historian and keeper of the ledger. It must thus date between March/April 1799 and Ebubekir's dismissal on 10 B AH 1214 = December 8, 1799.

labor and said that it would do well to encourage him – His Majesty had, after all, clearly meant to give a large reward. While Vâsıf was only too happy to take the usual sum from the treasury, moreover, he served with a full knowledge of the sultan's bounty and would accept whatever was seen fit. It is rather surprising in view of this effrontery that Vâsıf got anything at all. The fact that Selim granted him a "suitable reward" of 5,000 kuruş must be regarded as proof of his genuine esteem or need for the work.[92]

Flushed with this success, Vâsıf pushed ahead with his revisions and several months later, in June 1800, presented the complete work as a second volume of *Charms and Truths*. In another covering letter, he preened that he had recast Nûrî's account as proper history, with lessons from practical philosophy and additions to bring it up to date. Now he had written the whole of Selim's reign, he said, a feat of "boundless glory." The historian also used the occasion to deride his predecessors, who had been "pedestrian or even less articulate than Bâqil," a proverbial dimwit of Arabic literature. And while he claimed to have excelled them in prose, he at the same time begged the sultan to pardon his faults, which, quite naturally, were accidental.[93] We can safely say that Vâsıf's return on the chronicle – 3,000 kuruş, a pay cut due to the treasury's embarrassment – only slightly marred his good fortune. By this period, he had also been made chancellor, or *tevkî'î*, a prestigious

---

[92] Two archival documents detail this episode. In the first (BOA.HAT 14883), Ebubekir Paşa formally presented Vâsıf's two volumes and covering letter to the sultan; he added that "as His Excellency has clearly given all his energies to this history in both its prose and exact account, and as the arrangement follows your orders, it is yours to command should the work please your Majesty." In the margin, Selim voiced his approval, with some suggestions: "Good. He should collect all of this and make it a single volume. Have him bring together the episode of Mustafa Paşa and Ebuhûr [i.e. the 1799 fall of the Egyptian town of Abuqîr] and record it truthfully as one event. And he should prepare a clean copy of what he has now drafted in three to five months." In the second document (BOA.HAT 13274), Ebubekir Paşa replied to Selim's orders. He had explained them to Vâsıf, he said, who would set to work. But he then repeated at some length that the historian had "devoted himself utterly to this important task" and merited reward, ending with the words: "Trust that in my impudence to speak so boldly, I am your Majesty's absolute slave." Selim's laconic answer was to "give him a suitable reward." See also İlgürel, "Vak'anüvislerin Taltifleri," 187–188.

[93] Two copies of this cover letter exist in the historian's drafts: BOA.Y.EE 90, pp. 37, 39. It is also printed as an appendix in Cevdet, *Târih*, 1: 345. Vâsıf specified in the manuscript colophon (MEHÂSİN 3, fol. 278a) that the work was "the second volume of the *Charms and Truths of Relics and Annals*" and that a third installment would follow where the second ended.

if mostly symbolic post in the chancery. After his recent commissions, the promotion was a sure sign of favor and lifted him out of the treasury once and for all. Vâsıf was closer than at any point in decades to the coveted post of chief scribe, the pinnacle of a bureaucratic career. All was within his reach at last.[94]

---

[94] A decree, BOA.HAT 13652, records the final submission of the chronicle to the sultan, who again ordered a "suitable reward." We find some wrangling over the sum, though. A second document (BOA.AE.Slm 9539, dated 28 M AH 1215 = June 21, 1800) notes that while Vâsıf had got 5,000 *kuruş* for his last submission, it was impossible to give him another 5,000 on account of the "state of the imperial treasury." It suggests that he be remunerated at Nûrî's level: 3,000 *kuruş*. Kütükoğlu's claim ("Vekâyi'nüvis," 122) that Vâsıf submitted the work between February 6, 1802, and January 29, 1803 is in error; Vâsıf was dismissed as keeper of the daily ledger on 4 L AH 1214 = March 1, 1800 and became chancellor shortly after, on either 4 or 5 Za = March 30–31, after the death of the previous *tevkî'î*. See MEHÂSİN 3, fol. 271a; Fâtin, 432; Hammer-Purgstall, 3: 553; BOA. A.RSK.d 1623, p. 37; and Afyoncu, "Tevcihat Kayıtları I," 124.

7

The Height of Fame (1800–1806)

7.1 REFORM AND ITS DISCONTENTS, 1800–1802

It is fair to say that the last six years of Vâsıf's life, from 1800 to 1806, saw him reach the height of his career and personal fame. These were years when his powers as a historian matured and he at last molded a vision of the empire from the inchoate past, years when he ferociously defended Selim's reforms and savaged his opponents. These were years, moreover, when to do so he literally rewrote history. Yet, Vâsıf's last years also present us with an anticlimax. The historian had all that he desired: fame, wealth, royal favor, and, in 1805, the post of chief scribe. Was it enough? Like one of his own moral lessons, Vâsıf gathered these vain prizes only to see them turn to dust in his hands and die. His wealth – vast, if we believe reports – went unspent. As a chief scribe, he proved middling. None of his genius fitted him politically to the role, and he ended his brief term in discredit. His history and oeuvre survived, it is true, but unfinished and forever linked to his overweening arrogance and hubris. In the end, posterity would remember Vâsıf as someone whose flaws equaled or surpassed his immense talents, as a figure who could preach ethics and self-control, but not apply the lessons to himself. It did not matter that he was perhaps the greatest littérateur and historian of his age or that, over a long career, he had been an effective intellectual partisan of reform. He was either a hypocrite or, in some sense, a failure.

The turn of the nineteenth century for Vâsıf and his peers coincided with the French expulsion from Egypt, a victory that had less to do with Ottoman initiative than with Napoléon's missteps and British sea power. By the time Selim dispatched his forces in the spring of 1800, his army with

Yusuf Ziyâ Paşa and navy with Küçük Hüseyin Paşa, the French were already doomed. Nelson had destroyed their fleet at Abûqîr, and Napoléon's failure that spring to take Acre in Syria, held firmly by the governor Cezzâr Ahmed Paşa, a joint Ottoman-British fleet, and some of the sultan's new model soldiers, led him to abandon the project. He sailed for France, leaving the cleanup to his commander Jean-Baptiste Kléber. The rest was largely a matter of diplomacy. Old habits were starting to reassert themselves and Ottomans like the new chief scribe, Mahmud Râif Efendi, distrusted their allies and favored coming to terms directly with the French, their traditional friends. While Kléber agreed in early 1800 to evacuate his forces, the settlement fell apart under British and Russian opposition and Kléber's own assassination later that year. It was only after renewed hostilities that Ziyâ Paşa was able, with British aid, to force a final surrender. The French evacuated a besieged Alexandria on August 31, 1801; about a month and a half later, Küçük Hüseyin Paşa took formal control of the city. When the Ottomans signed a formal peace treaty the next year, reestablishing friendship with France, the so-called Triple Alliance was no more and diplomatic currents resumed their former course.[1]

Vâsıf, of course, followed these events from a safe distance in the capital. We can assume that he kept well-informed of affairs in Egypt through his new post as chancellor or tevkî'î, to which he was named in late March 1800 after the death of the previous holder, İsmet İsmail Efendi, and which afforded him a high level of access to both documents and ruling circles. This was an ancient duty. Also called the nişâncı, the chancellor affixed the sultanic seal, or tuğra, to decrees, letters, treaties, and patents in order to make them official. Traditionally he had been a top figure in the scribal corps, a member of the imperial council who kept the rolls of fief holders, safeguarded protocol, and led the bureaucracy as a whole. Past chancellors like Celâlzâde Mustafa (d. 1567) and Ramazanzâde Mehmed (d. 1571) had commanded respect for their deep knowledge of customary law, or kânûn; the historian Mustafa Âli, who coveted the position, had even likened their role in formulating kânûn to the şeyhülislâm's interpretation of holy law. If the post by Vâsıf's day had lost most of its functions to the chief scribe, then, it still retained a heady aura of prestige. The historian was now a member of the imperial council. He sat in the top rung of bureau chiefs and could join in major imperial ceremonies and

---

[1] Shaw, *Old and New*, 258, 271–282. See also Soysal, 278–314; and Süslü, "Rapports," 242–244.

religious celebrations. He also likely took pride in the post's storied history. It mattered rather less that Vâsıf was unhappy with the salary of some 6,000 *kuruş*, for, as far as we can tell, his duties were limited and the position a sinecure to support him in other tasks, especially his work as court historian.[2]

The first years of the century were in fact an intense period for Vâsıf's literary activity, most of it touching squarely on reform. The need to mount a defense of Selim's program had only grown since the foundation of the new model army and, while not yet overt or violent, its opponents worked insidiously through gossip and acts of protest like arson.[3] Vâsıf's colleagues knew that they had to make the case. The problem was that they disagreed over a host of issues, major and minor. It is within this wider reformist discourse – in relation to both supporters and critics of the "New Order" – that we must judge the historian's early nineteenth-century writings. Vâsıf wanted as much as any to create a workable framework for reform and had made a good deal of headway, but it is no surprise that he struggled to assemble the disparate parts. If anything, his difficulty was less a token of his own confusion than of a deeper intellectual incoherence in the empire.

Ottoman reform tracts from the early 1800s ranged from broadsides and propaganda to guarded studies that aimed, alternately, to publicize, defend, and criticize the sultan's program. As earlier, this literature asked what had gone wrong and how to effect a restoration. It focused its energies above all on ancient practice and the legitimate scope of "reciprocation" and reason. One instance of propaganda, Mahmud Râif Efendi's 1798 *Tableau des nouveaux règlemens de l'Empire ottoman*, parroted the government's official line and presented the New Order in glowing terms. Selim's circle appears to have used this work to introduce his reforms to European audiences and had it translated into French,

---

[2] According to an archival document (BOA.HAT 15168), Vâsıf was one of three candidates put forward for this appointment. Its leading language – noting his meritorious service as court historian and another candidate's prior engagement – shows that he was the favorite. See also MEHÂSİN 3, fol. 271a; BOA.A.RSK.d 1623, p. 37; and Afyoncu, "Tevcihat Kayıtları I," 124. Vâsıf would later complain (MEHÂSİN 5, 2: 184) in an offhand comment of the "chancellorship's small income." Two documents (BOA.C.DH 1632 and BOA.C.ML 21110) from his second term as chancellor show that he earned 504 ½ *kuruş* in the month of L AH 1216, 561 *kuruş* in Ca AH 1217, and a total of 6,620 *kuruş* for the year. On the chancellor, the so-called "müfti of *kânûn*," see Fleischer, *Bureaucrat*, 92–95, 214–221, 227–229; and DİA, s.v. "Nişancı." Kaya Şahin has recently published a biography of Celâlzâde: *Empire and Power in the Reign of Süleyman: Narrating the Sixteenth Century Ottoman World* (Cambridge, 2013).

[3] Yıldız, 110–121.

illustrated, printed, and distributed to foreign envoys. In it, Râif drew a stark textual and pictorial contrast between old and new. He claimed that the reforms had remedied a decay in Ottoman institutions caused by the neglect of Süleyman I's statutes, or *kânûnnâme*. Râif also touted a foreign language, French, and expressed the belief that modern science could only be acquired outside of the empire.[4] Seyyid Mustafa Efendi's *Diatribe de l'ingénieur Séid Moustapha* was a similar work. Like Râif's *Tableau*, the sultan's coterie had the *Diatribe* written in French and disseminated to European envoys. Seyyid Mustafa's key contribution was the importance that he attached to reciprocation. While there are questions over the tract's authorship and even over Mustafa's existence, the author, like Râif, lamented popular biases against the positive sciences and their use in modern warfare. To be sure, he argued, Ottoman weakness and European superiority stemmed from this attitude. The Ottomans lost because they failed to benefit from European knowhow and to observe reciprocation, which had been distorted by "la classe des idiots et superstitieux" and turned from a worldly into a religious issue. For Seyyid Mustafa, knowledge and reason were universal. What was more, scientific dominance could migrate. He therefore located the basic motor of civilization in reciprocation, which became something closer to a historical law than the mere transfer of technology. The empire's problem was not, then, a matter of recreating old institutions, but of restoring the precept of reciprocation over and above those wrongheaded boors who interpreted it as sinful innovation.[5]

Still other reformers, like Ubeydullah Kuşmânî and his *Kuşmânî on the Divinely Inspired Order* (*Zebîre-i Kuşmânî fî Tarîf-i Nizâm-ı İlhâmî*),

---

[4] The work was first published in French at the imperial press as *Tableau des nouveaux règlemens de l'Empire ottoman* (Üsküdar, 1798). Kemal Beydilli and İlhan Şahin have uncovered the original Turkish manuscript, entitled *Nümûne-i Menâzım-ı Cedîd-i Selîm Hânî*. See *Mahmud Râif Efendi ve Nizâm-ı Cedîd'e Dâir Eseri* (Ankara, 2001), esp. 121–155. See also Beydilli, "Islâhât Düşünceleri," 34–35; and Şakul, "Nizâm-ı Cedîd," 125–127.

[5] The imperial press in Üsküdar issued this work in French in 1803. It appeared in two later editions (in 1807 and 1810) at the initiative of the Parisian orientalist L. Langlès. Kemal Beydilli has found and edited a later Turkish translation in "İlk Mühendislerimizden Seyyid Mustafa ve Nizâm-ı Cedîd'e Dair Risâlesi," *Tarih Enstitüsü Dergisi* 12 (1987): 387–479. Joseph von Hammer-Purgstall once claimed that Seyyid Mustafa never existed and that the tract was written by the dragoman Yakovaki Argyropoulos for the chief scribe, Mahmud Râif: see Bernard Lewis, *The Emergence of Modern Turkey* (Oxford, 2002), 60 n. 43. In fact, Beydilli shows ("Seyyid Mustafa," esp. 392 ff.) that he did exist, if confused with another figure of the same name. See also idem, "Islâhât Düşünceleri," 34–35; and Şakul, "Nizâm-ı Cedîd," 127–131.

wrote polemical defenses of Selim's program which mocked opponents, exploited fears of Russia, and used scripture to refute charges that the reforms offended religion. Kuşmânî, for one, had pointed words for the Janissaries. Like Seyyid Mustafa, he saw reciprocation as a historical rule and continuous transfer of knowledge. Kuşmânî may have been a Nakşbendî-Müceddidî dervish, a politically active order who supported religious renewal. Other Sufis like Gâlib Dede advocated reciprocation in this way, as a religious principle, for the divine plan included all creation and sources of knowledge. One should borrow equally from Muslims as from infidels, from Moses as from Pharaoh. To do otherwise was to reject the divine plan and a form of unbelief. Vâsıf, too, as we shall see, would pen a vicious screed that belittled his opponents and pushed reciprocation to the level of historic principle.[6]

These treatises and polemics raise an important question: who exactly were Selim's opponents, Seyyid Mustafa's "idiots" and Vâsıf's "fanatics"? What were their arguments? It would be wrong to presume that they were a minority of extremists or to dismiss them outright as straw men. While such discontents are often absent from the written record, Vâsıf and his peers cast sidelights that allow us to say a certain amount about their reservations and why they resisted reform. Some people clearly and viscerally opposed the New Order. If the period's crises led many élites to give wider scope to reciprocation, for example, certain ulema at the same time hardened their stance on innovation. Reform for them undermined the faith and veered into heresy, unbelief, and treason.[7] They not unexpectedly denounced the New Order in religious terms and, as seen in reform tracts, charged the sultan and his circle with illicit innovation. We should note that this served to disqualify Selim as a restorer, or *müceddid*, who, it was thought, protected tradition from innovation. It is also of interest that after his 1807 deposition, a number of

---

[6] There are two recent editions of this work, whose title plays on Selim III's pen name İlhâmî, or "the divinely inspired." The first was published by Ömer İşbilir as *Nizâm-ı Cedîd'e Dair bir Risale: Zebîre-i Kuşmânî fî Tarîf-i Nizâm-ı İlhâmî* (Ankara, 2006). Aysel Yıldız included a second in her volume *Asiler ve Gaziler: Kabakçı Mustafa Risalesi* (Istanbul, 2007). See also Beydilli, "Islâhât Düşünceleri," 35–37; Şakul, "Nizâm-ı Cedîd," 135–140; and Yıldız, 11–21.

[7] This argument is expressed in the hadith, "He who imitates another people becomes one of them." See Christopher Tuck, "'All Innovation Leads to Hellfire': Military Reform and the Ottoman Empire in the Eighteenth Century," *Journal of Strategic Studies* 31 (2008): 484–487; and Heyd, "Ottoman 'Ulemâ," 70–77. While Üstün is right to criticize the view that opposition to reform was the result of inherent cultural conservatism (e.g. 78–86), there was, at the same time, a very real and heated debate over reform's religious legitimacy. See too Çelik, "Nizâm-ı Cedîd'in Niteliği," 579–580.

high-profile scholars signed an affidavit, or *hüccet-i şer'iyye*, denouncing the reforms as "unprecedented illegal innovations and reprehensible infidel imitations."[8]

Two other aggrieved parties were the provincial notables and Janissaries. As said before, by the late eighteenth century, many of the empire's provinces had fallen into the hands of local dynasts and magnates called *a'yân*. The New Order struck at these figures from several angles. Selim's desire to consolidate his rule over the empire was naturally a threat to their political standing, while his new revenue treasury undermined their economic power by diverting local revenues and made them obsolete as contractors. Not all notables lost out; those who worked with Istanbul stood to profit in the short term. However, *a'yân* who found themselves outside of the new fiscal and administrative networks tended to resist reform, while the sultan's long-term project of centralization challenged the power of all notables and even the stability of the New Order coalition.[9] The Janissaries also feared marginalization. More than provincial notables, the corps could make common cause with townsmen – many of whom had nominal places on the rolls – and could command a wide social base. Interestingly, one of Vâsıf's early nineteenth-century works hints that some disaffected Janissaries aped the ulema's anti-reform rhetoric. Marginalia in one copy supply their rebuttals, crudely using the same language of "innovation" and implying that the new army and its European drill harmed the faith. "Infidels work through trickery," said one imagined soldier. "This is effective but we are Muslims and trickery does not become us." Another note vowed that hand-to-hand combat was the only way to fight and that newer technology had, in fact, led to recent defeats: "Fooling with weapons is infidel business and to a Muslim infidel business is unbelief . . . They are the reason for our defeat, you see."[10] These claims aside, Janissary opposition was in part economic. The scores of individuals who held pay chits included craftsmen, merchants, bureaucrats, and even religious scholars, all of whom stood to lose from an expansion of the new army. Vâsıf and his peers inevitably cast such men and their qualms as self-interested. The New Order threatened livelihoods. Men linked to the old corps feared for their

---

[8] Âsım, 2: 46–49; and Heyd, "Ottoman 'Ulemâ," 69. Yıldız writes (457–472) on whether this affidavit justified military force in politics in order to oppose "innovations." Another anonymous tract charged (ibid, 181–183) that Selim's intention was not to reform Islam, but to "convert" it.

[9] Yaycıoğlu, 54–55; and Yıldız, 194–202.

[10] BOA.HAT 48106-A, notes nine, eleven, and twelve. Cf. HULÂSAT, 57–65. On resistance to the reforms from the Janissaries and others, see Üstün, 146–192; and Yaycıoğlu, 56–58, 62, 157 ff.

pay and used religion as a pretext, they claimed. As Vâsıf later put it, "these nitwits have never had any concern for our faith or country and know nothing of ritual purity, yet now they show a mighty anxiety for religion."[11]

A very different sort of critic emerges in literature from the center of power – reformers with ties to government. Critics-cum-reformers sympathized with Selim, but questioned the trajectory of his program, chiefly its focus on worldly goals. Ömer Fâik Efendi was one of this number. A low-level scribe, Fâik attended an 1804 meeting organized by Vâsıf's ally, Ahmed Fâiz Efendi, that appears to have been a "seminar" to push the reforms on the palace bureaucracy. In response to Fâik's questions, Fâiz had the scribe put his thoughts on paper in what eventually became the tract the *Old Order in the Abyss* or *Nizâmü'l-Atîk fî Bahri'l-Amîk*. The *Old Order* addressed thirty-two separate points, twenty-three devoted to outward order and nine to moral issues. Fâik felt that the empire needed military as well as all-purpose reform. However, he was disturbed by the luxury and caprice of Selim's inner circle and by what he considered their wrongheaded policies. Above all, he was convinced that the reforms, as they stood, exalted reason over the piety of the "old order." Fâik proposed "spiritual measures" like the public reading of religious texts, the improvement of religious education, and just rule according to holy law, arguing that the realm would prosper and defeat its enemies with these changes. The *Old Order* in this way replicated popular views of Ottoman exceptionalism and raised topics that were quite sensitive to the program's opponents; Fâik dared not publish it, feeling quite rightly that it deviated from sanctioned views and might endanger him.[12] Mehmed Emîn Behîç Efendi, who wrote the essay *Inspired Memoranda*, or *Sevânihü'l-Levâyih*, in 1803, was another critic-cum-reformer. Behîç served in a number of posts and was killed in 1809 as a result of his alignment with Âlemdar Mustafa Paşa, the author of an 1807 coup. Behîç believed the empire to be better prepared for reform than its European adversaries. He thus contrasted the Ottomans with the Russians, whom he called "dumb brutes incapable of learning the simplest matter in ten years, even should they be clobbered on the head."

---

[11] HULÂSAT, 62–63.

[12] This tract is available only in manuscript and an edited undergraduate thesis: Ahmet Sarıkaya, ed., "Ömer Fâ'ik Efendi, Nizâmü'l-Atîk" (Istanbul University, 1979). On the author and his work, see Beydilli, "Islâhât Düşünceleri," 37–42; Şakul, "Nizâm-ı Cedîd," 145–148; and Yıldız, 183–184. Fâik's concept of "moral reform" does not appear to be overly unique and parallels Vâsıf's "spiritual preparations," or *rûhânî tedârükât*, in MEHÂSİN 1, fol. 42b.

The empire would certainly succeed if they, the Russians, had managed. Yet while Behîç insisted that the basis of reform was holy law and stood against the Janissaries, who derided the New Order as infidel, he joined Fâik in criticizing the state of contemporary education and religious life. It is important to stress that both men, Fâik and Behîç, did not reject reform. Their works were not "eulogies" for the old order as much as careful critiques of the new, which reveal, moreover, major divisions in the government itself over reform.[13]

Vâsıf sided in these debates with the likes of Mahmud Râif, Seyyid Mustafa, and Ahmed Fâiz – with Selim's circle, of which he was a part – and used his pen to defend the reforms at length. While he still hoped for a moral and material restoration of the empire, Vâsıf was at the same time developing ideas that, if not wholly original, took tentative steps away from an immutable world order. He increasingly recognized the novelty of his era and was shaping a metaphysics to match his sense of dislocation. He also continued to make reciprocation a fundamental concept of reform: a universal, rational, historical, and legal precept that must guide the empire to a new political and military order and which, combined with the dynasty's innate virtues, would reestablish Ottoman dominance.

The main venue for Vâsıf at this stage remained his chronicle *Charms and Truths*, whose third volume he began in 1800 and which he was coming to see as a unified record of Selim's reign. It certainly kept him busy. Vâsıf spent much of 1800 and 1801 on the volume, installments of which he submitted each year in return for rewards.[14] His focus in these years was on the drama unfolding in Egypt and its wider meaning for the Ottoman world. For Vâsıf, victory over the French was proof of the empire's divine favor and the vindication of the sultan's reforms that he had predicted in the *Letter of Consolation*. The Ottomans on one hand

---

[13] Baki Tezcan reads Fâik's work as a "eulogy of the Old Order" (*The Second Empire*, 194 n. 8), which is a misinterpretation of the tract. Fâik and others like him were not members of an old guard; they were reformers who tried to influence the discourse from within. See Çınar, ed., "Es-Seyyid Mehmed Emîn Behîç"; Beydilli, "Islâhât Düşünceleri," 42–53; Şakul, "Nizâm-ı Cedîd," 141–145; and Yıldız, 183–184.

[14] Vâsıf called the work the "third volume" of his chronicle in poems at the beginning of MEHÂSİN 4, fol. 1b, and at the end of MEHÂSİN 3, fol. 278a. A similar reference exists in his drafts: BOA.Y.EE 90, p. 58. We also possess two cover letters that document Vâsıf's submission of parts of the volume. The first introduces events from M AH 1215 to S 1216 (May/June 1800–May 1801) and is found in BOA.Y.EE 90, p. 40; and in Cevdet, *Târih*, 1: 345–346. The second (BOA.Y.EE p. 38; and Cevdet, *Târih*, 1: 346) covers the period from S AH 1216 to S 1217 (May 1801–May 1802), with Vâsıf stating that he usually presented a year's worth of new events each year.

prevailed through God's grace. The French had lost their powers of *istidrâc* and could no longer resist the empire or its allies, and were forced by divine wrath to cede their conquests. On the other hand, Vâsıf credited Küçük Hüseyin Paşa for his prudent command and for agreeing to the evacuation. War being unpredictable in the world of generation and corruption, he said, the admiral had wisely chosen to avoid an uncertain battle or siege in favor of negotiation.[15] This mixture of human and divine causes set within a naturally volatile world was becoming characteristic of the historian's work. A second element, aggressive reform, was also present. In a passage on the navy, Vâsıf argued that the Ottomans must match new European technologies, and that it was "a duty for every individual that the dynasty respond in kind." This terminology is quite specific. Reciprocation here is an individual religious obligation or *farz-ı 'ayn*, a legal term that signifies something incumbent on all believers, rather than on only part of the community (*farz-ı kifâye*). Jihad, for example, was deemed a collective obligation except in dire emergencies, as in an invasion, when all individuals became liable. Vâsıf's claim implies a set of truly exceptional circumstances – namely, that the danger posed by not acting reciprocally endangered the empire's very existence. Yet he still held fast to the notion of fated Ottoman greatness. Vâsıf marked the victory in Egypt with poetry and at least two chronograms. One won him a gift of 2,500 *kuruş*. The second, marking Hüseyin Paşa's entry into Alexandria in the autumn of 1801, praised God for restoring Egypt to its proper place in the empire, which he declared to be specially blessed and even mentioned in the Quran.[16]

Vâsıf also tried to turn the French invasion into the subject of more intensive historical study. He wrote a short essay on the campaign around this time, probably soon after Küçük Hüseyin Paşa's return to Istanbul in December 1801, which he dedicated to the Grand Admiral and called the *Gestes of Hüseyin Paşa* or *Gazavât-ı Hüseyin Paşa*. This tract culled material from his chronicle to paint a fawning portrait. Relating the work to history as a moral and political tool, and especially to the cultivation of

---

[15] MEHÂSİN 4, fols. 74b, 87a, 89b-90a, 94a.

[16] MEHÂSİN 4, fols. 309a-309b. For the legal terms, see EI², s.v. "Farḍ"; and Kâtib Çelebi, *Kashf al-ẓunûn*, 1: 46. Vâsıf claimed (MEHÂSİN 4, fol. 81a) that he and others wrote chronograms for Selim on the reconquest of Egypt, his own winning special favor: "By way of description [*vâsıfen*] did I / Mark this conquest's date: Sultan Selim's men / Took Egypt with great effort [= AH 1216]." The second chronogram (ibid, fol. 95b) – "The return of the keys to Alexandria, by God's grace [= AH 1216]" – begins a section that describes a ceremony of prayer and thanksgiving at the imperial palace and ends with a longer poem on the empire's unique favor. Elgin (39) features a third chronogram.

the "experiential intellect," Vâsıf stated in his preface how he wished to celebrate the admiral's services and immortalize his "oceanic bravery." Of course, the more immediate aim was flattery. Vâsıf was very solicitous with Küçük Hüseyin Paşa in these years, writing him poems and depicting him alongside Selim III as a sort of second conqueror of Egypt. *Gestes* was part of this and, in truth, added little besides one or two new paragraphs. Vâsıf also refused or was passed over for a similar puff piece on Grand Vizier Ziyâ Paşa's role in Egypt, the later *Book of Light* or *Ziyânâme* by Darendeli İzzet Hasan, and wrote the epitaph for Hüseyin Paşa's tombstone after his death from dysentery in 1803.[17]

Proof that Vâsıf had still larger plans for the Egypt campaign comes through a note in the presentation copy of his *Letter of Consolation*. Here, Vâsıf signaled a desire to reuse the theodicy in a future work. The essay, he said, "would clearly serve with some small changes as a preface for a separate piece, God willing, that I shall write on Egyptian episode." It is a pity that we do not know more; Vâsıf seems to have abandoned the idea. It may be that he was asked to write the work that became the *Book of Light*, but had to put it aside. He also could have been referring to a long digression on the French Revolution in the second volume of *Charms and Truths*, where he adapted parts of the *Letter* to urge unity in the face of invasion and again predicted victory. Judging by a broadsheet in his drafts, Vâsıf might have intended to issue this piece as a printed pamphlet.[18] There is an even more intriguing possibility: a work that may represent an attempt by Vâsıf to place the invasion of Egypt into a larger historical framework. The manuscript in question is a pastiche of events from the second and third volumes of *Charms and Truths*, prefaced with

---

[17] GAZAVÂT, fols. 1a–2b, 7b, 8b–10a, 15a. We can plausibly date this work to late 1801 or early 1802 on the basis of Vâsıf's statement that he presented it to Hüseyin Paşa, which must have occurred after the latter's return to Istanbul. Sarıkaya has recently shown (ccxli–ccxlii) that the Vienna manuscript – explicitly attributed to Vâsıf – is the same as a work in the Egyptian National Library previously thought anonymous. Vâsıf's authorship is in any event obvious from the contents, even though he never identified himself by name. Darendeli İzzet said (*Ziyânâme: Sadrazam Yusuf Ziya Paşa'nın Napolyon'a Karşı Mısır Seferi (1798–1802)*, ed. M. İlkin Erkutun [Istanbul, 2009], 10) that Vâsıf could not divert energy from his normal duties to write a detailed account of Ziyâ Paşa's time in Egypt, for which reason he, İzzet, was appointed. Given that Vâsıf wrote a special history for Hüseyin Paşa, this explanation is unconvincing. The epitaph was a chronogram that encoded Hüseyin Paşa's death date: 23 Ş AH 1218 = December 8, 1803. See Nejat Göyünç, "Kapudan-ı Deryâ Küçük Hüseyin Paşa," *Tarih Dergisi* 2 (1952): 47–48; Hammer-Purgstall, 3: 553–554; and MEHÂSİN 4, fols. 235a–237a.

[18] TESLİYETNÂME, fol. 1b. Cf. MEHÂSİN 3, fols. 196a–217b. The adapted *Letter of Consolation* appears in fols. 213a–215a. See also the partial broadsheet in BOA.Y.EE 90, p. 33.

a truncated version of his *Letter*. Clearly unfinished, it ends with events in the spring of 1802. Is this Vâsıf's work on Egypt? There is no firm evidence that he assembled it, though, interestingly enough, at least one reference to his usual volume numbers has been removed.[19] Yet if it is the planned work on the invasion, it carries no small importance for Vâsıf's growth as a historian and as his first experiment with an interpretive scheme, applying the *Letter of Consolation's* germ – its insistence on God's benevolence and the dynasty's divine favor – to a broad sequence of Ottoman history. Either way, Vâsıf was clearly trying in the early nineteenth century to harmonize the empire's situation with what he knew and believed of its exceptionalism. His writing on the French invasion was another case of history as theodicy, in which an Ottoman victory was, and could be nothing less than, a vindication.

Despite his output and labor, we know with some certainty that the first years of the new century were difficult ones in Vâsıf's personal life. In February 1801, he was discharged as chancellor. While vexing, the loss of this sinecure was but a small bother for a man now used to the system of yearly rotation in office. However, what followed proved to be much more serious. On the night of March 30, a fire broke out in the house next-door to Vâsıf's in Yerebatan, temporarily occupied by Mabeynci Ahmed Efendi, and spread quickly through the neighborhood. More than ten homes burned before the fire was extinguished. Vâsıf's own loss was total, the destruction not only encompassing his home, but many of his cherished personal effects: "Some of the valuables and countless books that I had acquired in thirty years of state service burned while others fell prey to looters, who even carried off some cheap immovable property," he said. The historian then compared himself to the Persian poet Shifâ'î (d. 1627), who too apparently lost everything: "My despair at the looters was like the tale of the inheritance that Hakîm Shifâ'î split among his brothers."[20] For all his anguish, Vâsıf voiced particular regret at the loss of his books and papers. There could be few greater disasters for an intellectual than the loss of a library. While we do not know much about the size or content of Vâsıf's collection, it is possible to speculate on the basis of some contemporary examples. For instance, İbrahim Müteferrika had a personal library of 124

---

[19] İÜ TY nr. 6012, fol. 76b. I argued in my dissertation (27–28) that this manuscript is the planned work, but have since altered my view. There is really no way to tell.

[20] MEHÂSİN 4, fol. 57b. Arıkan (348) corroborates the date as 15 Za AH 1215. Both accounts agree that the fire started several hours after sunset. On Vâsıf's dismissal, see BOA.A.RSK.d 1623, p. 37; and Afyoncu, "Tevcihat Kayıtları I," 125. Vâsıf's allusion to Shifâ'î is obscure, but see Browne, 4: 256.

books at his death; Ebubekir Râtib Efendi owned 234 volumes on topics like warfare, politics, the natural sciences, and numismatics, in addition to a large number of maps; and the late poet and court historian Küçükçelebizâde Âsım Efendi (d. 1760) reportedly had thousands of books, though this number was surely high for the time. It would not be unreasonable to estimate Vâsıf's own library at several hundred volumes. Judging by his words, Vâsıf likely owned titles ranging from the classic Arabic chronicles of al-Ṭabarî and al-Wâqidî to standard works of ethics, philosophy, geography, politics, traditions, and law. He certainly had a copy of the famed jurist al-Mâwardî's *Conduct of Viziers* or *Qawânîn al-wuzâra*; he also had an autograph miscellany by the Kurdish scholar and historian İdrîs Bitlîsî (d. 1520). All of this was lost in the flames.[21]

With his home gone, Vâsıf was forced to impose on friends and patrons for assistance. For a time, he moved to the scenic Çamlıca area of Üsküdar, presumably with his family and extended household, where he stayed at the summer residence of the judge Hafîd Mehmed Efendi, a son of Mustafa Âşir, nephew of Abdürrezzâk Efendi, and client of Küçük Hüseyin Paşa. The historian must have carried out his duties from this temporary refuge. He was still living there in 1803, when he was visited by a precocious Austrian *Sprachknabe* named Joseph Hammer, the future orientalist and Freiherr von Hammer-Purgstall.[22] Vâsıf too sought help of a monetary nature. Presenting a part of his chronicle in 1801, he appealed to the Grand Vizier's proxy Abdullah Paşa for extra funds to help him rebuild. "While I should not presume on the endless favor that my patrons have showered on me, and which greatly shames me, it would be equally disrespectful to feign wealth in the face of their generosity," Vâsıf wrote.

To wit: the sudden misfortune that I have suffered by God's will surely entitles me to royal pity and compassion. I beg that a sum be added to the reward paid out

---

[21] E.g. MEHÂSİN 2, fol. 163a; MEHÂSİN 3, fol. 236a; and MEHÂSİN 4, fols. 318a-318b. Vâsıf made apologies in one passage of his history (MEHÂSİN 5, 2: 232) for the loss of a key document in the fire. He also remarked (ibid, 1: 180) on the size of Küçükçelebizâde's library, which he saw in person. Cf. Sabev, 110–127, 345–350; and Yeşil, *Ebubekir Râtib*, 241–243.

[22] Hammer-Purgstall (3: 553) offers no further details of their meeting apart from the location. Münîb confirms in *Devḥatü'l-Meşâyiḫ*, 2: 423, that Hafîd Efendi had a fine summer home in Çamlıca. Though their relationship is unclear, he and Vâsıf, as I have proposed above, might have been family by marriage; nor would it have been socially permissible for the historian's wife or unmarried daughters to live in the home of a male non-relative. Hafîd was likewise aligned with Küçük Hüseyin Paşa, to whom he dedicated a biographical work on the empire's grand admirals: *The Ship of Viziers* or *Sefînetü'l-Vüzerâ*. The manuscript edited by İsmet Parmaksızoğlu (Istanbul, 1952, p. 57) is dated 19 C AH 1218 = October 6, 1803, at Çamlıca.

yearly by the imperial treasury on the submission of parts of the dynastic chronicle, that I may build a place to house my wife and children and save us from homelessness.[23]

The petition was successful. Abdullah Paşa forwarded it to Selim, who in July agreed to give Vâsıf a large top-up on his usual reward. "The merciful sovereign looked with a kind eye on my piteous state and deigned to honor me with 5,000 kuruş," Vâsıf boasted. This extra sum raised his total pay for the installment to 7,500 kuruş and also seems to have excited some measure of jealousy among rivals at court. Ahmed Âsım, a rising talent who had lately won 5,000 kuruş for a Turkish translation of a dictionary, the Persian Lexicon (Qâmûs al-'Ajam), and who aspired to be court historian, claimed that Vâsıf was able to wheedle more than 20,000 per year from Selim for his chronicle alone. This was simply not true. Indeed, Vâsıf was earning thousands less than this amount even after he regained the post of chancellor in early 1802 and began to draw a regular salary, his affairs considerably eased. Yet Âsım's very likely malicious exaggeration reminds us that no one really knew what the man was worth in his lifetime. The fact that Vâsıf so often misrepresented his finances could have only fanned such rumors.[24]

7.2 REWRITING THE PAST, 1802–1805

By the early nineteenth century, Selim III's mind turned more and more to the past and to his legacy in Ottoman history. He already had a full account of his reign. Thanks to Vâsıf, the dynastic chronicle from 1789 onward was a cogent defense of reform in which he, the sultan, was the fulcrum, the empire's long-awaited renewer. Yet Selim was not content. He wanted something more – a sweeping vision to suit the values of his court – and in 1801, commissioned Vâsıf to edit the mid-century work of court historians like Mehmed Hâkim (1752–1766), Çeşmizâde Mustafa Reşîd (1766–1768), and Sadullah Enverî (1768–1774) for print as part of

[23] BOA.Y.EE 90, p. 40; and Cevdet, Târih, 1: 345–346.
[24] Âsım, 1: 257. Two archival documents (BOA.C.DH 1632 and BOA.C.ML 21110) indicate that Vâsıf made 6,620 kuruş as chancellor. With his special emolument and an appointment bonus of 120 kuruş (see Sarıkaya, xcvii, for this document), his gross income in 1801/2 was likely much closer to 15,000 than 20,000 kuruş. See also MEHÂSİN 4, fol. 57b, where Vâsıf wrote that Selim granted him 5,000 kuruş to help rebuild. Cf. BOA. C.MF 3963, dated 14–16 Ra AH 1216 = July 25–27, 1801, which says that the total award was 7,500. The remaining 2,500 kuruş seems to represent his base pay for the chronicle. Also Kütükoğlu, "Vekâyi'nüvis," 110 f.; and İlgürel, "Vak'anüvislerin Taltifleri," 188–189.

the increasingly vast *Charms and Truths*. "His Majesty cultivated the noble craft of history just as he ordered all of the Sublime State's affairs," said Vâsıf of this work.

He not only restored the custom of his great ancestors by recording his own reign, but he assembled the empire's history from the rise of the Ottoman dynasty to the year 1752 and assisted the craft of printing, nurturing it with noble hands. And as sixteen years up to 1769 were on the verge of being lost or destroyed, he had a royal inspiration: that these should be collected in the best form from existing works and printed in due course, God willing. He then gave this duty to me, the former chancellor Ahmed Vâsıf, still court historian and reporter on the affairs of every underling and superior, and raised my humble station with his generous command.[25]

According to Vâsıf, Selim was thus looking back in time. He was literally asking the historian to rewrite the past.

Selim's decision to revise these chronicles needs some explanation. In part, the commission reflected a belief that the post of the court historian had declined in both quality and essential function. Vâsıf argued that the institution had become so broken by his time that decades of history were in danger of being lost.[26] While this may seem like an odd view, insofar as Hâkim and his kind left many polished volumes, it is true that the *vekayi'nüvis* had fallen in popular esteem. Low-level scribes outnumbered stylists for much of the eighteenth century, resulting, not unexpectedly, in prose that read less as history than dry annal. They also lost access to information. Even the more adept Hâkim and Mehmed Edîb (both skilled poets) struggled under conditions that limited them, they complained, to daily events and lists of court appointments. Selim had no use for such dross. His reforms of the mid-1790s aimed to keep court historians informed and to serve a larger purpose of historical value, as did his orders in 1802, at Vâsıf's request, to provide regular news from Europe.[27] History should tell a connected and edifying tale. It is no

---

[25] MEHÂSİN 5, 1: 3. Vâsıf's identification as the "former chancellor" allows us to date the work to around 1801, for he had been dismissed from this post on 4 L AH 1215 (February 18, 1801) and regained it one year later on 3 L AH 1216 (February 6, 1802). See below for this appointment. The print edition's dates are incorrect. Cf. TSMK nr. 1405, fols. 2b-3a, the probable presentation copy.

[26] MEHÂSİN 6, fols. 4b-5a. His remarks above and in MEHÂSİN 5, 1: 280, are quite similar.

[27] BOA.HAT 5094. Hâkim's and Edîb's complaints can be found, respectively, in Bekir Kütükoğlu, "Müverrih Vâsıf'ın Kaynaklarından Hâkim Tarihi," in *Vekayi'nüvis Makaleler*, 146–147; and Çınar, 117–118. See also Kütükoğlu, "Vekayi'nüvis," 107–108; and EI², s.v. "Waka'nuwîs."

surprise, then, that the sultan would try to "improve" works that failed this standard. But why Hâkim? Why Enverî? We might do well to look for their significance in the turn-of-the-century empire. Namely, Hâkim and his successors had written in the years leading up to that great crisis, the 1768–1774 war, when the illusion of Ottoman power collapsed and the need for reform grew dire. The link between these events and the sultan's New Order was powerful. Selim also seemed to be making a deliberate play – as seen in his many revisions, his desire to restore the court historian's prestige, and his move to compile and print dynastic records – to control the recent past's interpretation. We do not know that Vâsıf played anything more than a technical role in these ambitions, but he may well have encouraged them. Vâsıf and Selim shared a love of moralistic history, after all, in addition to political concerns. Vâsıf's earlier editions of Subhî and İzzî had also put the dynastic chronicle in print up to 1752, the very date when Hâkim's work began.

Vâsıf set himself to this new task with energy, no doubt working from his retreat on the Asian shore at Çamlıca, and took some four months to finish Hâkim before moving to two minor authors named Çeşmizâde and Mûsâzâde. In late 1801, he sent the clean copy to the palace: "I have enriched this work with fine points, allusions, enlightening verse, easy and novel rhyme, and biographies of great men," he crowed. "Now with all want and humility do I submit it to your Majesty's threshold."[28] We can imagine that Vâsıf was both pleased and encouraged by the results of his labor, for Selim rewarded him (how much is not known) and bid him to add the work of Sadullah Enverî, next in the chronological series, to his revisions. This came despite a hectic schedule and early signs of ill health. Renamed chancellor in February 1802, Vâsıf, now nearly seventy, was working like a man half his age to record the empire's history on top of side projects and Selim's special commissions. Vâsıf spoke openly of his limits in an 1801 letter likely addressed to Abdullah Paşa or Küçük Hüseyin Paşa. "Would that I could see to all the sultan's affairs," he wrote. "Serving the empire is like an act of piety, it is true, but I am becoming very tired. Frankly it has made me ill."[29] Vâsıf

---

[28] MEHÂSİN 5, 1: 326–327. See also ibid, 1: 4, 280–281, 311. Çeşmizâde left behind a small chronicle; Mûsâzâde only a few now-lost fragments. Vâsıf also said (1: 4) that he edited the work of one Behcetî Hasan Efendi, but this is unlikely as Hasan wrote in the 1770s. See also GOW, 302, 304; and Karslızâde, 61.

[29] TSMA.E 10323, published in İLGÜREL, 401. The letter dates to his revision of Hâkim. Vâsıf was later renamed chancellor in the abortive appointments of 3 L AH 1216 = February 6, 1802, the day before which Abdullah Paşa took ill and died: MEHÂSİN 4,

also hinted at his health and mindset with a couplet, jotted in his drafts around 1800, that suggests he was struggling with an unnamed ailment, perhaps an ulcer or abscess: "… Salve this running wound / Cure this acute malady." Vâsıf overcame his fatigue and discomfort, however, and by late 1804, he had seen the revisions to press in a massive two-volume edition from the imperial printery. The fourth installment of *Charms and Truths*, it was an admirable feat.[30]

Vâsıf's 1752–1774 chronicle shows the full maturation of his powers as a historian and merits our close analysis. This is not to say the work is faultless; its quality is actually highly uneven. Vâsıf's revision of Hâkim was notably uninspired, for the reason that he detested and even blamed the work for his illness. Hâkim Mehmed Efendi had served as court historian for over thirteen years under Mahmud I (1730–1754), Osman III (1754–1757), and Mustafa III (1757–1774), and left behind two large volumes in the palace library. A poet and man of letters, he wrote a work that was unique in its mix of the ornate and the ordinary, in its blend of eulogy and verse with accounts of Istanbul's lesser social actors. Yet this had no merit to Vâsıf. Notes that the historian inscribed in the palace copy in Turkish and Arabic make it clear that he considered Hâkim's prose inept and his poetry tedious. "My God, man! Half the history is filled with this very verse!" read one. In others, Vâsıf quibbled with dates or grammar, like a word that was "a glaring error by the historian," or simply voiced pique: "My God!"[31] Nor did he appreciate Hâkim's methods. In a letter from the time, written after he had finished the first volume, Vâsıf said that he had had to purge the work, replace its "fatuous" content, and turn the whole of it into a digest. How could such a meager talent like Hâkim have ever become court historian, he wondered, especially in the cultured era of Grand Vezir Koca Râgıb Paşa? Indeed, Vâsıf wrote that the task discouraged him and made him ill: "the man's painful

---

fols. 107a-108b, 110b-111a. Sarıkaya also shows (xcvii n. 10) that Vâsıf got a 120 *kuruş* bonus on the occasion.

[30] Vâsıf said (MEHÂSİN 5, 2: 3) that he tackled Enverî on Selim's orders only after first submitting his revisions of Hâkim for reward; he identified himself at the time as "the present chancellor." The edition's colophon (ibid, 2: 315) bears a printing date of Ş AH 1219 = November/December 1804. See also Vâsıf's couplet in BOA.Y.EE 90, p. 63.

[31] Hâkim, *Târih*, TSMK Bağdat nr. 231, fols. 21b, 172b, 208b, 209a, 414b. Kütükoğlu first linked this copy to Vâsıf in "Müverrih Vâsıf," 140 n. 3, 143 n. 19. The marginal notes are in his distinct hand and also, in one, include his name. The second and smaller volume of Hâkim, TSMK Bağdat nr. 233, may also contain Vâsıf's notations. See further Madeline Zilfi, "Hâkim's Chronicle Revisted," *Oriente Moderno* 18 (1999): 193–201; DİA, s.v. "Hâkim"; GOW, 300–301; and Karslızâde, 60.

expressions make a healthy man sick, let alone wish to write!" he said.[32] Vâsıf repeated these sentiments in his preface – a vicious piece of hatchet-work. "Although Hâkim Mehmed Efendi was quite skilled and versed in the sciences," he began,

in the art of composition he was pedestrian and perhaps even less articulate than Bâqil. His chronicle, meanwhile, contained only state postings and dismissals; it ignored causes and avoided sensitive topics; it lacked the sound narration and moral lessons that are precepts of historiography; and its wretched style earned scholars' weariness and disgust.

According to Vâsıf, Hâkim's chronicle was unusable, its sources "inveterate liars" like the seventeenth-century travel writer Evliya Çelebi. Only by stripping it to a digest, removing its wild tales, and fixing its defects could he produce a better version, he claimed.[33]

What are we to make of this criticism? While Vâsıf has not escaped censure in his own right, his words must to some degree reflect a view of history that prized style, elegance, and lessons above all else, a concern that was moral just as it was rhetorical. There may be some truth to Vâsıf's charge that the work ignored causality, as Hâkim admitted in one manuscript to disregarding causes.[34] His dislike of the prose is harder to pinpoint. Although Vâsıf clearly felt Hâkim lacked good taste, he conceded that his "painful expressions" must once have been popular with readers.[35] Yet the key to the historian's disdain more likely lies in his overriding moral concerns. Vâsıf cultivated a philosophic brand of history in his heavy use of the ethical tradition and in his underlying epistemology. Hâkim's annalistic mode could not meet these aims and conveyed what, to Vâsıf, was little more than a morass of disjointed, useless detail. The only remedy for him was to demolish the work and rebuild, adding morals to make it "useful for both high and low." Of course, the wisdom of this method is debatable. Vâsıf's somewhat apologetic words in the final edition and elsewhere hint that he was not fully convinced of his success. He was right: his version of Hâkim is limp, tedious, and rife with error.[36]

---

[32] TSMA.E 10323.

[33] MEHÂSİN 5, 1: 4. Cf. the slightly different wording in TSMK Hazine nr. 1405, fol. 3a. Vâsıf said much the same in MEHÂSİN 5, 1: 280; and in TSMA.E 10323.

[34] Kütükoğlu, "Müverrih Vâsıf," 146 n. 35.   [35] TSMA.E 10323.

[36] Vâsıf told the recipient of a letter (TSMA.E 10323) that "... It is a fine history – I have rewritten what deserves to be included and added a good deal of lessons – and God willing it shall please the sultan. But in short I shall not presume, my lord." In the final edition (MEHÂSİN 5, 1: 280–281), he asked the royal reader specifically to forgive his mistakes: "I, this old servant, pray you to overlook my errors, which are unplanned and natural

Vâsıf voiced similar doubts about the man who had once been a colleague and rival at court: Sadullah Enverî Efendi. Enverî wrote his 1768–1774 chronicle on the war front, a vast work like Hâkim's that was less a philosophic history than a litany of Ottoman military disasters. It was at times colorful, at times uncensored, at times unblinking. Yet these merits did not move Vâsıf, who aimed a killing-blow in his preface. He said:

The account that Enverî Efendi left is filled with copies of letters and other marvels, his history a mass of errors arising from pervasive ignorance. The sultan saw, moreover, that he had wasted much ink on events unfit for history and so bade me, his humble servant, to rewrite the work like Hâkim's and others' and to correct its content and errors.

Vâsıf went on to claim that his service in the wartime chancery gave him more authority than Enverî. Nor was this the whole of his criticism. Vâsıf also attacked Enverî in asides for adding needless documents, neglecting details, giving poor descriptions of winter camp, and, elsewhere, for confusing key dates.[37] As before, it is hard to parse this criticism. Vâsıf may have had a malicious aim in that he held a grudge against Enverî, never quite forgiving his plagiarism in 1793. One peer, Ahmed Âsım, even went so far as to accuse Vâsıf of grandstanding and said that his revisions copied Enverî in everything "except for the preface."[38] Âsım had reasons for disparaging Vâsıf, though, not least being his wish to replace the aging historian. Instead, as with Hâkim, Vâsıf's criticism of Enverî was probably some mix of ambition, rivalry, and historiographic method. There is no question that Enverî was the less gifted stylist, his work akin to undigested reportage. His approach grated with Vâsıf's sense of selectivity, his literary scruples, and his belief that historians must check the value of reports for factual content and usefulness. Vâsıf hinted at this in his conclusion by comparing himself in eloquence to the famed Persian historians Vassâf and Juvaynî. Unlike less skilled peers, Vâsıf noted, he had also added precepts of morality and practical philosophy from which

---

slips of the pen." Kütükoğlu pointed out many of these omissions, slips, and errors in "Müverrih Vâsıf."

[37] MEHÂSİN 5, 2: 3–4, 77–78, 102, 210–211. Vâsıf also criticized Enverî in MEHÂSİN 6, fols. 11b-12a; and in a marginal note in ÖN H.O. nr. 105, fol. 99a.

[38] Âsım said (1: 258–259) as follows: "... Vâsıf's history followed the history Enverî Efendi wrote point by point. But while he clearly copied it verbatim, he convinced himself of his great care in selection and held the works to be totally different, so that it was greatly admired. In truth, they are no different except for the prefaces." Cf. Filiz Çalışkan, esp. 162–163.

readers might gain "pearls of wisdom" and, applying these by analogy, better themselves.[39]

If the historian's version of Hâkim was mediocre, however, his account of the 1768–1774 war may well represent his best overall effort. This is because Vâsıf clearly saw the potential of his subject matter. Still fresh in Ottoman minds, the war had been a dire defeat that raised the problems of the 1784 essay, 1789–1794 chronicle, and *Letter of Consolation* on a mass scale and offered up fodder for an extended historical odyssey. Vâsıf used it to explore major intellectual concerns; for the first and only time in a finished volume, he applied his philosophy – his views on the universe, change, and free will – to broach issues like reform, morality, peacemaking, and reconciling defeat with exceptionalism. Adding his own firsthand testimony, he created a chronicle that is a fine piece of interpretive history no less than it is a powerful argument for political reform.

The work's most obvious significance lies in its philosophic bent. Vâsıf's decades-long concern with free will had led him slowly but surely to experiment with historical models and frameworks, notably in his *Letter* and theodicies on the Egypt campaign. That this trend now reached a climax should not surprise us. Free will went hand-in-hand with early modern Ottoman reform. The focus on free will and action by writers like Vâsıf, Kâtib Çelebi, and İbrahim Müteferrika often underwrote pleas for bureaucratic and military programs, of which Selim's New Order was only the latest. So too must these ideas have had an effect outside of the political realm. By removing divine intervention, Ottoman thinkers not only pushed the limits of human will and reason in the empire's political life but argued, if we may use imperfect terms, for a more secularized or deistic way of viewing the world – one in which human rather than divine action creates outcomes.[40] Vâsıf did just this in his preface. He placed the war in a framework of the "universal" and the "particular," depicting it as a series of moral, human choices. He wrote:

---

[39] MEHÂSİN 5, 2: 314–315. Aksan likens Enverî's style to reportage in *Ottoman Statesman*, 111. Babinger for his part calls it (GOW, 320–322) "easily intelligible, if often clumsy and vulgar."

[40] Menchinger, "Free Will," 465. One finds fruitful parallels between this trend and developments in Europe, such as the shift among early modern scholars from sacred to profane history and from divine to "natural" or "secondary causes" (on which see Louis Dupré, *The Enlightenment and the Intellectual Foundations of Modern Culture* [New Haven, 2004], 187–228). We might also speculate that the search for human causes represented an emerging rationality in the empire or even, following Max Weber, a "disenchantment" of the Ottoman world. I owe these ideas to exchanges with Gottfried Hagen.

It is a point of philosophy for learned men that misfortunes – now peace and harmony, now misery and war – should at times appear on earth, for the universe is changeable and formed of atoms. These two states also depend on certain causes which, by God's will, lead people to quarrel. And so if we scrutinize the universal and particular events that have occurred in the world from man's creation till this age, each of them will be based on a cause. Everything issues from God. Yet if man's deeds have, in fact, absolutely no effect or influence on causes or the ability to influence the course of events, it is clearly the Lord God's divine custom to create a thing as an outcome of secondary causes. Indeed, this is close to what philosophers say: everything is contingent; what is contingent admits influence; and what admits influence cannot be without cause.[41]

Vâsıf argued that the war began because the Russians' reforms had made them bold. They grew powerful through *istidrâc* and invaded Poland, while the Ottomans tried to gain territory, "entered a serious matter of unknown outcome," and declared war.[42]

The preface put human action at the heart of events. Vâsıf again evoked a world of "generation and corruption" and "causes" in which God alone determined events, His causes unseen and unchangeable. Yet Vâsıf left room for action alongside God's will in the idea of secondary causes or *esbâb-ı zâhire*. The Ottomans could not have stopped Russia's rise, as that was a divine trial, but they might have resolved the situation with sounder policy. War was avoidable. The preface also signaled Vâsıf's intent to highlight secondary causes – the decisions behind movements, errors, and critical junctures – to show how things like poor provisioning and tactics ("particular events") led to a larger outcome: a calamitous defeat (a "universal event"). Vâsıf paused on the battles of Falça, Kartal, and Kozluca to probe Ottoman failings, for example. At Falça, a rout he had seen firsthand, the Russians had surprised the Ottoman army at dawn and drove them from camp with a large loss of life and matériel. While some blamed the rank and file and others the commanders, Vâsıf claimed that the loss had in one way come from immorality. The "inner truth" was that God let the Russians win in order to punish the army's wanton impiety. Yet Vâsıf also weighed Ottoman moral failings with their shortcomings in secondary causes like tactics, training, discipline, and provisioning. "On the other hand," he wrote,

Men who see the obvious will claim that the enemy followed the new rules of war; that they obeyed their officers and drilled regularly in all means of firearms; that they kept their men from luxury and rest; that they have no place in their forces for

---

[41] MEHÂSİN 5, 2: 4.   [42] Ibid, 2: 4–5.

the untrained and, most times, will beat out an untested, untrained, soft, and disorderly army.[43]

Vâsıf was no deist or secularist, of course. He upheld the proper theological view that God is the only true cause in the universe, upon whom humans must rely. Yet the two – the earthly and the divine – grew ever more entwined in his later work. While not a deist, it is possible to say that Vâsıf arrived at what amounted to the same thing: a view of history and causes set on a decidedly human scale. Urging a mix of action and moral renewal, his 1768–1774 chronicle made free will a basic problem through which the war and its outcome could be understood. We can also note that these lessons were not merely historical. Their reformist significance would have been plain to Ottoman readers in 1804.[44]

The latest installment of *Charms and Truths* is also notable for its treatment of peacemaking, another of the century's major intellectual concerns. Vâsıf had long tried to square the empire's martial ethos with its ever more meager battlefield returns. The aim was in part practical: how should the empire act? By the new century, Vâsıf had come to respect Europe's military dominance, won through reciprocation, and to retool his earlier arguments for peace. "War is unpredictable," his favored euphemism, pronounced the world to be innately unstable just as it rejected Ottoman legal reasoning and followed his psychological drift from the 1790s onward, when his youthful certainty gave way to doubt. Vâsıf had clearly lost faith in war. Yet he dared not admit this in so many words. If the empire could no longer face its enemies without risking defeat, at least for the time, it could not claim to be an exceptional military power. As his legal pretense gave way to philosophical resignation, then, Vâsıf inched closer to a Resmian view of war and to peace as a universal good rather than a temporary evil.

At the metaphysical level, we can see how the historian fit war and peace into his larger causal framework. The 1774 Treaty of Kaynarca had been a blow to the empire, and Vâsıf aimed both to explain why the treaty had been necessary and how it might have been avoided. His own position was clear: he felt that initial Ottoman refusals to make peace led to the more onerous Kaynarca. As in all things, for Vâsıf war and peace resulted on a universal scale from cosmic instability. This was why the 1768–1774 conflict moved generally toward peace: "The Lord God settled this world of generation and corruption with mankind," he wrote.

---

[43] Ibid, 2: 88–89.
[44] I draw this analysis from "Reformist Philosophy," 160–161; "Free Will," 458–459; and my dissertation, esp. 103 ff. See also Aksan, *Ottoman Statesman*, 151.

And as humans are by nature conflicted and hostile, we can deem the odd war between states as so much a point of philosophy. Yet the world is unstable. We know from its ephemerality that accidents – now peace and repose, now misery and war – will befall men on earth no matter how long a war may last. It was no doubt God's will that the war between the Sublime State and Russia yield to peace, and thus with truce and negotiation was the groundwork laid for a reconciliation.[45]

On a smaller scale, however, the chronicle asserts that humans do affect war. At Kartal, Marshal Rumiantsev had offered İvazpaşazâde Halil Paşa direct negotiations only to have the Grand Vezir defer to Istanbul, where the sultan's circle dismissed the proposal. Vâsıf rued this decision in an aside. War is unpredictable, he noted. Wise men (but especially Europeans) seek peace in war and try to secure victory whenever possible, so that the Ottomans refused peace for nothing but lost blood and treasure. Vâsıf then pressed this point by citing a gloss on the Egyptian scholar al-Suyûtî's *Lesser Collection* (*al-Jâmi' al-ṣaghîr*) that, if believers cannot win, it is a sort of victory to preserve Muslim life, territory, and property through peace. Past rulers knew this precept, but not so the Ottomans, he concluded – for "we surely would have gotten a much better settlement than Kaynarca had the empire agreed when the Russians sued for peace."[46] Vâsıf thus held that God ordained patterns of amity and enmity such that an enemy might grow threatening or friendly, but he also stressed that Ottoman decision-making forestalled peace and did great damage. He repeatedly stated that the realm's refusal to make peace led to death, destruction, and the harsh terms of Kaynarca.[47]

Peacemaking also forms a key theme of the work at a mundane level, as Vâsıf recounted bitter division in the Ottoman ranks. In fact, the dispute in his telling takes on nearly as much importance as the war itself and pits scribe against scribe, Ottoman against Ottoman, with opponents as much friend as foe. One issue again was securing an "honorable peace." When talks began in 1772, Vâsıf said that the empire desired terms "suiting its interests and abiding honor." What this meant in practice was contentious, however. While many at the front felt it wise to "sheath the sword of enmity" to salvage the empire's honor, a defiant opposition refused to give

---

[45] MEHÂSİN 5, 2: 196–197. See also "Reformist Philosophy," 161–163.

[46] MEHÂSİN 5, 2: 111–116. For more on these peace overtures, see RESMÎ, 56–57 (trans.), 111–112 (text); Aksan, *Ottoman Statesman*, 153–154; and Köse, 52–57. 'Abd al-Ra'uf Muḥammad al-Munâwî (d. 1621) glossed al-Suyûtî's work of hadith *The Lesser Collection*, in which the same scholar epitomized his larger *Collection of Collections* (*Jam' al-jawâmi'*). See EI², s.v. "al-Munâwî" and "al-Suyûtî."

[47] E.g. MEHÂSİN 5, 2: 115, 203–204, 225–226, 245–246, 305–307.

ground.[48] Vâsıf used the former chief scribe Yenişehirli Osman Efendi, with whom he had had dealings during the war, as a sort of vessel for these types. Osman had caused the collapse of talks that year at Foksani by his refusal to admit Tatar autonomy. He then became an extravagant critic of peace, deterred Vâsıf from his truce duties, and agitated for a return to war, scapegoating fellow negotiator Yâsinîzâde Efendi along the way. According to the chronicle, Osman acted from fear of militant ulema. Vâsıf hinted that many at court saw the proposed peace as dictated and against the law, especially for the Crimea, and actively undermined it.[49] He was joined in this view by Ahmed Resmî, who blamed the former chief scribe as well as high ulema at court who, he said, held an overly rigid view of Tatar independence and manipulated Mustafa III. The sultan, under their influence, then ordered the army back to war in the hope of defeating the Russians and winning a victorious peace.[50]

Vâsıf, of course, begged to differ with this opposition and depicted them as misguided and reckless. Early on, he quoted Muhsinzâde Paşa to contrast that vizier's caution with public disregard for the "unclear outcome and latent danger" of the war, repeating in his preface that the conflict was "a grave and unpredictable affair."[51] Here, Vâsıf's meaning was twofold – not only that the empire was unready for war, but that warfare itself is a risky venture. Given war's uncertainty, Vâsıf felt that policy was the best course and that the empire would have been better to secure peace. We can draw more cases like this from the heart of the chronicle. Following the failed conference at Bucharest, for instance, to which he was a party, Vâsıf digressed for two pages on talks between Abdürrezzâk Efendi and the Russian legate Aleksei Obreskov. When they reached an impasse, he wrote, Obreskov said in pique that his demands were the fruits of victory. What would the Ottomans do in his place? No doubt they would make impossible claims. Abdürrezzâk deftly replied with the story of Peter I's 1711 defeat on the Pruth River to Grand Vizier Baltacı Mehmed Paşa. Even with Peter surrounded in a forest, Abdürrezzâk said, the empire avoided bloodshed and accepted the Tsar's surrender in return for the port of Azov. For that Obreskov admitted that he, Baltacı Mehmed, was a wise vizier. He

---

[48] MEHÂSİN 5, 2: 197, 203–205, 207.

[49] MEHÂSİN 5, 2: 223–232. Cf. RESMÎ, 62–64 (trans.), 117–118 (text).

[50] MEHÂSİN 5, 2: 249–250. Cf. RESMÎ, 65–66, 72 (trans.), 119–120, 126 (text). See also Aksan, Ottoman Statesman, 156 ff. Vâsıf clearly used Resmî as a source and inspiration for parts of this work.

[51] MEHÂSİN 5, 1: 314–315, 2: 5. Vâsıf said that Muhsinzâde explained to him the reasons for his first dismissal from the Grand Vizierate one year, while the army wintered in Şumnu. Decades later, he added this first-person narrative to his chronicle.

feared a battle with desperate men "and so he did not lose his chance for victory: he chose peace."[52] Now, whether Vâsıf faithfully recalled this conversation matters less than its core message. The passage bolsters his defense of peace and shows that peacemaking, used judiciously, can be a wise and honorable path; nor is peace at odds with victory. Vâsıf inserted a third and final example at the signing of the Treaty of Kaynarca. In an aside, he pointed out how unfavorable the treaty was when compared to the terms offered at Bucharest. "It is obvious on the slightest consideration how much the Russians profited" in the final text, he said. Vâsıf then proceeded to a staggering pronouncement on war and peace:

There is no question in war that money is squandered on raising levies and that rebellion arises in the land through requisite, heavy imposts. Indeed, in warfare victory and triumph are but an illusion while the comfort and ease of peace are very real. And it is detailed in the books of philosophers who once graced this world that preferring the real to the fanciful, and the known to the unknown, were among their practices.

This statement – echoing at least one earlier Ottoman source – epitomizes Vâsıf's defense of peacemaking in the 1768–1774 chronicle: that war is unclear, unpredictable, unprofitable, to be avoided in favor of peace.[53] It is also the closest he came in the full span of his writing to a rejection of war and a radical, Resmian view of peace.

It is fair to say that Vâsıf finally and coherently synthesized a number of long-standing concerns in his work on the 1768–1774 war. His treatment of peace, for one, capped an intellectual shift with which he had struggled for thirty years. Leaving aside the older legal formula, Vâsıf now argued that war was neither a political nor moral imperative, but something to be evaluated and used, like any other tool, on the basis of reason. In doing so, he opened peace and war to wider human control. This does not mean Vâsıf rejected warfare in later life – while influenced by Ahmed Resmî, he never quite indulged in the same brand of radicalism. The key change to his thought was rather one of premises. To Vâsıf, the Ottomans could no longer guarantee the outcome of war and so must use it with care and

---

[52] MEHÂSİN 5, 2: 246–247. Ahmed Resmî reported having a similar discussion with Frederick II on Baltacı Mehmed Paşa during his Berlin embassy: Aksan, "An Ottoman Portrait," 75. See also DİA, s.v. "Prut Antlaşması."

[53] MEHÂSİN 5, 2: 306–307. Vâsıf had clearly read the anonymous "Dialogue between a Christian and Muslim Officer," where the latter credits these words to the architect of Karlowitz, Amcazâde Hüseyin Paşa: "Peace makes the realm prosper and the treasury increase and brings our men to heel. It is a pure blessing while the chance for revenge is but an illusion; and to prefer the fanciful to the real and the unknown to the known is, for philosophers, to be rejected." See Unat, "Bir Islahat Takriri," 109.

diligence; metaphysically and morally, war no longer had to be perpetual and peace, by the same token, was a virtue rather than a temporary evil. More outstanding, though, is the way that the work blends action, ethics, and theodicy into a stout defense of Ottoman exceptionalism. Vâsıf once again conjured a world in flux and an empire whose ills came from divine trial, both bound ultimately to God's will. But he also called for action. The work's central problem is free will and, by applying will to Ottoman history, it stresses our ability and duty as humans to act. For acting is not an idle choice. It is a moral one. Affirming the dynasty's uniqueness, Vâsıf held that future Ottoman success rested on action as well as moral responsibility. In this world, he asserted, trust, piety, and proper choice would deliver the empire and community of believers now and till the end of time.

It would appear that men at Selim's court saw the value of this work, or at least its use as an ideological stay for their reforms. Vâsıf claimed that the chronicle raised a stir with its 1804 printing:

As the realm's history from 1752 to the year 1774 was about to be lost to disarray among earlier historians, the sultan had me compile the said events carefully from the original sources, rewrite, and arrange them. Warming to the task, I crowned the history with a great many truths and had it printed at the imperial press. This took some months. Enthusiasts of prose and history then clamored high and low for copies and the head of the press, Abdurrahman Efendi, worked himself to exhaustion to meet the demand, a fine royal effort that pleased and obliged us all to pray for the sultan's long life and glory.

Vâsıf added that Selim, learning of the work's popularity, bid him to begin more revisions and bring the dynastic chronicle through the reign of Abdülhamid I. This, too, would be printed: "Hearing of popular demand, his Majesty ordered me to revise, purge, and print the empire's history from 1774 to his accession year 1789 as a sequel volume," he said.[54] The new project – a fifth installment of *Charms and Truths* – would have Vâsıf refit work by Sadullah Enverî and the lesser authors Behcetî Hasan Efendi and Süleyman Molla in addition to his own first (and unfinished) volume, edits that the historian had planned for over a decade. Vâsıf started this work in early 1805 and hinted at his aim by reusing a preface on historical epistemology, once written for Abdülhamid, before moving into events after Kaynarca. By autumn, he had a hundred folios. Drawing mostly on Enverî, but also on the authority of Abdürrezzâk and his own memory, Vâsıf felt that he had improved the work and added

---

[54] MEHÂSİN 6, fols. 5a-5b.

a good many philosophical and moral points. It would be a fine history and spread his fame.[55]

Whether true or exaggerated, Vâsıf's talk of fame reflected his inflated pretensions and increasingly grandiose sense of self. He continued to hold office as a senior statesman. Dismissed as chancellor again, the historian found a place as keeper of the daily ledger when the incumbent, Mustafa Râsih, died in September 1803, a position he retained until early 1805. We also see him writing poetry to the sultan in this period, as well as to influential figures like İbrahim Nesîm Efendi, one of Selim's inner circle, to whom he dedicated a chronogram in 1803.[56] Yet *Charms and Truths* was Vâsıf's main source of pride. He was coming to see his history as a work for the ages, himself as the empire's greatest historian. This conceit came partly from the work's scope. Vâsıf could now brag that he had forged a narrative for the full second half of the eighteenth century – that he had recorded the realm's history from 1752 onward "in a single stroke."[57] While this claim was premature, he surely intended to close any gaps and to realize his vision with the sultan's newest commission. Vâsıf was likewise starting to rank himself with cherished historians past and present. Ending his account of the 1768–1774 war, he wrote that his predecessors had marred their work with "tenebrous prose" and tasteless drivel. Such men were "crumbs for the mouths of men of talent" who paid no heed to state benefit, philosophy, or the rules of history, he declared. Vâsıf also prayed that readers would place him on a par with the Persian masters Vaṣṣâf and Juvaynî.[58] The fifth volume of *Charms and Truths* offered more room for self-praise. In his preface, Vâsıf listed Ottoman historians

---

[55] Ibid, fol. 5b. This work survives in a single and incomplete copy in the imperial palace, its text ending after one hundred folios. In it, Vâsıf recycled (fols. 2a-4a) the preface on history and intellect from his 1783–1787 volume. He also drew on reports from his late patron Abdürrezzâk Efendi (e.g. fols. 13a-14a, 18a, 100b) as well as from his own involvement in political events (e.g. fols. 6a-11b). Vâsıf's criticism of Enverî is here more subdued and limited to one complaint (fol. 12a): namely, that Enverî had not credited him for his 1774 negotiations with Rumiantsev.

[56] Vâsıf said (MEHÂSİN 6, fol. 171b) that he received no post in general appointments on 5 L AH 1217 = January 29, 1803. He replaced (fols. 211a, 247b) Râsih on 14 Ca 1218 = September 1, 1803, and was confirmed as keeper of the ledger on 4 L 1218 = January 7, 1804, before being turned (fol. 312b) from office one year later on 4 L 1219 = January 6, 1805. He again got a 120 *kuruş* bonus in 1804 (Sarıkaya, xcvii n. 12). Vâsıf wrote occasional poems in this period, as well: a chronogram for the Grand Vizier's proxy Mustafa Bey (fol. 110b); a eulogy and chronogram on the building of new palace privy chambers (fol. 189a); and a chronogram for İbrahim Nesîm (fol. 195b).

[57] MEHÂSİN 5, 2: 3–4, 315.

[58] MEHÂSİN 5, 2: 314. Cf. Millet Kütüphanesi nr. 608, fol. 166a. Vâsıf decried the overall state of learning, too. Describing a mid-century Grand Vizier who read Vaṣṣâf and other

against whom he wished to be judged and picked each one apart. "The history that Hoca Sadeddîn Efendi wrote has a sort of eloquent charm," he said, "but his prose disagrees with this era's scholars and, in truth, his repetition to balance rhymes is overdone and the work is full of Turkish and simple verse."

As for Mustafa Âli Efendi, he used odd words willy-nilly and his history lacks literary taste and substance. The works of Solâkzâde, Neşrî, Oruç Bey, Hadîdî, and Malkoçzâde are vulgar and wretched and their successors much the same. The late Naîmâ set the events that Şârih-i Menârzâde skillfully collected in the Imperial harem with key additions. Everyone enjoys his history. His successors Râşid Efendi and Çelebizâde Efendi each wrote fine and pleasing works, too. The quality of later chroniclers is quite clear from their histories; their bungled efforts are unmistakable to the skilled stylist.

By contrast, Vâsıf wrote that he coined "a new style neither simple nor obscure" for his work and added advice, morals, and precepts of practical philosophy where others in their ignorance had failed.[59] It is hard to miss the sense of grievance that fed these boasts. The historian mixed praise of Selim with complaints that he had been betrayed in the past by envy and royal disinterest, his work unnoticed and talent unrecognized. We also know that by 1804 or 1805, Vâsıf's ill health had led to talk of Ahmed Âsım as a replacement. The fact that Selim's favor gave him untold riches and fame, so he said, did little to soothe these wounds or his lingering resentment. Despite his bluster, Vâsıf could not bring himself to forget. He remained a deeply insecure man.[60]

The first years of the century saw Vâsıf involved in a number of side ventures, as well, minor works that often elaborated his chronicle's themes. Such was the *Book of the Monk* or *Râhibnâme*. Vâsıf wrote this treatise for Selim during his time as chancellor, either in 1800/1 or 1802/3, though we may link it circumstantially to his first term and the war against

---

works in office, he lamented (ibid, 1: 146–147) "how much urbanity was then valued, which is now counted as a fault."

[59] MEHÂSİN 6, fols. 4a-4b. Vâsıf was not always so negative in his appraisals. Apart from Naîmâ, Râşid, and Küçükçelebizâde Âsım, he spoke warmly (e.g. MEHÂSİN 5, 1: 51–52, 179–180; and 2: 7–9) of the mid-eighteenth-century historians Süleyman İzzî and Mehmed Subhî, calling the former's prose "prolix but still sweet of expression" and the latter a "paragon of the age."

[60] Vâsıf wrote in one work (MEHÂSİN 5, 2: 314) that prior to Selim, he had been undermined by the envious and that the talents he had acquired since youth were forgotten. He said in another (MEHÂSİN 6, fols. 4b-5a) that he had been jilted in Abdülhamid I's reign, when "the charms of my history went unnoticed and my talent unrecognized." See also Sarıkaya, cclvii n. 3.

the French in Egypt.[61] The *Book of the Monk* is an odd work. It is true that its subject matter, patience, is entirely in line with Vâsıf's ethical interests and that its aim of encouraging the sultan rests on familiar ideas of virtue and intellect in Ottoman moral philosophy. As Vâsıf wrote,

Some philosophers claim that all things have an essence and that patience is the essence of intellect, while others call patience a faculty or part of the intellect. Kingly patience too comes from firmness in all the heart's faculties. The first faculty is clemency, whose fruit is pardon; the second is prudence and mild words, whose fruit is the realm's welfare; and the third is bravery, which brings firmness. Patience means enduring bitter adversity. Its object is to bide one's time and to await a better opportunity.

Vâsıf argued that seemingly impossible things can be gained by patience. In more detail, he said that man's experiential intellect and ability to grasp sensibilia offer a vantage from which we might see the benefit or harm of an action. Applying these premises, we can then learn self-control and attain our desires.[62] While these ideas are common enough, however, their use in the moral tract is jarringly Machiavellian. The *Book of the Monk* tells of an ascetic or monk (*râhib*) in pre-Ottoman Byzantium who harbored a hopeless love for a princess, but won her hand and political power by falsely gaining the emperor's trust and ousting him. It is patience – but also ruthless deceit – that allowed him to succeed. Politics thus seems less like an adjunct to ethics in the work than the sort of amoral "politicking" that some Ottomans decried in Christian Europe. Vâsıf claimed to have translated the story from an obscure Arabic book called the *Hidden Pearl on the Ship Laden with Cargo* (*al-Durr al-maknûn fî al-fulk al-mashḥûn*), but one wonders if it was not the fruit of his own mind.[63]

---

[61] RÂHİBNÂME, fols. 2a-2b. Vâsıf was chancellor and court historian when he prepared this treatise. Given that it aimed to console and hearten Selim in the face of adversity, it seems logical to accept that the work coincided with a major political crisis, the most obvious being the invasion of Egypt. Vâsıf's papers also contain a more or less full draft: BOA.Y.EE 90, pp. 7–8.

[62] RÂHİBNÂME, fols. 1b-2a. KINÂLIZÂDE held (103) patience to be a subsidiary virtue of the cardinal virtue temperance in the concupiscent soul. He also listed (457–470) it as a "kingly virtue" along with ambition, good judgment, resolve, wealth, military leadership, and pedigree. See too Sariyannis' "The Princely Virtues," 121–144.

[63] RÂHİBNÂME, fols. 2a-10b. I have failed to locate this title in any of the standard bibliographical guides. While the story's themes of asceticism and moral restraint suggest a work on Sufism, and perhaps also a gloss, this is by no means certain. In fact, extant copies of the *Book of the Monk* do not even agree on a proper title. While the likely presentation copy calls the Arabic original *al-Durr al-maknûn fî al-fulk al-mashḥûn*, a later manuscript and print edition refer to it as the *Inviolable Pearl on the Ship Laden with Cargo* (*al-Durr al-maṣnûn fî al-fulk al-mashḥûn*): *Râhibnâme*, Atatürk Kitaplığı, Muallim Cevdet nr. 49, fol. 1a; and *Râhibnâme* (Istanbul, 1873), 4.

Vâsıf also helped a colleague, the chief scribe Mahmud Râif Efendi, in a new project at the imperial press. Râif valued European science and had spent four years in London as secretary to the Ottoman envoy, Yusuf Agâh, during which time he took an interest in geography, translated maps by the French cartographer Jean-Baptiste Bourguignon d'Anville (d. 1782), and even wrote a short geography in French. This last work is more notable today for its place in cartography and print than for content, for it followed the obsolete Ptolemaic cosmology, but at the time, its descriptions of Europe, Asia, Africa, and the Americas represented the Ottoman state-of-the-art.[64] Selim III published Râif's maps after his return to Istanbul. He also learned of the geography and had a dragoman named Yakovaki Argyropoulos translate it into Turkish for Râif, who was busy with official duties. It was then that Vâsıf became involved. The sultan wanted the geography – now called the *Handbook of Geography* or *Ucâletü'l-Coğrafiyye* – to be combined with modern European maps in a print edition, but felt that Yakovaki's translation was too unwieldy. He thus enlisted Vâsıf in 1804 to proof as well as introduce the text. Vâsıf and Râif pored over the prose, correcting, adding, and revising, while the historian put together a preface that linked the work to Selim's reforms and to the concept of reciprocation. Geography, said Vâsıf, a branch of mathematics, is as useful to rulers as to merchants in its reports of towns, roads, villages, and topography. That the Ottomans neglected it was due partly to sloth and partly to Muslim geographers like al-Idrîsî and Kâtib Çelebi, who, while skilled, "followed the ways of the ancients" and were hard to fathom. The craft only revived when Selim came to the throne, continued Vâsıf, for the sultan kept it close to heart and wished to spread the hard sciences throughout his empire. Mahmud Râif then took note and learned foreign languages in Britain as a way to "master geography's modern practice," the tenets of which he compiled in a small tract.[65]

---

[64] ATLAS, p. 1–2. See also Abdülhak Adnan-Adıvar, *Osmanlı Türklerinde İlim* (Istanbul, 1943), 188–189; Beydilli, *Mühendishâne*, 169–172; and idem, *Mahmud Râif*, 26–34.

[65] Vâsıf wrote (ATLAS, p. 1) that he undertook the task as court historian and keeper of the ledger; the combined atlas was then published in November 1804. Three decrees from the Ottoman archives also trace these events. The first two (BOA.HAT 1681, 5004) date to 1799/1800 and detail the d'Anville maps, showing Selim's interest in the project. According to the third (BOA.HAT 12436), Râif was later able to bring his geography to the sultan's attention and suggested that it act as a preface for the so-called *Great Atlas* or *Atlas-ı Kebîr*, based on maps by the Englishman William Faden (d. 1836). Selim thus had it printed: "I am very pleased with the printed work – well done!" he wrote. "Now have it bound with illustrations and made into an atlas ... My congratulations to the chief

The *Handbook* is a milestone in the empire's scientific literature. Geography had long been a popular subject with Ottoman readers, who consumed an ever-increasing number of atlases, descriptive geographies, travel accounts, and cosmographies in the seventeenth and eighteenth centuries. Early modern Ottoman scholars had begun to develop geography as a field in its own right, as distinct from history and cosmography, and as a useful science for war and government. Kâtib Çelebi made geography a key part of his intellectual project, for example. In preparing the first Ottoman world geography, the *Cosmorama* or *Cihânnümâ*, he praised the subject for its practical benefits, used European sources like Ortelius' *Theatrum Orbis Terrarum* and Cluverius' *Introductio in Universam Geographiam* alongside Islamic geographers, and translated and incorporated the Hondius edition of Mercator's *Atlas*. This trend continued with Abû Bakr al-Dimashqî's translation of Blaeu's *Atlas Maior* and İbrahim Müteferrika's printing activity, which included a number of geographical works. Vâsıf too knew the value of geography. In his embassy report, he had noted Spain's physical topography along with the longitude, latitude, and clime of each city, while in his chronicle, he argued that European success in trade and war came in part from geographic knowhow and urged Selim to teach it in academies. Vâsıf's claim that Europe had a tactical advantage over the empire in geography was not new, as we find it in the work of Kâtib Çelebi, al-Dimashqî, and Müteferrika. However, what Vâsıf and Râif did for the first time was to combine European maps with a descriptive geography drawn strictly from western sources and to the exclusion of Ottoman classics. Vâsıf's talk of the "ancients" and "moderns," an old trope in both Christian and Islamic ideas, is striking when we see how he privileged the latter over the former and European geography over his own intellectual canon. For him, al-Idrîsî and Kâtib Çelebi were passé. The empire had to borrow from Europe to regain its rightful place.[66]

scribe for still managing such things in hard times. May God bless him." A Phanariot, Yakovaki Efendi spoke Greek, Turkish, Arabic, Persian, French, Italian, and Russian and served as an interpreter in Istanbul as well as chargé d'affaires in Berlin. He wrote a number of works in later life, translated Montesquieu's *L'Esprit des lois* into Greek and Castéra's *Vie de Catherine II* into Turkish, and died in 1850 at the age of seventy-six. See "Jacques Argyropoulos," *Magasin Pittoresque* 31 (1863): 127–128.

[66] SEFÂRETNÂME, fols. 331b, 332b, 346a; and MEHÂSİN 2, fols. 166a-166b, 169a-170a. Bonner and Hagen argue that by the late eighteenth century, Islamic geographers had moved away from cosmography and mirabilia and were increasingly "dominated by Western sources and models": "Muslim Accounts of the *dâr al-ḥarb*," 4: 474–494. See also Pınar Emiralioğlu, *Geographical Knowledge and Imperial Culture in the Early Modern Ottoman Empire* (Surrey, 2014).

Still more noteworthy in its articulation of Vâsıf's agenda is a fiery treatise called the *Final Word to Refute the Rabble* (*Hulâsatü'l-Kelâm fî Reddi'l-'Avâm*) or the *Merits of the New Soldiery* (*Muhassenât-ı 'Asker-i Cedîd*). An anonymous polemic, we know that Selim had the historian write this work in 1803 or 1804 against certain "contentious imbeciles" who denounced his reforms as the "cause of all disorder."[67] The *Final Word* is in fact a dialogue between Vâsıf and imagined opponents, as he defended the New Order by placing it in historical context. "These despicable idiots have never left the city or traveled a single stage from home," he wrote.

They have never tasted adversity. They have never gone on campaign. They do not know what war and peace mean or what troubles the world now and in future days. Some of them do not even know about ritual purity and cannot read the creed without mistakes from start to finish – men solely in appearance, vile scum, prodigious morons who think that the New Order has caused all the world's problems and that, were it abolished and the old order restored, the universe would naturally right itself in five days.[68]

The reality for Vâsıf was rather one of flux, in which rulers must take care to guard their realms. The Prophet had advocated policy in the hadith "War is a trickery," for example, while the Janissaries who so strongly objected to reform had forgotten their own origins as an innovative and disciplined military unit. The point, then, was that threats to the empire should be met with action and by adapting to the enemy. All things being equal, history showed that armies with better training and strategy would prevail.[69]

Vâsıf aimed the *Final Word* at a wide readership and focused less on the universe's inner workings than elsewhere. Still, the work supports his major themes; we find a clear causal framework, a defense of reform as reciprocation, and an activism that is Vâsıf at his boldest and most belligerent. The historian raised his thesis in the preface. God created rulers as the "mundane cause" of world order, he wrote, which they must "defend from hostile violence." Since God placed many kings over the earth and made man naturally greedy, states flourish only to the extent that they uphold this order, while "those that ignore a neighbor's machinations are either wiped out or, in their carelessness, put utterly at his mercy, humbled, and impoverished."[70] Vâsıf then moved to establish

---

[67] HULÂSAT, 33. I discuss the work's authorship in the Appendix.   [68] Ibid, 75–76.
[69] HULÂSAT, 29–30, 45–49, 69, 80. For similar ideas, see Müteferrika, *Usûlü'l-Hikem*, 148–149; MEHÂSİN 2, fols. 26a-26b; and MEHÂSİN 3, fol. 216a.
[70] HULÂSAT, 29–30.

reciprocation as the basis for political order and Selim's program of reform. In response to Russian threats, he said, ministers urged the sultan to take defensive steps and to found a corps of regular soldiers. This was vital because the Janissaries, while they objected mightily, were engaged in all manner of trade and refused to accept discipline:

No matter how much we might doubt the threat, we cannot, God forbid, allow so cunning an enemy to catch us off guard. History tells us that many a state has been wiped out through insouciance and how ignoring the enemy's machinations and failing to supply timely troops and stores caused them to fall.

The new-style army would consequently protect and restore the realm, as its recent success in Egypt proved.[71]

Like Vâsıf's chronicle, the *Final Word* also depicts reciprocation as a key motor in Ottoman history – but with a twist. As earlier, Vâsıf held that the empire's decline began in the late sixteenth century when Christian states matched the Ottomans with gunpowder weapons and tactics based on professional soldiers, regular drill, and formations. This style of war neutralized Muslim bravery and gave the enemy an advantage. "We have most often lost since the invention of this new system of tactics," Vâsıf wrote, "because we could not use our sabres among the infidel as we wished."[72] The twist lies in the fact that the new warfare was itself a response to Ottoman innovation. Vâsıf claimed that Süleyman I had formed a regular infantry after a string of defeats – the Janissaries, of whom the era's rabble complained bitterly – but that these ceased to be élite and sultans up to Selim III had failed in their attempts at reform. Vâsıf of course knew that the Janissaries predated Süleyman by more than a hundred years; he was making a specious but useful point.[73] For one thing, the inaccuracy let him link a potent symbol of the Ottoman "Golden Age" and its most storied ruler to reciprocation. *Mukâbele bi'l-misl*, he implied, was a main factor in the dynasty's success. Trouble arose only when they ceased to observe it. Vâsıf's argument also made a mockery of his opponents. If they, the Janissaries, began as an innovative and trained unit, how could they now object to the New Order and refuse discipline?

---

[71] Ibid, 39–40, 43–44.   [72] HULÂSAT, 47–49. Cf. MEHÂSİN 3, fols. 38a-40b.
[73] HULÂSAT, 45–46, 49–50. On the treatise's historical errors, see Aksan, "Ottoman Political Writing," 39–40; Şakul, "Nizâm-ı Cedîd," 134–135; and Y. Hakan Erdem, "The Wise Old Man, Propagandist, and Ideologist: Koca Sekbanbaşi on the Janissaries, 1806," in *Individuals and Ideologies and Society: Tracing the Mosaic of Mediterranean History*, ed. Kirsi Virtanen (Tampere, 2001), 166–168.

In the *Final Word*, Vâsıf fashioned ideas that he had refined for years into a single shot of incandescent propaganda, one that would ideally silence naysayers once and for all. He again assumed that victory went to the best trained and prepared. The new army's "merits" depended on its ability to meet Christians like-for-like, something that the disorder, indiscipline, and obstinacy of the old corps made impossible. So too did Vâsıf accuse opponents of leading the empire to ruin. It was their refusal to cooperate that had caused recent defeats and the loss of the Crimea. Following his logic, reform and reciprocation fell as an "individual obligation" on all believers and inaction was not merely a personal failing but a betrayal of Ottoman *dîn ü devlet*:

We all know that the infidel is adept in every sort of battle and military drill and that we are wanting. This being so, is not your stubborn rejection of discipline a brazen insult to our faith and empire?[74]

By the early nineteenth century, then, Vâsıf and his circle had come to see reform as vital to the empire's physical and metaphysical wellbeing. Opposition to the New Order was not just wrong; it was perverse and criminal.

7.3 CHIEF SCRIBE, 1805–1806

By the year 1805, Ahmed Vâsıf had little left to achieve. The seventy-year-old was nearing the end of life as an elder Ottoman statesman, respected, if never well-liked, by his peers. He had made a mark in politics and penned one of the century's key histories, to say nothing of lesser efforts in poetry, ethics, or printing, and had done much to further the cause of reform. This does not mean that he was content. As an old man, Vâsıf still recalled the hope he had felt as a young scribe and the sting of seeing it go unrealized. He clung to his ambition just as he refused to forgive slights; and while he preened like a man half his age, he seems, deep down, to have been insecure and embittered. It was only fitting, then, that now, in August 1805 and in poor health, Vâsıf received the news for which he had waited a lifetime: he had been named chief scribe.[75]

---

[74] HULÂSAT, 41, 51.

[75] Âsım says (1: 257) that this posting took place in early Ca AH 1220 = late July/ early August 1805, while Fâik and Karslızâde (148 and 65) say it occurred in mid-1220. Ömer Câbî mentions it twice in *Târih-i Sultân Selîm-i Sâlis ve Mahmûd-ı Sânî Tahlîl ve Tenkidli Metin*, ed. Mehmet Ali Beyhan (Ankara, 2003), 1: 95, 97, but surrounding entries make it clear that he has confused the year with 1806. Cevdet dates (*Târih*, 8: 22) the appointment to 8 Ca = August 4, 1805. A palace daybook also says that

Vâsıf's term as head of the Ottoman bureaucracy was the high point of his career, but also something of an anticlimax. From a personal standpoint, it was the fulfillment of an old dream. Vâsıf to some degree must have reveled in the felicitations that came in verse from judges and scribes like Mehmed Münîb, Esîrîzâde Refî, and Sâdık Lebîd and from the court poet Antepli Aynî Efendi. He was also fêted by Seyyid Osman Sürûrî (d. 1814), the most prolific Ottoman chronogrammatist of the age, who wrote the following in his honor:

> Vâsıf Efendi whom scribes ever praise
> Got his heart's desire as chief.
> As his prose is fine, with a pearl I marked the date:
> Sultan Selim made his wordsmith *reis*.[76]

The event in other ways marked an end, however. Namely, Vâsıf would no longer have time for purely intellectual pursuits. If his posting as chief scribe let him put his ideas on politics, ethics, and statecraft into practice, in one last stretch of active life, it deprived him of what he seems to have loved best – writing, history, and the acclaim that it earned. Vâsıf had grown used to the sultan's favor. He did not wish to give up his place as court historian and resisted the idea of stepping down. It seems that when courtiers raised the issue of a successor, their choice again being Ahmed Âsım, Vâsıf bridled and vowed to hold both posts at the same time. This may be why Âsım called him "a rude and arrogant fool" and left us so unsavory a picture of the elder historian: "He was envious and mean," he said of Vâsıf years later. "Backstabbing and jealous, he would fly into a rage if he heard that the sultan had honored a man of letters or praised his work and would criticize him shamelessly."[77] While age and health did not allow it, Vâsıf's desire to remain the empire's court historian may also

---

Selim met with the Grand Vizier, İbrahim Nesîm, and "the new chief scribe Vâsıf Ahmed" on 12 Ca (August 8) and again with the Grand Vizier, Vâsıf, and *şeyhülislâm* on 21 Ca (August 17): Mehmet Ali Beyhan, ed., *Saray Günlüğü (25 Aralık 1802–24 Ocak 1809)* (Istanbul, 2007), 177. See also Hammer-Purgstall, 3: 553; and Schlechta-Wssehrd, 7.

[76] Sürûrî, *Divân-ı Sürûrî* (Bulaq, 1839), 245. Fâik and Karslızâde (148 and 65) record verse by Münîb, Refî, and Lebîd that all produce the date AH 1220: "In the year one thousand two hundred and twenty / Vâsıf Ahmed Efendi became *reis*"; "Vâsıf Efendi became captain of the ship of state"; and "Hail the erudite *reis*!" Sarıkaya has found (lxxxix n. 2) that Antepli Aynî also wrote Vâsıf a chronogram: "I gave good news to the scribes, a perfect date / Sultan Selim honored his servant Vâsıf as *reis*." The full poem is in Aynî, 264–265.

[77] Âsım, 1: 258. Sarıkaya draws (cclvii) the story of Vâsıf's replacement from a manuscript in which Âsım claimed that the historian "begrudged" him the post. While Sarıkaya is right that we must read Âsım with care, I feel that his portrayal of Vâsıf, while spiteful and

be why, when at last forced to step down in early 1806, his successor was not Âsım, but a nonentity named Mehmed Pertev Efendi. Ambition outstripped vigor. Keeping able talent at bay, Vâsıf put *Charms and Truths* aside with every thought of returning to it later. He never did; the work would remain unfinished.[78]

The discussion of Vâsıf's rise to the top of the scribal service begs a question: why now? Why, after so many years, was he made chief scribe? What had changed? To find an answer we must look to the realm's foreign and domestic affairs. While the 1802 Treaty of Paris had ended the war with France, it could not free the empire from its wider entanglements in Europe. Selim III was in an uneasy alliance with Russia, whose forces resumed hostilities with Napoléon in 1803. The formation of the Third Coalition in 1804 between Britain, Austria, and Russia further complicated matters; while the allies wished to press the Ottomans into closer cooperation against France in the Eastern Mediterranean and abroad, the French looked to win back their old friends and began to court them aggressively. This position – pulled between two armed camps – posed an added challenge because the Ottomans could ill afford war. Egypt had proved a fool's victory. The empire's situation deteriorated in only a few years to the point that whole provinces were effectively lost. Egypt, Syria, Albania, Serbia, large swaths of the Balkans – Vâsıf and his peers could only watch as they drifted out of the administration's orbit. Nor did reform slow this process. In fact, the New Order's showing in Egypt may have whetted the opposition, which moved into a more violent stage as the new model army gained in power and prestige. The Trabzon governor Mahmud Tayyâr Paşa's 1804–1805 revolt was at least partly driven by the formation of modern regiments in Anatolia, for instance. In Istanbul itself, Janissaries opened fire on officials in early 1805 after hearing that the new troops would attend the opening of an imperial

---

angry, is largely accurate. Certainly, the traits of envy, greed, pride, and selfishness pervade Vâsıf's biography.

[78] Seyyid Mehmed Pertev was the son of a time-keeper at the Sultan Ahmed mosque in Istanbul and had apprenticed in both the Anatolian accounts and receiver's offices. He later served as receiver (*amedî*) in the army and died in late September 1807. Mehmed Esad dates (in *Bağçe-i Safâ-Endûz*, ed. Rıza Oğraş [Burdur, 2001], 75) his appointment as court historian to R AH 1220 = September/October 1805. However, an archival document (BOA.C.MF 975) fixes the event to 1 M AH 1221 = March 21, 1806. See also Kütükoğlu, "Vekâyi'nüvis," 121–122; Cevdet, *Târih*, 8: 22; Karslızâde, 66–67; and Schlechta-Wssehrd, 9–10. According to Sarıkaya (lxxvi n. 6), Pertev moved to the receiver's office to gain access to state secrets, better his style and hand, and improve his accuracy in chronicling. His skill clearly left much to be desired.

mosque. The sultan could not even stop mutinous troops in his capital – he certainly could not risk a European war.[79]

The Ottoman bureaucracy thus did a balancing act to keep the empire neutral, appeasing Russia and Britain and encouraging France without taking either side. The first test of this policy showed its inherent dangers. In 1804, the French ambassador, Guillaume Brune, asked the Porte to recognize formally his master Napoléon's title of emperor. Couched as a demand, the request meant to force the Ottomans to pick a side and ideally move them closer to the new French empire, breaking with allies. Brune addressed the chief scribe Mahmud Râif Efendi, who now favored Russian interests but feared that France would go to war over a refusal. Selim, for his part, felt that Russia and Britain posed the bigger threat and ordered Râif to stall. When Brune finally presented an ultimatum – either the Ottomans recognize the French empire and close the Dardanelles and Bosphorus to Russian warships or he would quit Istanbul – Selim refused to answer. Brune left the city on December 22, 1804, severing diplomatic ties.[80] The upshot of this dispute was that the Ottomans drew nearer to Russia. Already the tsar's ambassador in Istanbul, Andrei Italinskii, had assured the Porte of his country's goodwill and willingness to renew their 1799 alliance. Taking this as an invitation, Râif sent Italinskii a request in mid-1804 to reopen the terms as part of a new treaty and began negotiations in February of the next year with a fellow scribe, İsmet Bey. The two sides talked for months. The basic treaty terms were not so much at issue as the empire's role in the alliance (which they insisted be purely defensive) and several secret articles that stupefied even the pro-Russian Râif. The tsar, Italinskii said, wished to station a 10,000 to 15,000-man army along the Danube in the semi-autonomous principalities of Moldavia and Wallachia. He also wished the sultan to grant his Christian subjects the same civil privileges and rights that Ottoman Muslims enjoyed, an exception being the poll-tax, and to allow the Russians to intercede on their behalf. Râif dared not accept and so told Italinskii. The talks reached an impasse in late July and early August, exactly when Ahmed Vâsıf unseated Râif as chief scribe.[81]

---

[79] On the empire's internal and diplomatic situation, see Shaw, *Old and New*, 283–331; and Yıldız, 121–136, 223–226.

[80] Shaw, *Old and New*, 332–333; Yıldız, 226–228; and Süslü, "Rapports," 244–246. See also Valeriy Morkva, "Russia's Policy of Rapprochement with the Ottoman Empire in the Era of the French Revolutionary and Napoleonic Wars, 1792–1806" (Ph.D. diss., Sabancı University, 2010), 310–313.

[81] Armand Goşu, *La troisième coalition antinapoléonienne et la Sublime Porte, 1805* (Istanbul, 2003), 14–18, 22–27. See also Yıldız, 228 f. On Italinskii, see MERSH, s.v. "Italinskii, Andrei Yakovlevich."

FIG. 7.1: Andrei Italinskii (d. 1827), Russian diplomat and ambassador to the Ottoman court.

If Vâsıf owed his new position in part to the ebb and flow of Ottoman diplomacy, he also profited from a timely shift in court factions. The sultan's circle not only disputed the treaty terms, but disagreed over the very wisdom of an alliance with Russia, their natural enemy, when the empire might align itself more closely with France or, better, remain aloof. In brief, the court had split into two factions after the 1798 invasion of

Egypt. The Grand Vizier, Yusuf Ziyâ Paşa, led a group who regarded the dual alliance with Russia and Britain as the empire's best hope for survival. These included Yusuf Ağa, the influential steward and confidant of Selim's mother, Mihrişah Sultan, and the chief scribe Mahmud Râif Efendi, whom the Russians had bribed and exploited though one Beyzâde Demetrius Mourouzi, agent and son of the prince of Moldavia. The second group favored France. Led at first by Grand Admiral Küçük Hüseyin Paşa, this faction fell into the hands of İbrahim Nesîm after the former's death in December 1803 and slowly wrested power from its rivals. In April 1805, Selim replaced Yusuf Ziyâ with Küçük Hüseyin Paşa's protégé, Hâfız İsmail Paşa. While some saw this as a ploy to calm popular anger over reform, the change came at a moment when Russian and Ottoman delegates had begun to discuss the treaty's secret articles. Italinskii reported that Hâfız İsmail acted for pro-French figures at court like Nesîm and Mustafa Reşîd and that he was little more than a pawn. What was more, the Grand Vizier began to lay the groundwork for Râif's dismissal, isolating the chief scribe and blocking the secret articles in spite of his protests. Râif's fall was thus seen as a rebuke, a sign that the sultan had tired of his too-cozy relations with the Russians.[82]

Was Vâsıf's promotion a token of political loyalties, then? To what extent did it signal the victory of pro-French forces and a pivot away from Russia? These were questions that arose in his first meetings with European powers. In early August, Vâsıf received the formal good wishes of envoys resident in Istanbul. It seems that after this ceremony, a British interpreter waylaid the chief Ottoman dragoman, Scarlat Callimaki, and asked the reason for Vâsıf's selection: namely, was it due to Râif's views on France? Callimaki reported the exchange to Vâsıf, who suspected a Russian hand and questioned the interpreter. "Did you ask such a thing?" he said. The interpreter did not deny it. "While we are pleased that you are chief scribe, your predecessor was not removed to make way for your appointment," he said. "We shall have misgivings if it was over the issue of Napoléon." Like any good politician, Vâsıf tried to deflect the question and dissemble his own views. He was happy to have the British ambassador's esteem, he said, and the empire's friendship was steadfast. The sultan had perhaps only wished to give the allies a modicum of doubt

---

[82] Shaw, *Old and New*, 371–374; Goşu, 27, 75–79; and Morkva, 323. On Yusuf Ağa, see Uzunçarşılı, "Nizam-ı Cedid Ricalinden Valide Sultan Kethüdası Meşhur Yusuf Ağa ve Kethüdazâde Arif Efendi," *Belleten* 20 (1956): 485–495.

in order to prove his fidelity, while he, Vâsıf, would both excel Râif as chief scribe and bring the two realms closer than before.[83]

Assurances aside, there is little doubt that the historian owed his rise to courtly intrigue and to the tack that peers expected him to take in directing the realm's affairs. Selim said publicly that he had removed Râif over delays in negotiation. This was a fiction. In private, he declared the former chief scribe to have been "misled" by a group of schemers, men who spread mistrust and forced the Russians to make unpalatable demands. According to Demetrius Mourouzi, Italinskii's informer, the sultan sacrificed Râif to quiet Ottoman statesmen who opposed the treaty's secret articles and chose Vâsıf as a more neutral figure – "learned but self-effacing" and without partisan bias. The instructions that Selim gave on Vâsıf's appointment appear to follow this version of Râif's fall. Namely, he ordered the chief scribe to conclude the alliance with all speed "in a way that does not violate the religious and political precepts or the laws of my empire."[84] Selim here referred to the proposed secret articles. It was a warning: do not repeat your predecessor's mistakes. As for Vâsıf himself, Mourouzi did not yet know his man. Vâsıf was a creature of faction. He certainly fraternized with pro-French courtiers like İbrahim Nesîm, Selim's privy secretary Ahmed Fâiz, and the late Küçük Hüseyin Paşa. An early biographer even identifies Nesîm and Ahmed Fâiz as his chief supporters in office. Nor was Vâsıf modest. He knew that he was well-qualified to be chief scribe, at least by Ottoman standards, and that he enjoyed repute as a one-time ambassador and skilled negotiator. European diplomats soon discovered his arrogant streak. Italinskii reported in October that he had to be guarded with Vâsıf about Mahmud Râif, for he deemed the two of them enemies and said that the historian "continually belittles Mahmud out of envy and rivalry."[85] True to form, Vâsıf ignored his past with Râif and whatever respect he had for

---

[83] The full conversation between Vâsıf and the interpreter, Berto Pisani, appears in the archival document BOA.HAT 4822. In a gloss, Selim wrote that Vâsıf should prevent the spread of gossip: "The chief scribe should be brief and to the point ... He knows the situation very well and how his predecessor acted. Let us see what he is worth. He shall act wisely and serve our faith and realm. God willing he will succeed."

[84] Goşu cites the original documents on pp. 27, 79–80. Shaw claims (*Old and New*, 374) that the death of Mihrişah Sultan deprived Yusuf Ağa of so much power that Nesîm was able to secure Vâsıf's position. However, Selim's mother did not die until October 16, 1805 – her death could not have affected the appointment.

[85] Italinskii to Adam Czartoryski, October 11, 1805, in Goşu, 85. In another letter from the same day, Italinskii also credited (167–169) Vâsıf's rise to a dispute between Yusuf Ağa and Ahmed Fâiz Efendi, who, he said, was Vâsıf's "kinsman" and sought his promotion. See also Âsım, 1: 257.

the latter's intellectual lights. The two were on different sides, in faction and politics, and he eagerly asserted superiority.

Vâsıf's first dealings focused on the empire's allies, Britain and Russia. In the days after his appointment, Vâsıf sent a letter to Prime Minister William Pitt over the expulsion of a British consul in Baghdad for "unfriendly" acts and to patch up relations between the empires. He also began to work with the ambassador, Charles Arbuthnot, to alter an existing commercial treaty and lower the import and export tariffs on British goods like textiles, spices, and metals, an agreement the two secured in January 1806.[86] But more urgent for the chief scribe were his talks with Russia. Italinskii was beginning to apply pressure and, in early August, declared that he had lost patience, calling for a final answer, yes or no, to the secret articles. Vâsıf promised to see to the matter and shortly reported that Selim would decide after meeting with close advisers. A few days later, the sultan gave his leave to negotiate. Citing loyalty and service, Selim wrote that he had chosen the historian to replace Râif "with my full leave to renew the treaty and, as matters stand, to add certain articles to ensure our security." Once Vâsıf and Italinskii decided the terms, he continued, they should set a time and place for the treaty's ratification.[87] Still, Vâsıf knew his master. However broadly he read his authority, he knew that Selim could not accept the secret articles for fear of domestic turmoil. The first meetings in late August and early September thus foundered on the same points. The Ottoman side of Vâsıf, İbrahim Nesîm, and Scarlat Callimaki refused to grant Christian subjects greater civil privileges or to allow Russian troops into the Principalities and made counterproposals; Italinskii for his part insisted on both of the terms or, at the very least, a compromise to demonstrate Ottoman goodwill.[88]

The talks lasted into the fall in spite of Vâsıf's increasingly open dislike for his partners. He distrusted the Wallachian and Moldavian Phanariots, especially Mourouzi, who he felt had planted the idea of allowing Russian troops on the Danube to weaken Ottoman rule. He also suspected Russian

---

[86] Vâsıf's letter to Pitt the Younger (BOA.HAT 52578-A) survives in a heavily edited draft in the Ottoman archives and is dated 5 C AH 1220 = August 31, 1805. A second document (BOA.C.HR 930) details changes to tariffs for fifty-seven items in the Ottoman-British commercial treaty and bears the date 21 L AH 1220 = January 12, 1806. While Vâsıf and Arbuthnot oversaw the latter, the Ottoman customs officer Hasan Ağa and the dragoman Pisani did most of the actual negotiation. See also Goşu, 108–109.

[87] Goşu, 27–28. Vâsıf's letter of accreditation survives in the Ottoman archives (BOA.HAT 12526) and is dated mid-Ca AH 1220 = mid-August 1805. BOA.HAT 12474 is a further copy.

[88] Goşu, 28–30.

motives, saying so openly. Vâsıf carried the memory of two wars and knew how tsarist policy operated. As he told Arbuthnot in September, Russia wanted to expand into the Black Sea basin and had already annexed the Crimea and Georgia. The same would happen if the empire let them into Wallachia and Moldavia. When Italinskii later accused him of bad faith, the chief scribe retorted that the Russians could only blame themselves if the Ottomans mistrusted them.[89] In fact, Vâsıf had reason to doubt the ambassador's sincerity. We know that Italinskii bribed Callimaki for information, much of it coming directly from the Porte, and used him to replace Mourouzi as an informer. In the meantime, he worked at the secret terms through a mix of threats and finesse. Italinskii first tried to manipulate the Ottomans with another Phanariot prince, Alexander Ypsilanti, who suggested to Vâsıf and Nesîm that local troops might guard the Principalities rather than the Russians. The chief scribe adopted and offered this measure as a compromise, unaware of its origin. But it did not matter. On September 9, Vâsıf, having met with Selim, informed the Russians that the sultan had had enough and would discuss the secret articles no further. Italinskii then gave an ultimatum: he threatened to quit Istanbul if the Ottomans balked and even hinted at the use of military force. After all, he noted transparently, the Tsar had a fleet on the Black Sea and an army on the Ottoman frontier. As the realm could ill afford to break with Russia, Vâsıf hastened to end the talks, accepted Italinskii's terms on September 14, and signed the treaty on September 23. The Ottomans in fact fared well – they had a purely defensive alliance without the worst of the secret articles.[90]

If Vâsıf played a key part in renewing the alliance, he did so out of a sense of duty and took no joy in embracing his old enemy as a comrade-in-arms. The historian hated the Russians. He preferred France. Indeed, Vâsıf found in the French chargé d'affaires, Pierre-Jean-Marie Ruffin, a man to his particular tastes.[91] Ruffin had spent long years in the Near

---

[89] Goşu, 38, 59, 81, 118–119.

[90] Goşu, 14–16, 31–42, 82–83. The final terms did not include civil or military concessions in the Danubian Principalities. For the French treaty text, see *Vneshniaia politika Rossii XIX i nachala XX veka: dokumenty Rossiiskogo Ministerstva inostrannykh del* (Moscow, 1961), 2: 584–589. The treaty bears the date 29 C AH 1220 = September 23, 1805. See also Morkva, 323–326.

[91] Born in 1742, Ruffin was the son of an interpreter to the French consul in Thessalonika. He went to Paris in 1750 as a *jeune de langues* and later served as an interpreter and diplomat in the Crimea and Istanbul. Ruffin also had a scholarly bent, held an honorary chair in Turkish and Persian at the Collège de France, and corresponded with well-known orientalists like Silvestre de Sacy, Joseph von Hammer-Purgstall, and Thomas-Xavier

East and had previously served the French embassy in Istanbul; a translator and orientalist, he knew Arabic, Turkish, and Persian and saw Vâsıf as
a sort of kindred spirit, whose promotion coincided with his own rise to
the head of the French mission. The two got along well. While Ruffin had
early doubts about the scribe's ability, knowing only his scholarly reputation, he made a good impression. In their first exchange, he flattered Vâsıf
as "a minister famed in Europe for his success in diplomacy and letters
and – still better in Muslim eyes – for his enlightenment, virtue, and loyalty
to his realm and sovereign." Vâsıf in turn sent copies of his chronicle and
embassy report to Ruffin, who collected manuscripts.[92] Ruffin's orders
were to block the Russian alliance, if possible. In early October, he
submitted a memo that attacked the treaty in terms of Ottoman law and
history and appealed to Vâsıf's "deep erudition." Calling the chief scribe
an "oracle of history," Ruffin noted that the empire always stayed out of
European wars and that the alliance had no basis in Islamic law. How
could they justify it? Several weeks later, he visited Vâsıf at home. Having
exhausted politics, Ruffin began to talk of Selim, whom he still recalled as
a young prince and for whom he felt "fatherly affection." "You bring
back pleasant memories," said Vâsıf. "But how old are you? We are nearly
the same age. You take me back to such fine times!" The chief scribe
wondered how those days – before wars and rebellion had sapped the
empire – could ever return. Ruffin, switching to Persian for privacy,
assured him that it was simple; the Ottomans must only act as they had
in the past and rid themselves of outside Russian influence. Vâsıf then gave
Ruffin two gold boxes as tokens of esteem, along with a vow that the
sultan and his ministry had only affection for their old ally of France.[93]

This is not to suggest the historian was especially "pro-French" or
a partisan of any foreign power, for that matter. His loyalty was to the
empire and himself. He chose the lesser evil to safeguard the realm, which
meant avoiding war at all costs and cultivating the best partners. That

---

Bianchi. He died in 1824. See Henri Dehérain, *La vie de Pierre Ruffin: orientalist et
diplomate, 1742–1824* (Paris, 1929–30), 2 vols.; and Thomas-Xavier Bianchi, *Notice
historique sur M. Ruffin* (Paris, 1825).

[92] Ruffin to Talleyrand, August 16, 1805, in *Documente privitóre la istoria românilor*, ed.
Eudoxin de Hurmuzaki (Bucharest, 1885), supp. 1, vol. 2: 319–321. See also Dehérain, 2:
16; and Bianchi, 49–50.

[93] Dehérain, 2: 16–18, 149. Ruffin submitted his memo to the Porte on October 6, 1805. His
meeting with Vâsıf took place on October 28. It is clear in this instance that Ruffin spoke
directly to Vâsıf in order to exclude interpreters. He also quoted an Arabic proverb at the
start of the audience to excuse his deafness: "The ear falls in love before the eye. She is also
punished first."

Vâsıf put personal feeling aside is clear from his encouragement of Ruffin even as he negotiated and signed the treaty of alliance with Italinskii. Ruffin only discovered this fact in late December when the two sides ratified the terms, and the news so shook the French interpreter that Vâsıf had to assure him that he, the sultan, and the Grand Vizier remained Napoléon's firm friends. The words rang hollow, of course. Vâsıf may have liked Ruffin and his flattery, but he happily kept him in the dark.[94] It is something of a surprise that Vâsıf also resisted bribery in his duties as chief scribe. To be more precise, he took money from all sides, but did not let it influence his position. Italinskii tried at one point to buy him. In a letter to the Russian foreign minister, Adam Czartoryski, the ambassador expressed hope that he could corrupt Vâsıf as he had Mahmud Râif. "Vâsıf's greed and small fortune led me to believe he would welcome some attention on my part," he wrote. "I decided to give him a thousand sequins, valued at 5,500 kuruş, and begged that he accept this small proof of my regard. For this kind gesture he made me show a good deal of gratitude." Italinskii at first thought that the payment had worked. "I have already seen results from this expedient. Vâsıf now shows more zeal, more goodwill in our affairs. I also hope that this will make him more open in his communication."[95] He was disappointed. Vâsıf's main impetus was not political – it was self-interest. He pocketed the money without softening his views on Russia and while accepting payments from other parties, gifts or bribes, including from the princes of Wallachia and Moldavia. While it is true that Ottoman bureaucracy operated on a degree of built-in venality, mostly in fees, sales of office, and "gifts" to superiors, Vâsıf's free behavior seems to have stood out even among his peers.[96] Ahmed Âsım said that he acquired a fortune in cash and valuables as chief scribe, with help from İbrahim Nesîm and Ahmed Fâiz. A later biographer added more poetically that he "took the liberty of hoarding huge sums, cutting himself a garment of whole cloth from the fabric of state." Some things do not change. Given Vâsıf's weakness for money, we may be sure that he did a fair share of graft in office.[97]

---

[94] Ruffin to Talleyrand, December 29, 1805, in Documente privitóre, supp. 1, vol. 2: 323. See Goşu, 72.

[95] Italinskii to Czartoryski, October 11, 1805, in Goşu, 83, 169.

[96] See Carter Findley, "The Legacy of Tradition to Reform: Origins of the Ottoman Foreign Ministry," IJMES 1 (1970): 334–357. He notes (353 f.) that the chief scribe not only got a large share of chancery fees, but also took a special due, called the câ'ize, which scribes paid in order to assume their posts.

[97] Âsım, 1: 257. See also Fâik, 148; and Cevdet, who repeats the phrase in his Târih, 8: 78. Vâsıf had ample chance for graft. For example, two documents (BOA.C.TZ 5558, 8476)

The effort to renew the Ottoman-Russian alliance soon unraveled, in any event, as news of Napoléon's latest victories on the continent reached Istanbul. Selim confirmed the treaty on October 11, 1805. Italinskii and Vâsıf exchanged ratifications two months later on December 30. By chance, however, that same night a courier came from Vienna with word of the French triumph at Austerlitz (December 2), the defeat of the joint Russian-Austrian army, and Austria's surrender. The news so stunned Selim that he called an emergency council; for his part, Ruffin began to press for a rapprochement between the empires. The Russians were a mutual enemy, he said. His master would never prejudice Ottoman interests and could even help them to retake the Crimea. The renewed alliance thus quickly frayed. In a letter dated January 10, 1806, the Grand Vizier congratulated his counterpart Talleyrand on the victory and called Napoléon emperor for the first time. "You see, sir," reported Ruffin, "that the Grand Vizier at last gives His Majesty the title of emperor. His Imperial Majesty has surely won it in the same short and brilliant campaign in which he subjected so many realms." The French pursued the advantage. A few days later, Ruffin sent Vâsıf a note to state his formal opposition to a renewal of the Anglo-Ottoman treaty, saying that he would return to Paris if again surprised. Ruffin and a colleague, Roux de Rochelle, also initiated deeper talks with the chief scribe and İbrahim Nesîm over a full restoration of diplomatic ties, which led Selim to agree to the imperial title in late February and to a mutual exchange of ambassadors that spring – Abdurrahim Muhib Efendi and General Horace Sébastiani de la Porta.[98]

---

show him transferring prebends to scribes in the imperial chancery worth, respectively, 16,160 and 43,830 akçe. They are dated 3 C AH 1220 = August 29, 1805, and 7 Z = February 26, 1806. By contrast, Ruffin tells a story so different from what we know of Vâsıf that it is hard to believe. In a letter to Talleyrand on August 16, 1805 (in *Documente privitóre*, supp. 1, vol. 2: 320–321), he wrote: "Vâsıf has already shown selflessness on becoming chief scribe. The princes of Wallachia and Moldavia are in the habit of making [the chief scribe] a free gift; the sum is fixed. The princes' agents doubled the amount in order to pay the new scribe court, but Vâsıf would only take his rightful half and sent the other back. The Greeks again doubled the surplus. He returned it all with scorn. May this test deter bribers!"

[98] Dehérain, 2: 18–23. See also Bianchi, 38–39; Goşu, 44–45; Morkva, 327–337; Shaw, *Old and New*, 334–335; and Bekir Günay, *Paris'te bir Osmanlı: Seyyid Abdurrahim Muhib Efendi'nin Paris Sefirliği ve Büyük Sefaretnamesi* (Istanbul, 2009), 204. Vâsıf's letter of accreditation for Muhib survives in "Ahmed Vâsıf à Talleyrand," BnF, Supplément turc nr. 1474 (1). A reply to a letter from Talleyrand, it is a large folio dated 5 C AH 1221 = August 20, 1806, and bears Vâsıf's seal impression in red wax.

What role did Vâsıf play in these events? We have reason to think that the historian advised Selim to counter the Russians with the French, for one, with one scholar claiming he "used successive reports of Bonaparte's recent military victories to win the Sultan over to his view." Nor did Vâsıf oppose recognizing Napoléon as emperor. After all, he felt, a stable French monarchy was much better than the excess of the Revolutionary régime.[99] Yet Vâsıf could not alienate the realm's official allies, who feared the French would try to shut them out of the Danubian Principalities and to close the straits to their warships, bottling up the Russian Black Sea fleet. These fears were well-placed. In early March, the Russians learned of activity at the northern forts of Khotin and İsmail, the garrisons of which were being reinforced and resupplied. However much he assured Italinskii of the empire's friendship and vowed to stamp out rumors of war, Vâsıf could not allay Russian fears. It did not help matters when he petitioned Italinskii in April to close the straits. The passage of Russian warships violated the empire's neutrality, he said, for the empire had only agreed to the measure in case of a defensive war against France. Italinskii rejected his arguments.[100] Vâsıf's missteps strained relations more. In an unguarded moment, in front of interpreters, he told the Wallachian prince Ypsilanti that he wanted to undercut Russian power on the Danube: "We are trying to undo the terms regarding your principality with French aid. God willing it will work," he said. Vâsıf later spoke too openly to Ruffin about his envoy Muhib's secret orders, news of which soon spread to the Russian and British missions in Istanbul. Peers attacked him for these indiscretions. Âsım said that Vâsıf, being proud and boastful, liked to impress visitors by reading aloud his memoranda and other documents that ought to have been secret. Muhib too complained about his lapses.[101]

---

[99] The scholar was Shaw in *Old and New*, 335. Cf. MEHÂSİN 4, fols. 269a-270b, 292a-295b.

[100] Two documents (BOA.HAT 14400, 15246) record Vâsıf's talks with Italinskii in March 1806, when the Russian envoy complained, among other things, that the empire's recognition of Napoléon broke their treaty. Italinskii relayed the chief scribe's assurances to Czartoryski on March 2 (in *Vneshniaia politika Rossii*, 3: 69–71), while Czartoryski replied on April 30 (3: 128) that he "cannot square Vâsıf's assurances and protests about the Porte's intent to maintain the alliance ... with the military activities they continue to hold on our borders." According to a third document (BOA.HAT 14672), Vâsıf petitioned Italinskii on the straits, but was ignored. The Russians flouted the closure by continuing to send warships. See also Morkva, 337–342.

[101] Âsım, 1: 94. Repeated in Cevdet, *Târih*, 8: 46–49. Muhib made similar charges (Günay, 212) in his embassy report.

As spring wore into summer, Vâsıf's ability to pilot the empire safely and to avoid war looked ever more doubtful. His health was failing. Now over seventy, Vâsıf suffered from an abdominal ailment that in time would force him from office and end his life. Nor, to be frank, was he a good chief scribe. Vâsıf's habits, character, and judgment – those of an arrogant courtier and intellectual – ill-suited the needs of the post and led him to make costly mistakes. If some of his policies had wide support, like closing the straits, other decisions proved disastrous for the realm in the long run. Chief among these was Vâsıf's part in a plot to depose the princes of Wallachia and Moldavia, Alexander Mourouzi and Constantine Ypsilanti, in favor of more pliant figures, an act that would break an 1802 Ottoman-Russian convention on the Principalities. Vâsıf loathed the two Phanariot princes. In 1805, he aided the recall of Alexander Suzzo, a Moldavian prince exiled two years before for pro-French leanings, which Italinskii protested. When the chief scribe pled ignorance, Italinskii claimed that he, Nesîm, and the Grand Vizier all stood to profit from the recall.[102] Vâsıf's aims are even clearer when we look at how he dealt with Ruffin that summer. Letters show that he deemed Ypsilanti a traitor and once told Ruffin's interpreter that he only tolerated "those dogs the Greeks" out of respect for İbrahim Nesîm and the sultan. "I will tell you a great secret," he added. "The sultan has sworn on the Quran that he shall deal with the two princes at the first word from his new ambassador in Paris."[103] In early July, Vâsıf refused a new French agent in Moldavia the title of "resident," as he said this would tacitly confirm the princes' sovereignty and the rights that Russia claimed there. Ruffin agreed. Napoléon saw the Principalities as a strategic territory and wished to help the sultan suppress his prior agreement, Ruffin said. By mid-month, he wrote to Talleyrand that "We can trust the current princes of Wallachia and Moldavia will be replaced by Prince Alexander Suzzo ... and the chief dragoman Charles Callimaki." The admission was staggering. It was little short of a declaration of war.[104]

---

[102] Italinskii to Czartoryksi, October 15, 1805, in Goşu, 169–172. See also Âsım, 1: 258; and Cevdet, *Târih*, 8: 79.

[103] Ruffin to Talleyrand, March 10, 1806, in *Documente privitóre*, supp. 1, vol. 2: 326.

[104] Vâsıf's refusal had to do with the status of the new French agent, Charles-Frédéric Reinhard, at the Moldavian court in Jassy. As diplomatic "residents" usually resided in the capital of sovereign powers, he pointed out, the title would hurt the sultan's claim to the territory. The letters are as follows: Vâsıf to Ruffin (French translation), July 3, 1806; Ruffin to Talleyrand, July 6, 1806; Ruffin to Vâsıf, June 6, 1806; and Ruffin to

The full crisis erupted in August, only shortly after Napoléon's ambassador Sébastiani reached Istanbul and while, in Edirne, a group of Janissaries and notables faced down Selim's new army. The empire was on the brink of foreign and civil war. Sébastiani had orders from Paris to seek an alliance; he was also to press the sultan to close the Bosphorus to warships, reassert control over the Danubian Principalities, and fortify his territories against Russia. It is in fact hard to say how well he succeeded in these aims, for, as we have seen, neither Selim nor Vâsıf and the Ottoman government needed much convincing. Vâsıf and Nesîm gave the ambassador a warm reception soon after his arrival. Over two evenings in August, they voiced goodwill and assured Sébastiani that he should have no doubts whatsoever that they, the empire and France, shared the same goals. Ever the rhetorician, Vâsıf made it clear where he stood: "Our two empires are in fact like one body," he said. "So natural is the trust and friendship between them that they cannot be divided in any way."[105] Whether moved by Sébastiani or simply ready to challenge the Russians, then, Selim made his decision and on August 24, had Vâsıf announce what everyone had long suspected – that he was deposing Mourouzi and Ypsilanti in favor of his own men, Suzzo and Callimaki. Italinskii was livid, though not terribly surprised, and immediately protested. On August 28, he submitted a demand that Selim reverse the move and observe prior treaties, pointing out the large Russian army massed on the frontier and threatening to leave Istanbul. The Ottoman response to this ultimatum was deliberate, even coy. Vâsıf met Italinskii in early September and, while vowing continued friendship, said that the sultan merely wished to protect his realm from internal chaos and French threats, an answer which failed to satisfy. Italinskii saw that Vâsıf was buying time. "I am not fooled by Vâsıf Efendi's alleged confidence," he wrote. "Nor will it change my views on the chief scribe's public and private feelings or those of the whole ministry, despite all the perorations and insults against France

Talleyrand, July 10 1806, in *Documente privitóre*, supp. 1, vol. 2: 341–342, 343–344, 345. On French policy in the Principalities, see J.D. Ghika, "La France et les principautés danubiennes de 1789 à 1815," *Annales de l'École libre des sciences politiques* 11 (1896): 321 ff.

[105] The meetings are recorded in two documents (BOA.HAT 14683, 15766) which, while undated, must come from the days after Sébastiani's arrival on August 10, 1806. See also P. Coquelle, "Sébastiani, ambassadeur à Constantinople, 1806–1808," *Revue d'histoire diplomatique* 18 (1904): 574–581; Dehérain, 2: 72–73; and Morkva, 347–350. On the so-called "Edirne Incident," see Shaw, *Old and New*, 345–350; Yaycıoğlu, 163–165; and Yıldız, 136 ff.

and protests in favor of Russia with which he followed our exchange."
The historian was again playing a double game, though the result was
now far more serious than his earlier factional intrigues. This time it was
war.[106]

It remains a sort of irony that Vâsıf never saw the fruits of his labor,
neither the war, nor the ensuing Ottoman defeat, nor the collapse of
Selim's government the following spring in the so-called Kabakçı
Mustafa rebellion. In late September, Italinskii demanded an answer
to his ultimatum. While the Ottomans gave in, agreeing to reinstate
Mourouzi and Ypsilanti, events had already moved well outside of their
control. In November, the Russians summarily invaded the Danubian
Principalities and occupied the settlements of Khotin, Jassy, Bender,
and Bucharest, while the Ottomans belatedly declared war on
December 24.[107] Vâsıf did not live to see this outcome, however.
Deemed the war's architect by one peer – a judgment that may overstate
his impact and underrate his ineptitude – he fell seriously ill in
early September and took to bed with his old abdominal complaint
and growing weakness. There was no hope of recovery. Despite doctors'
best efforts, we are told, the historian and chief scribe was unable to
return to his duties and worsened, relieved of his post and surrounded
by a grieving household. On October 16 or 17, 1806, he died. Vâsıf was
buried near the tomb of Selim's mother, Mihrişah Sultan, in Eyüp.
An idealized epitaph by Sürûrî marks his grave:

> Alas, Vâsıf Efendi has died.
>> Namesake of the Prophet,
> A humble wordsmith and
>> Good-hearted man was he.
> He ever strove for wisdom
>> While was life in his body,
> Recoiled from love of being chief scribe,
>> And turned his back on the world.
> He chose to be free from office,
>> Now henceforth blessed be

---

[106] Italinskii to Andrei Budberg, September 15, 1806, in *Vneshniaia politika Rossii*, 3:
319–320; and Italinskii to Budberg, same date, ibid, 3: 314–317. Yıldız includes the
Turkish translation of a petition (TSMA.E 5162, on pp. 876–878) that Sébastiani
submitted to the Porte on August 30. See also Morkva, 350–353; and Shaw, *Old and
New*, 351 ff.
[107] Morkva, 353–361; and Yıldız, 253–268.

That praiseful man's tomb.
He passed at a luminous time,
In October I marked the date:
A laudable wordsmith has died.[108]

---

[108] Sürûrî, 150–151. The latter adds (295) two more chronograms on his death. See also Âsım, 1: 135, 255; Cevdet, *Târih*, 8: 77–78; Fâik, 149; Fâtin, 432–433; Karslızâde, 65; Hammer-Purgstall, 3: 553; Sarıkaya, xciii-xciv, xcviii-xcix; and Schlechta-Wssehrd, 7. The chronology of Vâsıf's final days is hard to reconstruct. As far as we can tell, he fell ill in early September, for Italinskii wrote in a letter on September 15 (in *Vneshniaia politika Rossii*, 3: 314) that Vâsıf's sickness prevented an answer to Russia's ultimatum. Cevdet says (*Târih*, 8: 77) that he was replaced after twenty days of inactivity with Mehmed Gâlib Efendi in early Ş AH 1221 = October 14–23, 1806. As Italinskii makes no mention of Gâlib, Sarıkaya's claim (xciv) that Vâsıf was dismissed on 1 B = September 14 seems too early. The fact that Arbuthnot introduced Gâlib in a letter on October 30 (Public Record Office, FO 78–52, nr. 77, in Yıldız, 881–884) as the "new Reis Efendi of whom as yet I have said but little" strengthens this opinion, along with his relation of how Gâlib attained the post through Vâsıf's "incapacity and ill state of health." Vâsıf's death date is more certain. Although his tombstone bears the date 7 Ş = October 20, two new finds suggest either 3 or 4 Ş = 16/17 October. The first is an imam's diary that records his death twice as 4 Ş: Beydilli, ed., *Osmanlı Döneminde İmamlar ve Bir İmamın Günlüğü* (Istanbul, 2001), 183, 224. Sarıkaya also found (xcviii) a second date on the grave's left-hand side of 3 Ş.

Epilogue: Vâsıf as Ancient and Modern

In a way, Vâsıf was lucky to die when he did. He had lived a full life and passed away at home, naturally and peacefully, surrounded by bereaved family, friends, and servants. The end might have been far different had he lived longer. Sultan Selim was now losing his grip on the empire and could barely placate opponents of reform, the political and intellectual enterprise to which he had devoted his reign. Like the sultan and his still-living peers, Vâsıf would have seen his life's work unravel. The time, effort, and resources they had poured into reform came to nothing as their enemies moved to dismantle the New Order and restore a bankrupt status quo. The war that Vâsıf had provoked was also to end badly. While Selim would successfully repulse a British fleet from Istanbul and hold the Russians along the Danube, he fell from power in mid-1807 in an armed rebellion. It began as a mutiny at one of the Bosphorus forts. In late May, the former chief scribe Mahmud Râif visited a garrison of auxiliaries (*yamak*) at Rumeli Kavak to pay out quarterly wages and to ask the men to adopt the new model army's uniform and drill. The soldiers erupted in anger, slaughtering a hapless assistant. Râif tried to escape, but was captured and killed. Led by one Kabakçı Mustafa, the auxiliaries then joined forces with local Janissaries and called for an open revolt to end the sultan's "infidel innovations." In days, the rebels took over the city and demanded that Selim dissolve the New Order and surrender followers like İbrahim Nesîm, Yusuf Ağa, Ahmed Fâiz, and others for summary execution. Swayed by one Köse Musa Paşa, who had helped to stoke the revolt, Selim tried to save himself by capitulating and keeping his new-style soldiers in the barracks. He thus all but doomed his closest supporters, who were hunted down and murdered, and paved the way for his own deposition and imprisonment on May 29. In a little more than a year he, too, was killed in a counter-coup.[1]

Of course, few could have predicted these events at Vâsıf's passing. His death instead fed a good deal of rumor and speculation and even sparked a minor scandal over his net worth. It was usual for the Ottoman treasury to seize late servitors' estates. The sultans justified this confiscation or *müsâdere* as a legal prerogative, since statesmen were traditionally seen as slaves (*kul*) who owed their lives and wealth to the dynasty's goodwill. By the eighteenth century, the government had also come to rely on confiscation as a revenue tool and increasingly targeted artisans and the once-exempt ulema. Having decided on a seizure, the sultan sent treasury agents to inventory the estate. These scribes appraised any moveable goods, valuables, and ready cash, made a register, and held a sale to liquidate the assets. The treasury then took the revenue, after first making provisions for heirs and satisfying creditors. Selim moved on Vâsıf's estate more or less immediately. In the week after the historian's death, he ordered the keeper of the ledger, Râşid Efendi, to inspect the estate, find out what Vâsıf owned and owed, hold a sale, and pay off his heirs and creditors. Râşid was at work within days. Alongside staff from the religious courts, he began to compile data and calculated Vâsıf's debts to the imperial treasury. He finished the inventory about a month later, on November 16, 1806.[2]

The reason for Selim's interest seems to have been gossip: rampant "hearsay" about the late Vâsıf's personal wealth. We can get some sense of the magnitude of these reports from Ahmed Âsım, who used them to criticize the historian. "Oddly enough," he wrote a few years later,

Vâsıf was always begging for handouts from the palace and nobles and kept that vile habit to the death. Yet after he died, his estate yielded 100,000 *kuruş* worth of Spanish gold that he had brought back from Spain and another 800 purses of dinars he hoarded for himself. This caused quite a scandal. The Lord grant all of us contentment![3]

---

[1] Shaw, *Old and New*, 378–405. Yıldız treats these events in detail in her dissertation.

[2] Several documents detail these events. BOA.HAT 19 refers to Selim's appointment of and original orders to Râşid Efendi; BOA.C.ML 16852 concerns Vâsıf's debts to the treasury and is dated 17 Ş AH 1221 = October 30, 1806. Sarıkaya has also discovered (cclxiii-cclxvi) new documents related to the estate, including a register on its ready cash, income, and debts. See also DİA, s.v. "Müsâdere."

[3] Âsım, 1: 259, adds that the Spanish gold was kept under Vâsıf's personal seal. BOA.HAT 19 says that Selim ordered an inventory because the estate was a point of "hearsay." BOA.

Âsım put a fairly clear price on Vâsıf's cash holdings and likely reflects the estimates of local gossipmongers. A "purse" or *kese* was a fixed unit of account. It held 500 *kuruş*. According to Âsım, then, Vâsıf had 100,000 *kuruş* in Spanish gold and a further 400,000 in other coin for a total of 500,000 in liquid assets. For a better idea of this sum's real value, we may recall that at the turn of the nineteenth century, it took about fifteen *kuruş* to make one British pound sterling. Vâsıf would thus have had some 33,300 pounds apart from property and moveable goods – a little more than Georgiana Darcy's 30,000 pound legacy and a colossal fortune. Even if Âsım overstated the sum, it is clear that peers assumed Vâsıf to be fabulously wealthy.

The reality was a bit more complicated. Vâsıf *was* wealthy, especially for a scribe who had never risen to the highest posts in the realm like the Grand Vizierate. However, he was not nearly as rich as Âsım suspected and had large debts. In late 1806, the treasury reported that Vâsıf held 171,789 *kuruş* in cash and that the sale of his effects had raised a further 129,738 *kuruş*. This did not include the value of his home or adjust for his 95,000 in debts.[4] The government changed these figures as more informa- tion came to light and as the historian's creditors began to circle and call on the Porte for payment. Less fees, a later account put his cash assets at 161,000, his effects at 111,305, and his debts at 105,800 *kuruş*, while a further list set his proven and contested debts at 102,438 *kuruş*.[5] Much of what Vâsıf owed was for loans and luxury items. However, he also had debts for household goods, clothing, pens, paper, books, dowries, and his own funeral costs. The government "discounted" some of these and settled the rest for nearly 84,000 *kuruş*. Vâsıf's family also shared in the estate. Holy law provided for his widow and children, though Lebîb as a male got the largest sum, while the sultan gave a good deal more and let

---

HAT 2179 contains his own words: "They are gossiping about Vâsıf Efendi's estate. Let me see a register of all of his estate and debts. Submit it." See also Cevdet, *Târih*, 8: 79; and Schlechta-Wssehrd, 7.

[4] BOA.C.ADL 6334, dated 8 L AH 1221 = December 19, 1806.

[5] See BOA.HAT 19 and BOA.D.BŞM.d 6866. A series of petitions for outstanding sums date shortly after Vâsıf's death: BOA.C.ADL 681 (dated 27 Z AH 1221 = March 7, 1807) records the claim of a locksmith "Gregor" for 123 *kuruş*; BOA.C.ADL 1583 (11 Ş AH 1222 = October 14, 1807) asks for 147 *kuruş* on behalf of a wool-maker named Artin; BOA.C.ML 2052 (23 S AH 1222 = May 2, 1807) seeks payment of 1,000 *kuruş* for one Hüseyin Beyefendi; BOA.C.ML 19478 (11 L AH 1221 = December 22, 1806) places a claim of 55 *kuruş* for one Elhac Emîn; and BOA.C.ML 20656 (25 Za AH 1221 = February 3, 1807) seeks 9,560 *kuruş* for Vâsıf's "chief oarsman Togofil." On a more personal note, BOA.C.ML 27701 (17 N AH 1221 = November 28, 1806) records the stone-carver Mehmed's request to be paid 800 *kuruş* for Vâsıf's headstone.

them keep the family home in central Istanbul.[6] All told, the estate's total
value was 301,527 *kuruş*. Selim ordered Râşid Efendi to send the treasury
what remained after heirs and creditors had taken their share and then,
voicing ire, rebuked the dead:

> Vâsıf had to live on alms only a year ago and now look at this dishonesty! What
> a pity – this is not putting one's trust in God. The faithful hate prosperity; the
> world is treacherous. Yet a learned, frugal, poised statesman accumulates this
> much in one year, it seems! I wonder what the blighters who don't parade about
> the streets in finery are stealing? Good God!

As in life, so in death. Vâsıf's ill-gotten riches would occupy the probate
courts for some time.[7]

In death, Vâsıf's legacy also lived on in his children and his written
work – mainly the history *Charms and Truths*. We know that Lebîb lived
a productive life, for instance, becoming a high-ranking judge and minor
poet and finally dying in the city of Ṭâ'if near Mecca in 1837–1838.[8]
While the historian's widow disappears from our record, his two daughters Züleyhâ and Hanîfe pop up in sources as late as the mid-nineteenth
century, though not always for good reasons. Züleyhâ was part of an
unseemly scandal in 1817 with the daughter of the former *şeyhülislâm*
Mehmed Mekkî Efendi, whom she likely knew through her father and
who abused and publicly shamed a female slave. While details are few, the
sources hint at a lesbian affair and say that the slave's crime was "to
oppose the intimate liaison" between her mistress and Züleyhâ. Mekkî
Efendi's daughter retaliated by shaving the slave's head and confining her
to a leper hospital in Üsküdar, for which Sultan Mahmud II sent her, her
husband, and Züleyhâ into exile. Whatever the transgression, Züleyhâ
was pardoned in 1818. Late in life, she and her sister Hanîfe petitioned the

---

[6] Sarıkaya (cclxiv) breaks down the debts by percentage and lists the family shares as
follows: Vâsıf's widow Ümmü Gülsûm received 725 *kuruş*, his son Lebîb 2,030, and his
daughters Züleyhâ and Hanîfe 1,015 each. Moreover, Selim left (BOA.HAT 19) Lebîb
eight purses of *kuruş* and four purses each to the women. See also BOA.D.BŞM.d 7370.
Vâsıf had rebuilt his house in Yerebatan, as seen in an affidavit of sale from 5 B AH 1805
(September 29, 1805) for a water connection: in Ahmet Tabakoğlu, ed., *İstanbul Su
Külliyâtı*, vol. 10, *İstanbul Şer'iyye Sicilleri: Mâ-ı Lezîz Defterleri* (Istanbul, 1999), 5:
333–335. A second affidavit records his purchase of water from near the villages of Karka
and Ayapa for the home; that the document calls him chief scribe implies a date of 1805 or
1806. See ibid, vol. 25, *Vakıf Su Defterleri: Avrupa Yakası Suları* (Istanbul, 2002), 3: 321.
[7] BOA.HAT 19. Vâsıf's estate appears in probate records for the years 1806–1807: e.g. SSA,
Kısmet-i Askeriyye nrs. 827, 829 passim.
[8] Lebîb served as a judge in Bursa, Jerusalem, and Mecca. His poetry was notable enough to
be included in Fâtin's mid-century anthology. BOA.C.ADL 3682 records his posting as the
judge of Jerusalem and is dated to 28 Ş AH 1249 = January 10, 1834. See also SO, 3: 900.

palace as well, Züleyhâ for money to make the pilgrimage to Mecca and Hanîfe for a stipend to relieve her poverty. Both, of course, invoked the name of their late father.[9]

Vâsıf's written work had an "afterlife" of its own, too, though surely not in the way he had envisioned. He had boasted in old age of creating a great history, a work that would outdo his Ottoman rivals and equal the masters of medieval Persia. These hopes went largely unfulfilled. Vâsıf was still read and esteemed for a time. Apart from Âsım, early nineteenth-century Ottomans hailed him as a great stylist and deemed his history a literary achievement. Süleyman Fâik (d. 1838), a noted poet and biographer, wrote that "Vâsıf's skill in the rational and transmitted sciences and his mastery of poetry and prose is obvious from his eloquent history, *Charms and Truths*, which remains in use. He was famed for his originality and way with words." The author of a poetry anthology, Davud Fâtin (d. 1868), added that he had written "an elegant and coveted history."[10] We know also that the early volumes of *Charms and Truths* were reprinted twice in Egypt in 1828 and 1830, while the *Book of the Monk* appeared in pamphlet form in 1873. Still, Vâsıf's history fell by the wayside. The imperial press voiced bewilderment over its extent when it tried to issue a later volume in 1835–1836. Fifteen years from 1774 to 1789 had not been printed, the press director said, nor could he find the missing parts. Perhaps the imperial treasury had a copy? The palace sent a manuscript – very likely the last, incomplete volume – but the edition failed to materialize.[11] A still bigger blow to Vâsıf's dream of immortality came from Ahmed Cevdet Paşa (d. 1895). The greatest Ottoman historian of the nineteenth century, and maybe of all time, Cevdet was asked in 1853 to assemble the dynastic history from 1774 to 1826 from existing manuscripts and to pare, rewrite, and simplify the language for publication. He worked on the task for decades, combing the archives, drawing on fifty-five histories, and producing a classic and still used twelve-volume series. Cevdet got the best of Vâsıf in the end. He acquired the late historian's drafts and manuscript volumes, which he used for the years 1783 to 1805 and criticized frequently, at times harshly. Vâsıf thus met

---

[9] BOA.C.ML 23317 concerns Hanîfe's request for a stipend and is dated 18 N AH 1265 = July 28, 1849. BOA.İ.DH 2002 (6 Ca AH 1257 = June 26, 1841) contains Züleyhâ's petition and the reply granting her 5,000 *kuruş*. See also Sarıkaya, lxvi. For the scandal involving Züleyhâ, see BOA.HAT 24889, 25708; and Şânîzâde, 2: 813. Cf. Cevdet, *Târih*, 10: 239–240. Aysel Yıldız first brought this event to my attention.

[10] Fâik, 149; and Fâtin, 432.

[11] BOA.HAT 31287. See also Kütükoğlu, "Vekâyi'nüvis," 120.

the same fate that he had inflicted on Hâkim, Enverî, and others. His printed work survived, it is true, but readers who wished to know about later periods could simply consult Cevdet, whose content superseded his own and whose prose suited the simpler tastes of the nineteenth century. The empire was changing dramatically. So too was Ottoman literature. No one wanted to be a second Vaṣṣâf anymore, much less a Vâsıf, and the historian's star dimmed perceptibly in the century and more after his last breath.[12]

8.2 VÂSIF AND OTTOMAN HISTORY

The fact that later Ottomans mostly forgot about Vâsıf or failed to appreciate his work does not necessarily reflect poorly on his life, career, or literary talent. It would be unfair to deny him these things. While a deeply flawed man, Vâsıf rose from humble origins in the provinces to a high station and enjoyed a long and fruitful career; his success in breaking into the ranks and climbing to the pinnacle of the scribal service was itself remarkable and, if not unique, an increasingly rare feat for his time. Vâsıf was also one of the empire's brightest intellectual lights. His virtuosity in prose was unmatched and his work on ethics, politics, and history rank him as the preeminent Ottoman writer of the eighteenth century. If we deplore his greed and jealousy, we can at the same time admire his industry, ambition, literary skill, and force of character.

Vâsıf's diminished legacy instead had to do with his place at a crossroads in the empire's history. The historian belonged to a waning age. His was the last generation to grow up and be educated in the old ways and the first to see major change, to grapple with the problem of Europe, and to try to hold together a fractured world. Ottoman élites born in the early and mid-eighteenth century recalled a time when (so they thought) the empire had been prosperous and powerful, feared and respected by its enemies. Like so many others, Vâsıf breathed the intellectual traditions of a dynamic, confident, and mostly self-contained Ottoman culture. Europe to him seemed a world apart. His education had focused on the Islamic classics and he had

---

[12] The best work on Cevdet's history is Christoph Neumann's *Das indirekte Argument: ein Plädoyer für die Tanzīmāt vermittels der Historie: die geschichtliche Bedeutung von Aḥmed Cevdet Paşas Tarīḫ* (Münster: Lit, 1994). See also İlgürel, "Cevdet Paşa"; and Kütükoğlu, "Vekâyi'nüvis," 123–124, 131–133. Cevdet's seal marks and notes left by his son show that he gained possession of Vâsıf's drafts: see BOA.Y.EE, p. 1; Beyazıt Kütüphanesi, Nadir Eserler Bölümü nr. V3497–200, fols. 1a, 3a; and Millet Kütüphanesi, Ali Emiri layihalar nr. 74, unpaginated insert.

mastered the three languages of learning, poetry, and government – Arabic, Persian, and Turkish. He wrote history and poetry according to well-known Persianate models, idolizing men like Vaṣṣâf, Juvaynî, and ʿUrfî, and, despite great upheaval, he believed steadfastly in the realm's divine mission and favor. Future generations knew a different world. Vâsıf's children grew up in an empire ravaged by war and teetering near collapse, an empire that was bankrupt, unstable, and vulnerable. Europe and Christendom were more immediate, either as threats or potential sources of strength. Early nineteenth-century élites also began to look more to western languages and knowhow – to works of math, tactics, geography, engineering, and diplomacy – and less to the urbane wisdom of the past. This is not to say Vâsıf and his peers were the last of their kind. Ottomans continued to write court poetry, for example, and to believe in the dynasty's exceptionalism. The old ways persisted even as the empire started to emulate Europe and move into the modern era. Yet Vâsıf's generation was the last before this transformation. They were the last to live on the far side of the divide and the only ones to span it.

Seen through Vâsıf's life, the story of this generation leaves us in a position to look back and to survey the intellectual trends of the eighteenth-century Ottoman Empire. Vâsıf and his peers lived at a time of crisis. They were not the first Ottomans to lose wars and territory or to be humiliated by their enemies, but they were arguably the first to confront the collapse of the realm's ruling ideology. The dilemma was this: how could the empire fail? If God had sent the dynasty to spread and renew the faith, rewarding them with far-flung conquests, what had now changed? Why did God withhold His blessings? Was it a test or a punishment for sin? And what must they do to win back divine favor? Contemporary debates over reform, war and peace, theodicy, free will, and the limits of human reason all, to some extent, sprang from these questions. The period was hence one of considerable intellectual, existential, and moral anxiety. Yet far from paralysis, we have seen that the eighteenth-century crisis stoked ferment in élite ranks and generated a highly dynamic response. Continuity was perhaps the broadest theme of this reaction. Vâsıf and others did not radically re-examine old beliefs and institutions and, as it were, throw out the baby with the bath water to meet the century's challenges. While pragmatic, they tended to apply deeply ingrained, tested conceptual frameworks to their problems, like the ideas of a fixed "world order" and dynastic exceptionalism. These proved slow to change, but change they did.

For one thing, eighteenth-century élites clung to the pretense that the empire was unique and immune to the inexorable march of history. We have noted how political exceptionalism acted as a sort of linchpin in Ottoman ideology. Its focus on divine favor, justice, and martial superiority united the ruling class while imbuing them with poise and a deep sense of mission. Like any kind of exceptionalism or chauvinism, however, it could not easily admit shortcomings or adapt to long-term shifts in the empire's power.[13] When élites did address such concerns – a loss in war, an unfavorable treaty, economic or domestic hardship – it was to declare their belief in God's favor and often joined with a good deal of casuistry. These assertions became even more strained late in the century. Vâsıf and his peers sensed that reality did not match their expectations and, as though they could not withstand the psychological blow, they tried valiantly but vainly to save exceptionalism from collapse by framing the empire's ills as divine trials (istidrâc) and lessons in theodicy. At the same time, Vâsıf and like minds insisted that the realm's subjects could not remain idle. They reaffirmed the dynasty's unique character but with the caveat that success was part of a divine grand bargain; exceptionalism, they claimed, demanded action as well as moral responsibility.

Ottoman concern with causality, free will, and action during this period is a major and till now unwritten chapter in the empire's history, with wide implications. Whether in theology, history, or the political sphere, the theorizing of human deeds betrayed an acute anxiety over the human condition, the realm, and its ultimate fate. This was no isolated or academic discourse. It grew out of and fed élite efforts to salvage Ottoman exceptionalism, it met a deep emotional need, and it shaped many facets of eighteenth-century intellectual and political life. Deep down, Ottomans may have turned to the issue to find solace and to assuage doubts about the empire's future. Human will explained their plight. It also offered hope in the form of control. For one, we have seen how the men around Mustafa III, Abdülhamid I, and Selim III pushed an increasingly "activist" agenda and that their stance had much to do with politics. Vâsıf and his peers wished to rebut or pre-empt discordant voices, Ottomans who, for whatever reason, rejected free will. Some of these may have been "fatalists" with legitimate religious scruples; others likely used the rhetoric of fatalism to defend their material interests against the New Order or similar reforms. "Particular will" was a potent argument against

---

[13] This author hopes to study Ottoman exceptionalism and its long-term political, cultural, and intellectual consequences as part of a future project.

them and in favor of systemic reform. Yet it led to unforeseen ends, too. In placing human will and causes at the heart of his work, Vâsıf hinted at a secularized, human concept of history in place of the older mechanisms of sacred history. Ottomans had long viewed history as a story of moral choices, but had left room for God as author, actor, and judge. Vâsıf and others now shifted this focus and, while they did not exclude God, they made it clear that humans must act and take ownership for themselves in the world. The result was incidental but crucial: a wider scope for action and reason in all spheres of life.

We can see how human will touched other intellectual controversies in the debate over war, peace, and peacemaking. Eighteenth-century Ottomans began to retreat from a division of the world into "realms" of war and Islam. Vâsıf's early legalistic defenses of peace gave way by the 1790s to a more philosophic viewpoint, signaling his departure from the empire's martial ethos, as well as prefiguring a broader role for humans in the conduct of war. If warfare were "unpredictable," as Vâsıf came to argue, it meant that the Ottomans could not simply rely on victory as a predetermined, preordained outcome. They instead had to use care, prudence, and reason and often forgo the use of force. While such an approach had always been part of the empire's praxis and was, besides, firmly in its interest, it was not before much lag in the late eighteenth and early nineteenth centuries that ideology caught up with action. Vâsıf's generation was hence the first to assert the virtues of peace – or, put differently, of containing warfare – rather than treating it as a necessary evil.

The same period likewise saw fissures in that hoary bastion of socio-political stability, "world order (nizâm-ı 'âlem)." For the empire's thinkers and statesmen, "world order" without fail remained the framework to discuss society and political thought in the eighteenth century. Reform, meanwhile, was understood as nothing more or less than the restoration of that same order's internal balance. Ottoman reformers did not envision a radical break with the past or even smaller structural change, since for them, the main characteristic of world order was that it was, in theory, unchanging and unchangeable. Selim III and his camarilla therefore presented his reforms not as a new universal order, but as a restoration of the old: the renovation of a purely political order within nizâm-ı 'âlem. This debate turned on the related issue of human reason. How far might rulers use reason to solve political problems? As seen above, Selim and his allies legitimized rational reform by pushing ideas like "reciprocation (mukâbele bi'l-misl)," "ancient practice (kânûn-ı kadîm)," and "individual obligation (*farz-ı 'ayn*)" to new ends and limits, even to the point of bending rules of Ottoman political thought. Perhaps without fully appreciating it, they were undermining the supports of world order. Yet Vâsıf's kind did not totally carry the argument. We have it on good grounds that some Ottomans rejected the New Order as sinful innovation (*bid'a*), a religiously charged concept that denied the free use of reason and that vulnerable interest groups seized on. This is not to say the contest was entirely cynical. Many Ottomans, even some sympathizers, were skeptical about the rationalist direction of Selim's program and felt that it neglected spiritual, nonmaterial concerns. The presence of such a policy disagreement among the reformers themselves is important and indicates that, in the end, Selim had failed to build up a necessary consensus within his own government.

These are the intellectual trends of the Ottoman *fin de siècle*. But what larger points do they raise? What do they say more generally about late eighteenth-century Ottoman state and society? It is hard to deny that our picture is a dynamic and vital one. We have seen how Vâsıf and his peers responded to crisis upon crisis by reconsidering, altering, and redeploying major concepts, legal, ethical, philosophical, and otherwise. We have also observed how they were willing to tinker and in some cases to bend or break fundamental precepts of Ottoman thought. While many of the frameworks stayed the same, élites across society moved to find solutions to the empire's ills. Their approach may have been tentative and conservative, but one cannot call it dogmatic. Indeed, Vâsıf and his colleagues were eminently pragmatic in their stress of human action and reason and surprisingly flexible in the degree that they accepted change. Is it possible to talk of modernity during this time, then? Can one speak of a growing worldliness, rationalism, or enlightenment? Yes and no. It was during the late eighteenth century that storied conceptual frameworks began to fracture and crumble and that figures like Vâsıf first shook the tenets of Ottoman ideology to the core. But we should not overstate the effect. Vâsıf and his contemporaries wanted to restore rather than alter, to return to a tested model rather than create their own. They looked to the past. They were not aware that they had taken the first intellectual steps toward an Ottoman modernity, the full onset of which would come later in the nineteenth century with Mahmud II and his open emulation of Europe.

So too should we avoid overrating the flexibility of Ottoman élites. If they were dynamic and resourceful, they were also badly divided. Early modern Ottomans ruled by consensus and enacted limited reforms because they could not afford to alienate entrenched interests. Ambitious reformers like Selim III understood these challenges but, in the end, failed to bridge divisions and build up agreement for their programs. Exactly why this was so is an open question. Clearly the debate was a bitter one – so bitter that we are able to trace the period's rich intellectual history. Our sources exist in part because opposition needed to be countered in writing, or else why make the argument? However, we almost totally lack the story of this opposition and it is unclear that it can be recovered apart from what we learn, in distorted fashion, from hostile interlocutors. Do these opponents have a rival intellectual history to tell? What stopped them from forming a coalition with Vâsıf and his colleagues? Given what sources suggest about the breakdown of traditional frameworks and other devices of legitimation, and the absence of ready replacements, could it be that the Ottoman polity had at this date and in this guise simply become unworkable?

Ahmed Vâsıf serves an intellectual history of the late eighteenth- and early nineteenth-century Ottoman Empire because he was so personally invested in these issues. The youth from Baghdad grew into mature adulthood on the war front, in Istanbul and abroad, and witnessed the empire's failures from an often risky first-hand vantage; he survived successive sultans and governments, reformers and reactionaries, and reached old age as the voice of the most ambitious reform program ever attempted in the realm. It should come as no surprise that his career and written work convey the imprint of all of these changes, and that we must only take the trouble to learn his language, follow his arguments, and become sensitive to the nuances of his discourse to see the stakes and positions involved, on his side and others. Vâsıf in this way offers a panorama of élite Ottoman society during his lifetime, a microcosm of his world.

APPENDIX

On the Authorship of the *Final Word* to *Refute the Rabble*

One of the more intriguing works of political writing from the era of Sultan Selim III is the anonymous treatise the *Final Word to Refute the Rabble* (*Hulâsatü'l-Kelâm fî Reddi'l-'Avamm*), also known as the *Merits of the New Soldiery* (*Muhassenât-ı 'Asker-i Cedîd*), and popularly ascribed to a figure named Koca Sekbanbaşı.[1] The *Final Word* is of interest for several reasons. In content, it is a polemical attack on opponents of the New Order, Selim's military, fiscal, administrative, and social reforms, and so sheds light on arguments of the program's political and intellectual partisans, as well as those of its detractors. It is also refreshingly candid. Written in accessible Ottoman Turkish, the treatise takes the form of an imagined dialogue between the author and Janissary opponents whom he alternately coaxes and abuses, political screed that makes, quite frankly, for an entertaining read. Finally, the anonymous nature of the work is something of a puzzle. Who wrote it? Why? A convincing line of argument in recent years has turned toward our historian, Ahmed Vâsıf, the evidence for which I will briefly review and evaluate.

---

[1] The treatise has been published on several occasions: in Ottoman Turkish in the appendix to *TOEM* 37/42 (1910); in transliterated Ottoman in Hüseyin Namık Orkun, *Türk Hukuk Tarihi-Araştırmalar ve Düşünceler-Belgeler* (Ankara, 1935), 402–447; in transliterated Ottoman and modern Turkish in Abdullah Uçman, ed., *Sekbanbaşı Risalesi, Hulâsat el-Kelâm fi Red el-Avam* (Istanbul, 1975); in English translation in William Wilkinson, *An Account of the Principalities of Wallachia and Moldavia* (London, 1820), 216–294; and in French translation, based on the English, in *Tableau historique, géographique et politique de la Moldavie et de la Valachie* (Paris, 1821), 265–355. Unfortunately, no manuscript survey has been conducted or a standard text established. Kemal Beydilli intended to do a study of the work and its author but has, unfortunately, not yet published it. See his "Seyyid Mustafa," 388 n. 3. While I fully agree with Beydilli that it is not a "scholarly edition," I have used Uçman because it is the most widely accessible text.

The *Final Word* is a fairly short treatise – less than fifty folios in manuscript – with an enigmatic textual history. We know a few things about it with certainty. For example, internal evidence shows that it was composed on Selim's orders in the year 1803/4 (anno hegirae 1218) and that the author was very familiar with the sultan's reform program and with the workings of Ottoman bureaucracy. Although Ahmed Cevdet claimed that it was written by one "Koca Sekbanbaşı" to instruct the crown prince Mustafa, the work appears in content and tone to be propaganda aimed at rebutting the New Order's opponents rather than a more conventional mirror-for-princes. The author focuses on the Janissaries, with whom he engages in a combative dialogue and whom he both tries to win over through reason and berates, calling them "scum," "morons," "idiots," and other creative terms of abuse.[2]

Much less is clear about the identity of the author himself. While he makes a number of biographical claims in the work, including an age (eighty-seven years old), mention of two terms in Russian captivity, and a family connection to the Janissary corps, the value of this information has long been questioned by scholars. The last Ottoman court historian, Abdurrahman Şeref (d. 1925), ventured as early as 1917 that "no one has established who the author is, nor is it clear whether he was indeed a Janissary officer (*sekbanbaşı*) or some other intellectual or scribe."[3] There is one notable exception. The writer alleges that he was present in the Ottoman army during the summer of 1791 and participated in the mutiny at Maçin. This "Maçin Boycott," unprecedented in the empire's history, is documented in Chapter 5. After being routed that July, Grand Vizier Koca Yusuf Paşa began to negotiate with the Russians before being explicitly ordered back to the field by Selim. However, Yusuf Paşa's delegate had already signed a truce by the time these new instructions arrived. What is more, the other Ottoman officers defied the sultan and refused to comply. They then drew up a memorandum to justify their refusal, the Maçin petition, which they signed, sealed, and sent back to Istanbul. "Koca Sekbanbaşı" not only claims to have supported this boycott but, indeed, to have personally drafted the petition. The author

---

[2] The author himself says (HULÂSAT, 32) that "being ordered by His Majesty to write an essay, I composed this work in a short and simple style and called it 'A Final Word to Refute the Rabble'." Cf. Cevdet, *Târih*, 7: 289–290. Recent scholarship largely accepts the dating and rhetorical purposes of the work: e.g. Aksan, "Ottoman Political Writing," 38 ff.; Beydilli, "Islâhât Düşünceleri," 29, 35; Şakul, "Nizâm-ı Cedîd," 131–135; and DİA, s. v. "Koca Sekbanbaşı Risâlesi."

[3] *Hulâsatü'l-Kelâm fî Reddi'l-'Avamm*, ÖN H.O. nr. 220, insert to text.

of one work is therefore the author of both. When added together, these clues point to a partisan of reform in Selim's bureaucracy, who was with the imperial army at Maçin in 1791 and still active in the years 1803/4.[4]

Scholars over the years have proposed several candidates as the author of the *Final Word*, some more plausible than others. The work's near-contemporary English translator, William Wilkinson, attributed it to a certain "Tshelebi-Effendi, one of the chief dignitaries of the Ottoman Empire, Counsellor, Minister of State, &c." This name is largely meaningless – Çelebi and Efendi both signifying a "gentleman" in Turkish – but it does indicate that he, Wilkinson, did not take the work's biographical claims at face value. The modern scholar Niyazi Berkes believed that by "Tshelebi-Effendi," Wilkinson meant a specific figure: Köse Kethüda Çelebi Mustafa Reşîd Efendi (d. 1819), a statesman whose candidacy I will explore below.[5]

Another suggestion comes from a manuscript at the Austrian National Library in Vienna. Copied in the first half of the nineteenth century, Cod. H.O. 220 bears a flyleaf inscription declaring the work to be "the treatise that the late Hoca Münib Efendi composed" on the New Order reforms.[6] Ayıntâbî Mehmed Münib Efendi (d. 1823) was an influential religious scholar, judge, and poet during and after Selim's reign who held posts in the upper ranks of the ulema and wrote works of law, prosody, and biography. But could he have been Koca Sekbanbaşı? The German orientalist Franz Babinger thought so. Presumably using this manuscript, Babinger credited the treatise to Münib in his still widely consulted *Die Geschichtsschreiber der Osmanen und ihre Werke*.[7] However, Cod. H.O. 220 also contains an insert by the historian Abdurrahman Şeref that refutes Münib's authorship. Dated July 2, 1917, the note remarks that "while this treatise is attributed to Hoca Münib Efendi, it is known to history as that of Koca Sekbanbaşı."

No one has established who the author is, nor is it clear whether he was indeed a Janissary officer or some other intellectual or scribe. And if one considers that he says seven or eight lines from the end of the work, "I had reached my eighty-seventh year," the attribution to Hoca Münib Efendi, who did not live a long life, cannot be correct.[8]

---

[4] HULÂSAT, 61. Beydilli stresses the importance of this Maçin petition in "Islâhât Düşünceleri," 30; and in DİA, s.v. "Nizâm-ı Cedîd."

[5] Wilkinson, 216. Cf. Niyazi Berkes, *Türkiye'de Çağdaşlaşma* (Ankara, 1973), 502 n. 99.

[6] ÖN H.O. nr. 220, fol. 1a.   [7] GOW, 344 f.

[8] Şeref signed this insert (in ÖN H.O. nr. 220) and dated it according to the solar calendar to 2 Temmuz 1917 = July 2, 1917.

Şeref's "proof" against Münib is insufficient, as he trusted that the author gave his real age. The superannuated Koca Sekbanbaşı was more likely a fiction. Yet Münib was not in the imperial camp at Maçin in 1791 and could not have written the boycott petition. Nor is there strong evidence linking him to Selim's bureaucracy and reforms. In fact, some sources allege that while Münib benefited from the sultan's patronage, he opposed the New Order and aided the revolt that took him from power in 1807, or at least acquiesced to the rebels.[9]

In a recent article, the Turkish scholar Ali Birinci proposed yet another figure as the alter ego of Koca Sekbanbaşı, this time a military man named Tokatlı Mustafa Ağa. Birinci came to this judgment by combing the lists of Janissary officers, whom he then tried to match with the work's internal biographical information. His choice fell on Mustafa Ağa, a two-time Janissary Ağa who died in 1805 at the age of eighty-seven. This suggestion is highly doubtful, however, for Birinci not only failed to consult a number of sources, but uncritically accepted the author's claims about his own identity. A thorough critique by Kemal Beydilli has since demolished the argument, leaving us with little reason to accept Tokatlı Mustafa Ağa as the work's author.[10]

A more plausible choice is the above-said Köse Kethüda Çelebi Mustafa Reşîd Efendi. Reşîd is a strong candidate. A ranking minister and adviser to Selim, for whom he wrote a reform memo in 1791, he was at the Maçin boycott as the Grand Vizier's steward (*kethüdâ-yı sadr-ı âli*) and later served as the director of the special treasury dedicated to the New Order reforms (*defterdâr-ı irâd-ı cedîd*). Reşîd was a known partisan of reform who was still alive and active in 1803/4 and was highly informed about the Ottoman bureaucracy. He thus meets all the requirements for authorship. It is not surprising that scholars like Berkes, and at times Beydilli, have considered him to be the man behind Koca Sekbanbaşı, a case most recently made by Hakan Erdem. Erdem argues that, while no internal evidence links Reşîd to Koca Sekbanbaşı, he is the most likely candidate and even fits the tract's biographical details. "In my opinion, the two carriers perfectly tally with each other

---

[9] On Münib see DİA, s.v. "Ayıntâbî, Mehmed Münîb." Also Yıldız, esp. 457–472, 689–692. Münib wrote the famous *Hüccet-i Şeriyye*, a legal affidavit that justified Selim's deposition and denounced his reforms. He also appears to have collaborated generally with the rebels.

[10] Ali Birinci, "Koca Sekbanbaşı Risalesi'nin Müellifi Tokatlı Mustafa Ağa (1131–1219)," in *Prof. Dr. İsmail Aka Armağanı* (Izmir, 1999), 105–120. Cf. Kemal Beydilli, "Evreka, Evreka veya Errare Humanum Est," *İlmî Araştırmalar Dergisi* 9 (2000): 45–66.

and Koca Sekbanbaşı is perhaps a pseudonym for Mustafa Reşid," Erdem writes.

Koca Sekbanbaşı's hint that he had been a high ranking official since 1768/69 corresponds exactly with the date of the first important appointment of Mustafa Reşid when he became the official in charge of Istanbul *mukataas*. Similarly, Mustafa Reşid, too, could have claimed to have been associated with the Janissaries on two counts. His father was most probably a Janissary and he himself was at one point Secretary of the Janissary Regiments ... Therefore, it is possible that it was he, as the ex-Secretary of the Janissaries and the new Steward of the Grand Vizier, who wrote it.[11]

Erdem relies in this judgment on a partial draft of the *Final Word*, which he uncovered in the Ottoman archives in Istanbul and which he claims to be annotated by the author. This document is of interest, as it contains twenty marginal notes commenting on the text, at times in strong language, and also two dates: anno hegirae 1222 and Muharrem 1222. If indeed an author's copy, the document would thus prove key in resolving Koca Sekbanbaşı's identity.[12] It would serve to disqualify Ahmed Vâsıf, for example, an even stronger candidate who died a few months earlier in October 1806 (Şaban AH 1221). But it is far from certain that the notes are the author's. For one thing, as Erdem admits, they are not incorporated into any other copies of the *Final Word*, which one would expect if they indeed belonged to him. They also read less as additions than glosses on the text. In the third note, the annotator responds to the passage, "What need is there for these new troops of the *Nizâm-ı Cedîd*? There were no New Order forces when the House of Osman conquered the world with the sword!" He writes: "This is true. But in those times the infidel could also not load and fire fifteen cannon rounds per minute!"[13] The eighth note comments on the text's criticism of the Janissaries and their behavior on campaign, "Prove that you have acquitted yourselves or rendered the least service to our faith and sovereign." Here the annotator writes: "They are even at present thus, Muharrem AH 1222."[14] Finally, Erdem incorrectly assumes that the *Final Word* itself dates from AH 1222 or 1807/8 and that the partial copy and notes were prepared for Selim III for his approval. In fact, we know from the evidence mentioned above that the work was actually drafted in AH 1218 or 1803/4. Why, years later,

---

[11] Erdem, esp. 159–162. Beydilli gives a guarded assent to Reşîd Efendi in "Seyyid Mustafa," 388 n. 3. He has since revised his opinion. See also Şakul, "Nizâm-ı Cedîd," 132. For Mustafa Reşîd's life and career, see Yıldız, 853–854.

[12] Erdem, 164–165. The document is BOA.HAT 48106/48106-A.

[13] BOA.HAT 48106-A, marginal note 3.   [14] Ibid, marginal note 8.

would the author have made such notations for the sultan? If they are his additions, why do they not appear in later copies? It seems more likely that the notes are not the author's at all, but the jottings of an engaged, sympathetic reader.

Mustafa Reşîd has never been fully ruled out as the treatise's author. However, the best single piece of evidence yet uncovered points to another figure, Reşîd's colleague Ahmed Vâsıf. Vâsıf too meets all the requirements. His service in the Ottoman bureaucracy as a scribe, court historian, and ambassador, his open support for Selim's reform program, and his activity up to and past 1803/4 are all treated above. He was likewise at Maçin in 1791, returning from truce talks with the Russian general Nikolai Repnin on the very day that the boycott began. Vâsıf's involvement in both the Maçin petition and the *Final Word* is attested by a later author, Sahaflar Şeyhizâde Esad Efendi (d. 1848), in his celebratory account of Mahmud II's 1826 destruction of the Janissary corps, the *Roots of Victory*, or *Üss-i Zafer*. As shown by Beydilli, Esad quotes from the *Final Word* on the Maçin boycott and the New Order force's performance against Napoléon at the Battle of Acre and against Rumelian rebels, attributing authorship to Vâsıf in three places. In the first, he refers to Maçin as "that strange affair the late historian Vâsıf recorded," and says that "the same historian also relates that he personally wrote the said petition." Esad prefaces two later extended quotations from the work with the words, "as Vâsıf Efendi writes in his essay on the *Merits of the New Soldiery*" and "the historian Vâsıf narrates the following disaster in his essay." These attributions are explicit and carry great weight. It is no surprise that in recent years, scholars have more and more accepted Vâsıf as the man behind Koca Sekbanbaşı.[15]

While the weight of evidence points to Ahmed Vâsıf as the author of the *Final Word*, it is worthwhile to look for further clues. After all, Esad Efendi's attribution, while powerful, remains only one puzzle piece and is not necessarily decisive. We may also examine Vâsıf's case in light of some new considerations. These items are also far from definitive, but they serve

---

[15] See Esad, *Üss-i Zafer*, 119–120, 122, 124. Cf. HULÂSAT, 53, 61, 63–65, 81–87. Although A.P. Caussin de Perceval included these passages in his French translation (*Précis historique de la destruction du corps des Janissaries par le sultan Mahmoud, en 1826* [Paris, 1833], 240–241, 252), they escaped notice for over 150 years. Beydilli was the first to note them in "Sekbanbaşı Risalesi'nin Müellifi Hakkında," *Türk Kültürü İncelemeleri Dergisi* 12 (2005): 221–224. Since his article, scholars have begun to accept the connection. See, for example, Christine Philliou, *Biography of an Empire: Governing Ottomans in an Age of Revolution* (Berkeley CA, 2011), 189 n. 18, 206 n. 47; and DİA, s.v. "Vâsıf Ahmed Efendi."

on the whole to strengthen the claim that the court historian wrote the treatise. They can be split into three categories: further attributions of authorship, textual clues from Vâsıf's own writings, and close parallels between his ideas and those of "Koca Sekbanbaşı."

I have found at least two other direct attributions to Vâsıf in manuscripts of the *Final Word*. Ms.orient.oct. 3119 in the Berlin State Library's Oriental collection is an early and complete copy of the work with a colophon date of AH 1225 or 1810/11, collated with the contemporary tract *Kuşmânî on the Divinely Inspired Order* (*Zebîre-i Kuşmânî fî Tarîf-i Nizâm-ı İlhâmî*) by Dihkânîzâde Ubeydullah Kuşmânî. The *Final Word* occupies folios 54b to 83b of the manuscript. On folio 54a, just before the text, a hand different from the copyist has added: "The following treatise is the work of the late historian Ahmed Vâsıf Efendi's pen."[16] More interesting is a second attribution, found in the Atatürk Library's Muallim Cevdet collection in Istanbul. Manuscript K.228 once belonged to the historian Ahmed Cevdet Paşa. It dates from the mid to late nineteenth century and bears a note in the incipit page reading, "Vâsıf Efendi's *Final Word*."[17] This note is doubly significant because it drew a lengthy reply from Cevdet. "I once saw and studied a partial copy of this work in the papers of the late Ârif Hikmet Efendi," he wrote in the margin. "Judging by marginal notes left by certain persons the essay cannot be Vâsıf's, nor does its simple style resemble his prose. The said notes are also written in red in this copy's margins below." Cevdet then disputed the attribution in more detail:

While it is clear that two people wrote these comments, we do not know who they were. Passages in the original differ from those of this copy. It is thus possible that Vâsıf Efendi intended to create a new work by altering or amending certain parts. As for the author, he enlisted in the Janissaries during the reign of the late sultan Mahmud I, served for many years in the corps, and was promoted under Abdülhamid I to *sekbanbaşı* and died in 1804/5. The essay was written in reply to a letter that the crown prince Mustafa had sent to the wise Koca Sekbanbaşı.

To stress his point, Cevdet also crossed out the rubricated attribution to Vâsıf.[18]

---

[16] Staatsbibliothek zu Berlin Orientabteilung, Ms.orient.oct. nr. 3119, fol. 54a. See also Hanna Sohrweide, ed., *Türkische Handschriften, Verzeichnis der orientalische Handschriften in Deutschland* vol. 13, no. 5 (Weisbaden, 1981), 124: "von anderer Hand der Vermark, daß Vâsıf Efendi, wohl der 1221/1806–7 gestorbene Reichshistoriker, Autor der Schrift sei."

[17] Atatürk Kitaplığı, Muallim Cevdet Yazmaları nr. K.228, fol. 1b.

[18] Ibid, fols. 1a–1b. The copy contains red marginalia that refer to events after the death of Selim III and cannot belong to Vâsıf, but also corrections in black in at least two hands. The text is also noteworthy in that it lacks the usual concluding section on the New Order

These two attributions – perhaps three, if we count Cevdet's reference to an "original copy" – are of course not decisive. We cannot know when, by whom, or in what circumstances they were added to the manuscripts. The annotators may have been relying on Esad Efendi's statements in the *Roots of Victory* or on other independent sources of information. As we have also seen in the case of Münib Efendi, Ottoman readers sometimes got matters wrong. Still, the further attributions show that rumors of Vâsıf's authorship circled among readers from an early date, only two or three decades after his death. Nineteenth-century Ottomans were closer chronologically and culturally to the work than us and clearly felt that this idea was plausible. Some did not, however. The fact that Cevdet so strenuously objected and ascribed the work to "Koca Sekbanbaşı," both in the manuscript and in his own history, is telling. He knew of, but did not believe, the claims about Vâsıf's authorship.

More clues emerge from a textual comparison of the *Final Word* with Vâsıf's larger corpus of work. None of his writings have so far yielded a direct connection to the essay, though this is perhaps due to the volume of his output – thousands of pages on history, politics, poetry, ethics, and literature – nor have I found any reference to the *Final Word* in Vâsıf's papers, which contain drafts of his history, petitions, and fragments of poetry and have been neglected till now. It may be that I have missed something that will at last settle the question. However, for the time being, we can isolate certain passages that express similar ideas or are in close parallel. Several examples will suffice. In a portion of his history from 1794, Vâsıf boasted of how the Barbary corsairs terrified their Christian enemies, an observation that he said his time as ambassador in Spain confirmed. "The enemy's innate fear of the Algerians is obvious. I saw during my embassy how the Spaniards even quiet their children when they cry by saying things like, 'The Algerians are coming!'" The author of the *Final Word* used similar language to make a like point. "From the beginning the enemies of the faith were extreme cowards, timid and craven," he said. "They had never been able to withstand Muslim power, insomuch that they were wont to frighten their bastards in the cradle by saying, 'The Muslims are coming!'"[19]

Vâsıf and "Koca Sekbanbaşı" share a common ideological framework, as well. As treated above, Vâsıf by the 1790s began to see reform as a function

---

treasury and ends with an *istihrâcnâme*, a long poem that acts as a huge chronogram and yields the date AH 1313 or 1895/96.

[19] MEHÂSİN 2, fol. 50b. Cf. HULÂSAT, 74–75.

of the principle of "reciprocation" or *mukâbele bi'l-misl*. The Ottomans had grown powerful by borrowing tools and weapons from their enemies, he held, and only "declined" in power when they ceased to adapt; the Christian powers, on the other hand, avidly adopted Ottoman tactics and improved upon them. They thus developed a "new science of war" and gained decisive military advantage. "Koca Sekbanbaşı" argued along nearly the same lines. His historically inaccurate description of the Janissary corps – in his opinion a foundation of Süleyman I – is a case study in the effects of reciprocation and its implication: that Ottomans must innovate and adapt if they are to restore the empire's glory. Interestingly, Vâsıf and "Koca Sekbanbaşı" also linked the disorder (*fesâd*) that Selim's reforms were meant to remedy to the French Revolution. Both insisted that the chaos was not localized in the empire; it had spread around the world. "Koca Sekbanbaşı" wrote that "Disorder has broken out in France and they are eating each other's flesh. The Christian kings have declared war on the French and campaigned for ten or fifteen years ... But, you see, such troubles are not confined to Europe alone. Neither India, China, Arabia, Persia, nor the New World are now lacking in disorder and carnage." The chaos had likewise infected the European parts of the empire.[20] Vâsıf largely agreed: "The present disorder is not restricted to Muslim realms," he wrote. "The French sedition has spread far and wide in the habitable world; all countries have been affected territorially and economically and all inhabitants have suffered in one way or another."[21]

In sum, Vâsıf's authorship of the *Final Word* is not entirely certain and based mostly on circumstantial evidence. The work is anonymous. The author also makes biographical claims that are at odds with the historian's life and career. Yet there is good reason to believe, as did many contemporary Ottomans, that the author was no Janissary, but a member of Selim III's camarilla. Of the figures put forward, moreover, Vâsıf supplies compelling textual parallels; he best fits the text's underlying ideological framework; and he is explicitly credited with the essay by several later authors and readers. While more facts may well come to light, then, he is for the time being our most likely candidate for "Koca Sekbanbaşı."

[20] HULÂSAT, 35.   [21] MEHÂSİN 3, fol. 213a.

Glossary

Adab, Trk. *edeb*: Proper conduct or politesse. Refinement and training esp. in

1. A literary canon of humane, urbane subjects like history, poetry, proverbs, and witticisms as a prerequisite for scribal service.
2. Moral norms based on the Persianate ethical tradition of *hikmet-i 'ameliyye* (q.v.).

'Adâlet: Justice or equity. Ottomans sought personal justice in the systematic study of virtue; they saw political justice as an equitable balance in the social estates that formed *nizâm-ı 'âlem* (q.v.) or the "order of the world."

'Âdatullah, Trk. *'âdetüllah*: "God's custom." The idea that God chooses to make worldly events occur regularly as if by cause and effect. Miracles happen when God breaks this custom.

Ağa: Lord or master; a title given to ranking members of the palace service and military.

Akçe: Asper; a silver coin debased and out of use by the eighteenth century.

'Âlim: Singular of ulema (q.v.).

Amedî: Receiver. A bureau chief who handled ingoing and outgoing communications, the chief scribe's and chief steward's reports, and the Grand Vizier's correspondence with the sultan. A top chancery post in the late eighteenth century.

Anadolu muhâsebecisi: Anatolian accounts officer. A treasury scribe in charge of receipts for tax farms, pious foundations, and customs dues. In the eighteenth century, he also oversaw monies for troops and pensioners in the Aegean.

277

'Aql: Intellect or reason. In Islamic tradition, the part of the human soul that knows or thinks.

'Askerî: The ruling élite who protected the *re'âyâ* (q.v.) and paid no taxes. While traditionally "military" in origin, this group by the eighteenth century included soldiers as well as judges, jurists, scholars, and scribes.

A'yân: A notable or grandee. In the eighteenth century, it referred to

1. A man of influence in the provinces, elected by his community to act for the whole in matters of taxes, security, and local governance. A broker between center and periphery.
2. One of the quasi-independent rulers who arose in the Balkans in the late eighteenth century, at times founding dynasties or carving out petty fiefdoms; by and by a warlord, local leader, bandit, rebel, governor, fiscal agent, and entrepreneur.

Bâb-ı Âli: Sublime Porte. A name for the Grand Vizier's offices and, by extension, the Ottoman bureaucracy as a whole.

Baş muhâsebeci: Chief of the general accounts office. A treasury official tasked with most of the realm's income and expenditure. Third in rank after the treasurer and keeper of the daily ledger.

Bektaşî: A heterodox Sufi *tarîkat* (q.v.) closely associated with the Janissary corps.

Bey: A title for military commanders, governors, or the sons of viziers; popularly, any person of wealth or distinction.

Beylikçi: Director of the imperial council. An officer in charge of drafting and issuing all council decisions, orders, and edicts. A chancery bureau chief directly under the chief scribe.

Bî'at: see *cülûs*.

Bid'a: Religiously illicit innovation.

Büyük kale tezkirecisi: First fortifications officer. A minor treasury post that kept the rolls on the appointments and pay of the empire's garrisons.

Büyük rûznâmçe: Keeper of the daily ledger. A treasury bureau chief responsible for monies from the poll-tax, tax farms, pious trusts, and pensions. Second in rank only to the treasurer.

Çelebi: An honorary title given to clerks, scholars, bureaucrats, and other men of refinement.

Cizye muhâsebecisi: Head of the poll-tax accounts office. A minor treasury agent whose job was to prepare receipts for the collection of the capitation or poll-tax on non-Muslims.

Cülûs: The imperial accession, attended by certain fixed rituals. It included an enthronement in the second courtyard of the palace and ceremonial oaths of allegiance, or *bî'at* (q.v.). The sultan later traveled to Eyüp for the *taklîd-i seyf* (q.v.), to be girded with the so-called Sword of Osman.

Damad: Son-in-law; especially, a son-in-law of the sultan.

Dâr al-ḥarb: "Realm of war." A juridical concept signifying all lands outside the pale of Islam.

Dâr al-Islâm: "Realm of Islam." Lands under the rule of Islamic law.

Defterdâr: Treasurer. A high-ranking bureau chief and the chief financial officer of the empire.

Dîn ü devlet: "Faith and dynasty"; or less accurately, religion and state. A concept expressing the incorporation of an Islamic community in the Ottoman polity as well as subjects' loyalty thereto.

Divân: 1. The imperial council or other deliberative decision-making organs.
2. An anthology of poems arranged alphabetically and by form.

Edîb: A littérateur or intellectual versed in the corpus of *adab* (q.v., def. 1).

Efendi: Lord; a title of respect for scribes and scholars. Popularly, a gentleman.

Ehven-i şerreyn: The "lesser of two evils." Juristic preference that allows illicit actions in a state of duress or *zarûret* (q.v.).

Elçi: Ambassador.

Esbâb-ı zâhire: Visible or "secondary" causes. The apparent causal relationship between worldly events that follows *'âdatullah* (q.v.).

Farz: An obligatory act in Islamic law. It is divided into two major types:

1. *Farz-ı 'ayn*, a duty incumbent on every member of the Islamic community.
2. *Farz-ı kifâye*, a duty discharged by a part of the community for the whole, e.g. burying the dead or, under normal circumstances, jihad.

Ghazâ: War for the faith.

Ghazi: One who fights for Islam or pursues *ghazâ*.

Gurebâ-yı yesâr kâtibi: Secretary to the left-wing cavalry. A scribe attached to a corps of cavalry that guarded the army camp and train.

Hacegân: The upper-most echelon in the chancery and treasury; the level of bureau chiefs.

Halîfe: Junior clerk in a bureaucratic office, under the supervision of a bureau chief.

Halvetî: A Sufi order given to ascetic practices; popular in earlier centuries and closely linked to the dynasty.

Hikmet: "Philosophy" or "wisdom." A field of knowledge covering all things in their essence, both in mind and substance. It is usually split into two subgroups:

1. *Hikmet-i nazariyye*, or speculative philosophy, which deals with "pure" knowledge and fields beyond human volition, e.g. physics, metaphysics, mathematics, or astronomy.
2. *Hikmet-i 'ameliyye*, or practical philosophy, which deals with "applied" knowledge and fields within human volition, e.g. ethics, household economy, and politics.

'Ilmiyye: The learned religious institution; the ulema hierarchy of judges, jurists, jurisconsults, and *medrese* (q.v.) teachers. Led by the *şeyhülislâm* (q.v.).

İntisâb: "Connections"; a relationship of mutual benefit and obligation between a patron and protégé.

İrâde: Will, volition, free will. In philosophy, a faculty belonging to both humans and God as:

1. *İrâde-i cüziyye*, or particular will, imperfect human volition that relies on God's will.
2. *İrâde-i külliyye*, or universal will, God's volition as the *musabbib al-asbâb* (q.v.) and ultimate cause of all events in creation.

İstidrâc: Divine trial. In theology, when God grants infidels success to lead them to damnation and test believers' faith.

Jabriyya/mujbira: Fatalists or predestinarians.

Kâğıd-ı birûn emini: Director of the outer documentation office. A low-level bureau chief who supplied the treasury with writing supplies.

Kalemiyye: The bureaucracy; the scribal establishment divided into chancery and treasury.

Kalyonlar kâtibi: Galley scribe. An official in the arsenal who kept records and victualed ships.

Kânûn: 1. Dynastic law based on customary usage or decree and issued by royal prerogative, as a supplement to holy law.
2. The phrase *kânûn-ı kadîm*, "ancient practice," refers to legal and institutional usages that (in theory) ensured *nizâm-ı 'âlem* (q.v.) and the realm's integrity.

Kapudan-ı deryâ: Grand Admiral. The top-ranking officer in the Ottoman navy.

Kapu halkı: A great man's extended household.

Kapu kethüdâsı: Chief usher at the palace or in a vizierial household.

Kasb, Trk. *kesb*: "Acquisition." In Islamic theology, the idea that humans accept and "acquire" moral responsibility for acts created by God.

Kâtib: Scribe or clerk.

Kawn wa fasâd, Trk. *kevn ü fesâd*: "Generation and corruption." The process of creation where God at every moment creates, recreates, joins, and separates the universe's atoms. The basis of Islamic atomism/occasionalism.

Kese: "Purse." A unit of treasury account equal to 500 *kuruş* (q.v.) or 60,000 *akçe* (q.v.).

Kızıl elma: "Red Apple." A phrase referring in the eighteenth century to

1. A distant, mythical goal of conquest.
2. A byword for world domination.
3. The legendary and largely unstated place where Ottoman conquests would end.

Kızlar ağası: Chief black eunuch; keeper of the imperial harem. An influential palace figure in the mid-eighteenth century.

Kul: 1. "Slave," esp. recruited from the empire's subjects in the so-called "blood-tax" or *devşirme*. This sense was obsolete by the eighteenth century.
2. Any servant of the empire or royal household.

Kuruş: Piaster; the main silver coin during the eighteenth century, equal to 120 *akçe* (q.v.).

Mahlas: Pen name; a nom de plume.

Malikâne: Fief or lifetime freehold. Property transferred from the crown to a private person.

Mamlûk: "Slave," esp. military slaves that formed households and self-perpetuating ruling élites in Egypt, the Levant, and Mesopotamia.

Mecmû'a: Miscellany.

Medrese: A "college." A place of higher learning for religious disciplines and especially for training in the law.

Mekteb: Quran school; a school for the basics of Arabic literacy and grammar.

Mektûbî: Correspondence officer. A bureau chief who oversaw the Grand Vizier's confidential documents; in the eighteenth century, a prestigious figure under the chief scribe.

Mevkûfâtçı: Head of the suspended payments office. A treasury scribe in charge of property in mortmain trust as well as salaries in abeyance.

Mevlevî: A Sufi order; followers of Mawlânâ Jalâl al-Dîn Rûmî (d. 1273) famed for music and dancing. Also known as "Whirling Dervishes."

Mübâşir: An adjutant; an agent.

Müceddid: "Renewer." A figure who promised to end *bid'a* (q.v.) and restore the practice of the early Muslim community. See also *sâhib-i mia*.

Muhâsebe-i evvel: see *baş muhâsebeci*.

Mukâbele bi'l-misl: "Reciprocation." A legal concept that allowed Muslims to adopt an enemy's weapons, tactics, or technology to use against him.

Mukâleme kâtibi: Secretary to negotiations.

Münşeat: Epistolary manual.

Musabbib al-asbâb: "Causer of causes." A term referring to God as the creator of all events in the universe and as the higher cause of visible, secondary causes. See also *esbâb-ı zâhire*.

Müsâdere: Confiscation; expropriation. A legal prerogative held by sultans over their *kul* (q.v.).

Nakşbendî: A politically active Sufi order. Founded in Central Asia and widely popular among eighteenth-century reformers and bureaucrats.

Nizâm: Order, regime, regulation. A key political term used in several senses:

1. *Nizâm-ı 'âlem*, the "order of the world." A metaphysical concept expressing the whole of moral and political relations in just, harmonious balance.
2. *Nizâm-ı devlet/mülk*, "order of the dynasty/realm"; order in a strictly political sense.
3. *Nizâm-ı cedîd*, "New Order." Selim III's program of military, administrative, and fiscal reform.

Ordu kâdısı: Judge advocate for the army.

Paşa: A title given to viziers, governors, and high-ranking military commanders.

Qadariyya: Supporters of the idea of free will.

Re'âyâ: "Flock." Muslim and non-Muslim taxpaying subjects.

Reisülküttâb: Chief scribe; head of the chancery. In the eighteenth century, the chief scribe also directed the empire's foreign relations.

Sadaret kethüdâsı: The Grand Vizier's steward and chief deputy.

Sâhib-i mia: Centennial reformer; a *müceddid* (q.v.) who appeared at the turn of the century to restore the Muslim community.

Şân-ı devlet: The realm's "honor," esp. in the conduct of war and peace.

Sefâretnâme: Embassy report.

Serasker: A military commander-in-chief.

Seyfiyye: The military hierarchy, including soldiers, viziers, commanders, and governors.

Şeyhülislâm: Chief jurisconsult or mufti of the empire; head of the *'ilmiyye* (q.v.) and appointed directly by the sultan.

Silâhdar: Sword-bearer. A high-ranking page in the imperial palace.

Sırkâtibi: Privy scribe or secretary.

Siyâset: Rule, policy, governance. A term used in the following senses:

1. Punishment, esp. capital punishment.
2. Political rule as such, which might be "virtuous (*siyâset-i fâzıla*)" or "vicious (*siyâset-i nâkısa*)."
3. Types of political régimes, e.g. those based on divinely revealed law (*siyâset-i dîniyye / ilâhiyye*), human reason (*siyâset-i 'akliyye*), or a combination thereof.

Sufi: Muslim dervish or mystic.

Taklîd-i seyf: see *cülûs*.

Tarîkat: "Path"; a Sufi dervish order.

Tevkî'î: Chancellor; also called *nişâncı*. Formerly the highest figure in the imperial chancery. Overshadowed in the eighteenth century by the chief scribe.

Timâr: Prebend or military fief. A grant of usufruct from state lands or revenue sources worth less than 20,000 *akçe*.

Ulema: Plural of *'âlim* (q.v.). The bookmen, teachers, scholars, judges, jurists, and jurisconsults that staffed the realm's *'ilmiyye* (q.v.).

'Ulûm-ı 'akliyye: "Rational sciences." Fields of learning based on ratiocination, e.g. logic, philosophy, mathematics, and astronomy.

'Ulûm-ı nakliyye: "Transmitted sciences." Fields based on transmission from a source and taught in the *medrese* (q.v.), e.g. traditions, law, and exegesis.

Umûr-ı cüziyye: "Particular events." In theology, an event in which humans can exert their imperfect will or *irâde-i cüziyye* (q.v.).

Umûr-ı külliyye: "Universal events." An event linked to divine preordination that is beyond the influence of human volition.

Vekâyi'nüvis: Court historian. In the eighteenth century, a salaried official who wrote the empire's history in regular installments; usually a scribe or *'âlim* (q.v.).

Yamak: An auxiliary soldier.

Zarûret: Duress. A legal state whose presence permits illicit acts. See *ehven-i şerreyn*.

Zeamet: A type of *timâr* (q.v.) grant worth between 20,000 and 99,999 *akçe*.

Bibliography

WORKS BY AHMED VÂSIF

(N.B. This is not a full list. I give the main copies I have used with small letters and other copies or translations with roman numerals)

1. *Cedîd Atlas Tercümesi* (ATLAS)
   a) Râif, Mahmud. Tabhâne-i Hümâyûn, Istanbul, 1804.
2. *Divân*
   a) İÜ İbnülemin nr. 3692.
3. *Gazavât-ı Hüseyin Paşa* (GAZAVÂT)
   a) ÖN Cod. H.O. nr. 205.
4. *Hulâsatü'l-Kelâm fî Reddi'l-Avâm* (HULÂSAT)
   a) Uçman, Abdullah, ed. *Sekbanbaşı Risalesi, Hulâsat el-Kelâm fî Red el-Avam*. Istanbul, 1975.
      i) ÖN Cod. H.O. nr. 220.
      ii) Staatsbibliothek zu Berlin, Ms.orient.oct. nr. 3119, fols. 54b-83b.
      iii) Atatürk Kitaplığı, Muallim Cevdet Yazmaları nr. K.228.
      iv) In *TOEM*, suppl. volume.
      v) Orkun, Hüseyin Namık. *Türk Hukuk Tarihi-Araştırmalar ve Düşünceler-Belgeler*. Ankara, 1935. 402–447.
      vi) Wilkinson, William, trans. *An Account of the Principalities of Wallachia and Moldavia*. London, 1820. 216–294.
      vii) idem. *Tableau historique, géographique et politique de la Moldavie et de la Valachie*. Paris, 1821.
5. *Mehâsinü'l-Âsâr ve Hakâikü'l-Ahbâr*
   a) İstanbul Arkeoloji Müzesi Kütüphanesi nr. 355 (MEHÂSİN 1) (AD 1783–1787)
      i) İlgürel, Mücteba, ed. Istanbul, 1978. (İLGÜREL)
      ii) Staatsbibliothek zu Berlin, Ms.or.quart. nr. 1116.
   b) İÜ TY nr. 5978 (MEHÂSİN 2) (AD 1789–1794)
      i) Millet Kütüphanesi, Ali Emiri nr. 608.
      ii) BnF, Supplément turc nr. 508.

iii) TSMK Hazine nr. 1638.
c) İÜ TY nr. 5979 (MEHÂSİN 3) (AD 1794–1800)
   i) Sarıkaya, Hüseyin, ed. "Ahmed Vâsıf Efendi ve *Mehâsinü'l-Âsâr ve Hakâîkü'l-Ahbâr'ı*, 1209–1219/1794–1805." Ph.D. diss., Istanbul University, 2013.
d) İÜ TY nr. 6013 (MEHÂSİN 4) (AD 1800–1805)
   i) İÜ TY nr. 6012.
e) Istanbul, Tabhâne-i Hümâyûn, 1804. 2 vols. (MEHÂSİN 5) (AD 1752–1774)
   i) İÜ TY nr. 5972.
   ii) TSMK Hazine nr. 1405.
   iii) Caussin de Perceval, Armand-Pierre, trans. *Précis historique de la guerre des Turcs contre les Russes depuis l'année 1769 jusq'uà l'année 1774, tiré des annales de l'historien Turc Vassif-Efendi.* Paris, 1822.
f) TSMK Hazine nr. 1406 (MEHÂSİN 6) (AD 1774–1779)
6. *Müşkilât-ı Lugat-ı Vaşşâf*
   a) TSMK Hazine nr. 1448.
7. *Râhibnâme* (RÂHİBNÂME)
   a) TSMK Hazine nr. 386.
   i) Atatürk Kitaplığı, Muallim Cevdet nr. 49.
   ii) No publisher, Istanbul, 1873.
8. *Sefâretnâme* (SEFÂRETNÂME)
   a) TSMK Hazine nr. 1438, fols. 327b-354b.
   i) Menchinger, Ethan L., trans. "The Sefaretnâme of Ahmed Vâsıf Efendi to Spain (Ahmed Vâsıf Efendi'nin İspanya'ya Dair Sefaretnâmesi)." *Uluslararası Tarih Araştırmaları Dergisi* 2:4 (2010): 263–279.
   ii) Barbier de Meynard, A.C., trans. "Ambassade de l'historien turc Vaçif-Efendi en Espagne (1787–1788); traduit sur la relation originale." *Journal Asiatique* 5/19 (1862): 505–523.
9. *Tercüme-i Şerh-i Nevâbigü'l-Kelim* (NEVÂBİG)
   a) Süleymaniye Kütüphanesi, Pertev Paşa nr. 387.
10. *Tesliyetnâme* (TESLİYETNÂME)
   a) TSMK Hazine nr. 1625.
   i) Süleymaniye Kütüphanesi, Serez nr. 1890.

ARCHIVAL SOURCES

1. BOA, Istanbul
   a) A.DVNS.NMH.d 9
   b) AE.Abd 414, 532, 762, 884, 1064, 1216, 1487, 8795, 9384, 23342, 25728
   c) AE.Slm 4889, 5710, 9428, 9539, 11250, 11729, 11733, 12590, 12688, 12874, 14812, 14913, 14924, 14932, 15409, 17164

   d) A.RSK.d 1593, 1623
   e) C.ADL 681, 1583, 3682, 6334
   f) C.DH 1563, 1632, 2546
   g) C.HR 140, 930, 1285, 2548, 2938, 5748, 7849
   h) C.MF 939, 975, 2478, 3963, 8581
   i) C.ML 2052, 16852, 19478, 20656, 21110, 23317, 27701, 29999
   j) C.TZ 5558, 6637, 8476
   k) D.BŞM.d 4322, 5486, 6866, 7370
   l) HAT 19, 35, 1681, 2179, 4822, 5004, 5094, 5150, 8283, 10467, 11082,
        11187, 11579, 12436, 12474, 12526, 13135, 13274, 13652, 13957,
        14400, 14672, 14683, 14883, 15168, 15246, 15595, 15766, 24889,
        25708, 31287, 48106, 48106-A, 52143, 52578-A, 57475
   m) İ.DH 2002
   n) KK.d 57
   o) MHM.d 171, 197
   p) Y.EE 90
2) Beyazıt Kütüphanesi, Istanbul
   a) Nadir Eserler Bölümü nr. V3497-200
3) BnF, Paris
   a) Supplément turc nr. 1474 (1)
4) Millet Kütüphanesi, Istanbul
   a) Ali Emiri layihalar nr. 74
5) SSA, Istanbul
   a) Kısmet-i Askeriyye Mahkemesi nrs. 827, 829
6) TSMA, Istanbul
   a) Dossiers (d) 2057, 4819, 10363
   b) Documents (E) 201/1–3, 356, 3809, 5162, 7028/261, 10323

REFERENCE WORKS

Babinger, Franz. *Geschichtsschreiber der Osmanen und ihre Werke*. Leipzig,
    1927.
Brockelmann, Carl. *Geschichte der arabischen Literatur*. Weimar, 1898–1902. 2
    vols., 3 suppl. vols.
Browne, E.G. *A Literary History of Persia*. London, 1924. 4 vols.
Gibb, H.A.R., J.H. Kramers et al., eds. *Encyclopaedia of Islam*. 2nd edition.
    Leiden, 1960–2005. 12 vols.
Hammer-Purgstall, Joseph von. *Geschichte der osmanischen Dichtkunst*. Pest,
    1836–1838. 3 vols.
Hurmuzaki, Eudoxin de, ed. *Documente privitóre la istoria românilor*. Bucharest,
    1876–1922. 19 vols. and 2 supplements.
Kal'a, Ahmet, and Ahmet Tabakoğlu, eds. *İstanbul Su Külliyâtı*. Istanbul, 1997–
    2003. 34 vols.
Karal, Enver Ziya. *Selim III'ün Hatt-ı Hümayunları*. Ankara, 1942/46. 2 vols.

Karatay, Fehmi Edhem, ed. *Topkapı Sarayı Müzesi Kütüphanesi Türkçe Yazmalar Kataloğu*. Istanbul, 1961. 2 vols.

Lane, Edward. *An Arabic-English Lexicon*. New York, 2011. 8 vols.

Meninski, Franciscus. *Thesaurus Linguarum Orientalium Turcicae-Arabicae-Persicae*. Istanbul, 2000. 5 vols.

Parmaksızoğlu, İsmet, ed. *Türkiye Yazmaları Toplu Kataloğu*. vol. 34/4 *İstanbul Süleymaniye Kütüphanesi: Mustafa Aşir Efendi Koleksiyonu*. Ankara, 1994.

Redhouse, Sir James. *A Turkish and English Lexicon*. Istanbul, 2001.

Sâmî, Şemseddin. *Kâmûs-ı Türkî*. Istanbul, 1899/1900.

Sohrweide, Hanna, ed. *Türkische Handschriften*. In *Verzeichnis der orientalische Handschriften in Deutschland*. vol. 13, no. 5. Weisbaden, 1981.

Steingass, F. *A Comprehensive Persian-English Dictionary*. Springfield, VA, 2010.

Türkiye Diyanet Vakfı İslâm Ansiklopedisi. Üsküdar, 1988–. 40 vols.

Vneshniaia politika Rossii XIX i nachala XX veka: dokumenty Rossiiskogo Ministerstva inostrannykh del. Moscow, 1961. 17 vols.

Wehr, Hans. *A Dictionary of Modern Written Arabic*. Urbana, IL, 1994.

Wieczynski, Joseph, ed. *The Modern Encyclopedia of Russian and Soviet History*. Gulf Breeze, FL, 1976–2000. 61 vols.

WORKS IN ARABIC, OTTOMAN, AND PERSIAN

Afyoncu, Erhan, ed. "Târih-i Kırım (Rusya Sefaretnâmesi)." Master's thesis, Marmara University, 1990.

Altun, Abdullah, ed. "Said b. Halil İbrahim'in 'Tarih-i Sefer-i Rusya' Adlı Eseri: Transkripsiyon ve Değerlendirme." Master's thesis, Erciyes University, 2006.

Al-Aqhisârî, Hasan Kâfî. *Uṣûl al-ḥikam fî nizâm al-'âlam: risâla fî al-fikr al-siyâsî al-islâmî*. ed. Ihsân Şidkî al-'Amad. Kuwait, 1987.

Arıkan, Sema, ed. *III. Selim'in Sırkâtibi Ahmed Efendi Tarafından Tutulan Rûznâme*. Ankara, 1993.

Âsım, Ahmed. *Târih-i Âsım*. Istanbul, 1870. 2 vols.

Âsım, Necîb, ed. "Pîr Mehmed Efendi Muhtırası." *TOEM* 13 (1921–23): 134–160.

Ayıntâbî, Münîb. *Devḥatü'l-Meşâyiḫ: Einleitung und Edition*. ed. Barbara Kellner-Heinkele. In *Verzeichnis der orientalische Handschriften in Deutschland*. vol. 27, no. 2. Stuttgart, 2005.

Aynî, Antepli Hasan. *Antepli Aynî Dîvânı*. ed. Mehmet Arslan. Istanbul, 2004.

Al-Baghdâdî, Ismâ'îl Bâshâ. *Hadiyyat al-'ârifîn: asmâ al-mu'allifîn wa âthâr al-muṣannifîn min kashf al-ẓunûn*. Beirut, 2008. 2 vols.

Berker, Aziz, ed. "Mora İhtilâli Tarihçesi veya Penah Efendi Mecmuası." *Tarih Vesikaları* 2 (1942–43): 63–80, 8: 153–160, 9: 228–240, 10: 309–320, 11: 385–400, 12: 473–480.

Beydilli, Kemal, ed. *Osmanlı Döneminde İmamlar ve Bir İmamın Günlüğü*. Istanbul, 2001.

Beydilli, Kemal, and İlhan Şahin, eds. *Mahmud Râif Efendi ve Nizâm-ı Cedîd'e Dâir Eseri*. Ankara, 2001.

Beyhan, Mehmet Ali, ed. *Saray Günlüğü (25 Aralık 1802–24 Ocak 1809)*. Istanbul, 2007.

Câbî, Ömer. *Târih-i Sultân Selîm-i Sâlis ve Mahmûd-ı Sânî Tahlîl ve Tenkidli Metin*. ed. Mehmet Ali Beyhan. Ankara, 2003. 2 vols.

Çağman, Ergin, ed. *III. Selim'e Sunulan Islahat Lâyihaları*. Istanbul, 2010. "III. Selim'e Sunulan Bir Islahat Raporu: Mehmed Şerif Efendi Layihası." *İlmî Araştırmalar* 7 (1999): 217–233.

Çalışkan, Muharrem Saffet, ed. "(Vekâyi'nüvis) Enverî Sadullah Efendi ve Tarihinin I. Cildi'nin Metin ve Tahlili (1182–1188/1768–1774)." Ph.D. diss., Marmara University, 2000.

Canikli Ali. *Tedbîr-i Cedîd-i Nâdir*. ÖN Cod. H.O. nr. 104b.

Câvid, Ahmed. *Hadîka-i Vekâyi'*. ed. Adnan Baycar. Ankara, 1998.

Osmanlı-Rus İlişkileri Tarihi: Ahmet Câvid Bey'in Müntehabâtı. ed. Adnan Baycar. Istanbul, 2004.

Çeşmizâde, Mustafa Reşid. *Çeşmî-zâde Tarihi*. ed. Bekir Kütükoğlu. Istanbul, 1993.

Cevdet, Ahmed. *Mecelle-i Ahkâm-ı 'Adliyye*. Istanbul, 1882/83.

Târih-i Cevdet. Istanbul, 1891/92. 12 vols.

Çınar, Ali Osman, ed. "Es-seyyid Mehmed Emîn Behiç'in *Sevânihü'l-Levâyih*'i ve Değerlendirmesi." Master's thesis, Marmara University, 1992.

Çınarcı, M. Nuri, ed. "Şeyhülislâm Ârif Hikmet Bey'in Tezkiretü'ş-Şu'ârâsı ve Transkripsiyonlu Metni." Master's thesis, Gaziantep University, 2007.

Dombay, Franz von. *Mecmû'a*. John Rylands Library, Turkish MS nr. 51.

Dürrî, Mehmed. *Nuhbetü'l-Emel fî Tenkîhi'l-Fesâd ve'l-Halel*. TSMK Hazine nr. 1438, fols. 281b-296b.

Emîn, Mehmed. *Dercü'l-Vekâyi'*. Cairo Dâr al-kutub, 152 M. Tarîkh Turkî.

Enverî, Sadullah. *Târih*. ÖN Cod. H.O. nr. 105.

Târih. ÖN Cod. H.O. nr. 202.

Esad, Mehmed. *Mehmed Esad Efendi ve Bağçe-i Safâ-Endûz'u (İnceleme – Metin)*. ed. Rıza Oğraş. Burdur, 2001.

Üss-i Zafer (Yeniçeriliğin Kaldırılmasına Dair). ed. Mehmet Arslan. Istanbul, 2005.

Fâik, Süleyman. *Sefînetü'r-Rüesâ*. Istanbul, 1853.

Fâtin, Davud. *Tezkere-i Hâtimetü'l-Eş'âr*. Istanbul, 1854.

Al-Ghazâlî. *Mi'yâr al-'ilm*. Egypt, 1961.

Al-Ghulâmî, Muḥammad b. Muṣṭafa. *Shimâmat al-'anbar wa'l-zahr al-mu'anbar*. Baghdad, 1977.

Giray, Halim. *Gülbün-i Hânân*. Istanbul, 1909.

Günay, Bekir, ed. *Paris'te bir Osmanlı: Seyyid Abdurrahim Muhib Efendi'nin Paris Sefirliği ve Büyük Sefaretnamesi*. Istanbul, 2009.

Hafîd, Kazasker Mehmed. *Sefînetü'l-Vüzerâ*. ed. İsmet Parmaksızoğlu. Istanbul, 1952.

Hâkim, Mehmed. *Târih-i Hâkim*. TSMK Bağdat nr. 231.

Târih-i Hâkim. TSMK Bağdat nr. 233.

Haydar, Ali. *Dürerü'l-hukkâm şerhu mecelleti'l-ahkâm*. eds. Raşit Gündoğdu and Osman Erdem. Istanbul, 2000. 4 vols.

Ibn Khaldûn. *Muqaddima Ibn Khaldûn, prolégomènes d'Ebn-Khaldoun, texte arabe.* ed. M. Quatremère. Paris, 1858. 3 vols.

İpşirli, Mehmed, ed. "Hasan Kâfî el-Akhisarî ve Devlet Düzenine Ait Eseri Usûlü'l-Hikem fî Nizâmi'l-Âlem." *Tarih Enstitüsü Dergisi* 10–11 (1979–1980): 239–278.

İşbilir, Ömer, ed. *Nizâm-ı Cedîd'e Dair bir Risale: Zebîre-i Kuşmânî fî Tarîf-i Nizâm-ı İlhâmî.* Ankara, 2006.

İzzet, Darendeli Hasan. *Ziyânâme: Sadrazam Yusuf Ziya Paşa'nın Napolyon'a Karşı Mısır Seferi (1798–1802).* ed. M. İlkin Erkutun. Istanbul, 2009.

İzzi, Süleyman. *Târih-i İzzi.* Istanbul, 1785.

Al-Jabartî, 'Abd al-Raḥmân. *'Ajâ'ib al-âthâr fî al-tarâjim wa'l-akhbâr.* Bulaq, 1879. 4 vols.

Karal, Enver Ziya, ed. "Nizâm-ı Cedîd'e Dâir Lâyihalar." *Tarih Vesikaları* 1/2 (1941–1943): 104–111, 342–351, 424–432.

Karslızâde, Mehmed Cemaleddin. *Osmanlı Tarih ve Müverrihleri: Âyine-i Zurefâ.* Istanbul, 2003.

Kâtib Çelebi. *Kashf al-ẓunûn 'an asâmî al-kutub wa'l-funûn.* Beirut, 2008. 3 vols.
   Tuhfetü'l-Kibâr fî Esfâri'l-Bihâr. Istanbul, 1911.

Kesbî, Mustafa. *İbretnümâ-yı Devlet.* ed. Ahmet Öğreten. Ankara, 2002.

Kınâlızâde, Ali. *Ahlâk-ı Alâî.* ed. Mustafa Koç. Istanbul, 2007.

Al-Lubnânî, Salî Rustum Bâz. *Sharḥ al-majalla.* Beirut, 1986.

Al-Muḥibbî, Muḥammad Amîn b. Faḍl Allah. *Khulâṣat al-athâr fî 'ayân al-qarn al-ḥâdî 'ashar.* Cairo, 1868. 4 vols.

Al-Murâdî, Muḥammad Khalîl b. 'Alî. *Silk al-durar fî 'ayân al-qarn al-thânî 'ashar.* Beirut, 1997. 2 vols.

Müteferrika, İbrahim. *Usûlü'l-Hikem fî Nizâmi'l-Ümem.* ed. Adil Şen. Ankara, 1995.

Naîmâ, Mustafa. *Târih-i Na'îmâ.* ed. Mehmet İpşirli. Ankara, 2007. 4 vols.

Necîb, Mustafa. *Târih.* Istanbul, 1863–1864.

Nûrî, Halil. *Târih.* Beyazıt Devlet Kütüphanesi nr. 3369.

Öğreten, Ahmet, ed. "Nizam-ı Cedid'e Dair Islahat Layihaları." Istanbul University, 1989.

Osmanzâde Tâib. *Hadîkatü'l-Vüzerâ.* Istanbul, 1854.

Özcan, Ahmet, ed. "Kethüda Said Efendi Tarihi ve Değerlendirmesi." Master's thesis, Kırıkkale University, 1999.

Özkaya, Yücel. "Canikli Ali Paşa'nın Risalesi 'Tedâbîrü'l-Gazavât.'" *AÜDTCF Araştırmaları Dergisi* 7/13–14 (1969): 119–191.

Resmî, Ahmed. *Hulâsatü'l-İtibâr – A Summary of Admonitions: a Chronicle of the 1768–1774 Russian-Ottoman War.* trans. Ethan L. Menchinger. Istanbul, 2011.

Sâbit, Mahmud. *Târîh-i Cedîd-i Silistre.* ÖN Cod. H.O. nr. 102b.

Sâmî, Ebubekir. *Divân.* İÜ TY nr. 2836.

Şânîzâde, Mehmed Atâullah. *Tarih-i Şânîzâde.* ed. Ziya Yılmazer. Istanbul, 2008. 2 vols.

Sarıkaya, Ahmet, ed. "Ömer Fâ'ik Efendi, Nizâmü'l-Atîk." Istanbul University, 1979.

Şemdânîzâde, Süleyman. *Mür'i't-Tevârih*. ed. Münir Aktepe. Istanbul, 1976–1981. 3 vols.

Şener, Hasan, ed. "Hayrî: Hayatı, Edebi Şahsiyeti, Dîvânı'nın Tenkitli Metni." Ph.D. Diss., Fırat University, 1999.

Subhî, Mehmed et al. *Târih-i Sâmî ve Şâkir ve Subhî*. Istanbul, 1784.

Süreyya, Mehmed. *Sicill-i Osmânî*. ed. Nuri Akbayar. Istanbul, 1996. 6 vols.

Sürûrî, Osman. *Divân-ı Sürûrî*. Bulaq, 1839.

Taşköprüzâde, Ahmed. *Mawsû'at muştalaḥât miftâḥ al-sa'âda wa mişbâḥ al-siyâda fî mawḍû'ât al-'ulûm*. Beirut, 1998.

Tatarcık Abdullah. "Sultan Selim-i Sâlis Devrinde Nizâm-ı Devlet Hakkında Mütâlaat." *TOEM* (1916/17): 7/38: 74–88; 7/41: 321–346; 8/43: 15–34.

Taylesanizâde, Hâfız Abdullah. *İstanbul'un Uzun Dört Yılı (1785–1789): Taylesanizâde Hafız Abdullah Efendi Tarihi*. ed. Feridun Emecen. Istanbul, 2003. 2 vols.

Teşrifâtî, Hasan. *Târih*. ÖN Cod. H.O. nr. 230.

Tuman, Mehmed Nâil. *Tuhfe-i Nâilî: Divân Şâirlerinin Muhtasar Biyografileri*. eds. Cemal Kurnaz and Mustafa Tatcı. Istanbul, 2001. 2 vols.

Al-'Umarî, Muḥammad Amîn b. Khayr Allah. *Manhal al-awliyyâ wa mashrab al-aşfiyyâ min sâdât al-Mawsil al-ḥadbâ*. Mosul, 1967. 2 vols.

Al-'Umarî, 'Uthmân b. 'Alî. *al-Rawḍ al-naḍir fî tarjamat udabâ al-'aşr*. Baghdad, 1974–1975. 3 vols.

Ünal, Uğur, ed. *Kırım Hanlarına Nâme-i Hümâyûn*. Istanbul, 2013.

Uzunçarşılı, İ.H., ed. "III. Sultan Selim Zamanında Yazılmış Dış Ruznâmesinden 1206/1791 ve 1207/1792 Senelerine Âit Vekayi." *Belleten* 37 (1973): 607–662.

Vâsıf. *Eş-Şeyh Mehemmed Murâd Hazretleri'nin Sohbetleridir*. Süleymaniye Kütüphanesi, Esad Efendi nr. 1419, fols. 29b-44b.

Mecmû'a. İÜ TY nr. 1555.

Yıldız, Aysel, ed. *Asiler ve Gaziler: Kabakçı Mustafa Risalesi*. Istanbul, 2007.

Zaîmzâde, Mehmed Sâdık. *Vak'a-ı Hamîdiyye*. Istanbul, 1872.

OTHER SOURCES

Abou-El-Haj, Rifaat Ali. "The Formal Closure of the Ottoman Frontier in Europe, 1699–1703." *Journal of the American Oriental Society* 89 (1969): 467–475.

"Ottoman Attitudes Toward Peacemaking: The Karlowitz Case." *Der Islam* 51 (1974): 131–137.

"Ottoman Diplomacy at Karlowitz." *Journal of the American Oriental Society* 87 (1967): 498–512.

Aceituno, Antonio Jurado. "18. Yüzyılda Bir Osmanlı Elçisinin İspanya'yı Ziyareti." *Tarih ve Toplum* 36 (2001): 33–39.

Adnan-Adıvar, Abdülhak. *Osmanlı Türklerinde İlim*. Istanbul, 1943.

Afyoncu, Erhan. "Osmanlı Müelliflerine Dair Tevcihat Kayıtları I." *Belgeler* 20 (1999): 77–155.

"Osmanlı Müelliflerine Dair Tevcihat Kayıtları II." *Belgeler* 26 (2005): 85–193.

"Vekâyi'nüvis Tabirine Dair." *Türklük Araştırmaları Dergisi* 10 (2001): 7–19.

Ahıshalı, Recep. *Osmanlı Devlet Teşkilatında Reisülküttâblık (XVIII. Yüzyıl)*. Istanbul, 2001.

Ahmed, Shahab, and Nenad Filipovic, "The Sultan's Syllabus: A Curriculum for the Imperial Ottoman *medreses* Prescribed in a Fermân of Qânûnî I Süleymân, Dated 973 (1565)." *Studia Islamica* 98/99 (2004): 183–218.

Aksan, Virginia H. *Ottomans and Europeans: Contacts and Conflicts*. Istanbul, 2004.

An Ottoman Statesman in War and Peace: Ahmed Resmi Efendi, 1700–1783. Leiden, 1995.

Ottoman Wars, 1700–1870: An Empire Besieged. Harlow UK, 2007.

"The Question of Writing Premodern Biographies of the Middle East." In *Auto/Biography and the Construction of Identity and Community in the Middle East*. ed. Mary Ann Fay. New York, 2001. 191–200.

"War and Peace." In *The Cambridge History of Turkey*. Cambridge, 2006. 3: 81–117.

Akyıldız, Ali. "Osmanlı Bürokratik Geleneğinin Yenileşme Süreci: Yenileşmeyi Zorunlu Kılan Nedenler." In *İslâm, Gelenek ve Yenileşme*. Istanbul, 1996. 129–140.

Altun, Hilmi Kemal. "Osmanlı Müelliflerince Yazılan Kazâ ve Kader Risâleleri ve Taşköprüzâde'nin *Risâle Fi'l-Kazâ ve'l-Kader* Adlı Eseri." Master's thesis, Marmara University, 2010.

Anderson, M.S. "The Great Powers and the Russian Annexation of the Crimea, 1783–4." *The Slavonic and East European Review* 37 (1958): 17–41.

Arıkan, Zeki. "Fransız İhtilâli ve Osmanlı Tarihçiliği." In *De la Révolution française à la Turquie d'Atatürk: la modernisation politique et sociale. Les lettres, les sciences et les arts*. Istanbul, 1990. 85–100.

Aslan, Mustafa. "Kayserili Raşit Mehmet Efendi ve Divançesi." *Türkoloji Araştırmaları* 2/3 (2007): 40–58.

Atik, Kayhan. "Kayserili Devlet Adamı Dürri Mehmed Efendi ve Layihası." In *II. Kayseri ve Yöresi Tarih Sempozyumu*. Kayseri, 1998. 69–74.

Babinger, Franz. *Stambuler Buchwesen im 18. Jahrhundert*. Leipzig, 1919.

Bağış, A.I. *Britain and the Struggle for the Integrity of the Ottoman Empire: Sir Robert Ainslie's Embassy to Istanbul, 1776–1794*. Istanbul, 1984.

Barbir, Karl. "The Changing Face of the Ottoman Empire in the Eighteenth Century: Past and Future Scholarship." *Oriente Moderno* 18 (1999): 253–267.

Başaran, Betül. *Selim III, Social Control and Policing in Istanbul at the End of the Eighteenth Century*. Leiden, 2014.

Beckford, William. *Italy; with Sketches of Spain and Portugal*. London, 1835.

The Journal of William Beckford in Portugal and Spain, 1787–1788. ed. Boyd Alexander. Gloucestershire, 2006.

Berkes, Niyazi. *The Development of Secularism in Turkey*. Montreal, 1964.

Türkiye'de Çağdaşlaşma. Ankara, 1973.

Beydilli, Kemal. *Büyük Freidrich ve Osmanlılar: XVIII. Yüzyılda Osmanlı-Prusya Münâsebetleri*. Istanbul, 1985.

"Dış Politika ve Ahlâk." *İlmî Araştırmalar* 7 (1999): 47–56.

"Evreka, Evreka veya Errare Humanum Est." İlmî Araştırmalar 9 (2000): 45–66.
"İlk Mühendislerimizden Seyyid Mustafa ve Nizâm-ı Cedîd'e Dair Risâlesi." Tarih Enstitüsü Dergisi 12 (1987): 387–479.
"Küçük Kaynarca'dan Tanzimât'a Islâhât Düşünceleri." İlmî Araştırmalar 8 (1999): 25–64.
"Sefaret ve Sefaretnâme Hakkında Yeni Bir Değerlendirme." Journal of Ottoman Studies 30 (2007): 9–30.
"Sekbanbaşı Risalesi'nin Müellifi Hakkında." Türk Kültürü İncelemeleri Dergisi 12 (2005): 221–224.
Türk Bilim ve Matbaacılık Tarihinde Mühendishâne, Mühendishâne Matbaası ve Kütüphânesi (1776–1826). Istanbul, 1995.
"III. Selim: Aydınlanmış Hükümdar." In Nizâm-ı Kadîm'den Nizâm-ı Cedîd'e: III. Selim ve Dönemi. ed. Seyfi Kenan. Istanbul, 2010. 27–57.
Bianchi, Thomas-Xavier. Notice historique sur M. Ruffin. Paris, 1825.
Bilge, Mustafa L. "Vâsıf Tarihinin Üç Muteber Zeyli." In Prof. Dr. Şevki Nezihi Aykut Armağanı. eds. Niyazi Çiçek et al. Istanbul, 2011. 35–46.
Bilici, Faruk. "La Révolution française dans l'historiographie turque (1789–1927)." Annales historiques de la Révolution française (1991): 539–549.
Birinci, Ali. "Koca Sekbanbaşı Risalesi'nin Müellifi Tokatlı Mustafa Ağa (1131–1239)." In Prof. Dr. Ismail Aka Armağanı. Izmir, 1999. 105–120.
Bishai, Wilson. "Negotiations and Peace Agreements Between Muslims and Non-Muslims in Islamic History." In Medieval and Middle Eastern Studies in Honor of Aziz Suryal Atiya. ed. Sami A. Hanna. Leiden, 1972. 50–61.
Bond, Robert Charles. "The Office of the Ottoman Court Historian or Vak'anüvis (1714–1922): An Institutional and Prosopographic Study." Ph.D. diss., Stanford University, 2004.
Bonner, Michael. Jihad in Islamic History: Doctrines and Practices. Princeton, 2006.
Bonner, Michael, and Gottfried Hagen. "Muslim Accounts of the dâr al-ḥarb." In The New Cambridge History of Islam. ed. Robert Irwin. Cambridge, 2010. 4: 474–494.
Boogert, Maurits H. van den. Aleppo Observed: Ottoman Syria through the Eyes of Two Scottish Doctors, Alexander and Patrick Russell. Oxford, 2010.
Bruckmayr, Philipp. "The Particular Will (al-irâdat al-juz'iyya): Excavations Regarding a Latecomer in Kalâm Terminology on Human Agency and Its Position in Naqshbandi Discourse." European Journal of Turkish Studies 13 (2011): 2–20.
Burçak, Berrak. "The Institution of the Ottoman Embassy and Eighteenth-Century Ottoman History: An Alternative to Göçek." International Journal of Turkish Studies 13 (2007): 147–151.
Burguete, Francisco. Relación nueva en la que se describe el arribo y desembarco, que ha hecho en el ciudad de Barcelona el dia 28. de julio de este año de 1787. El Exc.MO Señor enviado de la Sublime Puerta Otomana... Valencia, 1787.
Butterworth, Charles. "Early Thought." In A Companion to Muslim Ethics. ed. Amyn Sajoo. London, 2010. 31–51.

Çalışkan, Filiz. "Vâsıf'ın Kaynaklarından Enverî Tarihi." In *Prof. Dr. Bekir Kütükoğlu'na Armağan*. Istanbul, 1991. 143–163.

Caussin de Perceval, A.P. *Précis historique de la destruction du corps des Janissaries par le sultan Mahmoud, en 1826*. Paris, 1833.

Çelik, Yüksel. "Nizâm-ı Cedîd'in Niteliği ve III. Selim ile II. Mahmud Devri Askerî Reformlarına Dair Tespitler (1789–1839)." In *III. Selim ve Dönemi*. 565–590.

"Siyaset-Nasihat Literatürümüzde Nadir bir Tür: Mısır'ın İşgali Üzerine III. Selim'e Sunulan Tesliyet-Nâme." *Türk Kültürü İncelemeler Dergisi* 22 (2010): 85–126.

Chambers, Richard. "The Education of a Nineteenth-Century Ottoman Âlim: Ahmed Cevdet Paşa." *IJMES* 4 (1973): 440–464.

Çınar, Alev. *Modernity, Islam, and Secularism in Turkey*. Minneapolis, 2005.

Clogg, Richard. "An Attempt to Revive Turkish Printing in Istanbul in 1779." *IJMES* 10 (1979): 67–70.

"A Further Note on the French Newspapers of Istanbul During the Revolutionary Period." *Belleten* 39 (1975): 483–490.

Conrotte, Manuel. *España y los países musulmanes durante el ministerio de Floridablanca*. Madrid, 1909.

Coquelle, P. "Sébastiani, ambassadeur à Constantinople, 1806–1808." *Revue d'histoire diplomatique* 18 (1904): 574–611.

Crone, Patricia. *Medieval Islamic Political Thought*. Edinburgh, 2004.

Darling, Linda. *A History of Social Justice and Political Power in the Middle East: The Circle of Justice from Mesopotamia to Globalization*. New York, 2013.

Davidson, Herbert. *Alfarabi, Avicenna, and Averroes on Intellect: Their Cosmologies, Theories of the Active Intellect, and Theories of Human Intellection*. Oxford, 1992.

Dehérain, Henri. *La vie de Pierre Ruffin: orientalist et diplomate, 1742–1824*. Paris, 1929–30. 2 vols.

Dilçin, Cem. "Şcyh Galip'in Şiirlerinde III. Selim ve Nizam-ı Cedit." *Türkoloji Dergisi* 11 (1993): 209–219.

Dupré, Louis. *The Enlightenment and the Intellectual Foundations of Modern Culture*. New Haven, 2004.

Eldem, Edhem. "18. Yüzyıl ve Değişim." *Cogito* 19 (1999): 189–199.

Elgin, Necati. *Üçüncü Sultan Selim (İlhâmî)*. Konya, 1959.

Emiralioğlu, Pınar. *Geographical Knowledge and Imperial Culture in the Early Modern Ottoman Empire*. Surrey, 2014.

Erdem, Y. Hakan. "The Wise Old Man, Propagandist, and Ideologist: Koca Sekbanbaşi on the Janissaries, 1806." In *Individuals and Ideologies and Society: Tracing the Mosaic of Mediterranean History*. ed. Kirsi Virtanen. Tampere, 2001. 154–177.

Eren, Ahmet Cevat. *Selim III'ün Biografyası*. Istanbul, 1964.

Ergene, Boğaç. "On Ottoman Justice: Interpretations in Conflict (1600–1800)." *Islamic Law and Society* 8 (2001): 52–87.

Ermiş, Fatih. *A History of Ottoman Economic Thought: Developments Before the Nineteenth Century*. London, 2014.

Erşahin, Seyfettin. "Westernization, Mahmud II, and the Islamic Virtue Tradition." *The American Journal of Islamic Social Sciences* 23 (2006): 37–62.

Fakhry, Majid. *Ethical Theories in Islam*. Leiden, 1991.

Ferdowsi, Abolqasem. *Shahnameh: The Persian Book of Kings*. trans. Dick Davis. New York, 2006.

Findley, Carter V. *Bureaucratic Reform in the Ottoman Empire: The Sublime Porte, 1789–1922*. Princeton, 1980.

"The Legacy of Tradition to Reform: Origins of the Ottoman Foreign Ministry." *IJMES* 1 (1970): 334–357.

"A Vision of a Brilliant Career." *Wiener Zeitschrift für die Kunde des Morgenlandes* 76 (1986): 95–101.

Fisher, Alan. *The Russian Annexation of the Crimea, 1772–1783*. Cambridge, 1970.

Fleischer, Cornell H. *Bureaucrat and Intellectual in the Ottoman Empire: The Historian Mustafa Âli, 1541–1600*. Princeton, 1986.

Fodor, Pál. "The View of the Turk in Hungary: The Apocalyptic Tradition and the Legend of the Golden Apple in Ottoman-Hungarian Context." In *Les traditions apocalyptiques au tourant de la chute de Constaninople*. eds. Lellouch and Yerasimos. Paris, 1999. 99–131.

Freytag, G.W.F. *Arabum proverbia, vocalibus instruxit, latine vertit, commentario illustravit et sumtibus suis editit*. Bonn, 1838–1843. 4 vols.

Gawrych, George W. "Şeyh Galib and Selim III: Mevlevism and the Nizam-ı Cedid." *International Journal of Turkish Studies* 4 (1987): 91–114.

Ghika, J.D. "La France et les principautés danubiennes de 1789 à 1815." *Annales de l'École libre des sciences politiques* 11 (1896): 208–229, 321–352.

Göçek, Fatma Müge. *East Encounters West: France and the Ottoman Empire in the Eighteenth Century*. New York, 1987.

Gölen, Zafer. "Reisülküttap Raşid Efendi'ye Göre İhtilal Sonrasında Fransa'nın Politik Yaklaşımları." *Toplumsal Tarih* 14 (2000): 12–15.

Görgün, Tahsin. "Osmanlı'da Nizâm-ı Âlem Fikri ve Kaynakları Üzerine Bazı Notlar." *İslâmî Araştırmalar Dergisi* 13 (2000): 180–188.

Goşu, Armand. *La troisième coalition antinapoléonienne et la Sublime Porte, 1805*. Istanbul, 2003.

Göyünç, Nejat. "Kapudan-ı Deryâ Küçük Hüseyin Paşa." *Tarih Dergisi* 2 (1952): 35–50.

Gran, Peter. *The Islamic Roots of Capitalism: Egypt, 1760–1840*. Austin, TX, 1979.

Gravina, Federico. *Descripción de Constantinopla*. ed. D. José Maria Sánchez Molledo. Madrid, 2001.

Griffel, Frank. *Al-Ghazali's Philosophical Theology*. Oxford, 2009.

Grunebaum, G. E. von. "The Concept and Function of Reason in Islamic Ethics." *Oriens* 15 (1962): 1–17.

Guilmartin, John F. "Ideology and Conflict: The Wars of the Ottoman Empire, 1453–1606." *Journal of Interdisciplinary History* 18 (1988): 721–747.

Hagen, Gottfried. "Afterword." In *An Ottoman Mentality: The World of Evliya Çelebi*. Leiden, 2004. 207–248.

"Legitimacy and World Order." In *Legitimizing the Order: The Ottoman Rhetoric of State Power*. eds. Hakan Karateke and Maurus Reinkowski. Leiden, 2005. 55–83.

"The Order of Knowledge, the Knowledge of Order: Intellectual Life." In *The Cambridge History of Turkey*. 2: 407–456.

"Osman II and the Cultural History of Ottoman Historiography." *H-Net Reviews* (2006).

Ein osmanischer Geograph bei der Arbeit: Entstehung und Gedankenwelt von Kâtib Čelebis Ğihânnümâ. Berlin, 2003.

Hagen, Gottfried, and Ethan L. Menchinger. "Ottoman Historical Thought." In *A Companion to Global Historical Thought*. eds. Prasenjit Duara et al. London, 2014. 92–106.

Hamadeh, Shirine. *The City's Pleasures: Istanbul in the Eighteenth Century*. Seattle, 2007.

Hathaway, Jane. "Rewriting Eighteenth Century Ottoman History." *Mediterranean Historical Review* 19 (2004): 29–53.

Heyd, Uriel. "The Ottoman 'Ulemâ and Westernization in the Time of Selim III and Maḥmûd II." In *Studies in Islamic History*. Jerusalem, 1961. 63–96.

Studies in Old Ottoman Criminal Law. Oxford, 1973.

Howard, Douglas. "Ottoman Historiography and the Literature of 'Decline' of the Sixteenth and Seventeenth Centuries." *Journal of Asian History* 22 (1988): 52–77.

Hurewitz, J.C. "The Europeanization of Ottoman Diplomacy: The Conversion from Unilateralism to Reciprocity in the Nineteenth Century." *Belleten* 25 (1961): 455–466.

İlgürel, Mücteba. "Cevdet Paşa Tarihi'nin Kaynaklarından Vâsıf Tarihi." In *Ahmed Cevdet Paşa Semineri: 27–28 Mayıs 1985*. Istanbul, 1986. 115–126.

"Vakanüvis Ahmed Vâsıf Efendi'nin İspanya Elçiliği ve Götürdüğü Hediyeler." *İÜ Edebiyat Fakültesi Tarih Dergisi* 46 (2007): 27–35.

"Vak'anüvislerin Taltiflerine Dâir." In *Bekir Kütükoğlu'na Armağan*. Istanbul, 1991. 183–192.

Imber, Colin. *Ebu's-su'ud: the Islamic Legal Tradition*. Edinburgh, 1997.

"The Ottoman Dynastic Myth." *Revue d'etudes turques* 19 (1987): 7–27.

İnalcık, Halil, and Donald Quataert, eds. *An Economic and Social History of the Ottoman Empire, 1300–1914*. Cambridge, 1994.

Itzkowitz, Norman. "Eighteenth Century Ottoman Realities." *Studia Islamica* 16 (1962): 73–94.

"Mehmed Raghib Pasha: The Making of an Ottoman Grand Vezir." Ph.D. diss., Princeton University, 1959.

Itzkowitz, Norman, and Max Mote, eds. *Mubadele: An Ottoman-Russian Exchange of Ambassadors*. Chicago, 1970.

Jack, Malcolm. *William Beckford: An English Hidalgo*. New York, 1996.

"Jacques Argyropoulos." *Magasin pittoresque* 31 (1863): 127–128.

Kafadar, Cemal. "The Myth of the Golden Age: Ottoman Historical Consciousness in the Post-Süleymânic Era." In *Süleyman the Second and His Time*. eds. Halil İnalcık and Cemal Kafadar. Istanbul, 1993. 37–48.

"The Question of Ottoman Decline." *Harvard Middle Eastern and Islamic Review* 4 (1998): 30–75.

Kayadibi, Saim. *The Doctrine of Istihsân (Juristic Preference) in Islamic Law.* Ankara, 2007.

Khadduri, Majid. *The Islamic Conception of Justice.* Baltimore, 1984.

War and Peace in the Law of Islam. Baltimore, 1955.

Khoury, Dina Rizk. *State and Provincial Society in the Ottoman Empire: Mosul, 1540–1834.* Cambridge, 1997.

Köhbach, Markus. "Die osmanische Gesandschaft nach Spanien in den Jahren 1787/88: Begegnung zweier Kulturen im Spiegel eines Gesandschaftsberichts." *Wiener Beiträge zur die Geschichte der Neuzeit* 10 (1983): 143–152.

Köse, Osman. *1774 Küçük Kaynarca Andlaşması.* Ankara, 2006.

Kramer, Martin, ed. *Middle Eastern Lives: The Practice of Biography and Self-Narrative.* Syracuse, 1991.

Küçük, B. Harun. "Early Enlightenment in Istanbul." Ph.D. diss., University of California, San Diego, 2012.

Kunt, Metin. "Derviş Mehmed Paşa, Vezir and Entrepreneur: A Study in Ottoman Political-Economic Theory and Practice." *Turcica* 9 (1977): 197–214.

Kurz, Marlene. *Ways to Heaven, Gates to Hell: Fazlızâde 'Alî's Struggle with the Diversity of Ottoman Islam.* Berlin, 2011.

Kutlu, Mehmet Necati. "İspanyol Belgelerine Göre İspanya Nezdinde Görevlendirilen (Eyüp'te Medfun) İlk Osmanlı Elçisi Ahmet Vâsıf Efendi." In *Tarihi, Kültürü ve Sanatıyla IV. Eyüpsultan Sempozyumu Tebliğler, 5–7 Mayıs 2000.* Istanbul, 2000. 106–111.

Kütükoğlu, Bekir. "Osmanlı Arşivleri ile Vak'anüvis Tarihleri Arasında Bağ." In *Osmanlı Arşivleri ve Osmanlı Araştırmaları Sempozyumu.* Istanbul, 1985. 123–125.

Vekayi'nüvis Makaleler. Istanbul, 1994.

Lagarde, L. "Note sur les journaux français de Constantinople à l'époque révolutionnaire." *Journal Asiatique* 236 (1948): 271–276.

Lalor, Bernard. "Promotion Patterns of Ottoman Bureaucratic Statesmen from the Lâle Devri until the Tanzimat." *Güney-Doğu Avrupa Araştırmalar Dergisi* 1 (1972): 77–92.

Landau-Tasseron, Ella. "The Cyclical Reform: A Study of the Mujaddid Tradition." *Studia Islamica* 70 (1989): 79–117.

Le Gall, Dina. *A Culture of Sufism: Naqshbandis in the Ottoman World, 1450–1700.* Albany, 2005.

Levy, Avigdor. "Military Reform and the Problem of Centralization in the Ottoman Empire in the Eighteenth Century." *Middle Eastern Studies* 18 (1982): 227–249.

Lewis, Bernard. *The Emergence of Modern Turkey.* Oxford, 2002.

"The Impact of the French Revolution on Turkey: Some Notes on the Transmission of Ideas," *Journal of World History* 1 (1953): 105–125.

The Political Language of Islam. Chicago, 1988.

Lindner, Rudi P. "Icon among Iconoclasts in the Renaissance." In *The Iconic Page in Manuscript, Print, and Digital Culture.* eds. George Bornstein and Theresa Tinkle. Ann Arbor, 1998. 89–107.

Mantran, Robert. "Baġdâd à l'époque ottomane." *Arabica* 9 (1962): 311–324.
Mardin, Şerif. *The Genesis of Young Ottoman Thought: A Study in the Modernization of Turkish Political Ideas*. Syracuse, 2000.
"The Mind of the Turkish Reformer, 1700–1900." In *Arab Socialism: A Documentary Survey*. Salt Lake City, 1969. 24–48.
Matuz, Josef. "Über die Epistolographie und Inšâ-Literatur der Osmanen." *Zeitschrift der Deutschen Morgenländischen Gesellschaft* supp. 1 (1968): 574–594.
Menchinger, Ethan L. "Free Will, Predestination, and the Fate of the Ottoman Empire." *Journal of the History of Ideas* 77 (2016): 445–466.
"An Ottoman Historian in an Age of Reform: Ahmed Vâsıf Efendi (ca. 1730–1806)." Ph.D. diss., University of Michigan, 2014.
"A Reformist Philosophy of History: The Case of Ahmed Vâsıf Efendi." *Journal of Ottoman Studies* 44 (2014): 141–168.
Mîr Khvând, Muḥammad b. Khâvandshâh. *The Rauzat-us-safa, or Garden of Purity*. trans. E. Rehatsek. London, 1891. 4 vols.
Mulledo, José Sánchez. "El viaje de Federico Gravina a Constantinopla en 1788." *Arbor* 180 (2005): 727–744.
Morkva, Valeriy. "Russia's Policy of Rapprochement with the Ottoman Empire in the Era of the French Revolutionary and Napoleonic Wars, 1792–1806." Ph.D. diss., Sabancı University, 2010.
Murphey, Rhoads. "Twists and Turns in the Diplomatic Dialogue: The Politics of Peacemaking in the Early Eighteenth Century." In *The Peace of Passarowitz, 1718*. West Lafayette, IN, 2011. 73–91.
Nasr, Seyyid Hossein. *An Introduction to Islamic Cosmological Doctrines: Conceptions of Nature and Methods Used for its Study by the Ikhwân al-Şafâ', al-Bîrûnî, and Ibn Sînâ*. Boulder CO, 1978.
Neumann, Christoph. "Decision Making without Decision Makers: Ottoman Foreign Policy Circa 1780." In *Decision Making and Change in the Ottoman Empire*. ed. Caesar Ferrah. Missouri, 1993. 29–38.
Das indirekte Argument: ein Plädoyer für die Tanzīmāt vermittels der Historie: die geschichtliche Bedeutung von Aḥmed Cevdet Paşas Tarīḫ. Münster: Lit, 1994.
Nieuwenhuis, Tom. *Politics and Society in Early Modern Iraq*. The Hague, 1981.
Öçal, Şamil. "Osmanlı Kelamcıları Eşarî miydi? Muhammad Akkirmânî'nin İnsan Hürriyeti Anlayışı." *Dinî Araştırmalar* 5 (1999): 225–254.
D'Ohsson, Ignatius Mouradgea. *Tableau général de l'Empire othoman*. Paris, 1788–1824. 7 vols.
Öksüz, Melek. "Ahmed Vasıf Efendi'nin İspanya Hakkında Görüşleri." *Türk Dünyası Araştırmaları* 154 (2005): 107–118.
Olson, Robert. *The Siege of Mosul and Ottoman-Persian Relations, 1718–1743: A Study of Rebellion in the Capital and War in the Provinces of the Ottoman Empire*. Bloomington, IN, 1975.
Önalp, Ertuğrul. "La crónica de Ahmet Vasıf Efendi, primer embajador turco en la corte española (1787–88)." *OTAM* 10 (1999): 175–191.
Ormsby, Eric L. *Theodicy in Islamic Thought: The Dispute over Ghazâlî's "Best of All Possible Worlds."* Princeton, 1984.

Ortaylı, İlber. "Osmanlı'da 18. Yüzyıl Düşünce Dünyasına Dair Notlar." In *Osmanlı Düşünce Dünyası ve Tarihyazımı*. Istanbul, 2007. 95–102.

"Türk Tarihçiliğinde Biyografi İnşası ve Biyografik Malzeme Sorunsalı." In *Osmanlı'dan Cumhuriyet'e Problemler, Araştırmalar, Tartışmalar*. Istanbul, 1998. 56–63.

Ortega, M. Helena Sánchez. "Las relaciones hispano-turcos en el siglo XVIII." *Hispania* 49 (1989): 187–195.

Öz, Mehmet. "Kânûn-ı Kadîm: Osmanlı Gelenekçi Söyleminin Dayanağı mı, Islahat Girişimlerinin Meşrulaştırma Aracı Mı?" In *III. Selim ve Dönemi*. Istanbul, 2010. 59–77.

Özoğlu, Hakan. *Kurdish Notables and the Ottoman State: Evolving Identities, Competing Loyalties, and Shifting Boundaries*. Albany, NY, 2004.

Pamuk, Şevket. *A Monetary History of the Ottoman Empire*. Cambridge, 1999.

Panaite, Viorel. *The Ottoman Law of War and Peace: The Ottoman Empire and Tribute Payers*. Boulder, 2000.

Paquette, Gabriel. *Enlightenment, Governance, and Reform in Spain and Its Empire, 1759–1808*. London, 2011.

Parmaksızoğlu, İsmet. "Bir Türk Diplomatının Onsekizinci Yüzyıl Sonunda Devletler Arası İlişkilere Dair Görüşleri." *Belleten* 47 (1983): 527–535.

Philliou, Christine. *Biography of an Empire: Governing Ottomans in an Age of Revolution*. Berkeley, CA, 2011.

Râif, Mahmud. *Tableau des nouveaux règlemens de l'Empire ottoman*. Üsküdar, 1798.

Redissi, Hamadi. "The Refutation of Wahhabism in Arabic Sources, 1745–1932." In *Kingdom Without Borders: Saudi Political, Religious, and Media Frontiers*. New York, 2008. 157–181.

Reichmuth, Stefan. *The World of Murtaḍā al-Zabîdî (1732–91): Life, Networks, and Writings*. Cambridge, 2009.

Rosenthal, Erwin. *Political Thought in Medieval Islam: An Introductory Outline*. Cambridge, 1962.

Rosenthal, Franz. *Knowledge Triumphant: The Concept of Knowledge in Medieval Islam*. Leiden, 1970.

"Sweeter than Hope": Complaint and Hope in Medieval Islam. Leiden, 1983.

El-Rouayheb, Khaled. *Islamic Intellectual History in the Seventeenth Century: Scholarly Currents in the Ottoman Empire and Maghreb*. Cambridge, 2015.

"The Myth of 'the Triumph of Fanaticism' in the Seventeenth-Century Ottoman Empire." *Die Welt des Islams* 48 (2008): 196–221.

Rousseau, J.-B. Louis Jacques. *Description du pachalik de Bagdad, suivie d'une notice historique sur les Wahabis, et de quelques autres pieces relatives à l'histoire et à la littérature de l'Orient*. Paris, 1809.

Voyage de Bagdad à Alep (1808), publié d'après le manuscrit inédit de l'auteur. Paris, 1899.

Russell, Alexander. *The Natural History of Aleppo*. rev. ed. London, 1797.

Sabev, Orlin. *İbrahim Müteferrika ya da İlk Osmanlı Matbaa Serüveni (1726–1746)*. Istanbul, 2006.

Şakul, Kahraman. "The Evolution of Ottoman Military Logistical Systems in the Later Eighteenth Century: The Rise of a New Class of Military

Entrepreneur." In *War, Entrepreneurs, and the State in Europe and the Mediterranean, 1300–1800*. Leiden, 2014. 307–327.

"Hattat İsmail Zihni Paşa: Life and Death of an Ottoman Statesman and an Inventor." *Journal of Ottoman Studies* 44 (2014): 67–98.

"Military Engineering in the Ottoman Empire." In *Military Engineers and the Development of the Early-Modern European State*. Dundee, UK, 2013. 179–199.

"Nizâm-ı Cedid Düşüncesinde Batılılaşma ve İslami Modernleşme." *İlmî Araştırmalar* 19 (2005): 117–150.

Salgar, M. Fatih. *III Selim: Hayatı, Sanatı, Eserleri*. Istanbul, 2001.

Salzmann, Ariel. "An Ancien Régime Revisited: 'Privatization' and Political Economy in the Eighteenth-Century Ottoman Empire." *Politics and Society* 21 (1993): 393–423.

Sarıcaoğlu, Fikret. *Kendi Kaleminden bir Padişahın Portresi: Sultan I. Abdülhamid (1774–1789)*. Istanbul, 2001.

Sariyannis, Marinos. "The Princely Virtues as Presented in Ottoman Political and Moral Literature." *Turcica* 43 (2011): 121–144.

"Ruler and State, State and Society in Ottoman Political Thought." *Turkish Historical Review* 4 (2013): 92–126.

Schlechta-Wssehrd, Otocar von. "Die osmanischen Geschichtsschreiber der neueren Zeit." *Denkschriften der phil. hist. Klasse der Kaiserl. Ak. der Wissenschaften* 8 (1856): 1–47.

Schulze, Reinhard. "Das islamische achtzehnte Jahrhundert: Versuch einer historiographischen Kritik." *Die Welt des Islams* 30 (1990): 140–159.

"Was ist die islamische Aufklärung?" *Die Welt des Islams* 36 (1996): 276–325.

Sendesni, Wajda. *Regard de l'historiographie ottomane sur la révolution française et l'expédition d'Égypte*. Istanbul, 2003.

Seyyid Mustafa. *Diatribe de l'ingénieur Séid Moustapha sur l'état actuel de l'art militaire, du génie et des sciences à Constantinople*. Paris, 1810.

Shaw, Stanford. *Between Old and New: The Ottoman Empire under Sultan Selim III, 1789–1807*. Cambridge, MA, 1971.

Shinder, Joel. "Career Line Formation in the Ottoman Bureaucracy, 1648–1750: A New Perspective." *Journal of the Economic and Social History of the Orient* 16 (1973): 217–237.

Sievert, Henning. *Zwischen arabischer Provinz und Hoher Pforte: Beziehungen, Bildung und Politik des osmanischen Bürokraten Râġıb Meḥmed Paşa (st. 1763)*. Ergon Verlag, 2008.

Silay, Kemal. *Nedim and the Poetics of the Ottoman Court: Medieval Inheritance and the Need for Change*. Bloomington, 1994.

Smiley, Will. "Let Whose People Go: Subjecthood, Sovereignty, Liberation, and Legalism in Eighteenth-Century Russo-Ottoman Relations." *Turkish Historical Review* 3 (2012): 196–228.

Soysal, İsmail. *Fransız İhtilâli ve Türk-Fransız Diplomasi Münasebetleri (1789–1802)*. Ankara, 1964.

Süslü, Azmi. "Un aperçu sur les ambassadeurs ottomans et leurs sefaretname." *AÜDTCF Tarih Araştırmaları Dergisi* 14 (1981): 223–260.

"Rapports diplomatiques ottomano-français, 1798–1807." *Belleten* 47 (1983): 237–279.

Telci, Cahit. "Osmanlı Yönetiminin Yeni Yıl Kutlamalarından: İstanbul Tekkelerine Muharremiye Dağıtımı." *Sûfî Araştırmaları* 3 (2012): 2–29.

Tezcan, Baki. "Ethics as a Domain to Discuss the Political: Kınalızâde Ali Efendi's *Ahlâk-ı Alâî*." In *Learning and Education in the Ottoman World.* Istanbul, 2001. 109–120.

"The Politics of Early Modern Ottoman Historiography." In *The Early Modern Ottomans: Remapping the Empire.* eds. Virginia Aksan and Daniel Goffman. Cambridge, 2007. 167–198.

The Second Ottoman Empire: Political and Social Transformation in the Early Modern World. Cambridge, 2010.

Thomas, Lewis. *A Study of Naima.* New York, 1972.

Toderini, Giambattista. *Letteratura Turchesca.* Venice, 1787. 3 vols.

Tuck, Christopher. "'All Innovation Leads to Hellfire': Military Reform and the Ottoman Empire in the Eighteenth Century." *Journal of Strategic Studies* 31 (2008): 467–502.

Turan, Osman. "The Ideal of World Domination Among the Medieval Turks." *Studia Islamica* 4 (1955): 77–90.

Türk Cihân Hâkimiyet Mefkûresi Tarihi. Istanbul, 1969. 2 vols.

Türkal, Nazire Karaçay. "18. Yüzyılın İkinci Yarısında Osmanlı-Fas İlişkileri: Seyyid İsmail ve Ahmed Azmi Efendilerin Fas Elçilikleri (1785–1787)." Master's thesis, Karadeniz Teknik University, 2004.

Unat, Faik. "Kırımın Osmanlı idaresinden çıktığı günlere ait bir vesika: Necati Efendi Sefaretnâme veya Sergüzeştnâmesi." *Türk Tarih Kurumu Kongresi* 3 (1943): 367–374.

Osmanlı Sefirleri ve Sefaretnameleri. Ankara, 1992.

Üstün, Kadir. "The New Order and Its Enemies: Opposition to Military Reform in the Ottoman Empire, 1789–1807." Ph.D. diss., Columbia University, 2013.

Uzunçarşılı, İ.H. "Cezayirli Gazi Hasan Paşa'ya Dair." *Türkiyat Mecmuası* 7/8 (1942): 17–44.

"Nizam-ı Cedid Ricalinden Valide Sultan Kethüdası Meşhur Yusuf Ağa ve Kethüdazâde Arif Efendi." *Belleten* 20 (1956): 485–525.

Osmanlı Devleti'nin Merkez ve Bahriye Teşkilâtı. Ankara, 1948.

"Sadrâzam Halil Hamid Paşa." *Türkiyat Mecmuası* 5 (1935): 213–268.

"Sultan III. Selim ve Koca Yusuf Paşa." *Belleten* 39 (1975): 233–256.

Woodhead, Christine. "From Scribe to Littérateur: The Career of a Sixteenth-Century Ottoman Kâtib." *Bulletin of the British Society for Middle East Studies* 9 (1982): 55–74.

Yalçınkaya, Mehmet. "Osmanlı Zihniyetindeki Değişimin Göstergesi Olarak Sefaretnamelerin Kaynak Defteri." *OTAM* 7 (1996): 319–338.

Yaycıoğlu, Ali. *Partners of the Empire: The Crisis of the Ottoman Order in the Age of Revolutions.* Stanford, 2016.

Yerasimos, Stéphane. "De l'arbre a la pomme: la genealogie d'un theme apocalyptique." In *Les traditions apocalyptiques au tourant de la chute de Constantinople.* 153–192.

Yeşil, Fatih. *Aydınlanma Çağında bir Osmanlı Kâtibi: Ebubekir Râtib Efendi (1750–1799)*. Istanbul, 2010.

"Looking at the French Revolution Through Ottoman Eyes: Ebubekir Ratib Efendi's Observations." *Bulletin of the School of Oriental and African Studies* 70 (2007): 283–304.

"Nizâm-ı Cedîd." In *III. Selim: İki Asrın Dönemecinde İstanbul*. ed. Coşkun Yılmaz. Istanbul, 2010. 103–121.

Yıldırım, Arif. "Karslı Davud (Davud-i Karsî) Efendi'nin İrade-i Cüz'iyye Anlayışı." *Ankara Üniversitesi Türkiyat Araştırmaları Enstitüsü Dergisi* 15 (2000): 189–199.

Yıldız, Aysel. "Vaka-yı Selimiyye or the Selimiyye Incident: A Study of the May 1807 Rebellion." Ph.D. diss., Sabancı University, 2008.

Zens, Robert. "In the Name of the Sultan: Hacı Mustafa Pasha of Belgrade and Ottoman Provincial Rule in the Late Fighteenth Century." *IJMES* 44 (2012): 129–116.

"Pasvanoğlu Osman Paşa and the Paşalık of Belgrade, 1791–1807." *International Journal of Turkish Studies* 8 (2002): 89–104.

Zilfi, Madeline. "Elite Circulation in the Ottoman Empire: Great Mollas of the Eighteenth Century." *Journal of the Economic and Social History of the Orient* 26 (1983): 318–364.

"Hâkim's Chronicle Revisted." *Oriente Moderno* 18 (1999): 193–201.

The Politics of Piety: The Ottoman Ulema in the Postclassical Age (1600–1800). Minneapolis, 1988.

Index

Other titles in the series